KV-579-034

MISCELLANY III

THE STAIR SOCIETY

MISCELLANY THREE

BY

VARIOUS AUTHORS

EDITED BY

Professor W. M. GORDON

WITH A PREFACE BY

Professor Emeritus GORDON DONALDSON
H. M. HISTORIOGRAPHER IN SCOTLAND

EDINBURGH
THE STAIR SOCIETY
1992

Published by

The Stair Society
16 Charlotte Square
Edinburgh
EH2 4YS

First published 1992

ISBN 1 872517 03 X

© 1992 The Stair Society

All rights reserved. No part of this publication may be reproduced, stored in a retrieval system, or transmitted in any form or by any means, electronic, mechanical, photocopying, recording or otherwise, without the prior permission of the Stair Society.

British Library Cataloguing-in-Publication Data.

A catologue record for this book is available from the British Library.

Typeset by Computing Services (University of Glasgow) Limited.

Printed by Martin's The Printers Ltd., Berwick upon Tweed

CONTENTS

PREFACE

Four of the seven articles in this volume, accounting for the great bulk of it, have their settings in what may be called the year of the Union of 1707. James Anderson (1682–1728) was the author of the *Historical Essay* which Dr Ferguson has edited. John Spotswood (1667–1728) is the subject of a carefully researched biography by Dr Cairns, who not only throws light on education in the law but reminds us that Spotswood was son of an advocate, grandson of a Lord President and great-grandson of an Archbishop (who held the office of Chancellor and was himself the son of a Superintendent or 'reformed bishop'). Lord George Douglas (?1667/68–?1693), well educated in the law – partly on the continent – acquired a library the riches of which are expertly analysed by Dr W.A. Kelly. These three men were contemporaries, while Lord Stair (1619–95) belonged to the previous generation, and Professor William Forbes, whose eulogy of Stair is shown by Dr Hector MacQueen to have derived mainly from Stair's own *Apology*, belonged to the following one.

But it is James Anderson alone who owes his place in this volume to his interest in the Union. The careers of the others illustrate the important truth that events which hit the headlines often had a limited effect on the life of the nation and on the lives of individuals. Almost as in 1745, when – so it was said – 'the industrious part of the nation did not quit their looms to dance after the Highland pipes', so it was in the run-up to the Union and in its aftermath. Whatever the political situation, John Spotswood went on publishing, lecturing on Scots and Civil law and running the Advocates Library, Lord George went on collecting books, and William Forbes went on assessing Stair.

Yet, despite this coincidence in chronology, there is a kind of timelessness about the studies in this book, and other articles besides those already mentioned are inter-related. Sheriff D.B. Smith's 'A sixteenth century legal opinion' produces from the National Library a 'Memorial and Opinion of Counsel' signed by thirteen advocates and used in 1574 in a process of apprising. Angus Stewart likewise produces, from the Barcaldine Muniments, 'A Memorial and Opinion', this time of 1762, by the future Lord Braxfield. This carries us to the familiar territory of the Appin Stewarts just ten years after the murder of Colin Campbell of Glenure and indicates some of the complications of West Highland landholding. This in turn leads directly to Mr A.I.B. Stewart's 'Regulation of Agriculture in Kintyre', which presents 'Acts of Neighbourhood' of 1653 and related 'Acts of Bailyierie' of 1672. These illustrate the problems and petty quarrels apt to arise between adjoining tenants and they at once recalled the 'Country Acts' of Shetland which I recently reproduced in *The Court Book of Shetland 1615–1629.*

Writing in 1992, when the Union achieved in 1707 is threatened with dissolution, one is apt to wonder if the United Kingdom will share the fate of Yugo-Slavia and if we may hear echoes of the poignant cry of a young Bosnian woman: 'For years we lived happily together and not it has come killing each other's babies. What is happening to us?' The debate on what may be called the Profit and Loss Account of the Union recurs, but James Anderson, writing in 1705, did not dwell either on the devastation and misery of the periods of war which preceded the Union or on the contrary blessings of peace. He chose instead to examine ancient documents bearing on the question whether the Scottish crown was 'imperial' or subordinate to that of England, dealing briskly with 'notorious falsehoods', 'romantick and incredible stories', often produced by 'juggling monks'. He advanced ingenious arguments, but perhaps too rarely raised his eyes from his charters to reflect on some realities in the medieval centuries. It was hard for 'patriots' like him to accept that King Edgar, with whose accession in 1097 the tenure of the throne by the English Margaretson line began, was a client of his English contemporary, that some Scottish kings did homage to English kings without apparently holding lands in England, or that Scottish kings were not anointed until 1331. To the scholarly examination of Anderson's controversies with English contemporaries Dr Ferguson brings his characteristic wit and customary pungency. The important fact remains that the debates preceding the Union gave an unparalleled stimulus to historical studies so that in the effect of the Union on Scottish record scholarship the profit far outweighs any loss.

The editing of the volume has been carried out by Professor W. M. Gordon, Literary Director of the Stair Society, for whose labours the members would wish me to express our united gratitude. Our thanks are also due to the Computer Publishing Unit of Glasgow University and its director, Professor Ken Browning, for assistance with typesetting and indexing and to Dr Douglas Grant for his help in seeing the volume towards publication.

GORDON DONALDSON

ILLUSTRATION

LIST OF ABBREVIATIONS

These abbreviations are supplementary to abbreviations appearing in the various contributions but do not include abbreviations used in James Anderson's *Historical Essay*.

Adv.	Advocates'
A.P.S.	*Acts of the Parliaments of Scotland*, edd. T. Thomson and C. Innes. 12 vols. (Edinburgh, 1814–75)
D.N.B.	*Dictionary of National Biography*, edd. L. Stephen and others (London, 1885–)
Fasti Ecclesiae Scoticanae	Hew Scott, *Fasti Ecclesiae Scoticanae*. New revised edition. 8 vols. (Edinburgh, 1915–50)
Jour. Leg. Hist.	*Journal of Legal History*
Jurid. Rev. [N.S.]	*Juridical Review [New Series]*
N.L.S.	National Library of Scotland
North. Ire. Leg. Quart.	*Northern Ireland Legal Quarterly*
Oxf. Jour. Leg. Stud.	*Oxford Journal of Legal Studies*
R.P.C., 1st ser.	*Register of the Privy Council of Scotland*, 1st series, edd. J. Hill Burton and D. Masson. 14 vols. (Edinburgh, 1878–98)
R.P.C., 3rd ser.	*Register of the Privy Council of Scotland*, 3rd series, edd. P. Hume Brown and others (Edinburgh, 1908–)
R.S.S.	*Registrum Secreti Sigilli Regum Scotorum*, edd. M. Livingstone and others (Edinburgh, 1908–)
S.R.O.	Scottish Record Office
Sc. Hist. Rev.	*Scottish Historical Review*
Yale Law Jour.	*Yale Law Journal*

JAMES ANDERSON'S *HISTORICAL ESSAY* ON THE CROWN OF SCOTLAND

Reprinted, with an Introduction by

WILLIAM FERGUSON, B.A., M.A., PH.D.,

Department of Scottish History, University of Edinburgh

INTRODUCTION

The Career of James Anderson

James Anderson, man of law and doyen of Scottish record scholars, was born at Edinburgh on 5 August 1662. Within two months of his birth family circumstances deteriorated when his father, the Reverend Patrick Anderson, became one of the outed presbyterian ministers for refusing to conform to the Restoration church settlement. The hardship and bitterness this led to were to be major influences on James Anderson, and if his life and work are to be understood these topics need some elucidation. An outline of the career of Patrick Anderson thus becomes necessary.

Patrick Anderson was born about 1627, graduated M.A. at St Andrews in 1648, and was inducted to the parish of Walston near Biggar in Lanarkshire in 1655.[1] Today his old church still stands though no longer in use; but when Master Patrick first took charge of this pleasant country parish in the Upper Ward of Clydesdale it was a new building. The trim little kirk, so typical of its period, bears the inscription, 'Give God the onlie Honour and Glory, Anno 1656'. Master Patrick himself may well have chosen that motto, for certainly its eclectic defiance of all earthly powers inspired him throughout life. The living had been in the gift of the dean and chapter of Glasgow ever since 1292,[2] but in 1656 neither archbishop nor patron had any function, nor, indeed, any legal existence. When they were restored after 1660, Mr Patrick, obeying his parish kirk's motto, refused to accept their authority, and on 1 October 1662 he was thrust out of his charge.

Ten years later Patrick Anderson was one of the indulged, who, while refusing to accept the full episcopalian system, were assigned to parishes

---

1 *Fasti Ecclesiae Scoticanae*, i, 262.
2 Ian B. Cowan, *The Parishes of Medieval Scotland* (Scottish Record Society, 93, Edinburgh, 1967), p. 206, for the parish's early history. The patron whose right was restored at the Restoration was Christopher Baillie.

under strict conditions for their future good behaviour.[3] He was ordered first of all to Kilbirnie and then latterly to Dreghorn, both Ayrshire parishes and remote from his old charge at Walston.[4] But, like others in his situation, he was lax in observing the strict terms of indulgence.[5] Living up to his old kirk's motto, Patrick Anderson, at considerable risk to himself and hardship for his family, defied the laws of the land to 'Give God the onlie Honour and Glory'. Probably it was financial difficulty that had induced him to accept indulgence, for his beliefs on church and state obviously did not change. He did not reside at Kilbirnie. Instead, in 1674 he was hauled before the privy council for holding conventicles at Boghall, Biggar, and in his house at Potterrow in Edinburgh. Later it was discovered that he was corresponding with notorious dissidents like John Welsh, Gabriel Semple and other intercommuned persons of lesser note. His numerous offences are itemised in the *Register of the Privy Council*, and later they earned him a niche in the hagiological histories of Kirkton and Wodrow.[6]

Patrick Anderson was first named in the act of the privy council of 12 March 1673 concerning indulged ministers who had failed to take up residence in their places of confinement.[7] For repeated offences he was sent in April 1678 to the Bass Rock, which the king had recently bought from the Duke of Lauderdale and converted into a state prison.[8] There Patrick Anderson and other recalcitrants, including the celebrated James Fraser of Brae, were ordered to be held until they found caution and promised to remove from Edinburgh. Anderson's caution was set at 2,000 merks, a large sum, but he may not have been entirely without means. In 1659 he, with his wife, Margaret Threipland, had sasine of the corn mill at Biggar, and in 1663 they got a fresh sasine of the same to include their children.[9] He also had a house in Potterrow Port, Edinburgh, which later belonged to his son James, the antiquary. Somehow the necessary sum was put up, and he was released from the Bass. But there was no change in his conduct. He removed the requisite five miles from Edinburgh, but only as far as Dalkeith, where he later got into trouble for setting up an illegal meeting-house. The

---

3   For the Declaration of Indulgence of 1669, see *R.P.C.*, 3rd ser., iii, 38–40. Patrick Anderson was included in the second indulgence of 1672 – see Rev. James Anderson, *The Martyrs of the Bass* (Edinburgh, 1848), p. 260. For an interesting but not always accurate account of Walston and Patrick Anderson, see *New Staistical Account of Scotland*. 15 vols. (Edinburgh, 1845), vi, 846–67.
4   *Fasti Ecclesiae Scoticanae*, i, 262.
5   Ian B. Cowan, *The Scottish Covenanters 1660–1688* (London, 1976), p. 81.
6   James Kirkton, *Secret and True History of the Church of Scotland from the Restoration to the Year 1678*, ed. C.K. Sharpe (Edinburgh, 1817), p. 337; and Robert Wodrow, *History of the Sufferings of the Church of Scotland from the Restoration to the Revolution*, ed. Rev. R. Burns (Edinburgh, 1829), ii, 264.
7   *R.P.C.*, 3rd ser., iv, 34.
8   Rev. Thomas McCrie, jr., in *The Bass Rock its Civil and Ecclesiastical History* (Edinburgh, 1848), p. 17.
9   *Fasti Ecclesiae Scoticanae*, i, 263.

Duchess of Buccleuch threatened him with the wrath of the privy council and he had to desist from house conventicling. Nevertheless, he continued to oppose the regime until, in covenanting phrase, 'the Deliverance came' with the Revolution of 1688. Patrick Anderson was a keen Revolutionist, strong for the presbyterian discipline and the political theories of George Buchanan, and these views his son James inherited.

A popular call returned Patrick Anderson to Walston in July 1689, and this was confirmed by the act of parliament of 25 April 1690 restoring 'the Presbyterian Ministers who were thrust from their churches since the 1st of January 1661'.[10] He was, then, one of the 'antediluvians', as those veterans were called. But he was not long destined to enjoy his restoration nor to share any further in the triumph of his Zion. He died on 22 July 1690, aged about 63.

Patrick Anderson had a numerous family by Margaret Threipland, of whom James was to be the most distinguished. But a daughter Mary also has a claim to fame. She married in 1678 David Pitcairne of Dreghorn, advocate, and their daughter, Eleanor Pitcairne, was the mother of the great Scottish ecclesiastic, historian and academic, Principal William Robertson of the university of Edinburgh. James Anderson, the antiquary, was thus grand-uncle to William Robertson, the historian. The link with the Anderson family was further strengthened by Robertson's marriage to his cousin, Mary Nisbet, whose mother was Mary Pitcairne, sister to Robertson's mother, Eleanor Pitcairne.

In the circumstances, James Anderson's early life could not have been easy. Nevertheless, he was well educated and graduated M.A. at Edinburgh in 1680. He is then said to have studied law as an apprentice to Sir Hugh Paterson of Bannockburn, an eminent W.S., but when he was admitted to the Society of Writers to the Signet on 6 June 1691 he was described as being 'apprentice to Robert Richardson'.[11] The branch of the law in which he specialised called for the ability to read and understand old instruments, and their study came to interest him above all else. From being incidental to his profession research into old charters became the passion of his life, and soon Anderson was noted for his palaeographical skills and his knowledge of history. He found congenial company in Edinburgh where Sir Robert Sibbald and Sir James Dalrymple were kindred spirits. In particular he enjoyed the friendship of Captain John Slezer, a Dutch artillerist turned Scottish topographer and author of a remarkable work, *Theatrum Scotiae*, which contained fine engravings of castles, palaces and towns. Slezer's career might have served as a salutary warning to Anderson, for the ever enthusiastic captain sank his savings in magnificent publishing ventures on the strength of promised government help that never materialised. The doleful

---

10   *A.P.S.*, ix, 111.
11   *Register of the Society of Writers to Her Majesty's Signet* (Edinburgh, 1983), p. 10.

lesson went unheeded, even though Anderson, who acted as Slezer's legal agent, in 1701 had had to dun the captain for payment of fees due and Slezer had to seek sanctuary at Holyrood.[12] All the same, Anderson in time was foolish enough to neglect his profession in favour of scholarship, lured on by government promises that proved to be as illusory as those that had ruined Slezer. Even before the event occurred that was to determine his future and lead him to prefer antiquarianism to the practice of law, historical research was increasingly taking up his time.

Through Bishop William Nicholson of Carlisle, a notable English anti-quary, Anderson learnt of important Scottish material at Durham, which, by the courtesy of the dean and chapter, he was permitted to peruse. Lists of holdings were exchanged between Durham and the Advocates Library at Edinburgh. The latter, keen to augment its holdings, asked Anderson to inspect and report on charters of Scottish interest held at Durham. It was while he was engaged on this congenial task that a friend wrote to him from Edinburgh in September 1703 urging him to hasten home, as his wife, the daughter of an advocate John Ellis of Ellistoun in West Lothian,[13] was sick and his family were all longing to see him. And, adds the writer omi-nously, 'your clients miss you'.[14] While he was 'on his pilgrimage', as Anderson dubbed it, he was not only transcribing old documents that threw some light on the early history of Scotland but also carrying thence an inventory of the Coldingham writs held by the cathedral chapter of Durham, which he was shortly to present to the Advocates Library in Edinburgh.[15] Anderson lingered on in Durham, fascinated by the splendid collection of charters, and charmed by the kindness and courtesy of its custodians.

In fact, the decisive moment of James Anderson's life was at hand. In 1703 the differences between Scotland and England over the succession question were reaching a critical stage. The crisis had arisen with the death in July 1700 of young William, Duke of Gloucester, last surviving child of Princess Anne. The death of this eleven year old boy virtually destroyed the succession laid down at the Revolution by the parliaments of England and Scotland. Anne was the undoubted legal successor to King William, whom she succeeded in March 1702, but her health was uncertain and the possibility of future progeny out of the question. With Britain at war with France over the Spanish Succession (a war that was really also the War of the British Succession) the descent of the crown had to be agreed in order to counter French and Jacobite schemes. The problem began to be addressed even before the outbreak of war. By the Act of Settlement passed in 1701 the English parliament sought to solve the problem by devolving the succession

---

12   *Analecta Scotica*, 1st ser., ed. James Maidment (Edinburgh, 1834), pp. 49–51.

13   G.F. Black, *The Surnames of Scotland* (New York, imp. 1974), s.v. Ellis, p. 243.

14   N.L.S., Advocates MS 29.3.4, fo. 22, 21 September 1703.

15   James Anderson, *An Historical Essay, Shewing that the Crown and Kingdom of Scotland is Imperial and Independent* (Edinburgh, 1705), pp. 44, 50–51.

on the nearest protestant heir of the royal Stewart blood. After Anne, the right of succession was to go to Sophia, Dowager Electress of Hanover, and her issue, the aged Sophia being a grand-daughter of James VI and I. The Hanoverian succession settled the question, but only as far as the kingdoms of England and Ireland were concerned, for by an application of Poynings' Law the act of 1701 applied in Ireland as well. But English statutes were of no avail in Scotland. The awkward fact was that only an act of the Scottish parliament could determine the succession to the crown of Scotland, and this fundamentally important fact was upheld by numerous precedents. Thus, in 1703 Scots of all political persuasions were convinced that their crown was imperial and independent. This fact, they claimed, had been recognised for centuries, and similarly with the fact that only the parliament of Scotland could regulate the succession to the crown. There is no need to recite here the evidence that upheld this conviction in order to appreciate the shock felt by most Scots when a revived English claim to superiority over Scotland was advanced by some English publicists in a bid to preserve the Union of the Crowns with or without reference to the parliament of Scotland.[16]

A moment's reflection will show that in this matter much more than antiquarian patriotism was involved. Nor is it in the least mysterious that Scots lawyers should have been particularly sensitive about this issue. The fundamental point is that had the Scottish crown been subject to English overlordship then Scots law as a separate and distinctive legal system could never have developed. The situation in Scotland would have become what it became in Ireland and Wales, where native laws and customs were swept aside by English Common law. Clearly, this has not happened in Scotland, and that obvious legal fact is in itself a sufficient vindication of the independence of the Scottish crown. Proof of this vital point is to be found in the aftermath of an earlier succession problem, that which was posed in Scotland by the death of Margaret, the Maid of Norway, in September 1290. Edward I of England masterfully manoeuvred to get himself recognised as the Superior and Lord Paramount of Scotland basing his claim on numerous alleged precedents. Most of the Competitors, including John Balliol, the successful claimant, accepted the king of England's gambit, but, in the upshot, Balliol, who was adjudged by Edward to be the rightful heir to the vassal crown of Scotland, was ruined because of his refusal to allow Scottish cases to be determined by his superior in his courts. The long and bitter Scottish War of Independence then began.

The next revealing piece of evidence comes from 1305. In that year, having apparently crushed all opposition in Scotland, Edward I issued an Ordinance for the Government of that country.[17] In it the ancient kingdom

---

16 For the general background, see William Ferguson, *Scotland's Relations with England: a Survey to 1707* (Edinburgh, 1977), pp. 197–99.

17 For the Ordinance, see E.L.G. Stones, *Anglo-Scottish Relations 1174–1328: Some Selected Documents* (London, 1965), pp. 120–29. It is curious, however, that the usually meticulous Professor Stones should translate the French word 'terre' as 'realm', thus running against the obvious tenor of the document.

of Scotland was reduced to 'la terre d'Escoce,' a lordship just like Ireland and with the king of England as its lord. The 'land' of Scotland was to be governed on Edward's behalf by his nephew, John of Brittany, just as at the time John Wogan acted as Chief Governor in Edward's lordship of Ireland. The actual provisions for the government of 'la terre d'Escoce' that were laid down in the Ordinance of 1305 are usually described as statesmanlike.[18] Insofar as Scots were granted some share in the administration, it was to that extent politic. The legal implications of the proposed new regime, however, are rarely touched upon. True, Lord Cooper discusses the Ordinance of 1305 at some length but mainly to refute the notion that Edward I was the author of the *Regiam Majestatem*.[19] The most penetrating assessment was made by Sir Maurice Powicke who noted the reduction of Scotland and the dire prospects this opened up for Scots Law.[20] Powicke was absolutely right in his judgment.

Under the Ordinance of 1305 the customs of the Scots and Brets [Britons] were forbidden, and the laws introduced in Scotland since the time of David I, largely Anglo-Norman in origin, were to be amended in the light of reason and by reference to King Edward I. If the great Edwardian statutes, and particularly those of *De Donis* and *Quia Emptores*, had been extended to Scotland, could Scots law possibly have developed as it did?[21] Only an unqualified negative can answer that hypothetical question. The evolving English Common law must inevitably have triumphed, just as it did in Ireland and Wales. Subinfeudation would have ended and the law of property in land would have taken a very different turn. Indeed, it seems the safest of speculations that if the Ordinance of 1305 had remained the basis of government in Scotland there would have been no need for the Stair Society.

Those imponderables are not irrelevant to James Anderson's life and work. In the first three or four years of Queen Anne's reign the problem of the succession led to stormy proceedings in the Scottish parliament. There was a noticeable raising of nationalistic temperatures in both kingdoms, and some bitter controversies ensued. In particular much acrid pamphleteering was occasioned by the angry session of the Scottish parliament in 1703. The

---

18   W. Croft Dickinson, *Scotland before 1603* (3rd edn., revised and edited by A.A.M. Duncan, Oxford, 1977), pp. 159, 161.
19   Lord Cooper, *Regiam Majestatem and Quoniam Attachiamenta* (Stair Society, 11, Edinburgh, 1947), Introduction, pp. 10–16.
20   Sir Maurice Powicke, *The Thirteenth Century* (2nd edn., Oxford, 1962), pp. 711–12.
21   For the Edwardian statutes, see Sir Frederick Pollock and Frederic William Maitland, *The History of English Law before the Time of Edward I* (2nd edn., Cambridge, 1923), i, 337, 355, 608n; ii, 19, 22–24; and F.W. Maitland, *The Constitutional History of England* (Cambridge, impr. of 1948), pp. 24–25, 86.

opposition routed the government, pointedly ignored the Hanoverian succession and seemed to aim at ending the Union of the Crowns.[22]

In point of fact, the question of the locus of sovereignty and the government of the three kingdoms in the British Isles had already arisen. It was a question whose historic moment had come: one of the English pamphleteers, William Atwood, a lawyer and former Chief Justice of New York, had already argued for the superiority of the English crown over that of Ireland, and by implication over that of Scotland as well.[23] Atwood came to believe that the concept of one imperial crown in the British Isles (that of England, naturally) could be invoked to overcome all the current difficulties about the succession. So he set out to refute the claims of George Ridpath, a Scottish Whig based in London, who in 1695 had published a translation of Sir Thomas Craig's hitherto unpublished Latin treatise 'De Hominio'. This tract, a sturdy defence of Scottish independence, resolutely rejected English claims to suzerainty over Scotland.[24] As the constitutional crisis between England and Scotland deepened Ridpath eagerly joined the fray and published an inflammatory account of the session of the Scottish parliament in 1703.[25] He proved that the Scottish parliament alone had the right to regulate the succession to the Scottish crown, and in so doing he threw down the gauntlet to the antiquaries of England. The best of the English antiquaries had better things to do and ignored the challenge. But the political pamphleteers rushed to join the fray.

In 1703 James Drake, a satirical physician, published a spoof *Historia Anglo-Scotica*, which, in spite of its pretentious title, was written in good vigorous English. In it he lampooned Ridpath's edition of Craig's 'De Hominio' and took every care to depict the Scots as preposterous clowns. Today, the most ridiculous aspect of Drake's amusing performance is its history, which is very much of the '1066 and All That' kind. But the Scottish parliament in 1704 was not entertained by Drake's drolleries and voted that his offending so-called *Historia* should be burned by the common hangman of Edinburgh.[26] Undeterred by this, the irrepressible Atwood brought out a large ill-digested tract which asserted, in the most arrogant and contemptuous

---

22 The best account of the pamphlet warfare is still James Mackinnon, *The Union of England and Scotland: a Study of International History* (London, 1896), chaps. VIII and XIV, though, oddly, Mackinnon scarcely notices Anderson.

23 William Atwood, *The History and Reasons of the Dependency of Ireland upon the Imperial Crown of the Kingdom of England* (London, 1698). For the background to these controversies, see William Ferguson, 'Imperial Crowns: a Neglected Facet of the Background of the Treaty of Union of 1707,' in *Sc. Hist. Rev.*, liii (1974), 22–44.

24 George Ridpath, tr. Craig, *Scotland's Sovereignty Asserted* (London, 1695). For Ridpath, see *Miscellany of the Abbotsford Club* (Edinburgh, 1833), i, 354 ff., and *D. N. B.*

25 Anon. [George Ridpath], *An Account of the Proceedings of the Parliament of Scotland which Met at Edinburgh, May 6, 1703* (Edinburgh, 1704).

26 *A.P.S.*, xi, 66, and App., p. 21.

terms, the *continuing* superiority of the English crown over Scotland.[27] True, in an attempt to ingratiate himself with the Scots, Atwood claimed to be of Scottish descent himself and to be writing to serve the true interests of the land of his ancestors. Amid the storm of abuse that his work gave rise to in Scotland no one seems to have noticed that the surname 'Atwood' is the English equivalent of the Scottish 'Boece'.[28]

Atwood's *Superiority and Direct Dominion of the Imperial Crown of England* was intended to refute Craig and Ridpath, and it certainly succeeded in abusing those authors as well as nearly every Scottish historian who had ever penned a line. It is, in fact, a bewildering performance, at once clumsily argued, absurd in its contentions, and shapeless to the point of incoherence. Anything at all that could be bent to serve Atwood's purposes was treated as irrefragable evidence. Facts rose or fell, took root or were scornfully dismissed, according to whether they could be made to support Atwood's thesis. The work was a late and very bad example of a traditional genre that was rather going out of fashion: it was a typical disputatious flyting treatise. In substance it was little more than a rehashing of the English chronicles liberally garnished with fabulous history. As long as Atwood stood, so did Geoffrey of Monmouth and his tall tales of early Britain. Certainly, Atwood's work had at times a rough vigour of style, but any sense that it might adventitiously throw up tended to be lost in the shapeless muddle of misconceived argument and wild assertion. In all this, sophistry was Atwood's chief weapon. His attempted rebuttal of Ridpath's neat exposure of a forged charter of Malcolm Canmore, in which homage was allegedly made to Edward the Confessor for the kingdom of Scotland, shows Atwood at his determined worst. It was a mere mish-mash of eccentric nonsense and pseudo-antiquarian lore which well deserved Anderson's stricture that 'there's no supporting of Forgeries, unless by gross Absurdities'.[29]

But, amid his lucubrations, Atwood in an evil moment for himself cited James Anderson in support of his contention that certain early charters at Durham proved Scotland's dependency on the crown of England.[30] Incensed by this, but still reluctant to engage in controversy, Anderson hurriedly wrote *An Historical Essay, Shewing that the Crown and Kingdom of Scotland is Imperial and Independent.* James Anderson was obviously stung to patriotic wrath by Atwood's historical vandalism. The *Historical Essay*, then, though on the whole sober and restrained, is not without its angry

---

27 William Atwood, *The Superiority and Direct Dominion of the Imperial Crown of England, over the Crown and Kingdom of Scotland, and the Divine Right of Succession to such Crowns Inseparable from the Civil* (London, 1704). For Atwood, see *D.N.B.*

28 G.F. Black, *The Surnames of Scotland*, n. 13 above, s.v. Boyce, p. 94.

29 Anderson, *Historical Essay*, p.30.

30 Atwood, *Superiority and Direct Dominion*, p. 253; cf. Anderson, *Historical Essay*, 'preface' and p. 2.

passages and occasional descents into the gutter. But controversy is calculated to subvert even the best intentioned.

Quite apart from the leading part that it played in the homage controversy, Anderson's *Historical Essay* is of considerable importance in Scottish historiography. It is the pioneer exercise in record scholarship, and that is where its true and enduring value lies. Anderson, in short, represented a completely new approach to the study of Scottish history, and one that was to make a very great contribution to the subject. Others before him had, of course, consulted records, but none with the critical expertise that Anderson brought to bear on them. That expertise he derived from close study of the principles laid down by Jean Mabillon, the great French record scholar, whose seminal work *De Re Diplomatica*, first published in 1681, virtually created palaeography and diplomatic.[31] The influence of the indefatigable French monk pervades the *Historical Essay*. Anderson fairly sings Mabillon's praises,[32] an ironical touch considering the many scathing references the *Historical Essay* contains to monkish impostures. But although Anderson tried to apply the principles of Mabillon, his *Historical Essay* was nevertheless a *pièce d'occasion*, written at speed and hurried through the press. It was evidently hoped that it would appear in 1704, and, indeed, some copies of it give 1704 as the year of publication. In the event, it did not appear until early in 1705, for, to the last, Anderson was busy checking and verifying his material. He was in correspondence with Ridpath, Atwood's old foe, and told him that he was having trouble with certain charters at Durham which seemed to indicate Scotland's dependency on England in the time of William Rufus. But, he wrote, 'It was the cause of my Countrey ... and much prudence was requisite in such an affair'.[33] To the last he was uneasy about Edgar's relationship with Rufus, though convinced overall that Edgar, styling himself 'Basileus', could not have been a vassal king. He also asked Ridpath to inform him of any stylistic lapses, and particularly to point out any obvious Scotticisms. Literary minded Scots of that period were unhappy with written English, though blithely indifferent to the fine nuances of the spoken tongue.

Ridpath was pleased with the *Essay* as far as its general tenor and its substance were concerned. He showed it to James Tyrrell at the Herald's Office, and together they rejoiced at Atwood's discomfiture. Tyrrell, who had earned a rebuke from Anderson for some ill-judged strictures on Craig, expressed regret if he had given offence, and Anderson, it seems likely, mollified his criticisms. In general Ridpath was enthusiastic about the *Essay*, but recommended that Anderson should clearly state in his conclusion that he had not written against England or the English. Judging from the anodyne

---

31 The best account in English of Jean Mabillon (1632–1707) is an essay by Dom David Knowles in his *The Historian and Character and other Essays* (Cambridge, 1963), pp. 213–39.

32 E.g. *Historical Essay*, pp. 32–3.

33 N.L.S., Adv. MS 29.3.4, fo. 37, James Anderson to George Ridpath, 9 January 1705.

conclusion to the *Historical Essay* as published, Anderson took this advice to heart. As to style, Ridpath thought it passable. As a matter of fact, it now appears very variable. Anderson only rarely managed to free himself from the involved and sometimes obscure Latinate periods beloved of seventeenth-century writers of English, but in some passages he breaks into direct and spirited modern English of the kind that had been pioneered by John Dryden. Overall, however, he never achieved the easy flow of words that characterised Ridpath, or, even more conspicuously, Andrew Fletcher of Saltoun. He was not helped by the abysmal standards of his printer, the redoubtable Mrs. Anderson, no relative, whose productions were notorious. All the same, miserable piece of book production though it was, the *Historical Essay* as it finally appeared was much better than the general output of the press operated by the relict of Andrew Anderson, King's Printer.[34] Working against the clock, the author had evidently slaved hard over the proof-sheets and somehow managed to get the termagant to make the necessary corrections. Ridpath's sole caveat was about a few Scotticisms. Most such were not serious and, if anything, added savour to the work: 'For Scotticisms,' Ridpath wrote to the author, 'your book would not have been Genuine without them, only I wish that some of the Grosser ones, which are inseparable from your Law education had been corrected, such as Severals, Notour &c., for here they never say anything other than several and notorious'.[35] Unwittingly perhaps Ridpath had touched on the source of much of Anderson's power – namely, the fact that, like so many notable Scottish historians, he had been educated in the law and was able to apply his legal training to the evaluation of historical evidence.

Anderson's book was joyfully received in Scotland where the verdict was that it had annihilated Atwood and Drake and their offensive views. The Scots, obviously prejudiced though they were, were right to award the palm to Anderson, for the scholarship that he displayed was far superior to any shown by his antagonists. In an eloquent passage he proclaimed the new credo of the historian: 'Of all Proofs in History,' he wrote, 'none are so concluding and pointed as Charters: They speak for themselves, and need no Rhetorical Embellishments and Flourishes to perswade; Which hath

---

34   For a brief notice of the Anderson press, see William Ferguson, *Scotland: 1689 to the Present* (Edinburgh, edn. 1987), pp. 98–99, and references. Mrs Anderson sometimes used her maiden name, Agnes Campbell.

35   N.L.S., Adv. MS 29.3.4, fo. 40, George Ridpath to James Anderson, 24 February 1705. Robert Wodrow later also conjured Ridpath to school him out of Scotticisms, for he feared that his style would not 'answer the taste of this age'. Ridpath freely advised: cf. *Miscellany of the Abbotsford Club*, i, 413; Burns's 'Memoir of Wodrow' in *Hist. of the Sufferings*, i, pp. vii-ix; and ibid., p. xli, Wodrow's Preface (1721), where he hoped English readers would bear with him, 'though I come not fully up to the propriety of the English language, nor to the accuracy and neatness of their writers'.

made ancient Charters and Records, so much the study of this inquisitive Age: For Histories being overgrown with Legends of Miracles and Visions on the one hand, and larded with many Romantick Fables and Traditions on the other, there was no safe way left, to correct what's amiss, to clear what's obscure, and to add what's wanting, but a diligent search into records and ancient Muniments'.[36] This was an ideal statement of the case, and, of course, Anderson was well aware that the records could only yield up their secrets to those who were proficient in the arts inculcated by Mabillon. Most readers at the time most likely cared little for such arcane quiddities; but patriotic Scots could only applaud Anderson's comforting conclusions which dispelled the hateful thought of homage. So taken was the Scottish parliament with the *Historical Essay* that its author was publicly thanked for performing such a great national service, and it was ordered that he should receive a grant of £4,800 Scots to further his studies, while for good measure Atwood's book was condemned.[37] At the same time a like reward was granted to James Hodges, 'who hath in his writeings served the interest of this Nation'.

Atwood attempted a reply to Anderson but the wordy tome that he produced consisted largely of a tedious and long-winded repetition of his previous wild assertions.[38]

Anderson was elated by his triumph, and, relying on the promised support of the Scottish parliament, he set about preparing his great projected work, the *Diplomata Scotiae*. His business began to suffer and he was obliged to dip into his own purse in order to meet the expense of collecting charters and seals. The work of engraving, too, was costly. In November 1706 he submitted a report of his labours and the expenses incurred to a committee of the parliament, which reported favourably on his activities. They had seen 'impressions' of twenty-four charters with many seals, all 'very happily imitated'; and 'They did likewise consider curious Tables, prepared by the Author, to be engraven on large Plates ready polished, for explaining the Characters [i.e. letters] of the Several Ages; and the Abbreviations and Contractions so frequent in ancient Charters and Manuscripts; to which the Author is to add useful Notes and Observations'. The expense incurred was adjudged 'modest and reasonable', but the complete work would be very expensive; so the £590 sterling of his own money, a large sum for those days, should be reimbursed, and he should have in addition £1,050 Sterling, 'to enable him to complete the said work, with the same Beauty and Exactness that he has begun it'. The parliament approved of the report and accepted its recommendations.[39]

---

36 Anderson, *Historical Essay*, p. 15.
37 *A.P.S.*, xi, 221, 10 August 1705.
38 William Atwood, *Superiority and Direct Dominion etc....Reasserted* (London, 1705).
39 *A.P.S.*, xi, 427–28, 12 February 1707; printed also in Anderson's *Diplomata Scotiae*, ed. T. Ruddiman (Edinburgh, 1739), p. V.

It is quite clear from this report that Anderson had already envisaged the lines on which the *Diplomata Scotiae* would run. Incidentally, prominent members of the committee which reported so favourably on the project were Sir John Lauder of Fountainhall, a noted lawyer historian, and Sir David Dalrymple, advocate.

Another Dalrymple, Sir James, had also published a work in 1705 entitled *Collections concerning the Scottish History* in which he also was concerned with vindicating the independence of the crown and the church in Scotland. Dalrymple, a younger son of the great Stair, had been working on his *Collections* on and off ever since the English bishops Lloyd and Stillingfleet had in the 1680s challenged Hector Boece's account of the antiquity of the royal line of Scotland. In the preface he states that he had written most of his treatise when 'Mr Atwood's book came to my hand, bearing the most false and arrogant title of *The Superiority and Direct Dominion of the Imperial Crown of England, over the Crown and Kingdom of Scotland'*. Dalrymple's preface was largely given up to a long rambling refutation of Atwood's claims, which, Dalrymple believed, were founded on 'meer whim'. Much that Dalrymple had to say, however, was also conjectural and far removed from sober history. But he recognised, and gratefully acknowledged, the value of Anderson's work.[40]

Just as in the case of Slezer, however, the money promised to Anderson was never paid. Nor did he ever recover in full a sizable sum of his own money that he spent on the great work that he projected on Scottish palaeography and diplomatic. It is a shabby story, and it pretty well ruined James Anderson's life. After 1707 the British parliament and government felt that enough money had been paid to secure 'the end o' an auld sang,' and that whatever was due to Anderson ought to come out of the Equivalent, the large sum assigned by the Treaty of Union to pay the debts of the Scottish government and sundry other charges. But in the crucial opening years of the union Anderson lacked political interest, and so, while a Tory government was in office, had no hope of securing repayment. A 'Memorial to the Queen' was equally fruitless.[41] From the 'Memorial' it is clear that he intended to produce a working manual of Scottish palaeography. Not only would it contain facsimiles of charters and seals but also an alphabetical table of abbreviations and contractions, together with explications of unusual or difficult words 'to make their Reading more easie and intelligible; Seeing nothing does more to discharge Gentlemen and ingenious Persons to inspect old Writs than the difficulty of reading them, and the not knowing the Meaning of some obsolete Words'. Teachers of

---

40   Sir James Dalrymple, *Collections concerning the Scottish History, Preceeding the Death of King David I, in the Year 1153 wherein the Soveraignty of the Crown and Independency of the Church are cleared; And an Account given of the Antiquity and Priority of the Scottish-British Church, and the Noveltie of Popery in this Kingdom* (Edinburgh, 1705), pp. VI, XLIII.
41   Edinburgh University Library, MS La. II.101.A, 'Anderson's Memorial'.

palaeography today follow Anderson's precepts, and the above important passage shows that his projected *Diplomata* was more practical and less philosophical than the work that was finally published by Ruddiman.

Much of Anderson's time after 1707 was spent in London trying to get the help he had been promised. His wife and family remaining in Edinburgh added to his financial difficulties and he was forced to redouble his efforts to obtain government help. In about 1708–9 he apparently sought the vacant post of Historiographer Royal for Scotland, an ill-remunerated position for which he was eminently well qualified. Among his papers there is what purports to be a copy of a writ issued by Queen Anne directing that letters patent for his appointment as Historiographer should pass the Great Seal. It recites his qualifications for the post, stresses the encouragement and the promises he had received from the parliament of Scotland, and, what Anderson would have prized most, orders that he should have open and free access to all state papers and such private muniments as might throw light on his investigations into ancient Scottish charters and seals. But, for some unknown reason, the application failed. No such warrant passed the Great Seal, and Anderson is not listed among the Historiographers Royal for Scotland.[42]

Particularly disappointing for Anderson was the treatment that he received from the leading Tory minister, Robert Harley. Harley, a keen collector of books and manuscripts and reputedly a great patron of letters, played a peculiarly mean role. It was one that was in keeping with his contemptuous attitude to Scotland and the Scots. As Chancellor of the Exchequer in 1711 Harley dismissed protests from Scottish M.P.s against a proposed duty on Scotch linen with the sneering remark that when England granted the Scots the Equivalent she had bought the right to tax them.[43] But to begin with Harley encouraged Anderson with promises of help, and he even gulled that unfortunate supplicant into paying for his own likeness to be drawn and hung in Harley's magnificent library along with those of other eminent scholars. Harley accepted the portrait, graciously hung it in his library, and then promptly washed his hands of the importunate Scottish Whig. After the Tories fell in 1714 and the Whigs engrossed power, Anderson, a staunch Revolutionist and Hanoverian, expected better treatment. At first the change of regime that followed the death of Queen Anne led to an improvement in his fortunes. Thanks to the triumph of the Argyll interest in 1715 he was appointed Deputy Postmaster-General for Scotland. This brought him a modest competence of £200 per annum and he was enabled to take up residence in Edinburgh once more, to the relief of his longsuffering wife who had encountered difficulties with a bevy of unruly

---

42   Ibid., fo. 15. Anderson does not figure in the Scottish Record Office's 'List of Minor Offices – Lists of Appointments to the office of Historiographer Royal'. Nor does he figure in Denys Hay, 'The Historiographers Royal in England and Scotland', in *Sc. Hist. Rev.*, xxx (1951), 15–29.

43   *The Lockhart Papers*, ed. A. Aufrere (London, 1817), i, 327.

daughters. The position of deputy postmaster-general, however, was arduous and fraught with problems. The postal system in Scotland was in its pioneer phase, with roads and communications primitive and the bulk of the post carried by foot. Anderson introduced the horse post, at first between Edinburgh and Stirling, then latterly, in spite of opposition from his superiors in London, between Edinburgh and Glasgow. The work of the deputy postmaster-general was made even more difficult by the outbreak of the Jacobite Rebellion of 1715-16. Nonetheless, Anderson coped well with all his troubles and frustrations, and he managed to lay the foundations for a faster and more efficient service.[44] But in the autumn of 1717 he was curtly dismissed with no reasons given for his dismissal. It was, in fact, a consequence of the fall of his patron, the Duke of Argyll, who was divested of all his offices. Anderson was one of the Argathelian office-holders who fell with the duke.[45]

Anderson then had to return to London once more in an attempt to 'make interest' and repair his fortunes. His eldest son Patrick, by then a qualified solicitor, was left to manage his father's legal practice in Scotland, of which the main work was factorage of the Campbell of Calder estate on Islay. The factor's duties were carried out by Patrick Anderson aided by his brother-in-law John Allan, who was married to James Anderson's daughter, Jean. The correspondence dealing with this topic makes interesting but on the whole doleful reading. A succession of bad harvests hit the estate hard. There was widespread poverty and distress, in which Allan and his wife also suffered, and for James Anderson the factorship of Islay could not have been a very profitable business.

Anderson found himself in the unfortunate position where his income was diminishing while his expenditure, not least on his scholarly pursuits, steadily mounted. He built up a superb and expensive collection of books on history and genealogy. At the same time his outlay on the engraving of his charters and seals also increased. By 1718 he was in financial straits, and tried to raise money by canvassing for subscriptions of the *Diplomata* both in Edinburgh and London. It is of some interest that one of those with whom subscriptions could be lodged was Thomas Ruddiman, librarian of the Advocates Library in Edinburgh.[46] Insufficient subscriptions were put up, and Anderson, with more zeal than discretion, continued to spend money

---

44   See A.R.B. Haldane, *Three Centuries of Scottish Posts: An Historical Survey to 1836* (Edinburgh, 1971), chap. II. Curiously, Haldane does not seem to have been aware of Anderson's work as an antiquary but simply refers to him as an Edinburgh W.S., which rather weakens an otherwise interesting account of Anderson as deputy postmaster-general.

45   All this is reflected in Anderson's correspondence in N.L.S., Adv. MS 29.1.2. For the political background to the fall of the Duke of Argyll and the triumph of the Squadrone, see William Ferguson, *Scotland: 1689 to the Present* (Edinburgh, 1987), p. 138.

46   Douglas Duncan, *Thomas Ruddiman: a Study in Scottish Scholarship of the Early Eighteenth Century* (Edinburgh and London, 1965), p. 41.

he could ill afford on his cherished project. On it he positively refused to economise. He insisted on the engravings being done by John Sturt, the leading London engraver of the day who excelled in reproducing calligraphy. At that taxing work Sturt was best, and correspondingly expensive. But Anderson was determined that the *Diplomata* should be of the highest possible quality in every respect. Such perfectionism, of course, added to his financial troubles, and after 1719 Anderson's life was one long struggle with poverty. He was frequently dunned for bills, particularly by booksellers, and even, in the nicest possible way, by the excellent but impecunious Sturt.[47] Indeed so hard pressed was Anderson that in 1721 he tried, though unsuccessfully, through his friend Sir Richard Steele, the essayist, to sell his treasured library to George I.[48] A catalogue that he drew up and had printed about this time shows that it was a very fine historical collection, containing good editions of all the main chronicles, English and Scottish, and such seminal works as Rymer's *Foedera* and Madox's *Exchequer.*[49] The collection was later sold in lots, many of the items being purchased for the Advocates Library and the rest being dispersed – a rather mournful story.[50] To add to Anderson's frustration another Memorial of 1723 pleading with government to honour the pledges given to him came to nothing.

All this while Anderson drudged on as a literary hack in London, and the money earned in this way helped to defray expenditure on the *Diplomata.* Through no fault of James Anderson's that national undertaking was rapidly becoming a national disgrace. There was, indeed, something heroic about James Anderson and his complete dedication to the great national obligation that had fallen to his lot. Not only was he overworked, weighed down by frustration and dogged by poverty, but his life was also latterly saddened by family cares.

His wife seems to have been a nervous and querulous woman who found it impossible to cope single-handed with a large brood. It is difficult not to sympathise with her, though her incessant complaints must have frayed Anderson's nerves. No doubt part of the trouble was that the family was a large one. Anderson had three sons (Patrick, James and the baby of the family Billy), and six daughters (Mary, Anne, Jean, Janet, Margaret, and Elizabeth who died of fever in 1719). Anne and Mary were flighty and caused a lot of worry; Margaret married George Crawford, who at his father-in-law's instigation wrote a valuable work on the *Scots Peerage;* Janet set up

---

47   For John Sturt, see article in *D.N.B.* For some revealing correspondence between Sturt and Anderson, see James Maidment, *Analecta Scotica*, 1st series (Edinburgh, 1834), pp. 94ff.

48   Maidment, op. cit., 1st ser., pp. 18–20, and 2nd ser. (Edinburgh, 1837), pp. 355–56.

49   A copy of the catalogue, which is entitled *Libri de Rebus Britannicis, scilicet, Anglicis, Scoticis et Hibernicis* (pp. 56), is N.L.S., F.7. e. 30.

50   See Maidment, op. cit., 2nd series, p. 356 n*; and Douglas Duncan, op. cit. n. 46 above, p. 27: wrote Ruddiman of Anderson's library, 'He has the best Collection of not only Scottish but English historians of any I know'.

in a millinery business in Edinburgh, worked hard and prospered; and Jean was married to John Allan and lived on Islay. Of the sons Patrick was steady and hardworking, James was a scapegrace who had to be shipped to Bombay as a midshipman, and of Billy nothing is known. It was on Patrick that James Anderson chiefly relied to tend to affairs and try to help his mother to run the household.

So straitened were Anderson's circumstances, and so severe the privations of his family, that shortly before he died of apoplexy in London in 1728 he even had to pledge to Thomas Paterson, a friend who had loaned him money, the plates of the engravings that had cost him so dear. It looked as if the *Diplomata* were to remain a chimera, and it looked as if James Anderson's failure was complete. He seemed to have failed as a man of business, as a family man, and as a scholar.

Sadly, Anderson's tragedy did not end with his death. He was to be traduced beyond the grave following the eventual publication of the *Diplomata* in 1739, edited and enlarged, at Paterson's behest, by Thomas Ruddiman, keeper of the Advocates Library and by then a successful printer and publisher as well as a distinguished Latinist and antiquarian.[51] But it must be made clear at the outset that the derogation of Anderson was not the work of Ruddiman. Ruddiman and Anderson had known each other well, and their friendship was cemented by a respect for each other's abilities. But, though this did not affect their personal relations, they differed deeply in politics and religion, matters which in eighteenth-century Scotland could produce the most bitter rancour. Anderson, from Edinburgh, represented the Whig and presbyterian tradition, whereas Ruddiman hailed from Banffshire and clung throughout life to the episcopalian and Jacobite beliefs of his birthplace. In spite of their strongly held convictions and aversions, however, both were decent men and tolerant in practice.

As far as James Anderson was concerned we get an interesting glimpse of his innate kindness and tolerance from a note later compiled on the Anderson family. It appears that the Reverend Master Patrick, a devoted presbyterian, had a nephew, David Anderson, minister at Perth, who was an equally zealous episcopalian.[52] In spite of their religious and political differences they remained on good terms. At the Revolution their fortunes underwent a reversal of roles. Mr Patrick was restored to his kirk, but Mr David was on 3 September 1689 deposed for refusing to pray for William and Mary. An ex-regent of Humanity at St Andrews, he then kept a school at Perth until he died in 1697, leaving behind him in straitened circumstances a widow and a young family of two sons and a daughter. The claims of kinship overrode religious prejudice. James Anderson 'took the sole charge' of young Andrew Anderson, thus adding to his own extensive brood, and bred him up to the legal profession. The writer of this note was Andrew Anderson's grandson, and he spoke glowingly of James Anderson. Thanks

---

51   For an excellent account of Ruddiman, see Duncan, op. cit., n. 46 above.
52   *Fasti Ecclesiae Scoticanae*, iv, 204, 234.

to him, wrote John Anderson, the Andersons had become a legal family. James's son Patrick became a solicitor, and so did Andrew; Andrew's son David, and the compiler of those interesting but scrappy notes, Andrew's grandson, became Writers to the Signet.[53]

Ruddiman, who had long looked forward to the appearance of the *Diplomata*, was distressed at Anderson's failure and the fate of his plates which in 1729 were sold at auction for £530. Ruddiman subsequently leapt at the chance to prepare them for publication, and the result was the magnificent folio volume of 1739 that is familiarly known as *Diplomata Scotiae*.[54] As a tribute to Anderson's beliefs and Ruddiman's tolerance the work was dedicated to King George II. The dedication, however, was signed not by Ruddiman but by Patrick Anderson, James's son. Ruddiman must have personally detested that dedication, but suffered it to stand in the hope that Patrick might thereby gain a lucrative sinecure. Something may have come of it, for latterly Patrick Anderson was comptroller of the stamp duty in Scotland. But, in spite of his personal political beliefs, Ruddiman must also have appreciated, even if his Jacobite friends could not, that the dedication was appropriate in that the House of Brunswick represented the line of the ancient Scottish kings and also had a distinguished reputation for its patronage of history and historians, as the career of the great German polymath, Gottfried Leibnitz, had at one point demonstrated.

But such a dedication at that particular juncture was bound to raise Jacobite hackles. It seemed to the Jacobites to mar an otherwise admirable work. Jacobite hopes, in fact, revived in 1739 with the outbreak of the War of Jenkins' Ear between Britain and Spain, a conflict that widened out to bring Britain and France to blows. Ever since 1716 the Jacobites had hoped and prayed for a renewal of war between Britain and France, with the latter emerging victorious and restoring the Old Pretender. Things did not, of course, work out like that. The Old Pretender's hopes were dashed at Dettingen on 27 June 1743 when George II himself led his troops in the field, to date the last occasion on which a British sovereign was to do so.[55] And, of course, the romantic failure of the 'Forty-Five' buried Jacobite hopes irretrievably. Literary Jacobites took it out on James Anderson. They were quick to insinuate that the glory of the *Diplomata* was Ruddiman's alone. That Ruddiman furnished much, if not all, of the elaborate introduction is undeniable. It is further undeniable that he took every care to produce in fitting form one of the greatest works of Scottish scholarship. But to some

---

53   Edinburgh University Library, MS. La. II. 451/2, fo. 98, 'Notes on the Anderson Family by John Anderson'; see too *Register of the Society of Writers to Her Majesty's Signet* (Edinburgh, 1983), pp. 9–10.

54   The full title of this important work is *Selectus Diplomatum et Numismatum Scotiae Thesaurus ... Jacobus Andersonus Scriba Regius ... auxit et locupletavit Thomas Ruddimannus, A.M.* (Edinburgh, 1739).

55   Basil Williams, *The Whig Supremacy 1714–1760* (2nd edn., revised by C.H. Stuart, Oxford, 1962), p. 242.

commentators, and most notably George Chalmers, that apparently was not enough.

Like Ruddiman, Chalmers hailed from the north-east of Scotland, and, again like Ruddiman, he had been educated at King's College, Old Aberdeen. He had been baptised in the Church of Scotland but later joined the Church of England and displayed a bitter hatred of presbyterianism. He also developed a fixation about Mary, Queen of Scots, for whom, crusty old bachelor though he was, he acquired an overwhelming idealistic passion. Mary became to him a perfect symbol of pure and ill-used womanhood. For her sake he abominated the Reformation and all its works, and the sole remnant of Calvinism to which he clung was the belief that God marked out the elect by making them prosperous.[56] Chalmers revered prescriptive right, worshipped authority, dreaded revolution and hated all who questioned the *status quo*. His experience of the American Revolution, his championing of the landowners of Maryland, his belief in slavery and detestation of abolitionism, all predisposed him to dislike James Anderson, the shiftless champion of presbyterianism and constitutional government. James Anderson, in fact, represented most things that George Chalmers loathed, and Chalmers, a fierce dogmatist, was not the man to hide his prejudices. Thus, in his *Life of Ruddiman*, Chalmers, himself an antiquary of note,[57] went out of his way to make frenzied attacks on Anderson. His aim, quite clearly, was to minimise Anderson's contribution to the *Diplomata* and to the study of Scottish history as a whole.

According to Chalmers, Anderson was an impudent, improvident charlatan, who had taken umbrage at critical remarks about George Buchanan contained in Ruddiman's great edition of Buchanan's works, and had even dared to join a Whig society that was formed in Edinburgh to combat Ruddiman's strictures.[58] Anderson, so the diatribe ran, had gone from bad to worse and latterly had contributed to the Marian controversy, in quest of truth, as he sanctimoniously claimed, but, as it seemed to devoted Marians,

---

56 See Grace Amelia Cockcroft, *The Public Life of George Chalmers* (New York, 1939).

57 George Chalmers (1742–1825) produced many works of great industry but of mixed quality. His chief work is *Caledonia: or a Historical and Topographical Account of North Britain from the most ancient to the present Times*. 7 vols. (new edn., Paisley, 1887). It was first published in 1807, and it contains much valuable material.

58 George Chalmers, *The Life of Thomas Ruddiman* (London, 1794), pp. 74–78. In his edition of *Buchanani Opera* (1715), Ruddiman had in fact corrected many misprints and obvious errors as well as controverting Buchanan's strictures on Mary, Queen of Scots, and attacking his political theories in general. Anderson compiled extensive notes in Latin combating Ruddiman's views, but in the event he never published his own projected edition of Buchanan. The notes are in N.L.S., Adv. MS 31.6.2, 'Materials for a preface to an edition of George Buchanan's works by J.A. (c.1719–c.1729)'.

in no spirit of knight errantry. In 1727–28 he published four volumes of original source material entitled *Collections Relating to the History of Mary, Queen of Scotland.* The title alone condemned the work as far as Chalmers was concerned. He found it astonishing that Mary should be referred to as 'Queen of Scotland'.[59] But Mary herself did so on occasion. A notable instance of such royal carelessness occurred at the time of her marriage to Darnley. In a proclamation of 28 July 1565, 'Marie, by the grace of God, Quene of Scottis' ordered that on her marriage she and her new husband should be styled 'King and Quene of Scotland, conjunctlie'.[60] People, and particularly English people, often talked of kings and queens of Scotland, and the usage was not unknown in the Scotland of Anderson's day.[61] In the Appendix of documents to his *Historical Essay* Anderson in his headings to the documents as often as not referred to the 'king of Scotland,' although he scrupulously preserved references in the texts to 'Rex Scottorum'. It was largely thanks to the success of William Robertson's *History of Scotland,* which was first published in 1759, that by the end of the eighteenth century 'king or queen of Scots' became accepted conventional usage. It had not always been so in the past; and, indeed, in the charters themselves sometimes the contracted form, 'Rex Scot', begs the question.[62] In sum, although the title 'king of Scots' was the most common designation, 'king of Scotland' was not unknown. In the early eighteenth century, too, with Scottish historians trying to break into the English market, there was a tendency to follow English usage, and this seems to have been the case with James Anderson.

It was typical of Chalmers to make a massive indictment out of a mere change of usage. As befitted such a slender case, the charges that he brought against Anderson were all vague and general. The *Collections*, he held, were poorly done and ill-received. Indeed, according to Chalmers, Anderson was lucky to die before the wrath of the critics descended on him, and Chalmers evidently felt that it was his duty to make up for the delinquent author's providential escape by smearing his reputation. The burden of the long and tedious charge was that Anderson was ignorant, unscholarly, bigoted and unfair in his treatment of Mary. But not one specific instance of any of these bad faults was produced by Chalmers. Indeed, on this topic Chalmers was rabid and rather disgusting. The judicious verdict of a recent student of the age-old Marian controversy puts matters in a very different light. Professor Ian Cowan finds much to praise in

---

59   Chalmers, *Ruddiman*, p. 156, n. 'O'.
60   *R.P.C.*, 1st ser., i, 345–46.
61   Cf. Anderson, *Historical Essay*, pp. 65–66. Andrew Fletcher often used the terms king or prince of Scotland.
62   E.g. in *The Acts of William I: King of Scots 1165–1214*, ed. G.W.S. Barrow (Edinburgh, 1971), p. 126 and p. 128, we have 'W' Rex Scott.'; but on p. 132, William is styled 'Rex Scocie', and similarly on p.156. Both the latter charters conferred grants in England, and possibly that would account for their following English usage. But cf., p. 169, where 'Willelmus Rex Scocie' confirms the property and privileges of Dryburgh Abbey.

Anderson's *Collections*, and not least the work's calm impartiality.[63] Chalmers, however, never missed an opportunity to asperse Anderson, condemning his fecklessness and hinting at, but never specifying, alleged inaccuracies in Anderson's transcripts. This sustained smear paved the way for the grand conclusion that, were it not for Ruddiman, nothing would have come of the *Diplomata*. Chalmers concludes his long diatribe by stating that 'Inquiry will easily find that Ruddiman performed more at the age of sixty-four, in one twelve-month, than Anderson had done, during the vigour of his life, in twenty years'.[64] Anderson had apparently only contributed the plates (hocked at that!); as if those magnificent engravings, far from being the enduring strength of the *Diplomata*, were mere pretty pictures.[65]

Informed inquiry today would have to reverse Chalmers's judgment: the engravings, not the introduction, are the parts of the *Diplomata* that are still essential to the study of Scottish palaeography and diplomatic. The introduction was, indeed, a veritable *tour de force* in its day, and from its frequent attacks on Buchanan it was clearly the work of Ruddiman. It strikes the historian of today as being diffuse and speculative in a way that typified Ruddiman, the literary scholar, rather than Anderson the record scholar. The introduction to the *Diplomata* went to great lengths to suggest that the use of charters in Scotland was known in the tenth century, but for this contention scarcely any hard evidence can be produced. Ruddiman's concern here, though, was not with record evidence as such. His chief purpose was to establish the antiquity and primacy of the bishops of St Andrews. He concluded, 'I have remained the longer upon these observations, not only that I might demonstrate, that the use of charters was more ancient among us, than some perhaps have thought; but also that I might throw light on our history, in settling the age and succession of the bishops of St Andrews, and make it clearer than hitherto has been done'.[66] But his case rests not on an examination of record evidence, of which there is practically none, but on ingenious and sometimes far-fetched arguments drawn from the medieval chronicles. Of hard proof not a vestige is to be found. Thus, according to Ruddiman, Gregory the Great, an early king of Scots, as related by Fordun bestows gifts upon the church which are confirmed by Pope John VIII, and from this Ruddiman concludes, 'That the priviledges and liberty granted to ecclesiastics by king Gregory, was committed to writing may be easily believed, from what Fordun says, of their being confirmed by pope John

---

63   Ian B. Cowan, *The Enigma of Mary Stuart* (London, 1971), pp. 20–21.
64   Chalmers, *Ruddiman*, n. 58 above, p. 159.
65   In the preface to his *Collections*, vol. i, p. vi, Anderson states that 150 plates 'are already engraven by the ingenious Artist and incomparable Letter Graver, Mr John Sturt'. For some details, see Sturt's letters to Anderson in Maidment, *Analecta Scotica*, 1st series, pp. 94–99.
66   *Diplomata*, ed. T. Ruddiman, Praefatio, sect. XVIII; translated, Anon., *An Introduction to Mr James Anderson's Diplomata Scotiae* (Edinburgh, 1773), p. 41.

VIII'.[67] This seems plausible enough; but an awkward circumstance rears its head. Can we believe in King Gregory? The historian today has to take a Dickensian view and consign Gregory the Great, like the redoubtable 'Mrs 'Arris', to limbo.

Anderson was well versed in the chroniclers and frequently invoked their works, but usually much more circumspectly than this. The kind of soft circular argument that Ruddiman employed so freely was not favoured by Anderson. James Anderson, a veritable dryasdust, liked to base his arguments on firm parchments. Indeed, his life was devoted to establishing the authenticity of the record evidence, and, in doing so, he was, in Thomas Carlyle's phrase, the 'true poet.'

The first twenty sections of Ruddiman's 'Introduction' would find few supporters today. They are far too speculative and dogmatise too much from flimsy evidence. He fared better when he dealt with the middle ages proper where he could follow the principles laid down by Anderson and the guidelines furnished by the *Historical Essay.* Ruddiman honestly admitted this. He praises Anderson's pioneer work in enabling genuine charters to be distinguished from forgeries. He states correctly that this was the principal need that the author of the *Diplomata* intended his work to serve. He rightly observes that 'The learned Anderson, well knowing this, had principally in view to publishing this work, that he [the student] might be able to judge from specimens of undoubted charters, for some centuries, concerning the authenticity of others, which have the appearance of the writings of these centuries'.[68] He lauds Anderson for exposing Atwood's enormities, which were based on notorious forgeries, and then proceeds to discuss the evidence pertaining to the homage question just as Anderson had done. He evidently intended only to summarise Anderson here, but again garrulousness takes over and spoils the effect. Ruddiman, unable to forget his undying devotion to the House of Stewart, launched out on a tedious and unnecessary defence of the legitimacy of the Stewart line. At excessive length he proved what was already known, namely, that the offspring of Robert II's first marriage were legitimate, a matter already dealt with by Father Lewis Innes. The chief value of Ruddiman's introduction, in fact, lies in its closing sections dealing with Scottish coinage and monetary values; but here, too, some crucial corrections have had to be made.[69]

It is certainly curious that Chalmers, who frequently in his *Life of Ruddiman* disparaged Anderson's *Historical Essay,* failed to notice that work's obvious bearing on the *Diplomata.* The *Diplomata* grew naturally out of the *Essay.* Most obviously, the *Essay's* influence is detectable in its Appendix of documents, for there are printed some of the items that were

---

67   Ruddiman, *Diplomata*, Praefatio, sect. XIX; translated Anon, *Introduction etc.,* p. 43.
68   Ruddiman, *Diplomata*, Praefatio, sect. XXIX; tr. Anon, cit., p. 62.
69   See R.W. Cochran Patrick, 'Note on Ruddiman's Table of the Value of Silver Money Coined in Scotland,' in *Proceedings of the Society of Antiquaries of Scotland,* x (1872) (Edinburgh, 1875), 34–42.

later reproduced in Sturt's engravings for the *Diplomata,* including the seal of Edgar 'Basileus Scottorum' that has since been repeatedly reproduced.[70] But, of course, the appendix of documents to the *Historical Essay* illustrates the essay's chief theme, that of homage, whereas the *Diplomata* aimed at a wider coverage and gave specimens of the styles of charters used by the kings and nobility of Scotland at different periods. Nonetheless, the family resemblance between the items in the appendix to the *Historical Essay* and the documents portrayed in the *Diplomata* is too close to be accidental. They were all the work of James Anderson.

It was unfortunate that Chalmers's view of James Anderson came to prevail and was accepted by the Victorians, who felt instinctively that such a one as Anderson who had enjoyed little material success must have been a shiftless ne'er-do-well. Ruddiman, on the other hand, greatly appealed to the Victorians. From the point of view of upward mobility he was everything that Samuel Smiles could have desired. From humble origins he had become not just a famous scholar but also an outstanding success as a man of business. Thus Chalmers's innuendoes against James Anderson tended to be regarded as facts, again with no evidence adduced, in such influential works as Chambers's *Eminent Scotsmen* and Anderson's *Scottish Nation.*[71] *The Dictionary of National Biography,* coming at the end of the Victorian age, was more cautious and left the matter open. Of late, however, the absurd virulence of George Chalmers's diatribe against James Anderson has been noted and deplored.[72] The present writer's examination of the matter has led to the conclusion that Chalmers's case against Anderson simply does not stand up to factual analysis. The pity is that George Chalmers's splenetic nonsense should have reigned so long unchallenged.

The Importance of the 'Historical Essay'

It only now remains to assess the importance of the *Historical Essay.* In it James Anderson made a significant new departure in Scottish historiography by adopting a more stringent approach to documentary evidence and advocating the methods of Mabillon in establishing the value of such evidence. He also made full use of the best English historical scholarship of his time, of which, as Professor Douglas has reminded us, there was no lack. Indeed, in England it was a great age of historical scholarship and pioneering

---

70   There is an excellent copy of it taken from Anderson's *Diplomata* in Gordon Donaldson's *Scottish Kings* (London, 1967), p. 8; *Diplomata,* VI, Charta Eadgari Regis.

71   The decline can be charted. Alexander Chalmers, *The General Biographical Dictionary* (London, 1812), ii, 182–83, gives a favourable account of James Anderson and brushes aside George Chalmers's aspersions. But later nineteenth century works were censorious; e.g. William Anderson, *The Scottish Nation; or the Surnames, Families, Literature, Honours, and Biographical History of the People of Scotland* (Edinburgh, 1860), i, 125–26; and *Chambers's Biographical Dictionary of Eminent Scotsmen,* ed. T. Thomson (London, 1864), i, 54–55.

72   Duncan, *Ruddiman,* n. 46 above, pp. 132–33.

re-appraisal.[73] Anderson freely availed himself of the work of English historians, frequently citing John Selden, Sir Henry Spelman, George Hickes, Thomas Rymer, Thomas Hearne, James Tyrrell, Bishop Nicholson, and many others.

James Anderson's *Historical Essay* was, in short, the performance not only of a skilled pioneer palaeographer and diplomatist but also of a learned historian who was steeped in the best historical works of his time. Myth and fable had little appeal for him. He frequently denounces the stories of Geoffrey of Monmouth whose twelfth-century *Historia Regum Britanniae* gave an incredibly detailed and wholly imaginary account of early Britain, and whose tall tales were woven into subsequent chronicle histories of England, though contemptuously rejected by John of Fordun.[74] Yet, though the historical tide has long turned against Geoffrey, he dies hard.

Recently the present writer was astonished to be adjudged mistaken in holding that the concept of an imperial crown appeared in Scotland earlier than in England.[75] The critic, Dr Arthur Williamson, has evidently been beguiled by Geoffrey of Monmouth whose views were staple items of Tudor propaganda. There is no space here to deal with the matter at length, but the imperial tradition for England on which Dr Williamson bases his case never had any existence outside the charmed pages of Geoffrey's masterpiece of whoppers. In the case of Scotland the concept of an imperial crown is a matter of record. The Scottish act of parliament of 1425 speaks for itself: 'It is ordanit be ye king with ye consent and deliverance of ye three estats that all and sindry ye kingis liegis of ye realme lief and be governyt under ye kingis lawis and statuts of this realme allenarly and undir na particular lawis na special privilegeis na be na lawis of other countreis nor realmis'.[76] The act of 1469 regulating notaries in Scotland makes precisely the same claim, which by definition categorises an imperial crown, when it

---

73   David C. Douglas, *English Scholars 1660–1730* (2nd revised edn., London, 1951).

74   Anderson, *Historical Essay*, p. 131. For Fordun and Geoffrey, see Laura Keeler, *Geoffrey of Monmouth and the Late Latin Chroniclers 1300–1500* (Berkeley and Los Angeles, 1946), pp. 76–80; but, as Professor Keeler notes, Fordun rejects Geoffrey's fables only to make way for whoppers of his own.

75   A.H. Williamson in *New Perspectives on the Politics and Culture of Early Modern Scotland*, edd. John Dwyer, Roger A. Mason and Alexander Murdoch (Edinburgh, n.d.), pp. 35, 54 n. 15, vaguely animadverting on Ferguson, art. cit. n. 23 above, *Sc. Hist. Rev.* (1974).

76   *A.P.S.*, ii, 9. This, says Ranald Nicholson, *Scotland: the Later Middle Ages* (Edinburgh, 1974), p. 309, was an omnibus measure that stressed the jurisdictional independence of Scotland. No such measure, of course, stressed the jurisdictional independence of Ireland. The import of this act of 1425 has always been recognised, as by Stair's great contemporary, Mackenzie of Rosehaugh, who held that 'This Act was made to exclude all Pretensions of the Emperor or Pope, and all laws made, or Privelegeis operated by them'. Sir George Mackenzie, *Works* (Edinburgh, 1716), i, 176.

opens, 'Oure Sovran lord has ful Jurisdictione and free Impire within his Realm'.[77] James Anderson was correct in regarding those statutes as proof that Scotland had an imperial crown, and he was right to cite Selden in support of his judgement.[78] Much more evidence bearing on the issue could be adduced but will have to lie over until another occasion.

Overall, Anderson proved the case for the independence of Scotland and its possession of an imperial crown. He was right to conclude that homage was only given under duress and never freely conceded. But the evidence of the Durham charters, which troubled Anderson somewhat, is still perplexing. Experts today differ on the all-important question of the authenticity or otherwise of King Edgar's charter of 1095 in which homage is admitted.[79] The matter is a very difficult one, for of the early career of Edgar little is known for certain. Anderson perhaps tended to see the problem too much in the light of later developments, failing to note that the general circumstances of Edgar's situation pointed towards the likelihood of his having accepted Rufus as his overlord for Scotland.[80] But if Edgar did pay homage to William Rufus for Scotland he seems to have made light of it, and certainly his successors did not feel bound by his submission. The case was quite otherwise, and William the Lion's enforced homage in 1174 merely underlines the point. William had to be a captive of the king of England and bereft of choice before he accepted Henry II as his overlord for Scotland. Thus, as far as Edgar's charter of 1095 is concerned, the state of the evidence still calls for an open verdict.

On other matters Anderson was sometimes wrong, as when he attempted to rebut Matthew Paris's claim that the kings of Scots did homage for Lothian. The correct response here would have been simply to state that no record of such a homage exists. Instead, Anderson argued desperately that the 'Laudonia' in question was located in Northern England, and on this matter he came perilously close to Atwood's wild mode of argument. On the vexed question of the *Regiam Majestatem*, too, he rather tied himself in

77   *A.P.S.*, ii, 95. John Selden, *Titles of Honor* (London, 1614), p. 27, quoted this act, and observed that it proved that the crown of Scotland was among those 'not subject or subordinat to any, but God'.

78   Anderson, *Historical Essay*, pp. 79–80; John Selden, *Titles of Honor*, (London, 1614), pp. 26–27; Anderson probably used the third and enlarged edition of this work that was published at London in 1672, where the relevant passage is on pp. 20–21.

79   Sir Archibald C. Lawrie, *Early Scottish Charters prior to A.D. 1153* (Glasgow, 1905), No. XV, pp. 12–13 and notes pp. 246–49, regarded Edgar's charter as spurious; A.A.M. Duncan upholds its authenticity in 'The Earliest Scottish Charters', *Sc. Hist. Rev.*, xxxvii (1958), 103–135; G.W.S. Barrow, *The Anglo-Norman Era in Scottish History* (Oxford, 1980), p. 153, n. 43, feels that the text may have been tampered with; and Joseph Donnelly, 'The Earliest Scottish Charters?', has even stronger reservations about Lawrie XV, in *Sc. Hist. Rev.*, lxviii (1989), 1–22.

80   On the confused situation in Scotland following the death of Malcolm Canmore in 1093 see the excellent treatment in A.A.M. Duncan, *Scotland: The Making of the Kingdom* (Edinburgh, 1975), pp. 124–28.

knots. In the end he agreed, though gingerly, with Skene that the *Regiam* was put together in the reign of David I, and so before the time of Glanvil. Craig, on the other hand, had considered those books to be 'no part of our Law, but taken from Glanvil, and wrongly imposed upon us'. Anderson confessed to being puzzled (always a sign of grace in a historian), but in the end hesitantly accepted Skene's view. A measure of national *amour propre*, which in the *Essay* clearly shines through the author's modest protestations, doubtless helped to ensure this conclusion. Modern scholarship rejects Anderson in this matter. But then, as far as the conundrum of the *Regiam Majestatem* is concerned, who can be said to be right?[81] And, of course, not only is Homer known to nod, but even Mabillon to err.[82] Nonetheless, with the sources known to him and the tools at his disposal, James Anderson wrought to considerable purpose.

When it appeared in 1705 Anderson's *Historical Essay* was highly regarded. But once the Treaty of Union of 1707 took the urgency out of the homage controversy (not least by creating the imperial crown of Great Britain) the *Essay* was rather lost sight of. Partly, too, this was the result of the fact that record scholarship was not the forte of the philosophical historians who dominated the study of history in the mid-eighteenth century. Disputes about controversial points in charters appeared trivial to the lofty minds of the Enlightenment. Indeed, they did not find much to interest them in the Middle Ages, which they regarded as periods of childish barbarism, best summed up as 'Goth against Goth'. The opening sentence of William Robertson's *History of Scotland* makes the attitude of the Enlightened ones crystal clear: 'The first ages of the Scottish History are dark and fabulous. Nations, as well as men, arrive at maturity by degrees; and the events which happened during their infancy or early youth cannot be recollected, and deserve not to be remembered'.[83] But, interestingly enough, Anderson's *Historical Essay* is one of the few sources noted by Robertson in his skimpy treatment of early Scotland.[84] Robertson, too, unlike David Hume, consulted manuscript sources and had the habit of adding illustrative documents in appendices in the manner of his grand-uncle, James Anderson. Anderson's influence, then, did not just stem from the *Diplomata*, where there was some dispute about the extent of his labours and an unjust tendency to favour Ruddiman.

The *Historical Essay*, even although little mentioned after 1707, was also influential. And the reason for its influence was simple. It was the first

---

81 Anderson, *Historical Essay*, pp. 132ff. There is a discussion of varying assessments of the *Regiam* in George Chalmers, *Caledonia* (new edn.), ii, 727–33. More modern treatments are, Lord Cooper, *Regiam Majestatem and Quoniam Attachiamenta* (Stair Society, 11, Edinburgh, 1947); A.A.M. Duncan's brilliant re-appraisal, 'Regiam Majestatem, a Reconsideration', *Jurid. Rev. (N.S.)*, vi (1961), 199–217; and an interesting general survey of the problem in David M. Walker, *The Scottish Jurists*, (Edinburgh, 1985), chap. 2; cf. also his *A Legal History of Scotland*, vol. i (Edinburgh, 1988), pp. 108–21.

82 Knowles, *Historian and Character*, n. 31 above, p. 235.

83 William Robertson, *The History of Scotland* (new edn., London, 1794), p. 1.

84 Robertson, op. cit., p. 8.

piece of historical writing produced in Scotland in a distinctively modern mode. If a historian today felt the need to examine the question of homage vis-a-vis Scotland and England, he would, if he was any good at all, end up with a study similar in many ways to that which Anderson published in 1705; and, unless he was an unbelievably bad historian, he would be quite unable to emulate Atwood's *Superiority and Direct Dominion of the Imperial Crown of England.*

That, indeed, is the magnitude of James Anderson's achievement: he made a great contribution to the nascent sciences of palaeography and diplomatic, and at the same time contributed substantially to the development of modern historiography. History was to be about proof and not ranting triumphalism.

Note on this reprint

No attempt has been made to modernise spelling, punctuation or syntax. The text reproduced here is, as far as possible, a straight reprint. As such, it might be of some interest to students of historiography; and perhaps even more to students of English, illustrating as it does the difficulties that educated Scots of the period enountered in writing what was for most of them still a strange language. James Anderson, like Thomas Ruddiman, represented the last generation in Scotland that was more comfortable writing in Latin than in English. Their work in English, consequently, shows many awkwardnesses that the Augustan Scots of the next generation successfully overcame. The contrast between Anderson's English prose and that of his grand-nephew, William Robertson, is extremely instructive.

The opportunity has been taken, however, to correct some obvious misprints; but since there was no recognised standard of spelling in Anderson's day, it may be that some misprints have inadvertently been allowed to stand. Also the excessive and idiosyncratic italicisations in the original printed text have not been reproduced. They distract the reader to no real purpose, and italics have been used in this reprint only to give the titles of books and to render Latin phrases.

The valuable Appendix to the *Historical Essay,* consisting of twenty-six documents, has, reluctantly, been omitted. This has been done partly to save space and partly because the main items are readily available in better texts in modern collections. Thus Edgar's charter of 1095 (familiar as Lawrie XV in Sir Archibald C. Lawrie's *Early Scottish Charters* (Glasgow, 1905); the Ednam charter of Thor Longus; the Treaty of Falaise; the Quitclaim of Canterbury; and the Declaration of Arbroath (to note the chief items in Anderson's Appendix), can all be found, translated into English, in Professor Gordon Donaldson's invaluable *Scottish Historical Documents* (Edinburgh, 1970).

Finally, I should like to express my gratitude to Professor Alexander Fenton, Director of the School of Scottish Studies in the University of Edinburgh, for making available to me the School's copy of Anderson's *Historical Essay,* and to Professor G.W.S. Barrow, head of the Department of Scottish History at Edinburgh, for use of his copy of the *Diplomata Scotiae.*

AN HISTORICAL ESSAY, SHEWING THAT THE CROWN AND KINGDOM OF SCOTLAND, IS IMPERIAL AND INDEPENDENT

By JAMES ANDERSON

THE PREFACE

TO Appear in Print, in this mannerly Age, without Dedication or Preface, may be thought Unbecoming.

FOR Dedication, I must own, The performance is so small and mean, That it made me unwilling, to offer any trouble to a Patron; And I presume The Independency I maintain, has for Patrons, all true SCOTS-MEN, yea all Sincere well wishers, of the peace and quiet of Britain.

FOR Preface, less may be said, Because some parts of the ensewing Treatise are introductory; wherein I have accounted for my undertaking of this province: That it was rather necessity than choice:

BEING thus, I hope any failures in the performance will be the more easily pardoned; especially when my only aim is, to use my endeavours in the service of my Countrey. And I'm very sensible this Subject is already managed; and may be yet handled by others; with much more advantage:

BUT some, whose sentiments I regard, were pleas'd to think, That the Charters mention'd by Mr. Atwood, the author of the Treatise of, *The Superiority of England, over Scotland,* were what might be most amusing and observable in that Book; And he having flung me in, to vouch the most material of these deeds, I was necessarly obliged to answer; And BEING NAMED, AS A Witnes, my Testimony cou'd be given by none but my self.

THIS was the pressing motive, which engag'd me in this undertaking in relation to the Charters, and if to confirm, what's said of them, or to give light in this affair; I have launched out a little into other things; I hope it will not be thought foreign to the purpose.

OUR Independency hath of late not only been attacked in Historical Treatises first, by Doctor Drake, and then by Mr. Atwood: But also we're insulted by a scurrilous reviling Pamphlet, set furth under the title of *Select Fables.* And beside ther's very lately published a plagiary *Treatise of the Account of Scotland &c.* Where to make it more current, the Title Page is dabled with, *Light to the Dependency.*

THO' we're thus abus'd by some, yet several worthy English Authors, as Cambden, Coke, Spelman, Selden, Temple, and others speak with Civility and respect of Scotland: And if the Calumnious Treatises asserting the Homage, shou'd only come in the hands of the Knowing, They were little to be regarded; But they may fall in the hands of some well meaning persons Neighbours and Strangers, who may be misled by bold assertions and glittering proofs.

THIS oblidges Us by the necessity of self defence, after repeated attempts upon the Soveraignty of our Crown, to vindicat our just right of

Independency, and to lay open the unbecoming Artifices, that have been used in the Claim of Homage.

THE design of this Treatise, is to evince, That the Crown and Kingdom of Scotland, is Imperial and Independent; and that the pretences for the Homage Claim'd by England from Scotland, are chiefly founded upon Forgeries, vitiated or patcht up Laws, Fables, and extorted acknowledgments: which are the very shrewd signs of a bad Cause.

IN this Essay I have bore a little closs upon the Monks, Because they were the Incendiaries, who hatched that Claim, and deckt it up, with the gaudy and deluding dress of Fable, to perswade, that the Homage was due in the more distant and remote ages; and colour'd it with the abominable Juggle of Forgery, in the later times.

THIS Claim for sometime was managed only by word; But at length these monkish Devices occasioned a very long and bloody War, wherein was sacrificed the lives of several Hundred Thousand Christians, who exercised the most barbarous cruelties upon one another.

UPON these things, no Good Man can look back, without the height of horrour and concern: wherefore the reviving of this Claim is the proper office of a Firebrand:

THIS hath made me, in some measure, treat Mr. Atwood beyond my inclination; For tho' a calmness of temper, ought to accompany all disputes, with civil and candid Authors; yet he having no place among such, It wou'd be an injury to ingenuous enquirers, to place them and him upon a level; and to give the same treatment, to the modest, and to the extravagant.

TO this performance, I have given the Title of an Essay; For it becomes my years and experience, rather to enquire than to decide; and upon good reason and proof, I shall be very ready to retract, and frankly own my escapes.

FOR excuse, of what's amiss, in method and expression; I might lay claim to some ordinary pretences; But I rather throw my self upon the civility of the Reader: what I have Essay'd for the Service of my Countrey; Is with my Heart and Hand, without any by-end: and I have cloath'd my thoughts with such expressions as my low attainments did suggest, to make them intelligible, which is all I desire.

TO enforce my positions, I have brought testimonies, from some of the best English Historians; or else have voucht them by Charters, Seals and Records, and for illustration have placed them in an Appendix; being for the most part taken from the Originals; and if in the Transcribing of ancient deeds; wherein the Sillabication is different from what is now used; there may be any mistakes, especially in Letters, I hope to be excused:

AND upon the whole, seing I have charg'd the Invention and Revival, of the claim of Homage, upon particular persons; I may with freedom plead and expect; That what's amiss in the ensewing Essay, may be turn'd upon myself, and not upon my Countrey.

I HOPE none who considers, That the following Essay, Is chiefly concerning Ancient Charters, will think I turn my thoughts in a by-Road, when the knowledge of Writs is so agreeable to my Profession: And I acknowledg,

That for some time, my spare hours have now and then been imploy'd in Collecting of Copies of Charters, and of other Writs old and new, from Originals, Records and otherwise, and in excerpting from them, and I have made some Remarks upon the Form, Characters & Seals of Ancient Charters; For to understand them, is what I pursue, in matters of Antiquity.

TO this enquiry I was allur'd and invited by the sentiment of a great Master of our Laws and Stiles, the Learn'd and Judicious Lord Dirlton, exprest in his advice to an eminent Peer and Officer of State, about the Study of our Law; where this great Man Regrates, that the knowledg of writs is so much slighted, and says, that the careful perusal of them, is a Great Introduction to understand the grounds of our Practick.

IF then in a research into the Rudiments of my Employment, any discovery hath falln in my way for the service of my Country; It gives me the greatest content: And in case hereafter I make any publick appearance, it will probably be, In relation to the Formula's and Stiles of Scots Writs Ancient and Modern.

An Historical Essay, shewing, That the Crown and Kingdom of SCOTLAND, is Imperial and Independent.*

It might be thought, That all Contest concerning the HOMAGE claim'd by England from Scotland, was long ago laid aside, and, at most, was to be used as the Diversion of the Learn'd and Curious, and not to be applyed to any present Circumstance of Affairs; but one Mr. Atwood, a Lawyer, has taken upon him to Revive this Debate, in a Book published of late, under this Blustering Title, *The Superiority and Direct Dominion of the Imperial Crown and Kingdom of England, over the Crown and /2/ Kingdom of Scotland:* Where he handles the Argument, with an Inference and Tendency, of the outmost Import and Concern to a Kingdom.

IN this Book, I was much surpriz'd, to find my self dropt in as an Evidence, to vouch some Original Charters and Grants by our Kings, In which (says this Author) Homage for the Kingdom of Scotland is so fully own'd, That it's hoped may prevent all further Denial, in a Matter so evident.[1] And that one of these Original Charters, puts the Homage beyond all Question, and will Convict all of wilful Blindness, who pretend not now to see the Superiority of England over the whole Kingdom of Scotland.[2]

WITH what Manners, Mr. Atwood who was altogether unknown to me, as I presume, I was to him, hath adduc'd me as a Voucher, I shall not notice; Only being occasionally at London, when this Book came Abroad, I enquired into the Character of him who had assumed so mighty a Province, and was credibly Informed, He was late chief Justice of New-York, laid aside for Practices best known to himself; That he was a bold Undertaker, and /3/ whose greatest Encouragement and Expectation in this Work was from the Bookseller; And if the Sentiments which many of his Learn'd and Ingenious Countreymen have of him, and of his Performance were known, They would render the Book altogether contemptible.

I WOU'D willingly have communicat to more able Hands, what I knew in Relation to these Charters which Mr.Atwood mentions for proving the Homage; But since he has named me as an Eye-witness of the most important of them, I'm bound to publish what I know of the Matter, lest a Consequence of Acquiescing in the Authors Relation might be drawn from my silence, and I think my self the more under this Duty to my Countrey, because perhaps, of any Scots-man, I have had the best Opportunity to inspect these Charters, from which Mr. Atwood so Dogmatically infers the Homage of our Kings; And herefore I cou'd neither Decline nor delay, to Contribute my weak Endeavours, to Vindicat the Honour and Memory of some of the best of our Kings, from being stain'd, with a base and voluntar Surrender of their Soveraignty, and with Entailing a Servitude /4/ upon their People; And to let the World know what Injury is done to our Ancient and

---

*   In the footnotes, references to page numbers in Anderson's original text are
     put in the form 'P.2' to distinguish them from other page references.
P.2   (1) p. 253 (2) p. 542.

Independent Crown, by notorious and repeated Forgeries of the Charters and Seals of our Monarchs.

BEFORE Entry upon the Consideration of these Charters, I hope it will not be unacceptable to give a short hint of the Design of this daring Book, and of some remarkable Passages in it; Which I'm confident will justify and make good the Character given of the Author.

THIS forward Man under the imaginary Pretence, of our being Homagers to England, contendeth, that by the Act of Setlement of the English Crown, we are pre-determined in the Succession and Entail of our Crown, as a Consequence of our Homage, and in very plain Terms says, That whoever duly succeeds to the Crown of England, will be ipso facto Rightful King or Queen of Scotland,[1] And this being a bold Position, and needing support, our Author to act the true part of an Incendiary, calls in the Crown and Kingdom of England to be his auxiliaries, as /5/ being interested in the Controversy by the Judgment of two old wise Parliaments;[1] and condemns the Moderns for giving up this Plea.

HE Treats our Crown with the slighting Terms of supposed Imperial Crown,[2] and subordinat Crown,[3] Yea annexed to the Crown of England,[4] And he gives to our Monarchs, the undervaluing Title of Nominal Kings[5] and of *Sub-reguli* and Vice-roys[6] and is pleased to compliment us, by asserting the Honour of Subjection as our Right.[7]

HE takes upon him to charge them, who set up for the Soveraignty of our Crown, with Impiety; and Impudently says, That such a Liberty as is now contended for by them who set up for Patriots in Scotland, is contrary to GOD's Law, requiring Submission to that Imperial Crown under which he has placed them, and to their own most valuable Interests, as Men, and Reform'd Christians, and that they cannot assume this Liberty, without Impiety to GOD and their Countrey:[8] And that this Duty of Submission /6/ flows, from Scotland's being an undoubted Member of the English Monarchy;[1] And that the Act of Parliament of England has setled our Crown as an APPENNAGE to the Crown of the Monarchy:[2] And in maintaining our independency, he taxes us with being immoderately fond of a mistaken point of Honour;[3] And advances a step yet higher, and says, That the denying this right of Homage must now necessarly be grounded on French Counsels.[4]

THIS fanciful Author is so self conceited, to think, that His endeavours cannot faill of having good effect with any, but the Nonjurers in both Kingdoms, And will tend to the conviction of the Generality of the Scotch Nation, who are not too deeply engaged with France;[5]

LEST his Arguments should not prevail with us, He falls to Threatnings, and asks us, If with Justice we can retain Lodoney? (i.e. Lothian) or if it will become England to give up the Dependence of Scotland? And then he

---

P.4   (1) p. 4 & 562.
P.5   (1) p. 4 (2) p. 2 (3) p. 557. (4) p.4 & 226. (5) p. 15. (6) p. 4. (7) p. 49. (8) p. 559.
P.6   (1) 559. (2) ibid. (3) p. 597. (4) p. 570. (5) p. 575.

descends to particulars, That if we shou'd withdraw our allegiance from the Succession of England, /7/ And set up as an Independent Kingdom, from that time, all who are born in Scotland would be aliens to England, and Lands which otherways might have descended to them, wou'd Escheat to the Crown of England;[1] And for instance, He is so very unmannerly, as to name a most eminent and Noble Peer, whose Heirs, he says, may thereby chance to lose a considerable Estate in England.

THIS Lawyer, to Sum up the evidence, and to shew his extraordinary faculty in commenting, He insinuats, that the denying his Doctrine is no less than high Treason; And is so charitable as to advertise all concerned to notice their danger, as not being aware of the plain Import of the Act of Parliament, which makes it high Treason by any overt Act, to derogat from that Right to the Crown of England and its Appennages, which is ascertained by the Act of Setlement;[2] And this Author positively asserts, That Scotland is an undoubted Member and Appennage of the English Monarchy: So the consequence is obvious.

THIS and a great deal more such /8/ stuff, is to be found in this Book by any who will throw away so much time as to peruse it.

AGREEABLE to these Notions, are Mr. Atwoods Sentiments of Authors. He charges the Moderns in General with oversight, and preconceived opinions, and gives very unbecoming characters to many Learned Men, both Scots and English: he is indeed very favourable to Jeoffrey of Monmouth and Harding the Poet: and the Stories of Brutus and King Arthur are in great credit with him.

TO trace and answer all the whimsies, inconsistencies and extravagancies of this confus'd Author is not to be expected, But only that I shou'd touch what may give light in this matter, especially in relation to the Charters and Laws adduc'd for proof of the pretended superiority.

THAT the Kings of Scotland were subject in Homage for their Crown to England, has by degrees creep't into some English Histories; The most allowable ground of the mistake is, That our Kings, in ancient times, being very assisting to the English against their cruel Enemies the Danes, and that, for this and other considerations, The /9/ Kings of England did at different times bestow upon them some Northern Counties, and there were Leagues between the two Kings, whereby, perhaps the Scots were to assist the English on occasion: But even for these Counties, there is little or no evidence of Homage until after the Conquest.

THE more ancient and most approv'd English Historians recount nothing disagreeable to this; for in them, I presume, we will not find HOMAGE or HOMAGER before the days of the Conqueror; But other Historians of a later date, either by a design'd stretch to palliat the encroachments, made by some of their Monarchs, upon the Soveraignty of our Crown, or by lame Information, and confounding ancient Things with Modern Terms,[1] have

---

P.7   (1) p. 571. (2) p. 568 & 569.
P.9   (1) Spelman *Gloss. ad Voc. Homagium* p. 296. pen fin. No. Ed.

enlarg'd the Homage pay'd for what our Kings possest in England, to be also of the Kingdom of Scotland. Thus by Sophistry, drawing the fallacious consequence of a general from a Special.

THE Kings of Scotland, so long as they had Possessions in England after the Conquest, did justly pay Homage for them: But that any of our Kings did /10/ ever voluntarly acknowledg the King of England, as Superior and Overlord of their Crown, was alwise and still is denyed.

IT has indeed been the fate and misfortune of some of our Kings and Nobles when in Captivity, or by Compulsion and Force, to own the King of England as Superior; And have not the English Kings done the like to others, if not worse? But even these acknowledgments, have been renounced and released as Extortions and Injuries.

AMONG all the English Historians of any credit, Holinshed in his voluminous History, leads the van of the Homage-mongers, and hath mustered up all he could scrape together on the Subject, from other Writers, or which his own Invention could produce.[1]

THESE endeavours to eclipse the Glory and Liberty of Our CROWN, and NATION, by a fictitious Homage, enflam'd the Zeal of the Learn'd and Judicious Sir Thomas Craig of Riccartoun, to Write an elaborat Treatise concerning this Homage, wherein this brave Patriot hath refuted all pretences of Homage, for the Kingdom of Scotland, by solid Reasons, and by clear Answers to the Instances given in History, and hath made plainly appear, that /11/ any Homage pay'd by our Kings to England, was for the beneficiary Counties they enjoyed in that Kingdom. This Treatise was originally Written in Latine, and was of late acurately Translated, by our ingenious Country-man, Mr. George Ridpath, who in his preface, hath demonstrat the Forgery of a Charter of Homage, by King Malcolm the 3d, commonly called Canmoir, of which more afterward.

I'M sorry to find the Learn'd and Ingenious Mr. Tyrrel, in the entry of so great an undertaking of the general History of England, to pass so severe, and I must say, unjust censure, upon our Craig, That in his Treatise of Homage, there be as many Errors as Lines: He is also blamed by others, for expressing too much heat against Mr. Hollinshed.

OUR Craig's learning and judgment hath, with so much justice, gain'd him an establish'd reputation, both at home and abroad, that his performances are judged equal to, if not above any of their kind; & where may we be allowed to discover the heat, which is said to be natural in Scotsmen, if not in defence of the Soveraignity and Independency of our ancient Crown, and Kingdom.

/12/THE claim of Homage, did for a long time ly dormant, until King Henry the 8th of England, made War against his Nephew our King James the 5th; And he emitted a declaration in 1542 wherein he expatiats on this Homage, which he pretends was due, by proofs from History, Instruments

---

P.10   (1) Vol. 1. cap. 22, p. 116.

and records: And in the reign of his Son Edward the 6th, this Claim was enquired into, but the glorious Queen Elizabeth was so far from entertaining any such thoughts, that to prevent any jealousie, she published a Declaration in the contrair:[1] And the Succession of our Kings to the English Throne, with the repeated Commissions for uniting of both Kingdoms, seemed to bury this dispute.

BUT last year (1703) Dr. Drake published (as he says) a posthumous Treatise of an anonimous Author, concerning the Scottish & English History, under the title of *Historia anglo-scotica*, wherein are interspersed accounts of Homages, said to be performed by several of our Kings, by deeds under their seals, chiefly founded on the authority of Harding the English poetical Historian, who was a notorious Forger as shall be hereafter related.

/13/ THO several Historians, in the threed and course of their History, have mention'd this Homage; yet never any did undertake the argument singly by it self, until Mr. Atwood published his Book, from a whimsical fancy of his own, that it might serve a turn; And to make his undertaking the more favourable, he tells that he is descended of Scots progenitors.

IN the days of our learned Craig, the most pregnant proofs of the Homage, were adduced from History, for albeit the Declaration of War, by Henry the 8th, speaks of several Deeds & Instruments of Homage, under the Seals of our Kings, yet there is none particularized, except the base and known instrument of subiection of Baliol, and therefore this worthy Gentleman saith, If any Man can produce deeds for this Homage, write by either party or Charters and ancient Monuments, corroborated by their Seals, then they have something, to which they may give Credit.[1] And the Learned Sir George Mackenzie is of the same Sentiment,[2] and without peradventure Charters are the most sure and convincing proofs.

/14/ MR. Atwood fancies, that he has answered all Sir Thomas Craigs Arguments: But with how great weakness, & with how many inconsistencies, is at first view apparent: And thinking to gain the cause by Sir Thomas's own concession, he pretends to answer the Objections, made by Mr. Ridpath against King Malcolm's Charter,[1] and for support of it, make an induction of several other Charters, and above all, of some in the Archives of Durhame, & with a singular civility brings me in to vouch them.[2]

THIS, upon the Consideration before mentioned hath drawn me to give my Testimony, which I shall endeavour to perform with all Candor, having no design, either to Ingratiat or offend, but to make a free and impartial Enquiry after Truth; For tho' I'm a Native of Scotland, yet I must own the many Civilities and Favours, of the brave English Nation, and that the ingenious persons there, who favour'd me with Converse or Correspondence, did express their dislike, of Mr. Atwoods Enterprize, and as a demonstrative Evidence of their Indignation against it; & of their sincere Love of Truth, did

---

P.12   (1) In January 1568.
P.13   (1) *Scotlands Soveraignty Asserted*, p. 202. (2) *Treatise of precedency & Herauldry*, p. 9.
P.14   (1) p. 219. (2) p. 253.

without any disguise or reserve /**15**/ communicat to me, when I was in England, and since my return, Transcripts of any Writings I desir'd for giving light in this matter.

OF all Proofs in History, none are so concluding and pointed as Charters: They speak for themselves, and need no Rhetorical Embellishments and Flourishes to perswade; Which hath made ancient Charters and Records, so much the study of this inquisitive Age: For Histories being overgrown with Legends of Miracles and Visions on the one hand, and larded with many Romantick Fables, and Traditions on the other, there was no safe way left, to correct what's amiss, to clear what's obscure, and to add what's wanting, but a diligent search into records and ancient Muniments; And all persons, of true worth and Generosity, frankly communicat and lay open these Noble store-houses, which are so very useful for the discovery of Truth. But even in these valuable and rich Treasuries are to be found false Deeds, of which some are contriv'd with more, and some with less Artifice; And therefore are not implicitly to be relyed upon, but are to be examin'd, and may be disprov'd by Form & Character, /**16**/ which in ancient Times was very uniform, in the respective Periods of Time; and by Seals since they were us'd, and by the Witnesses and other pregnant Circumstances.

THE most corrupt Mint-house of Charters were the Cloysters; Here the idle and luxurious Monks devised mischievous Forgeries, to enrich themselves, & to agrandize their Monarchs, that they might be protected by them in their unjust Spoils: And these cuning Serpents instil'd in Men of Honour and Arms, that it was below them to be subject to the Drudgery of learning to Read and Write, and so keept the Knack to themselves; For of old none but Church-men were Clerks and Notaries, which encourag'd and Embolden'd them in such *Leger de main* and Jugling Tricks: And Discoveries are frequently made of Forg'd Deeds: And especially in the Archives of Religious Houses, which were in the Custody of the Monks, for nothing in former times was proof of Monkcraft, And all prudent Men will narrowly canvass ancient Charters, when adduc'd in any matter which touch Interest and Credit of a privat man, but much more, when they call in Question the Soveraignity of a Crown and Kingdom.

/**17**/ EVEN credulous Mr. Atwood, when he finds a Charter in his way, of our King Robert the 2d, while he was Steward of Scotland, he then charges the Priests of the Scots Colledge at Paris with forging of it (as being expert at that Trade) for no other Reason, but because that Robert, when Steward, used the Plural Number in his Charters,[1] which is no mark of Forgery; For tho' the English Nobility use not the Plural Number, yet ours do: Blind Zeal makes many a stumble, and it's pretty comical in Mr. Atwood, when he meets with any thing to his Purpose, from a Monkish Historian, he Avouches it as Gospel; But when the Pope, the infallible Father is on our side, he calls his Authority Hells-fire.[2]

P.17　(1) p. 514. (2) p. 101.

AMBITIOUS Princes, never wanted a Pretence to Overtop their Neighbours, when their Power was able to second their Inclinations, and bad men are ever ready to justifie the Practices of their Kings by unbecoming Methods: Of this, we are an Instance, when to colour a Pretence, for Wreathing a Yoke of Servitude upon us, The Knight errant Adventure of Brutus /18/ a true Trojan, who in the Days of Ely and Samuel, Dispossest the Giants, the then Inhabitants of this Ile: and the fabulous Division of Britain among his three Sons, with a Condition of Homage by the Younger to the Elder; And the Cant of the Romantick Victories, of the famous King Arthur, over a long Tribe of Kings, Dukes, Kingdoms, and Provinces; And the ridiculous Miracle of the Thumping Stroke of King Athelstan's Sword, slapping a great Gap an Eln long in a flint Rock near Dumbar, after a Prayer, to honest St John of Baverly, to shew he was true Superior of Scotland: and the vain Whim, of Edgars being row'd over Dee, with eight Kings as Watermen, are all devised by the Monks, and used as Evidences to support the Homage for the ancient British and Saxon Times,[1] and a parcel of forg'd Charters, vitiated or patched up Laws, and extorted Acknowledgments of Superiority, are brought in as a counter-part for the later Times.

I MUST own, Mr. Atwood hath brought me, upon a very undesirable Province, by naming me as an Eye-/19/witness of some Charters of Homage. These are edg'd Proofs against the Honour of my Countrey; From which, there is no protection or Defence, but a Recrimination of Forgery, and the Publishing of some things, which, at first were only design'd for privat use: To this I'm Compell'd by the natural Law of Self-defence. And our Gracious Queen in her last Letter, to our Parliament,[1] hath shown a great concern, for the SOVERAIGNTY OF OUR CROWN, which clearly evinces Her Majesties Dislike, of any Insults made upon our Independency.

NONE seem to have suffer'd more, by abominable Monkish Devices, than some of our Kings, whose Charters and Seals have been frequently Forg'd and Counterfeited, to Favour an imaginary Homage; And I presume, it may justly be thought, That if a Tract of Forgeries can be Demonstrat, it will render all Proofs from history, in this Matter very suspected; seing it furnishes good ground to believe, That the Historians, who mention this Homage are either Vitiat by Interpolations, for such Corruptions are not to /20/ be question'd, when Forgeries of Charters and Seals are practised: Or otherways, it may be rationally suppos'd, that the Historians have been Misled by Reports, and Informations, arising from these Counterfeit Deeds.

TO Consider all the suppos'd Saxon Charters, mentioned by our Author, is not worth the while, tho they did bear Homage, because they are the Testimony of a Party: But there's nothing in them, from so much as a strain'd Inference can be made, but from the big and swelling Titles of the Granters, which they might assume, or the Monks Hammer out at Pleasure.

P.18   (1) *Vide Epist. Edw. I ad Papam.*
P.19   (1) In June 1704.

IT'S meer Whim in Mr. Atwood to think, that from Caedwalla's designing himself in a Charter (tho Genuine) *Deo disponente Rex*,[1] without any Limitation implyed his Soveraignty of Britain, for this Caedwalla is reckon'd among the Kings of the West Saxons, and Predecessor of the memorable Ina, who was the first imagin'd Monarch of Britain, and for the clearer Manifestation of his Right, was e'en dignified and chosen by an Angel, according to the jumbled in sections, of the Laws ascrib'd to King Edward the /21/ Confessor,[1] Which Laws our Author adduces as potent Evidences of the Homage; But it's easy to make appear, that the Paragraphs of these Laws pointing at the Homage, are newly wedg'd in, and are a spurious after-growth; and so of a piece with Fable and Forgerie.

THE next charters are from Athelstan and Edgar of England, with some flourishing Titles not worth the notice. Our Author seems not to want some Suspicion of Edgar's Charters,[2] and Mr. Tyrrel is more plain in the Matter.[3] The most important Charter of Edgar, which supports the Titles of Athelstan, and of all Athelstan's, Edgar's and Cnuts Charters, bears the most extensive Titles, and is the Charter cited by the Author elsewhere,[4] I'm afraid will not endure the Touchstone, which brings all the rest under gross suspicion. And it is remarkable, this Charter begins thus; *Altitonantis Dei largislua Clementia, qui est Rex Regum & Dominus Dominantium, ego Eadgarus Anglorum BASILEUS, omniumque Regum, insula /22/ Oceani que Britanniam circumjacent, cunctarumque nationum que infra eum includuntur, Imperator & Dominus, &c.* which may be Translated thus, By the bountiful mercy of GOD, who thunders from on High, who is King of Kings and Lord of Lords, &c. O execrable villany! What wou'd not these Monks do, who dared to front a falsehood, with the lofty and glorious Titles of the All-seeing JEHOVAH: And the charter of this Edgar, transcribed by our Author, with the Subscriptions of so many Kings,[1] it at first view smells rank of the Cloyster, and is nothing to the purpose; for its empty to think, that any persons Witnessing a Deed, doth infer their subjection to the granter.

WHATEVER Mr. Atwood may say, of feudal Tenures in England before the conquest, yet they are positively disprov'd, by a very Learn'd and Judicious Antiquary, the famous Sir Henry Spelman, in his Treatise of Tenures, wherein he tells, That the Conqueror, after the Example of Hugh Capet of France, made Feuds Hereditary; and that the Feudal words in the Charters cited by Ingulfus, are not such in the /23/ Original Saxon, but only Translated with Terms adapted to the Norman customs;[1] And this great Antiquary, who was so very conversant in ancient deeds and records, challenges any, to shew him a charter in the Saxon Tongue before the conquest, wherein any Feudal word is apparently expressed.[2]

P.20　(1) p. 144.
P.21　(1) Lambards *Archaionomia* fol: 137. (2) p. 537. (3) *Hist.* Vol I. Book 6. p. 12. (4) p.194. dependence of Ireland.
P.22　(1) p. 197.
P.23　(1) *Reliquiae Spelmanneanae* p. 5. (2) ibid. p. 8.

IF then Feudal Tenures were not in England, until after the conquest; It's a demonstrative proof, of the Forgery of our Malcolm's Charter to the Confessor, yea fully redargues, the demanding or giving any Leige Homage before the conquest: Our Author forseeing this, blames Sir Henry Spelman of Bigotry;[3] which shews him a perfect Stranger to his Writings: In all which, there breaths a remarkable modesty, worthy of imitation: And he also tacitly insinuats a jealousie of these Remains being Genuine; But there's no ground of Suspicion, being so like their Father Sir Henry Spelman: And the Treatise of Tenures, is Printed from a fair Copy in the Bodleian Library, Corrected by the Authors hand;[4] And these Remains are published, by a very Learn'd /24/ & Industrious Editor, the Reverend Dr. Edmund Gibson, who has singularly oblidged this Age, with Publishing these and other venerable pieces of Antiquity and History. But Spelman is not singular in these thoughts, he is seconded, by a very Learned and Assiduous Judge in Antiquity, the Reverend Dr. Hicks, who is scurvily treated by our snarling Author; but the Doctors great skill in ancient Writes, is so notour, that his opinion is of much weight; And the great and laborious work, which is quickly expected from him, and his ingenious associat Mr. Wanley will be a great help in the Study of ancient Writes, and assist to discriminat the genuine from the spurious.

THE next Charters which come to the field, are these of our own Kings; Here are the Champions of the Cause; And the first is a very plain Charter of Homage, said to be granted by King Malcolm the third of Scotland, commonly called Canmoir to Edward King of England, generally stiled the Confessor, who was the Predecessor of William the conqueror.

I'M unwilling to cloy the Reader, by giving the Charters, and some /25/ other important Writs in this contraversy at length; But shal endeavour faithfully to rehearse, what seems most material in them; and for the satisfaction of the curious, shall subjoyn full Copies in an Appendix.

THE Charter of Malcolm Canmoir is among the Archives in Westminster, and was engraven by Direction of the Learn'd Mr Rymer Her Majesties Historiographer, But without any design, to enforce the Homage, or to use it as a genuine Charter, as may be seen, from his first Letter to the Bishop of Carlile,[1] Where it's evident, Mr. Rymer look't upon it as a Forgery: And tho' our Author frequently makes honourable mention of the Historiographer, and that very deservedly, yet he doth never in the least insinuat, That Mr. Rymer by causing this Charter to be engraven, design'd thereby to vouch the Homage.

THE Substance of this Charter is,[2] That King Malcolm and his Son Edward Earl of Carrick and Rothesay, own'd that they held the Kingdom of Scotland of Edward the son of Ethelred King of /26/ England, Leige Lord of Scotland, as their Predecessors are well known to have done, according to the ancient Records of the Crown; And that the Charter was granted at York,

---

P.23   (3) p. 25. (4) *prefat. ad reliquias.*
P.25   (1) p. 18. (2) *Vide ad longum* in append: Num. 1

in the 9th Year of King Malcolm's Reign; with consent and advice of Margaret his consort, and of Edgar Atheling her Brother, and of several other Nobles of Scotland.

THIS Charter, as is said before, is disprov'd by Mr. Ridpath, in his Preface, to the Translation of Sir Thomas Craig's Treatise of Homage, by several Arguments, and especially by this; That Queen Margaret, and her Brother Edgar Atheling, are consenters in this Charter, and yet this Queen was not Married to King Malcolm; nor did she & her Brother come to Scotland till after the Conquest, and so after the death of the Confessor, to whom this Charter is granted; And thus, It was impossible, that Edward the Son of Malcolm could joyn in a Charter with his Father, when he was not born.

OUR Author attempts to answer Mr. Ridpath's Objections, and to this Choking one, he faintly says, That the English Historians, do only relate Queen Margaret, and her Brother's going to /27/ Scotland, *in transitu*.[1] Whereas ther's nothing in these times more remarkable, than their leaving the Court of the Conqueror, and coming to Scotland; And it is a passage very memorable; for Edgar Atheling was the true and undoubted Heir of the English Crown, and in Vindication of his Right, he & his Brother in Law our King Malcolm with a numerous Army of Scots, in conjunction with some eminent Persons of the English Nobility and Clergy, who had come with, or after him to Scotland, made an Inroad as far as York.

THE right Reverend and Learn'd Bishop of Carlile, in the Historical Library of Scotland, owns that Mr. Ridpath has deservedly expos'd, and convicted this Charter of several Notorious and undenyable marks of Forgery:[2] And the worthy Prelate tells us, That among the Lord Longueville's Collections, is a Charter under this Title Homagium factum Edwardo filio Ethelred, A.D. 1043; And says, It's the very same with that publish'd by Mr. Rymer.[3]

THIS piece of Justice, done us by the Learn'd Bishop, has mightily /28/ exasperat our Author against his Lordship; and to support the Charter of Malcolm, by making the different dates of the two Copies agree, Mr. Atwood will shew his Knowledg in Chronology, by the difference between the Dionysian and Evangelical Computation; Which he thinks Salves all the Difficulty of the different Dates; For between these two Æras, there is 22 years, and he reckoning, that our King Malcolm came to the Crown in 1056, and adding thereto nine years, because of this Charter being dated in the ninth of his Reign, makes 1065, from which 22 being subtracted, there arises 1043, which exactly quadrats with the charter of the Lord Longueville, and thus both Dates are very agreeable; And our Author is so vain of this mighty Turn and Discovery, That with an assuming air, he says, Thus we have a demonstrative Evidence of the Truth of both Records, one as an Original, and the other as an Exemplification.[1] But our slippery footed Author, who is

---

P.27 (1) p. 221. (2) p. 278. (3) ibid. p. 281.
P.28 (1) p. 217.

pleased without any ground to charge others with Inadvertency, commits here a most manifest Blunder; /29/ For most Historians reckon by the Dionisian Æra; And according to them, Malcolm was King in 1056 or 1057, and was kill'd at Anwick in 1093; and the Dionisian year 1057, was by the Evangelical Computation 1079; So, our Author falls, in the gentle Escape of taking Subtraction for Addition; and drops into a petty Chronological Mistake of 44 years, or thereby: That the Dionisian Calcul is 22 short of the Evangelical, is clear from Marianus Scotus,[1] Gervasius Derobornensis,[2] and Florence of Worcester,[3] Which last, our Author cites, for the different way of Computation: And if Mr. Atwood had been pleas'd to look upon that Author, he wou'd find, that in the 1043, according to the Evangelical Æra, Cnute was King of England; And that in the Dionisian year 1043, and for several years after, Makbeth was King of Scotland; So by both Computations, this Charter must be a Forgery; The Granter and Receiver not being Cotemporaries: And further, if the Rambler, had glanc'd upon his Voucher Florence, for the Year /30/ 1068 Dionisian, and 1090 Evangelical, he wou'd find this Author telling us, That Edgar Atheling and his Mother Agatha, and his two Sisters Margaret and Christian went to Scotland: How will our Author make this agree, with the Charter in any view? And much more, if it be consider'd, That it must be several Years after this; For Edward a Son of the Marriage, between our King and his Queen this Margaret, is consenting. And if the Death of Malcolm be consider'd, that it was in 1093 Dionisian year, and in the 1115 Evangelical year; And that in 1043, he had Reign'd nine Years, and had a Son capable to consent to a charter; Mr. Atwood will make our Malcolm, a very ancient Gentleman: But there's no supporting of Forgeries, unless by gross Absurdities.

LEST this Charter shou'd be found an Imposture, our Author strains his Fancy to palliat the Matter, by telling us, that if it be counterfit, it must have been counterfited by the Scots to justifie their Claim to a Kingdom of Scotland:[1] Which is a Notion so very Fantastical, and an Original of Mr. /31/ Atwood, that it merits no Answer.

THO' what's already said, be more than sufficient, to demonstrat this Charter to be counterfeit; Yet there be several other clear Marks of Forgery in it.

FIRST, The Character of this Charter, is by hundreds of Years, after our Malcolm's Time. Besides in the nice Criticisms of ancient Writs, The Syllabication of *Scotorum* in this charter is wrong; For it is with a single T. whereas, in old genuine Charters, it is writ with a double TT.

SECONDLY, Malcolm speaks, in the plural Number; Which in his Days, and for many years after, was not us'd by the Kings of England, nor by our Kings: For tho' the first using of the plural Number by the Kings of England be not brought down so low, as the Reign of King John, according to the

---

P.29   (1) *Chron. lib.* I. cap. 10. (2) *Inter decem Scriptores* p. 1338. (3) *Lib. 2 & deinceps.*
P.30   (1) p. 539.

opinion of the Learn'd Lord chief Justice Coke, noticed by the Right Reverend Bishop of Carlile,[1] yet it will not by far run so high, as the time either of the Confessor or Conqueror. But

THIRDLY, To this Charter is appended a Seal with a plain Coat of Arms; Bearing the Armorial Ensigns of Scotland, viz. A Lyon Rampant, /32/ within a double Tressur. Flowr'd and Counter-flower'd with Flower de Lis's: Which for Illustration, I have caused to be engraven, and is a demonstrative evidence of Forgery: For it may be questioned, if in these days, Seals were affixed to Charters in England. Ingulphus, who was for many Years, in the Conquerors Court, both before and after he came to England being his Secretary in Normandy, and was made Abbot of Croyland, when he came to England, and so may be thought to know the customs of these times, tells us, That the Normans changed several Customs in England; and among others, That they condemn'd the old Custom, of the Solemnities of Writings which was by Subscriptions with Golden Crosses, and other sacred Marks; (whereof there were sundry in Ancient times) and also tells us, that they call'd Writings which before went under the name of *Chirographa,* charters: and constitut the Solemnities of Charters, in the Impression of Seals upon Wax, in presence of three or four Witnesses ingrost in the Deed.[1] And of this the learn'd Mabillon takes /33/ particular notice, in his most curious Treatise *De Re Diplomatica.*[1] However it may with great Assurance be said, That before the conquest, & for many years after it, neither the Kings of Scotland, nor of England, us'd Seals in their Charters, bearing Armorial Ensigns, of which more afterward. And at present, it shall suffice to notice, that the Conqueror's Seal, had not any Vestige of Arms: Which is evident, from a Copie of it, as appended to a Charter given us, by the very Learn'd Selden; in his Notes upon Eadmerus.[2]

THE falshood of this Charter is also apparent; By considering the time, when our King Malcolm, was Married to Queen Margaret: Turgot their Cotemporary, prior of Durham, and afterwards Bishop of St. Andrews, Who wrote their Lives, saith, They were Married in 1067 or 1070,[3] And with him other English Historians agree: And thus after the Conquest; How then cou'd King Malcolm, with consent of his Queen, pay Homage to the Confessor; when he was a long time in his Grave, before their Marriage? So this Charter /34/ is a most manifest Forgery, by variety of proofs.

THIS Charter of Homage, by King Malcolm, not being able to keep ground of it self; Our Author brings in as he thinks, a mighty support and Reinforcement, from an Original Charter, of our King Edgar, the Son of this Malcolm, and from other Original Charters granted to the Abbay of Coldingham, now kept in the Dean and Chapter's Treasury at Durham; And if we believe him, This Charter of Edgar is free from all possible Imputation

---

P.31 (1) *Engl. Hist. Lib.* part 3. p. 9.

P.32 (1) *Hist. Ingulphi edit. oxon.* 1684 *inter Vet. Script. rerum Anglicarum tom. I.* p. 70.

P.33 (1) p.169. (2) p.166. (3) Selden: *in prefat. ad decem Scrip.* p. 24.

of Forgery,[1] And will give the Decisive stroke, in this contraversy; And remove all suspicion of Forgery, of the Charter of King Malcolm, the Father of Edgar.

TO make way for the more easie belief of this doughty proof; our Author ushers it in, with a brief Abstract, of the History of these Times; to this purpose.

KING Malcolm Canmoir, with his eldest Son, being kill'd at Anwick in Northumberland, Dufenal or Donald his Brother became King; And was set aside by Duncan, Malcolm's Bastard Son, who mounted the Throne, with /35/ assistance of the English: But the Scots, would not suffer Duncan to continue to Reign, until he sent the English Home, (a brave Evidence of the Homage indeed). And in a little time after Duncan was kill'd by his Subjects, & Donald Restor'd.

THEREAFTER the King of England issued his precepts, requiring all his Vassals, to attend him at Christmas Court; If they expected his peace and protection; but Donald slighted this Protection; and the poor infortunate Prince, having committed an unpardonable piece of stubbornness & ungratitude, by not undertaking a long Winter Journey of 600 Miles, in going and coming, to keep Christmas with his Superior, he must be Proscrib'd and dethron'd: Wherefore, about Michaelmas 1097, The King of England sent a great Army to Scotland, under the command of Edgar Atheling and subdued it, and made Edgar, the Son of King Malcolm and Queen Margaret, and the Nephew of Edgar Atheling King of Scotland.

THEN our Author produces the nailing Evidence; The Charter of this our King Edgar, owning the Homage for the Kingdom of Scotland: and confirming the Charter of Malcolm; /36/ Which being of great Importance, he ingrosses it at some length,[1] and I have also given a Copy of it, and more full in the Appendix.[2]

IN this Charter, our King Edgar, Owns, that he did possess the Kingdom of Scotland, by the Gift of his Lord, William King of England; And with consent of his said Lord King William, he gives to GOD Almighty, and to the Church of Durham, and to the glorious Bishop St. Cuthbert, and to William Bishop, and to the Monks of Durham, and their Successors, the Mansions of Berwick and Coldingham, and several other Lands which his Father Malcolm had: And this Charter bears, to be granted in presence of William the Bishop, and Turgot the Prior and others, and is marked with the Crosses of Edgar, and of his Brother and Successor, Alexander and of other Nobles.

TO Enforce the Authority of this Charter, our Author cites a Letter published in the Appendix to the 2d Volum of the *Historie of the Reformation of England*.[3] Which Letter was writ by Tonstal Bishop of Durham in the Reign of /37/ Edward the 6th, to the Lord Protector Somerset, and to the Council of England, in answer to a Letter from them to the Bishop, ordering him to search his Records, for any thing that might clear Edward the 6th's Title to

---

P.34 (1) p. 252.
P.36 (1) p. 248. (2) Numb. 4. (3) p. 106. Num. 9.

Scotland: In that Letter, the Bishop assures the Protector and Council, That he had found many Homages by the Kings of the Scots, to the Kings of England, and sent them Copies of these Homages; and Reminds the Protector, of an Original Charter, under the Seal of Edgar king of Scots; Which the Bishop says, he shew'd once to the Lord Maxwell in presence of the Protector; and that, he the Bishop, had also found a confirmation by William Rufus of Edgar's Charter, and to establish the Faith of all these Deeds, our Author sets down a Charter of King John to the Prior and Monks of Durham, confirming the Grants of all Lands made to them, and among others of Coldingham, according to the Charter of Edgar, King of the Scots.[1]

THESE glaring Proofs, of the Homage, so pufft up our Author, That, with an Air of Assurance, he determines /38/ the Controversy; Because, he thinks that by these Charters the Homage was made evident, & put beyond Denyal and question, and condemns them as blind who will not now see the Superiority of England over Scotland: And he Attacks Mr. Ridpath for concealing these clear Evidences of Homage,[1] related in the History of the Reformation; for that he had Impugn'd the truth of Malcolm's Charter, because it was not mention'd in that History; And then he falls on the Bishop of Carlile, for favouring our Independency, and disproving Malcolm's Charter, when he had published a List of our Kings Grants to Coldingham, kept at Durham, Wherein the Homage is so manifest:[2] And to Rivet the Matter, he is pleased to favour his humble Servant, with the obliging Office, to be Voucher of these ancient and powerful Proofs, of our Subjection, and Homage: And that it may be thought, we were very concern'd about these Charters, he says, I was sent from Scotland to inspect them.[3]

I PRESUME to think, that few /39/ or none, except our Author, wou'd have adventur'd to publish, such pointed and convincing Proofs, in an Argument of such Concern; And when an Inference, of the greatest Import, is drawn from it; Without a very nice and strict Enquiry: Which our Author cannot pretend to, for his Voucher, for this invincible Proof and Charter, is a Copy set down, in the 45th Leaf of the first Volum, of the *Monasticon Anglicanum:* And with all Respect to the Memory of the Learn'd Compilers, it is handed to the World, with an unaccountable Blunder and Mistake: For the Introductory Paragraph runs thus; *In Tempore Regis Willielmi primi, & Willielmi Dunelmensis Episcopi, Edgarus Rex Scotorum, dedit Sancto-Cuthberto, & Ecclesiae Dunelmensi, Coldingham-Schyre; Sub eo qui sequitur Tenore;* Which Paragraph, may be thus Translated. In the Days of William the first, King of England, (viz. the Conqueror) And of William Bishop of Durham, Edgar King of Scotland, made a Grant to St. Cuthbert, and to the Church of Durham, of Coldingham Shire, of the Tenour following: And then comes the charter. Here is a manifest Error, for it's /40/ notour and uncontested, that William the first, dyed in September in the year 1087, and was

---

P.37 (1) p. 251.
P.38 (1) p. 250. (2) p. 252. (3) p. 253.

Buried, at Caen in Normandy, Ten or eleven years, before our Edgar was King; And this cou'd not but stare any Man broad in the face, who pretends to know the least thing of these Times. And our Author, in the third or fourth Line, before he sets down a Copie of this Charter, Remarks, that Edgar became King in the year 1097:[1] Which was in the tenth year, of the Reign of William the second called Rufus: How then cou'd our Edgar, after he was King, grant a Charter of Homage, in the days of a King, who before Edgar began to Reign, had rested full ten Years in his Grave: But good Mr. Atwood having already, as a specimen of his Chronology, taken Subtraction for Addition; he may be excus'd for not observing a difference, between first and second: And if the Printer shou'd be blam'd, and this slip reckon'd among the Errata; yet I am afraid, this plausible pretence, will not preserve, the credit of that charter. For what if William Bishop of Durham, in whose /41/ time also the Editors of the *Monasticon*, make this Charter to be granted; yea more, who is a Witness in it; be found in *Limbo patrum*, before our Edgar was King; Who as such granted it? Will not our Author shew himself a very cautious Spark? And yet he takes upon him, to censure the Learn'd and worthy Bishop of Carlile; As being unwary in publishing a List, of these charters at Durham, without consulting the Originals: This indeed is the hight of impudence, and the treatment, of the right Reverend Prelate, is still more abusive, when, it's sure, there is no Original, Extant at Durham of the Charter of Edgar; which is Copied in the Monasticon, and Transcrib'd by our Author; and consequently this Charter, neither is, nor cou'd be placed, in the List published by the Bishop. Ther's indeed at Durham a Charter of Edgar under Seal; And is probably what Bishop Tonstal shew'd, to the Protector Somerset, and to the Lord Maxwell: Which in the detail shall be accounted for. But our Author is so muddy, to confound the Copie in the Monasticon, with this Charter under Seal, and even this Charter under Seal, is not in /42/ the List, that was communicat to the Learn'd Bishop: and in all the five Charters of this our King Edgar, in that List, There is not one Sillable, or the least appearance or shadow, of Homage, by our Kings: But rather clear marks of their Soveraignity: As will be hereafter manifested.

OUR Author is also very injurious, to the Ingenious Mr. Ridpath; For he in the preface, to his Translation of Craigs Treatise of the Homage, only undertakes to disprove the Charter of Malcolm; Which being Engraven by Mr. Rymer's direction, might give him to think, it was designed for proof of the Homage: But there being no motion, about Edgar's Charters, It was not in his Road, to nottice them. And if our Author had that quality, which he thinks, others want; He would have notticed, That when the right Reverend Author of the History of the Reformation, Doctor Burnet, now Bishop of Sarum, one of the great Ornaments of the Reform'd Church, And of our Countrey; did publish Bishop Tonstal's Letter, in relation to the Homage; he at the same time, subjoyns a Letter, from the Nobility and Gentry of

---

P.40   (1) p. 247.

Scotland, to the Pope; As a /43/ counter-proof and Evidence, of our Independency.[1]

IF the Bishop of Carlile, and Mr. Ridpath, think it worth the while, They are by far more capable than I, to vindicat themselves, in these particulars; But for truth's sake, I think my self bound, to do them this piece of Justice.

WHAT is already said, I hope, is sufficient, to remove any appearance of Homage, from the Charters at Durham; As they're manadged by Mr. Atwood: but he having brought Bishop Tonstal's Letter in the field, Which perhaps may be of that weight, to incite some abler hand, to peruse the Records at Durham, and put some Charters kept there, which were granted to the Abbay of Coldingham, in a more agreeable dress; and by this Revive and set on foot, a new ground of Dispute; I shall therefore candidly relate, what Charters and Records I did see there, which have the least shew of Homage; And place them in the most favourable light, that my capacity can reach; And with all Submission, shall /44/ offer some Remarks upon them, chiefly founded on the Authority of English Historians.

THE Abbay or Priory of Coldingham, being a Cell of the Monastery of St Cuthbert of Durham, The Repository of the Archives of that Abbay, was justly in the Treasury of the Cathedral of Durham: And I must beg the Readers favour, before I open what I did see in these Archives, in Relation to the Homage; To be allowed, to give some passing account of the Religious House at Coldingham; And of my Pilgrimage to Durham, to visit the valuable Reliques of our Antiquities there.

I WILL not trouble the Reader, with Discanting upon the Antiquity of this Place of Coldingham: That it is supposed to be the *Colonia* mention'd by Ptolemy,[1] nor with the Accounts given of *Coldana, Colludum,* or Colludesburg, which is also thought to be Coldingham, and was a very ancient Monastery of Monks and Nuns; Wherein the famous Virgin Queen, tho' twice Married, Ethelfrida became Religious, who is Recorded with many /45/ Encomiums by the venerable Bede;[1] Nor with the History of the Fire from Heaven, that destroyed this Monastery, for the promiscuous Conversations of the Monks and Nuns related by the same Author:[2] Nor shall I enter upon the Conjecture, suggested by the Learn'd Selden; That from this *Colludum,* a large and fruitful Seminarie of Priests, did the *Culdei* take their Name:[3] Nor yet with the account of the second Conflagration, at this place of a Nunnery, burnt by the Danes under their terrible Chiftians and Tyrants, Hinguar, and Hubba; After the Nuns, to preserve their chastity, had disfigur'd their Faces, by cutting off their Noses, and Upper-Lips:[4] Nor of the mistake of a Modern Historian, who places Coldingham, in York-Shire. These things being somewhat Forreign to my purpose; But shall

---

P.43   (1) Appendix to the *Hist. of the Reform.* 2 Vol. Num. 10.

P.44   (1) *Camb: Brit: Scotia.*

P.45   (1) *Hist.Eccl.Lib.* 4. cap. 19. (2) cap. 25. & *Sim.Dunelm. inter X Script.* p. 16. (3) *prefat. ad X Script.* p. xi. (4) Math.Westm. *ad annum* 870.

briefly touch, what concerns the History, of the Abbay or Priorie of Coldingham; To which the Grants at Durham, do Relate.

/46/ THE Religious House at Coldingham, of which some Vestiges yet remain; Was founded by our King Edgar the Son of Malcolm Canmoir, and his good Queen Margaret, who began his Reign in 1098; And in the Ruins of this old Fabrick; There's yet a part of it to be seen, called to this day Edgars-Hall.

THE Church of Coldingham, was dedicated to the Virgin Mary; As a Cell of the Church of St. Cuthbert of Durham; This is Evident by many Charters granted to Coldingham, wherein the donatory Clause runs to St. Mary, and to St. Cuthbert, and to the Monks of Durham, at Coldingham.

AT the Dedication of this Church, according to the devotion of these Times, King Edgar made an offering upon the Altar, of several Elemosinary Gifts, to the Church of Coldingham; and bestowed other Donations upon it, which are to be seen in his Genuine Charters; set down in the Appendix.[1]

THE founding of this House, by King Edgar, to the Honour of St. Cuthbert, is confirm'd by two ancient Charters made by one Thor, an eminent person in those days, who, apparently, /47/ for his Stature, had the Epithet given him of *Longus*, and is a Witness, in the Charter of Edgar, that relates to the Dedication: Those Charters of Thor do mention, that he, with Assistance of his Prince King Edgar founded the Church of Eadnaham in Honour of St. Cuthbert; Which Church was ever a part of the Spirituality of Coldingham. And the Seal appended to these two Charters, seem to me worthy of Remark; For it is done, in a Convex Form, and the Impression is so clear and fine, that it evidently Demonstrats the nice Engraving of the Seal; From which, I hope, it may be inferr'd that in ancient Times, we have had exquisit Artists, even equal with our Neighbours: And for satisfaction of the Curious, I have given in the Appendix, a Copy of one of those Charters, and of the Seal;[1] But far short of the Original.

THE Prior of Coldingham was presented by the Convent of Durham, and was admitted to the Spirituality, by the Arch-Bishop of St. Andrews; And to the Temporality, by the King of Scotland.

/48/ BY Progress of time, this Abbay, or Priory of Coldingham, came to be among the most extensive and richest Benefices of this Kingdom: This will be evident, if we either consider the many Donatives of Lands, made to it, by the Grants at Durham; Or the Rental of this Benefice, given up, in Pursuance of the Act of Assumption in 1561; Wherein is a considerable Revenue, both of Temporality and Spirituality.[1]

THE Right Reverend Bishop of Carlile, oblidged the Learn'd World, with a most useful and desirable Work of *an Historical Library of England*; which met with a Reception, suitable to so good an Undertaking: And his Lordships Goodness and Generosity, was not circumscribed, to his own

---

P.46   (1) Numb. 2.
P.47   (1) Numb. 6.6.
P.48   (1) *Secundum Copiam penes Auth.*

Country; But extended even to us, in an excellent Treatise published by him, under the Title of *An Historical Library of Scotland*; Wherein we have many things laid before us, worthy of Perusal and Remark: And among other valuable Matters, his Lordship gives us, A List of the Charters of several of our Kings and Nobles granted /49/ to the Abbey of Coldingham, kept in the Dean and Chapter's Treasury at Durham, communicat to him by the Reverend Doctor John Smith Prebendary of Durham,[1] a very worthy Person, who beside a rare Talent of Preaching, and other suitable Qualifications of a Divine, is indued with many becoming Accomplishments of a Gentleman. To those two Learn'd and worthy Persons this Nation is much obliged, by letting us know, where so many of our valuable ancient Deeds and Writings be; Which by their being justly lodg'd at Durham have escap'd the repeated miserable Fates, that most of our ancient Charters and Records have undergone; first, by the general Havock and designed Extirpation of our Memory, by Edward the first; Who carried off or destroyed all the Marks of our Antiquity, and Independency; Yea even the Rights of our Lands, that came in his Clutches, with the famous Library kept at Restennet.[2] Next by the burning of the City of Edinburgh, by the English under the Command of the Duke of Lancaster, and /50/ thereafter by the Destruction, or Transportation of the most of what was left, by the Popish Clergy, at the Reformation: and lastly, by the carrying up of our Records to London, in the late Civil Wars, and the Disaster, that befel them, in their Return; Which are Subjects too Melanchollly, to be furder insisted upon. To Return then:

THIS Hint given of so many ancient Charters at Durham, induc'd me when I was occasionally traveling that Road, to desire the favour of a sight of them, which was allow'd in a most obliging Manner; Where beside those in the forementioned List, I observed a great Store and Collection of other Charters and Deeds, granted to Coldingham.

TO make some Acknowledgment, for this Favour, there was sent hence to Durham, a List of the large and valuable Collection of Manuscripts, in the Library of the Honourable Faculty of Advocats of Scotland. And in Return, there came thence to this Faculty, a full and curious Repertory or Inventory of all the Grants at Durham made to Coldingham, in a most exact method & worthy of Imitation. And I was /51/ favour'd, with the Office of presenting it; Which was most kindly received, by this Learn'd Society, with all Thankfulness, truly due to the Reverend and Learn'd Clergy of Durham, for so valuable and acceptable a Present.

ALONG with those Correspondences, was a free and frank Offer on both sides, suitable to Persons of Learning and Generosity, of Communication of Notes or Transcripts.

THE Repertory, sent hither, contained so rare and fine a Collection of Charters, by our Kings, Nobles, Clergy and Gentry, that it justly excited a Desire, to have them inspected: And I was desired, by some of the Learn'd

---

P.49 (1) p. 363. (2) Spotswood *Church Hist. ad ann.* 1300.

Faculty, and other Worthy Persons, to undertake this province; And was the more easily prevail'd with, because this choise Collection consisted of ancient Charters; And the Knowledge of their Form, was agreeable to my Profession; And useful to any, who may have occasion to inspect or inventary Charter-chists* (*Repositories of Writings); So; in this Undertaking was the united Views of Divertisement and Improvement; And there was no Design or Prospect, to make particular Enquiry, concerning any Charters or /52/ Deeds, relating to the Homage; But meerly to inspect so large a Store, of our Antiquities: Which upon many Occasions, might prove useful.

IN September 1703, I went to Durham, and stayed some days, where I was favour'd, with very obliging Civilities and Courtesies, from the Right Reverend and Right Honourable Lord Bishop of that See, My Lord Crew; And from the Honourable Master Dean; and Reverend Chapter of Durham; who were pleas'd to use me, with the greatest Humanity, so natural to that Learn'd and worthy Body of Clergy: And their favours to me, upon this and other occasions, are equally above my thanks, and expression. And as an Indication of their generous and Communicative Disposition, and of their respect to my Countrey; did with great cheerfulness, lay open to me the great store of Scots Charters and Writings in their custody.

THIS good Office will be the more apparent, by a short Recapitulation of the Charters to be seen here.

THE most Ancient, is a Charter of King Duncan; Which being singular in some things, my Honor'd Friend Sir James Dalrymple is to Publish /53/ it with Observations.

IN this curious Collection, are several Original Charters of our Kings, Edgar, Alexander and David, the Sons of King Malcolm Canmoir, and of his good Queen Margaret: Here be likewise some Original Charters of this King David, before he came to the Crown, when he had the Title of *Comes*; Several Charters of his Son Henry, also Stiled *Comes*; Who dyed before his Father; Many Charters of King Malcolm the 4th, commonly called the Maiden, and of King William, the Sons of Henry, several Charters of King Alexander the second and third; And some Charters of King Robert the Bruce; and of his Son King David the 2d; And of King Robert the 2d and 3d, and of our King James the first.

IN these Royal Deeds, are to be found as Witnesses, the Predecessors or Branches of many Noble and Ancient Families, and among others of the Families of Graham, Lindsay, Home, Bruce, Erskin, Lundie, Livingston, Hay, Keith, Maxwell, Giffard, Frazer, Ramsay, Seton, Somervill, De Quinci, Riddel, Swintun, Hastings, Berkley, Lauder, Coburn, Baliol, Sibbald, Moubray, Wardlaw, Arm-strong, Crawford, Haige, &c.

/54/ AMONG these numerous Grants, are many Charters of the Great, Ancient, and Noble Earls of March and Dumbar, with their Seals for several Generations; Some of which bear evident Marks of Antiquity: There be also some Charters of Robert Duke of Albany; And of the Earls and Countes of Douglass, Marr and Murray.

IN this Noble Collection are the two Charters formerly mention'd granted by Thor Longus; And Charters by several other Persons of Note;

Such as, Willelmus de Lindesey, Eadward de Lastalrig, Willelmus de Veteri Ponte, Guaterius & Clarebaldus de Olifard, Willelmus de Mordington, Everardus de Pencatlaht, Walterus de Bois, Radulfus de Bonkill, Willelmus de Vallibus, &c. Who are also Witnesses in severals of the Royal Charters.

HERE are two Original Charters, granted by King David, commonly called Saint David; To the Predecessor of Swintun: Wherein he is termed *Miles*, and is to hold his Lands as freely, as any of the Kings Barons.

IN this Treasury is to be found, a great number of Charters, Granted or Witnessed by the Predecessors or Branches, of many of our Ancient Families /55/ and Sirnames; Especially of those who ly nigh to the South Borders; Such as, of the Name and Family of Aiton, Blakader, Aldcumbus, Nisbet, Scot, Quickswuide, Alderngave, Paxtun, Hedenham, Birkenside, Purrock, Chantun, Fleming, Jedwire, Prendergest, Lambertun, Kinkborn, Reington, Wiseman, Lumsden, Dunning, Happer, Stampard, Cogane, Ploumer, Hebburn, Houborn, Beniston, Trere, Billingham, Laysingam, Stuts, Trereman, Bruning, Scryppe, Page, Edinton, Hale, Lowlen, Routbyry, Lumlayea, Merington, Hamer, Hutley, Frebern, De la tale, Golin, Scrimerston, Goclin, Newbiggen, Coleman, de Candela, Kinoreside, Preston, Witeslay, De Hert, Gray, Lethem, Waddell, Park, Feryng, Spens, Atkinson, Wardlaw, Brun, Russel, Ralston, Bellcrayk, Ridpath, Lermonth, Hart, Dale, Lettell, Smelholm, Purvas, Eccles, Crumbe, Becket, Papedy, Goodwin, Reuel, Burdun, Gourly, Ewing, Edger, Steinston, Fenton, Curry, Newton, &c.

THERE be here some Donors, & Witnesses, named by their Offices; As Cancellarius, Dapifer, Senescallus, Camerarius, Constabularius, Marescallus, de pincerna, de Sigillo, Clericus, Capellanus, Coronator, de Camera, Scriptor, Cantor, Braciator, /56/ Faber, Elemosinarius, Hostiarius, Cocus, Celerarius, Portarius, Pastor Prepositus, Janitor, Forrestarius, Vicarius, de la Wardrobe, Mason, &c.

IN the Recital, of those Families, Sirnames, and Offices, I have observed no order of Time; But placed them, as they fell in my way; Without any regard to their Precedency.

HERE are also some Grants, of the Kings of England, and Bulls of Popes, with curious and intire Seals, inclosed in Wooden Capsulas.

HERE be many ancient Charters, of the Bishops of St. Andrews, Robert, Arnald, Richard, Rodger, Willelm, David, Gamelin; and Deeds by the Chapter of St. Andrews; And two Charters by the Bishops of Glasgow, Jocelin, and William.

HERE are also some notable Deeds by some Abbots, Priors and Arch-Deacons, and their Officials.

HERE are many Deeds, of the Bishops, Priors and Convents of Durham, And of the Priors, and Convent of Coldingham; And so well have these Deeds been preserved, that the Seals of all these Church-men are intire; And of the most Ancient and Remarkable /57/ of them, I did take Draughts, and it's worthy Notice that there's a Tract of Seals, of the bishops of St. Andrews; With this Inscription, upon the Ring: SIGILLUM ———— EPISCOPI SCOTTORUM; This in some Measure, supports the Independency of our Church; Which is already clear'd by the Learn'd Sir Robert Sibbald, who will be seconded in that Argument, by the Honour'd and knowing Sir James Dalrymple.

IN this Store, there be several ancient Rent-Rolls; Upon the back of one of them, is the Exposition of some Feudal Words and Terms; And with these Rent-rolls are joyn'd some Tacks, Acts of Court, and Index's of some Deeds, that have been produced in Process.

HERE are the Services and Retours, of the heirs of many of the Vassals of Coldingham; And several Agreements and Setlements, made with the Prior and Convent, of diverse kinds.

HERE be some *Processus in Curia Romana:* And among others a very full and tedious Process, against Patrick and John Homes; Containing great variety of Matter and Writings.

THERE are also in this Store, many /58/ publick notorial Instruments, of different Kinds; As of Appeal, Agreement, Induction, Protestation, Transumpt, Inspection, Transcription, Admission, Citation, Constitution of Procurators, &c.

THERE be likewise some Missives, Indentures, Memorials, and many Copies of Writings.

IN brief, there's in this valuable Collection, about 90 Royal Charters and Grants; About 52 Deeds, by Nobles and Barons, about 266, by Gentlemen; About 131 by Popes, and other Religious Persons and Houses; and about 130 other Original Deeds and Copies; Which will amount in all about the number of 670.

THESE Charters are yet more valuable, and the favour of the Reverend Clergy of Durham more obliging, when it is considered; That our Records, having as is said, undergone and suffer'd many misfortunes; Ther's here yet preserved, the Original Charters of three of our Kings; Whereof we know no other Originals extant: And further, here and here only, so far as is yet known, is to be had, a /59/ full and compleat series of the true and Genuine Seals undefac'd, of our Kings, since Malcolm Canmoir, to our King James the second; And with much civility, I was allow'd to take draughts of them, which are of great import; For at first view they serve, to discriminat the Genuine Charters of these Kings, from such as are spurious: And however these things may to some seem dry and Barren, yet even these Seals protect us from Forgery, yea as will hereafter appear, they establish our Independency, and these Charters let us know, our forms in Ancient times, and in them are Witnesses, which support the Authority and Antiquity of our old Laws; And they furnish us almost, with a full List of our Officers and Ministers Civil and Ecclesiastick, for a long tract of time: And they even give us some hints, of our Ancient Government, and of the Antiquity and import of some Offices and other things, which our Historians have not toucht.

WHEN I tell these things, I presume I need not enlarge upon the civility of the truely Great and mighty English Nation in General, or of the worthy and Learn'd Clergy of Durham in particular; Those free and frank /60/ my good Countrey-Men, whenever occasion offers, will make grateful acknowledgments, and returns of these favours, to that Reverend and Learn'd Body; And its the only favour, I owe Mr. Atwood, that he has furnish'd me with an opportunity, to make my publick and deserv'd acknowledgment, of their endearing civilities.

HAVING thus digress'd, I return to my purpose, concerning what Deeds I saw at Durham, that may insinuat or carry any umbrage or suspicion of Homage, by the Kings of Scotland, to the Kings of England: What occur'd to me was as follows:

IN this Treasury, Ther's an old Copy of the Charter of Homage already mention'd granted by our King Edgar, set down in the *Monasticon*, and transcrib'd thence by our Author; Whereof I have given the Substance, only this Copy at Durham is more full; For it contains moe Subscriptions and Witnesses, with this general; In presence of a great multitude of French and English: And Likewise this Copy bears, that the Deed was made, that year wherein William the /61/ Son of the great William made a new Castle before Babbenburch upon Robert Earl of Northumberland; and condescends upon the Seal appended to this Charter.[1]

THERE is here also, a Charter by the same Edgar under Seal, and probably was the Charter shown by Bishop Tonstal to the Protector Somerset, and to the Lord Maxwell, which is yet more positive about the Homage; For in it, Edgar in the most plain terms, acknowledges William King of England, to be Superior of the Kingdom of Scotland; And by this Deed, gives most of the Lands mention'd in the preceeding Copie, By licence of his Superior to William the Bishop, And Turgot the Prior, and to the Monks of Durham, and their Successors, and bears date at Norham in presence of the said William King of England, Superior of the Kingdom of Scotland, and in presence of the said Bishop and Prior, and several others; And of a great multitude of French, English and Scots; To this Charter is appended a Seal, whereupon is King Edgar on Horseback, with a Sword in his right Hand, and a shield /62/ in his left, charged with the Arms of Scotland, within the Border of France; which appears by the Copy of this Charter, and Seal set down in the Appendix.[1]

THERE's moreover at Durham, two Charters, or rather a Duplicated Charter of King William Rufus the Son and Successor of William the Conqueror; Who in the Copie of Edgars Charter is called William the Great. By these duplicats, That King William gives to Bishop William, and the Monks of Durham, the Lands contain'd in the forementioned Copie, which Edgar the Son of Malcolm King of Scotland, gave to them, with his consent: According to the duplicated Charter at length placed in the Appendix.[2]

BY a Duplicated Charter is meant, a Charter whereof there is two Originals, and I have seen severals of them, both at Durham, and in my own Countrey; And sometimes there are three Originals; which probably was for Caution, in case of accidents; and frequently there is some little difference among these Originals, in the Teste or witnessing Clauses.

/63/ IT may from these Deeds at Durham be thus argued for the Homage, That the duplicated Charter of William Rufus contains the very

---

P.61   (1) Vide Apend. Num. 4.
P.62   (1) Numb. 3. (2) Numb. 5.

same Lands, with these in the copy of Edgars Charter, without any alteration: And tho there be only a copy of Edgars Charter, to which the King of
England's Charter relates, yet it is Ancient, And the Original might be lost, or
deliver'd up, in Pursuance of the Releases of Homage; And also tho it be
not Recorded, in an Ancient Cartuary; yet there be some Charters in this
Record; That are now wanting, which shews some Originals are lost or mis-
carried, and the Charter of Edgar yet extant under Seal, tho' it be not to be
found in this Cartuary, & may labour under suspicion, yet it might upon the
loss of the true old one been foisted in: And the Original duplicated Charter
of King William of England, being relative to Edgar's charter; and expressly
mentioning, That the grant of Edgar was done with his consent; seem
strongly to support the Copie; and may give ground to think, there was
once an Original, and therefore, this duplicated Charter may be thought still,
to retain some Tincture of Homage.

/64/ THOSE things do sufficiently justifie the Letter of Bishop Tonstal,
and it may be thought, that of any thing yet said, they bid fairest for the
Homage: And were such proofs and evidences suggested with Temper, and
in season, they might be ascribed to a due research into the Justice of the
Clame of Homage.

SEING then, I have given those Charters the most favourable dress, and
colour, that my weak capacity could attain, I hope I may with the more freedom, be allowed to make some Observes upon them. And

FIRST as to the Copie of Edgar's Charter of Homage, tho' it appear
somewhat Ancient, yet this Charter not being ingross'd, in the ancient
Cartuary and Record, where there's to be found five Genuine Charters of
this same King Edgar, makes the Copy of less Faith and Credit; and the five
genuine Charters yet extant, have not the least shadow of any Homage; But
in the contrair they do bear clear marks of Soveraignty, of which afterward.

IN the next place; Is it to be supposed that if ever there had been any
Original, of this Copie, That the Monks, /65/ who were the keepers and
Registers of the Deeds ingrost in the Monasterial Cartuaries, wou'd have
noticed and ingross'd five Charters of our Edgar, and omitted a sixth? Which
not only made our King and Kingdom dependent of their King; but also
contain'd all the Lands in the other five Charters, and a great many moe, of
far greater value: There be likewise some other things to condemn this
Copy, which coincide with the duplicated Charter of K. William Rufus of
England, and therefore I shall proceed to the consideration, of the Charter
of Edgar under Seal.

THIS Charter, as is before said, acknowledges the Superiority, in very
flat and positive Terms: And if this were a true deed, it wou'd put the
Homage, beyond denial; but this Charter and Seal, bears many Marks of
Forgery, as first, the Character and Sillabication is modern, and in it are also
several modern Words and Names which at first glance clearly discover it to
be counterfit. Secondly, Edgar speaks in the Plural Number, whereas the
Plural, as hath been already said, was not then used, either by the Kings of
Scotland or England; And Edgar /66/ in all the five genuine Charters, uses
the Singular; And all true Charters made by Kings and Princes, in those

Days, I presume, will support this Assertion. Thirdly, The Seal of the Charter is counterfit and false, for it's not only altogether different from the Seals of the genuine and true Charters of Edgar, but also it bears inconsistencies with the Seals then used; For upon the Seal, appended to this Charter, Is a Coat of Arms, which at that time, were not used upon Seals in Britain: And Richard the first, was the first of the English Kings, who used Arms upon his Seal: And he began to Reign eighty nine years after the Death of William Rufus; In whose time this Charter of Edgar is said to be made. In those Days the Seals of both the Kings of Scotland and England, did bear the King, sitting in this Throne, holding a Scepter, sometimes a Globe in the one hand and a Sword in the other; And if they used a Counter-seal; The King was riding on Horse-back, carrying a Banner Display'd or a Sword in his Dexter, and a plain Shield in his Sinister; & sometimes the King is upon Horse-back in the Seal, and Inthroniz'd in /67/ the Counter-Seal: And in Process of Time, they charged their Seal with their Arms, and sometime after, they adorned the Mantlings and Trappings of their Horses, with their Armorial Ensigns.

I HOPE, I will not be thought by this to impeach the Antiquity of Arms, and of the Gentile Science of Herauldry; My Assertion only is, that in the days of our King Edgar, and for some time after, Arms were not us'd upon Seals in Britain: And I presume this will not be denyed by any who are conversant in those Matters, and will not be controul'd by a Witness.

IF the before mention'd Charters of our Kings Malcolm and Edgar, and their Seals were Genuine, they would infer three Things, which I judge will not be granted by our Neighbours. First, That our Kings us'd the plural Number (which according to the great Selden was introduced for the further Illustration of the Majesty of Princes)[1] before the Kings of England used it. Secondly, That our Kings, had Seals with Armorial Bearings, before them. Thirdly, That We were /68/ anciently in League with France. This being evident by the Border of France, encircling Our Royal Arms; Which is the acknowledg'd Bage, of the ancient League; And how cou'd We be Dependent and Subject, if We contracted Alliances with Forraign Princes, yea even with the Enemies of our Superiors? This had been a just Cause of Forefeiture of Our Crown.

IN the next place, As to the two Charters of William Rufus King of England, or rather Duplicated Charter (for they are both the same, except that one of them hath Witnesses and the other wants) mentioning that Edgars Grant of Coldingham, to St. Cuthbert of Durham, was with the Consent of this English King; They be also lyable to Exceptions, As

FIRST, They are granted by one interested in a plea & Cause, which they support; and none can vindicat and prove their Right of Dominion by their own naked Assertion.

NEXT, they relate to a Charter of Edgar, Which is not extant, and its a received maxim *Non Creditur Referenti nisi constet de Relato.*

P.67   (1) *Titles of Honour* cap. 7.

AND further, in nicety, this consent may be thought to imply no more,
/69/ Than that the Warry Monks of Durham being English-men, procured a
consent from their King; to receave Donatives, from a Neighbouring Prince,
and who was frequently at enmity with him: And they had the more
Reason, to procure this consent, Because the Lands Gifted, did ly upon the
Boundaries of the two Kingdoms; and thereby, were exposed to frequent
Hostilities: And accordingly we find, That the Monks of Coldingham being
reduced to great Straits, by having their Stores consumed by Incursions; The
Monks of Durham, in consideration, that Coldingham was a Cell of Durham,
made Application to King Henry the 6th or 7th of England for Protection,
which he granted, by a Writ under his Privy seal, yet extant at Durham; And
it was very suitable, to the cunning of the Monks, to be thus secured, in all
events by the Kings of both Realms.

I CANNOT omitt to let the candor and Justice of the Clergy of Durham
be known, who in the Repertory of the Deeds of Coldingham, have marked
the Charter of Edgar under Seal, as suspected, and did not place and rank it,
among the other Charters of this /70/ King: Had the Archives of Durham,
been alwise in such faithful and worthy hands, as they now are, There had
no proofs of our Homage been brought from them: and I'm perswaded,
That nothing is more acceptable to the Learn'd and worthy Clergy of
Durham, than the discovery of truth, and the exposing of what contains Lye
and Forgery, especially when it contributs to justifie the innocent: And the
deeds impugn'd are already laid open to the World in the *Monasticon*. And
in Bishop Tonstals Letter to the Council of England.

TO come closs then to the matter, admitting the Copie of the Charter
set down in the *Monasticon*, and Transcribed by our Author, and the Copie
at Durham, To have been taken from an Original, yea admitting the Original
to be extant, and joyning with it the Charter yet Extant under Seal, And
cementing all together with the Duplicated Charter of William Rufus, and
even waving the Exceptions already offer'd amongst them, yet nevertheless
none of them seem Genuine and true; But with the greatest appearance are
counterfit, by some obvious circumstances plainly related by /71/ the most,
if not all the English Historians, Ancient and Modern, who treat of those
times. For

IT is evident, by the abstract I have given of these Charters, and by the
full copies subjoyn'd in the Appendix; that all of them are granted to
William Bishop of Durham, who can be no other, but he who is commonly
called, Willelmus de Carilefo; and likewise he and Turgot Prior of Durham,
are placed among the Witnesses in the two supposed Charters of our Edgar,
insinuating Homage.

THIS circumstance alone plainly discovers all these four deeds to be
spurious, for this Bishop William had left the Land of the living, long before
our Edgar was King of Scotland: So that it was impossible, that a true Deed
cou'd be granted to this Bishop after his Decease; nor cou'd the departed
Prelate Witness it.

THE Bishop nam'd in these Charters, can be no other, but Willelmus de
Carilefo, for there was none of this name Bishop of Durham before nor after

him, until the year 1143, That Willelmus de Barba or Barbara was made Bishop of Durham, and is called William the /72/ second,[1] which clearly demonstrats, That this other William was the first; Nor was any Bishop William Cotemporary with Turgot the Prior, who succeeded Aldwin in the Priors Office in 1087, but this Willelmus de Carilefo; which is ascertain'd not only from his own History of the Church of Durham, where he relates the time of his coming to be prior and of the promotion and death of this Bishop,[2] But also from this, That for the space of near thirty years before, and for as many years after the beginning of the Reign of our Edgar, and the death of William Rufus (in whose conjunct Reigns these Deeds, if true, behoved to be granted) there were only three Bishops of Durham, to wit, Walcherus, this Willelmus de Carilefo, and Ranulphus: This is clear from the History of the Church of Durham, written by this very Turgot the Prior, and published among the *Decem Scriptores*, under the Name of Simeon Dunelmensis and by his Continuator, and by the account given of the Bishops of the /73/ See, in the *Anglia Sacra*, and in Malmesbury's treatise *De Gestis pontificum Angliae*, published in the *quinque Scriptores post Bedam*: and is confirmed by the Saxon Chronicle, Florence of Worcester, the Annals of Simeon of Durham, and other English Historians: So that the Bishop William mentioned in these Charters, must be this Willelmus de Carilefo.

THAT this William Bishop of Durham was dead a considerable Time before our Edgar was King is most evident, by the unanimous Testimony of the English Historians; Turgot tells us, he died in King William Rufus's Court at Windsor in January 1096,[1] and the like We have from the Annals of Durham[2] and they give us the very day of his Sickening; For its known, That in the Monasteries, there were Obituaries kept with great care and exactness: With them may be joyn'd the Testimonies of the Saxon Chronicles; Florence of Worcester, Simeon of Durham, Hoveden,[3] and other English Historians, who all tell us, that /74/ this Prelate died at Windsor in January 1096; and some of them relate a notable Passage of his humility; In discharging his Body to be interred near the Glorious Body of St Cuthbert; and the same Historians[1] tell us, That about Michaelmass in the year 1097 our Edgar and his Uncle Edgar Atheling, with some auxiliary Forces went from England to Scotland; and having expelled Donald, he became King, and his Reign is reckoned to commence in 1098, which demonstratively evinces, That our Edgar, was not King in the Lifetime of this Bishop William, and by consequence irrecoverably Sinks the Faith of these Charters.

THIS Exception against the suppos'd Charters of Edgar, and the Duplicated Charter of William Rufus of England, is so clearly and fully voucht, That more need not be said, yet to show, That Forgeries generally go upon three it may be further excepted.

P.72 (1) *Anglia sacra* tom. I. p. 712 & 718 (2) *Inter X Scrip.* p. 49, 52 & 58.
P.73 (1) *Inter X. Script.* p. 58. (2) *Anglia Sacra* tom. I. p. 704. (3) *Omnes ad annum* 1096.
P.74 (1) *ad annum* 1097.

THAT the Copy at Durham of Edgar's Charter, bears, That it was made that Year wherein William the second made a new Castle before Bebbanburgh* (*Bamburrow) upon the Earl of Northumberland, /75/ Which could not be, For here again the above Historians[1] in one voice tell us that this new Castle which they call Maleveosin, or ill Neighbour was built, and that Babbenburgh was besieged some years before Our Edgar was King, how then cou'd he before he was King, make Grants or Homage?

THIS kind of Date clearly evinces the cunning and Artifice us'd in the Contrivance of this Copy, For in ancient Charters, we find sometime the date pointed furth by remarkable Facts for Example, there's a Grant by King David the First to Coldingham, made in that year, wherein the King of France and many other Christians went to Jerusalem; And there's another Charter by the same King to Melross bearing date, in the second year after the Captivity of Stephen King of England: And in a Charter granted by King Malcolm the Maiden, to the Predecessor of the ancient Family of Innes, it is said to be granted, at Christmas ensuing the Kings Receiving Sumerled into Favour.

MOREOVER there lyes a special /76/ Exception against the Charters of William Rufus, for being Duplicats, the one falling the other follows; In that which bears Witnesses, Willelmus Cancellarius is placed as a Witness, who, I presume, was never heard of before in the Reign of this King, and the before mentioned Historians Florence of Worcester, the Saxon Chronicle, Simeon of Durham, Hoveden,[1] and other English Historians, ancient and modern and with them the Learn'd Sir William Dugdale, who in his ingenious Treatise, Intituled, *Origines Juridicales*, hath collected and published a List of all the Cancellaries since the Conquest, say, That Robert Bloet Bishop of Lincoln was Cancellar to this King William five years before Edgar came to the Throne, and he survived King William many years.

THE Suspicion of Edgar's Charters, importing the Homage is increas'd, and our Crown and Kingdom is evidently Imperial and Independent by five Original Charters of this King Edgar, yet extant at Durham, and recorded in an ancient Cartuary there, which in their /77/ Form and Seal bear clear marks of Soveraignty.

FOR, First, in the Direction, they run in these Words, *Scottis et Anglis*, preferring the Scots to the English; which had been unjust if our King had been a Vassal of England, for his Kingdom, Thus to set the Sons of Ismael before the Children of Isaac, and to prefer the Offspring of the bond-woman, to the Posterity of her that was free: So the placeing of the Scots before the English, in the direction, seems to imply, We are not Dependent; And tho' Our King had been so Debonaire, to put the English first; Nevertheless that wou'd be no Note of our Subjection to the English, more than of theirs to France by the French being frequently set before them in the Direction of ancient English Charters.

P.75   (1) *ad annum* 1095.
P.76   (1) *Omnes ad annum* 1093.

NEXT the Seal appended to these genuine Charters bears this Circumscription, YMAGO EDGARI BASILEI SCOTTORUM, which is a clear Indication of Soveraignty; For where did ever a Vassal King, call himself *Basileus*. This was the exalted Title by which the Emperors of the East and West, strove to distinguish themselves, from all other Kings and /78/ Princes,[1] And is one of the lofty Titles of the Kings of England adduced to prove the Superiority; And this very Seal of Our King Edgar seems very valuable, as being an Ancient Voucher, and a most convincing proof of our Crowns, being of old reckon'd and own'd as Imperial, and shews the Rashness and Ignorance of our Author, who say's our Crown is a supposed Imperial Crown, and had never this name, but in an Act paving the way for a Popish Successor,[2] And it's against Reason to think, that a King, who assumed and bore the Title of *Basileus*, would own himself Subject to another Prince; and I wou'd fain know what more express marks of Soveraignty can there be, Than that our Kings used the same Title with Emperors, And its observable that the Composers of this Copy of Edgars Charter of Homage, to shew their craft have added the description of his true Seal, appended to the five Genuine Originals; But when they come to enumerat the words in the Ring or the Circumscription, they have thought /79/ fit to leave out the word *Basilei*, as being very disagreeable to an Homage, and substitut *Regis* in it's place.[1]

WITH all Submission I conceive, that the very useing of this Title, *Basileus*, is an unanswerable and pointed proof of our Independency, and puts the Soveraignty of Our Crown beyond all Question, and clearly evinces, that even in the days of Our Edgar, who by patcht up deeds is represented as a cringing Homager; Our Crown and Kingdom was Imperial and Independent; And further, this Title serves to convict all the Stories and Charters of ancient Times, concerning the Homage for Scotland, of Fable and Forgery, it not being presumable that Our Edgar wou'd assume a Title, which did not of right belong to him and his Predecessors; and the Presumption is the stronger, that there be Charters with a seal bearing this title, granted to the Monks of Durham, who were English, and that these Grants ever were and still are lodged in the Archives of that place.

THAT in the Import and Significance of the Word *Basileus*, I may not /80/ be thought Dogmatick or Daring, I skreen my self with the Authority and Countenance of the great English Selden, and whoever will be pleas'd to look upon the second chapter of the first Book of his Learn'd and curious Treatise of *Titles of Honor*, will there find Reasons and Instances, to demonstrat, that this Title is an infallible Mark of Soveraignty and independency, and in the last Paragraph of that Chapter which is in Relation to the opinion of some Civilians, who think this Title of *Basileus* or *Imperator*, in the Stile of other Princes is an injury to the Emperor of Germany who is commonly known by that name, and is of right Lord of the whole World on Earth,

---

P.78　(1) Seldens *titles of Hon*. B. I. Cap 2. § 5. (2) p. l.
P.79　(1) Append. Numb. 4.

upon this occasion, we have the plain Sentiment of this Learn'd Antiquary, which is so much to the present purpose, that I repeat his Words, But it is most clear (saith this Great Man) that neither Anciently, nor at this day, there is any such Title, as Lord of the whole World, really due to him, And that diverse other Princes, as the King of England, SCOTLAND, France, Spain, besides others have their Supremacy, Acknowledging no Superior, but GOD himself, and may every way as justly as the /81/ Emperours of Rome be stiled Emperours, or by any other name, which expresses the fullest height of Honour and Dignity. Here the King of Scotland is Rank'd equally Imperial and Independent with the three most puissant Kings of Europe; This Learn'd Author also in the same Paragraph cites the 3d Chapter of the 5th Parliament of our King James the third, wherein it is ordain'd *that our King has full Jurisdiction, and free Empire in this Realm,* and its observ-able, that when in the subsequent chapter, this Learn'd Author occasionally mentions, the Monkish Story of Edgar of England as Steersman, and eight Kings, as his Watermen their wafting over Dee, and the Story of Athelstan, he gives no positive opinion of his own, but only fairly cites the Authors, pro and con in that matter: and of these more, when the fables used in this dispute come to be considered; only by the bye, it may be noticed, That however some of the old Stories favouring the Homage, related in the Ancient English Historians, and rehearsed by Edward the first, in his Letter to the Pope, are laid aside by some as fabulous, not being Tenible, yet such is the enlarged appetite /82/ of Mankind after power and glory, That we're very ready to swallow any thing, that carries possibility, without chewing; and no Ancient evidence or Story, of the Grandeur and Glory of the Kings of England, and of their Soveraignty over our Kings, pass more Glibb with some of the Moderns, than this story of Edgar of Englands being rowed over Dee, by the King of Scots and by seven more Princes as his Vassals; and the mighty Speech, made by him to his People on this occasion; and Mr. Atwood says,[1] That Edward the first was so mightily pleased with this entertaining passage, That in his Letter to the Pope he dwelt upon it: Nevertheless it is plain, that this very Story, is a meer Fable and Monkish Invention; For in the Saxon Chronicles published by Mr. Wheloc, is related all the memorable things in this Kings Reign, which are mention'd in the other Edition of that Chronicle, except this chimerical pomp, there being not one Sillable of this Glorious passage:[2] So the first hint we have of it, is in the Edition of that Chronicle, published /83/ by the Reverend and Learn'd Dr. Gibson; where its said, six Kings met this King Edgar at Westchester, and entred into a League with him, to assist him by Sea and Land;[1] without naming who they were, or mentioning any other Circumstance whatsoever: But by the days of Florence of Worcester; Simeon of Durham, William of Malmesbury, and Hoveden,[2] They are degraded from Kings to *Subreguli,*

P.82 (1) p. 193. (2) edit. Cant. an. 1643. p. 559.
P.83 (1) *ad An.* 973. p. 122. *ubi dicitur: ad Laegeceaster ei obviam venerunt sex Reges & omnes cum eo foedere pacto polliciti sunt sese Cooperarios futuros terra marique.* (2) *Omnes ad Annum* 673 D.

and a Whim is trumpt up of Edgar's going into a Barge, and holding the Helm, while they row'd him over Dee, and that there might be a competent Set of Watermen, their Number is advanced to eight: Whereof three get Titles, and of them the King of Scots leads the Vann. Besides a powerful Speech is brush'd up for the Majestick Pilot. And by the Time of Mathew of Westminster; there's Titles fitted to the other five; and to make the Story more serious, or rather the more to prophane it: He tells us, that this open /84/ Manifestation and Declaration of the Soveraignty of the King of England, was accompanied with divine Services.[1] Mr. Holinshed and other Moderns think this Story so glorious for their Nation, that they set it down at large, and discant upon the Titles of these utopian Oar-tuggers.

BY this, we may see what Faith and Credit is to be given to English Historians, when any passage serves to exalt and aggrandize their Prince, and lessen others: For, admitting our King and other Princes, according to the last Edition of the Saxon Chronicle, entered in a League with Edgar of England, to assist him by Land and Sea; yet from thence to infer Homage or Subjection, were to banter common Sense and Reason: But the fanciful Monks, can from a League extract a Feudal Contract; they can make eight Subreguli out of six Kings, they can turn Allies* (*Co-operarii terra marique) unto Vassals by Land, and Water-men by Sea: They can make their Kings deliver Glorious Speeches, which were never spoken; /85/ and can dub Princes and give them Titles, that never had any Being, but under a shaven Pate.

THIS plainly shews how these Monks fitted their Histories to the Gust of these Dark and Superstitious Ages; and that the ancient Evidences of the Homage are wholly wrapt up in ridiculous Fables; It also lets us know how Crazy the Claim of Edward the first was, when founded upon such whimsical Fancies.

HOWEVER the dreaming Monks, who were valued according to the Measure they possessed of the endearing Talent of Fable and Juggle, might allow themselves in such Licentious Scribling; Yet its amazing to find any Moderns, entertain and publish, such vain Whimsies of one of their Kings making eight Princes, Tarrs, and of converting his Royal Barge to a Gally, from an Imagination, that these things are for the Glory of England.

SEING then most of the ancient English Historians, and some Moderns are so mightily charm'd with this beautiful Landskip of the Glorious Magnificence and Soveraignty of their King Edgar; I have for Vindication /86/ of Truth, and of the Honour of Our Kings, let its Colours be known, and set them in a true Light.

HAVING thus by Digression made a Trip to Westchester, to behold the Grand-Royal Interview, and the splendid Water-work there; I return to our own Historians to see what Light they afford us about our Edgar's Homage to William Rufus of England.

P.84 (1) *Ad annum* 973.

IF we turn to our own Historians, and review the Reign of our King Edgar, we will find somethings related very disagreeable, if not altogether inconsistent with his owning of the King of England as his Superior, in any Grants to Coldingham, or in any other respect.

BUCHANAN says, That Coldingham was formerly the Monastery of St. Ebbe, and was transferred by King Edgar to Durham, in the 7th Year of his Reign,[1] which was 5 Years after the Death of King William Rufus; For Edgar began his Reign in 1098, and William was killed in 1100, when he was Hunting, by the accidental Shot of an Arrow.

THIS account of Coldingham, seems /87/ to be supported by Bede, and other English Historians who mention Coldingham, as I've hinted: And our Learn'd Countrey-man's Sentiment, is confirmed by several Grants made to Coldingham, after it was transferr'd to Durham, wherein the Donors give Lands to St. Mary, and to St. Cuthbert, and to St. Ebbe; And among others is a very ancient Deed, by Edward the Son of Peter of Restalrig *Baro Regis Scotie.*

TURGOT, and from him Fordon, as appears by an ancient Copy of his History, belonging to a worthy Gentleman, and with much Civility communicat to me, wherein *Turgotus* is prefixed to most of the Chapters, in relation to the History of his time: and from Selden we understand, That there is a Copy of Fordon's History in the Cotton Library, having Turgot's name in the beginning of several Chapters concerning Queen Margaret and Her Children,[1] whereof Edgar was one: and after Turgot and Fordon, Hector Bois[2] give us the account and Reason of Edgar's bestowing Coldingham and its Appennages, upon St. Cuthbert /88/ of Durham; Which tho' it savour of the dark and blind Devotion of those Times, yet its worthy Remark and-wholly overturns any Thoughts of his Homage: According to these Historians, Our Edgar in his way from England to Scotland, having rested at Durham, St. Cuthbert appear'd to him in a Vision, and desired him to be of good Courage, and carry with him St. Cuthbert's Banner, and his Enemies shou'd flee before him; And he shou'd sit upon the Throne of his Ancestors; Which Advice this good Prince follow'd, and upon displaying of the St's Banner Donald who had usurped the Government, and his Forces fled, and were defeat: And Edgar was placed upon the Throne of his Father Malcolm.

THIS devout King Edgar being very mindful of Saint Cuthbert's good offices, did grant to the Monks of Durham, Coldingham, with it's Appennages, and he also gave to Ranulf Bishop of Durham, Berwick,[1] who proving thereafter ungrate and perfidious to Edgar his benefactor, he justly resum'd the grant of Berwick.

/89/ THIS account of Edgar's Grants is the more remarkable, that in probability it flows Originally from Turgot, who was Prior of Durham when Edgar was solaced by this Vision, and also when he as a Testimony of his

P.86   (1) *In Hist. lib. 7. ad Reg.* 89.
P.87   (1) *Praefat. ad X. Script:* p. 24. (2) *Hist. Scot. lib.* 12. *penes finem.*
P.88   (1) Fordon, Boeth; & Leslie *ad Regn: Edgari.*

Gratitude to St. Cuthbert, made these Genuine Grants to the Monks of Durham.

HEREBY likewise the true Charters of Edgar, which are granted to the Monks of Durham, are strengthen'd, and the Grants made to Bishop William are disproved; For by Turgot, we here understand that Edgar's Donatives to Durham were made in the time of Bishop Ranulf who was the only Bishop of that See, In the Reign of our King Edgar; For the English Historians tell us, That this See was Vacant for three Years, after the Death of Bishop William:[1] And that King William Rufus in the last Year of his Reign, gave this Bishoprick to that Ranulf the Squeezer of the Clergy, and Devourer of their Revenues; And his Memory is Transmitted to Posterity by the Monkish Historians, with /90/ the most odious Character.

THAT this was the true Motive of Edgar's granting Coldingham to Durham, is more plausible, than to think it was done to Testifie his Gratitude to his Succourer, William Rufus, who did not much value such a Complement; He being a notorious and Sacrilegious Pillager of Church Revenues, and none was so subservient to him, in these bad Practices, as Ranulph Bishop of Durham; And this King is said to have had one Arch-Bishoprick, two Bishopricks and twelve Abbies in his hands at his death.

IT'S Sure, That William Rufus was assisting to Edgar, an injured Prince and Neighbour, and furnished him with some Troops, to vindicat his just Right to the Crown of Scotland; This Assistance is much magnified by some English Historians, but Buchanan calls them only *Modica Auxilia*,[1] And not improbably; For it's to be Remembered, That when Edgar came with his Uncle Edgar Atheling to Scotland, William of England was going over Sea to Normandy, where he stayed for some time; And thus it's /91/ presumable, he had not much Force to spare; Again Edgar was invited Home, and encouraged by the Nobles of Scotland, as their true Prince:[1] And it might be thought no bad Politick in this King of England, and in Henry his Brother and Successor; when this King was going from England to Normandy, and leaving behind him a disoblidged People, and an abused and provocked Clergy, To dispatch Edgar Atheling, and his Nephew Our Edgar to Scotland, and thereby secure his Government; For Edgar Atheling was the true and undoubted Heir of the English Monarchy, and our Edgar was agen his presumptive Heir; and so sensible of this Right was Henry the first of England, the immediat King after Rufus, who for his great Enduements was called Beauclerk, That to strengthen his Title to the Crown, he with much Affection courted Mawde the Sister of our King Edgar, and the eldest Daughter of King Malcolm Canmoir, by his good Queen Margaret; and Married her after repeated refusals given by her, to the interposing Friends;[2] /92/ And this King Henry having only a Son called William who was Drown'd, and a Daughter of that Marriage, the Empress Mawde; He pre-

P.89   (1) Sim. Durh. *inter X. Script.* p. 59. & 224. *Et Anglia Sacra* vol. 1. p. 705.
P.90   (1) *Lib.* 7. *ad Reg.* 89.
P.91   (1) Buch. *Hist. Reg. Lib.* 7 *ad* 89. (2) Math. Paris *ad annum* 1101.

sented her to his People, as descended by her Grand-mother the Queen of Scots, of the true Blood Royal of England; and it is uncontravertible That by the death of Edgar Atheling without Issue, the Kings of Scotland, were the true Heirs of the English-Saxon Monarchy; And when our King James the sixth, succeeded to the Crown of England; He was not only the Heir of York and Lancaster, in the Right of his Great-Grand-Mother Margaret, the eldest Daughter of King Henry the 7th of England, and of his Queen Elizabeth; But also in this our James, and no sooner, was conjoyn'd and center'd, the true Heir of the Saxon and Norman Regal Race, upon the Throne of England.

WHAT the rear Author or concluder of the *Chronicon Saxonicum* saith, concerning Edgar, That he was made King *sub ditione Regis Anglie*,[1] Is not worth the noticing, for without a nice enquiry of the Import of the phrase, This seems only to be a flight of the /93/ Author, for when the Charter and Seal of this King, and also of the King of England, have been counterfit, to make this our Edgar, a Vassal of England for his Crown; It's not to be thought that a Historian of those days wou'd boggle at an amusing Innuendo, or a transcriber startle at an interpolation, And the faith of this part of the Chronicle is the less; If it be consider'd, that from the Preface of the Learn'd Editor Doctor Gibson, and from the account given of this Chronicle by the worthy Bishop of Carlile,[1] it appears, none of the Copies of this Chronicle used by Mr. Wheloc, or Doctor Gibson, nor some other Copies nam'd by the Bishop, do reach to the Reign of our Edgar, except one, given by Arch-Bishop Laud, To the University of Oxford; And which is thought, did anciently belong, to the Monastery of Peterburgh; But to oppose History to History, besides what is already said, It's highly Improbable, that Edgar pay'd any Homage, to the King of England; For neither Florence of Worcester who Survived Edgar about 12 /94/ years, And thus cotemporarie with him, nor yet Simeon of Durham, nor Hoveden, have in their Histories one Sillable of subjection by Edgar, to William of England, and none of them are so favourable to us, That it may be thought, they industriously overlook't it, and Florence and Simeon may Rationally be suppos'd, to know this Affair: For the first was Edgar's closs cotemporary, and the last was a Monk of Durham, who cou'd not be ignorant of Edgar's Homage if there had been any deeds granted by him to the Monks of Durham,importing homage; and this still enforces the Arguments disproving these Deeds.

ANY acknowledgment of Homage by Edgar, will yet further appear Improbable, if we consider some Historical passages of that time, and particularly one very remarkable, wherein our own, and all the English Historians agree; And tell us, That Duncan, Edgar's natural Brother dispossess'd Donald his Uncle, by the assistance of England and Norman Forces; And assum'd the Government, but the Scots, wou'd not allow him to continue in the exercise of it, unless he removed the English and Normans out

---

P.92   (1) p. 206.
P.93   (1) *Engl. Hist. Lib.* Vol. 1. p. 114.

of SCOTLAND. This /95/ memorable and uncontested passage is a very clear Historical proof of our Independency, and from it we may understand; How zealous our brave predecessors were, to preserve our Liberties, by guarding against any Appearances of having them Impair'd, by Foreign power and influence: It is also observable, That the Historians tell, that Edgar was a very good prince, that he Reign'd and dyed in peace. and in the affection of his Subjects, which had never been, If he had surrender'd his Soverainty.

THUS I hope the Crown and Kingdom of Scotland, is acquit from any Homage, by the before mention'd Charters of King Malcolm, and of his Son King Edgar, which are manifest Forgeries, by the Verdict of English Historians: And it seems worthy of notice, That in Edward the first's Letter to the Pope, he uses as a powerful argument for the Homage, the very words of Edgar's supposed Charter, which are, that William Rufus gifted him the Kingdom, and Bromton in his Chronicle, has the like expression,[1] Hence we see the design, /96/ use and effect of these spurious deeds in former times.

THESE falshoods of themselves alone, are sufficient to Wound and Blemish the Claim of Homage, but the promoters of the Cause have not rested here; For as I hinted in the entry of this Treatise, we are furder of late upbraided, in a Book published by Doctor Drake, with some moe certificats of Homage, said to be under the Seals of our King; which I shall briefly consider.

THIS Physician under the specious pretext, That by Fortuitous Means, There was Transmitted to him a valuable Historical Treatise, written by one long agoe Deceased; He last Year oblidged the World, with the Publication of this new discovered Treasure, under the Title of *Historia Anglo-Scotica*, And to this new Adjective, He adds the inviting words, an Impartial History.

THE Doctor is pleased to own no further share and office in this matter, but of Midwife, and of handing this desirable Work to the World; And ushering it, with a Prefatory Dedication.

IN the second Paragraph of this /97/ Introduction, The Doctor shews his design in bringing to light this non-such History, by telling; The intermixt affairs of England and Scotland, afford us a part of History, not only of entertainment, but at this Critical juncture of particular use to all that are studious of the knowledg of the interchangable Rights and Pretensions of these two Crowns, upon each other; Which no Book that he knows of, is of so great help to, as the following piece, This plainly opens the design of this Master-piece, And the more, that in the Title Page, Homages lead the Van of a Trainband of many particulars, which are there enumerat.

IT might be thought digression, to enter upon consideration of the Doctors preface, where in so narrow a compass, he goes backward and foreward; by making first a conjecture about the date of this new discovered Manuscript, and enforceing his guess with Reasons, and then in immediatly plainly Retracting it, from a clear passage in the Book it self; Bless me! did

---

P.95　(1) *Inter X Scrip.* p. 990.

the Doctor write his Preface, before he knew what was in a Book he composed, at least that he published; No sure, for in the Title Page, he tells the World, it was Extracted from the /98/ best Historians of England, and in the Preface, that he collated it with the best accounts of the several Reigns, that he could procure, Or was he in a mighty hurry and haist to publish it, and were his thoughts so disjoynted; That he cou'd neither favour himself, nor his Reader; To Transcribe his Preface, or dash out a Paragraph, but choose rather to continue an Error, and to add a *Peccavt*: There be also in this prefatory Dedication, some other things which seem not altogether dispensed *Secundum Artem*. And whether the Doctor be the Mask'd composer, or only the Abettor of this mighty performance, is much the same and not worth Enquiry. For at best it's the Child of an uncertain Father long ago deceased, which brings it under the suspicion of a Bastardly performance.

THE Doctor of late, hath got a mate in the Trade of dark dealing and of posthumous midewifry: The under deck Authour and Publisher of the *Select Fables;* For tho' they want the Doctors name, yet have some tincture and Scraps of his politicks; by telling the World, that the Author is dead, /99/ and that it was unfair to soften his expression.[1]

THESE Publishers have thought fit, to show so much respect and duty to the innocent dead, as to make them the beasts of burden, of their passions and designs: For the Fabulors Brat it was some thing agreeable, to make Mother viper deceased, to make way for the envenom'd brood; And by these Fables we know, who speaks in the skin of the dead.[2] But what need had the Doctor of a cloak for an Impartial History, unless he thought convenient to make himself, dead, that he might enbalm and Aromatize his performance with Encomiums in a Preface, that were not to be expected from any other hand.

EVEN Mr. Atwood the Busy Homage-monger, has acted a part of more candor and courage, by owning his performance, and not suffering it to be exposed, to the imputation of being Bastard or Foundling.

THE Laws of Scotland,[3] and the Rules of good manners, restrain us from any reviling or scandalous expressions /100/ against England; But we're unequally met by some of our Neighbours, and by none have we been more abused, than by the Ridiculous scoffs of this Scurrilous Taleteller; who insults us, by telling, That England hath an ancient and just Right of Soveraignty over us, and power to assert it when ever they please;[1] and Lampoons Scotland by the Fable of the Ass in the Lyons skin;[2] and yet more bitterly by the Fable of the unequal match;[3] which last seems to have been devised, in consequence or compliment of an insulting proverb; But before such Proverbs or Fables be applyed to us, they who use them, wou'd do well to raze out of their Annals and Records, the Marriage Suits made by Edward the first, and Henry the eight, for their Sons; and the Repeated Commissions for Union, or else convert those things also unto Fables: They

---

P.99   (1) Preface to the *Select Fables*. (2) p. 40. (3) 20 Parl. Jam. 6. cap. 9.
P.100 (1) *Select Fables* page ult. (2) p. 40. (3) p. 61.

might also remember who sits upon the Throne, and if they be above History yet they may call to mind, the Fable of the Eagle and the Beetle e'en set down by the Tale-teller in his /101/ Select Collection,[1] as taken from Aesop, with his own, and L'estrange's witty Reflections;[2] For by the most enlarged Comparison, our Neighbours will not be exalted above the Eagle, nor we depress'd below the Beetle.

ANOTHER dark-dealer the publisher of the late Plagiarie Treatise, entitled, *an impartial account of the Affairs of Scotland, &c.* to make it more current, has thrown in into the Title page, Some remarkable Instances that may give light into the Dependency of Scotland, on the Crown of England; which is mere juggle: For in this Book, there's nothing has the least Tendency to Homage; Only there's a passing hint of a Rumor spread abroad by the Partisans of our Queen Mary, of a secret Bargain between Queen Elizabeth, and the Earl of Murray for making Scotland a Province of England, and that our Q. Mary has promised the like her self,[3] both which have no Fundation but Imagination; For in the Entry of this Essay, I have noticed a Proclamation by Queen Elizabeth, to prevent jealousies between the two Nations; and /102/ now for clearing of this matter I have placed a Copy of the Proclamation in the Appendix[1] and as for our Queen Mary it's known a meanness of Spirit, was never reckon'd her Infirmity, and perhaps the Suspicion of her entertaining a Claim of Soveraignty, of something more than of Scotland, did hasten the fatal Exit, of that unfortunate Princess; But to Return to the consideration of Dr. Drakes impartial History.

IT commences with the History of the Reigns of Malcolm Canmoir, and William the Conqueror, and so about the year 1066, and ends in the Reigns of the two Maries of Scotland and England.

IN it we are promised the interwoven History of the two Kingdoms, in that tract of Time in such an impartial manner, that the most prejudic'd Scot can't arraign the Author of Injustice, who by his candid Relation of things, Will silence the most unreasonable litigious Advocat for Scotland;[2] But I'm afraid this Character given by the Doctor of this Performance will be *anapar-* /103/ *tes equales*, with his prefatory Conjectures.

AMONG the Maters toucht in his Treatise, there's never wanting positive Assertions of the Homage, beginning with the Homage of Malcolm Canmoir, and ending with the Homage of our King James the first, and almost in every Reign it's said, That our Kings did Homage to the Kings of England; for the Kingdom of Scotland, which they testified under their Seals.

THIS Authors common place-book for these Homages is Harding, a very famous Historian, eminently endued with the two recommending Faculties of Ryming and Forgeing; He lived in the Reign of our James the first, and of Henry the sixth of England, and is the oldest of this Authors Vouchers, and the only person we find upon his Margin for the Homage, until the Reign of our James the first, where there's joyn'd with him a yet

---

P.101 (1) p. 28. (2) L'estrange's *Esop Fab.* 378. p. 345. (3) p. 276 & 277.
P.102 (1) Numb. 10 (2) prefat. Ded[i]cat.

greater Novice, Edward Hall the Historical Master Fashioner, the Cream of whose Annals, consists in telling the Habits and Fashions of Cloaths worn in the several Reigns: For other Matters in the Reign of Henry the sixth and downward, we find upon the Margin /104/ of his Treatise, Holinshed, Polidore Virgil, Lesly, and some others of a very late date; And yet the Doctor says in the Title page, That this History is extracted from the best Historians of both Nations; and in his Preface, That it is collated with them: By these things in all Submission, the Doctor doth not much advance his Character as an Historian, nor doth he justice to his Countrey, which hath many more ancient, valuable and creditable Historians.

IT must be own'd, that whoever inclines to make a pudder about the Homage, cannot use any Author more fitting their Purpose and Design than Harding: But lest by so many alledged Testificats of the Homage, under the Seals of our Kings, Trimm'd up in this treatise, which is Gilded with the alluring Title of an *Impartial History*, faithfully Collected and Collated, any should be misled to the belief of the Homage; And to vindicat the just mark of Indignation put by my Countrey upon this Book, and to quell the Banter of the Satyrical Mythologist, who says *We Burn Books that we can not Answer*,[1] Upon these considerations I'm /105/ necessitat to open another black and Melancholly Scene of a Bundle of Forgeries contrived to support the imaginary Homage; And here I must again own the Civility and Ingenuity of the English; Because, from a very Worthy and Learn'd Gentleman and Historian, who had inspected the most valuable Records of his Country, I had the first nottice of these forg'd Deeds; And the account he was pleased to give me concerning them was in substance, thus:

JOHN Harding a Poet and Historian, was an inveterate Enemy to Scotland, and pretended, That he could Recover unquestionable Proofs of our Homage to England: And enters in a Contract with the then Treasurer of that Kingdom, for procuring of them, and gets some Money in hand, and a promise of more upon performance of the Indenture; Upon this he comes to Scotland, and finding himself disappointed, he or some of his Confederats patches up a bundle of Charters with Seals by our Kings, and other Deeds owning the Homage, as due by our Kings for Scotland to the King of England, and returns home with them: But not without a Parcel of Lyes to /106/ make the matter plausible. And he, good man, pretended, That he was in peril of his life, and incurably mutilat in bringing off those precious Deeds; And to make them appear the more valuable, he said, he was offered a considerable Sum by James King of Scotland to deliver them up to him, Wherefore Harding upon his giving in these Charters to the Treasurer, He was acquit of the Indenture, and was farther rewarded with a Pension of Twenty Pound Sterling during Life, which was a considerable Sum in those Days: This Discovery being generously made me, I cou'd not (tho' free of any Caution or Restraint from my Friend) have allow'd my self to publish, until I found this account confirm'd by some Paragraphs of Mr.

P.104 (1) *Select Fables* p. 48.

Tyrrel's Introduction to the third Volum of his *General History of England*,[1] where he mentions some Charters of Homage which were forged by this Harding, and tells they were delivered to the Earl of Shrewsbury Treasurer to Henry the Sixth, conform to a Memorandum enter'd in the Exchequer Books; And says these forged Charters are still /**107**/ preserved among the Archives in the Chapter-house at Westminster, in several Boxes, in the great Chist, entitled SCOTIA, and for the Truth of the Matter of Fact, he places in the Margin the Learn'd Historiographer Mr. Rymer for his Voucher; And I was yet farther confirmed in this Matter by the deed of Pension, granted by Henry the 6th in the 36th year of his Reign, to this notorious Forger Harding, whereof a Copy is subjoyn'd in the Appendix,[1] and in it some part of this black History is related; And it's observable, That besides some Charters particularly mention'd, to be deliver'd up by this Harding, ther's added this general, and many other notable Evidences demonstrating the Superiority of the King of England over Scotland.

IT'S not my Inclination, to defend but where we're attack'd, wherefore I have forborn to publish & disprove any particular Deeds, to which this Gift of Pension doth relate, and I hope none will enterprise to abett and justifie them, & thereby force me to expose & demonstrat these deeds to be scandalous Forgeries: For to me it's a most undesireable /**108**/ task, to lay open the Injuries done us, in relation to the Claim of Homage; But it were to rivet this claim to be altogether Silent, when there is no Restraint nor mark of Displeasure, put upon so many calumnious and unworthy Treatises, which question and arraign her Majesties Soveraignty of Scotland, and the Independency of her ancient Kingdom.

THESE notorious Forg'd Deeds speak so loud and plain of themselves, That they need no Commentary or Reflection, only it's very rational and natural to think, That when some of our Neighbours have been so easie in such late times, as of King Henry the 6th to admit of any thing that favour'd of the Homage; and to glutt over so many Forgeries, without enquiry; Yea liberally to gratifie the Hatchers of such Iniquity, and to defile the noblest Repository of the most valuable Archives of England, with an abominable cluster of falsehoods; There is little or no Faith to be given to the Stories of more ancient and dark Times.

IN the same Introduction Mr. Tyrrel likewise disproves upon good grounds the aforesaid Deed of Homage, said to be granted by our King James the first /**109**/ to Henry the sixth, in the second year of his Reign, and set down at large in the Chronicle of Mr. Hall, and thence transcribed by Doctor Drake,[1] And it's also Transcribed by Mr. Atwood,[2] And Mr. Tyrrel in this Introduction says, that in this Volum of his History, he has disproved as spurious, a Charter of Homage by our David the 2d, To Edward the 3d Transcribed by Doctor Brady in his History, and we hope very justly; For tho' it was the Misfortune of these two Princes to be Prisoners in England,

---

P.106 (1) P. 9 & 10.
P.107 (1) Numb. 7.
P.109 (1) p. 208. (2) p. 326.

yet its known, They wou'd not redeem their Liberty, by a Surrender of their Soveraignty; Nor probably wou'd their people have received them, if they had done Homage to the King of England, & when King James was in the hands of the English, his people gave powerful Assistance to the French against them, and he being desired by the King of England to deal with his Subjects, to forbear this assistance, it's recorded with what Boldness and Magnanimity this excellent Prince behaved and express'd himself, and this is e'en particularly notic'd by Doctor Drake,[3] /110/ And yet in a few Leaves after, he setts down a most solemn Deed of Homage by this King, which is very disagreeable to this brave Prince's Character and Deportment, and had this Homage been so solemnly perform'd, in so great and numerous a presence, viz. three Dukes, two Arch-Bishops, twelve Earls, twenty Barrons, and about two hundred Knights and Esquires,[1] without all peradventure, it had been ingrost, as Mr. Tyrrel well observes, in some unquestionable Record: For these favours we are obliged to Mr. Tyrrel, Yet in this introduction, he makes some little insinuation of the Homage, from the acknowledgments made by the Competitors for our Crown, in the days of Edward the first, And says, It was then the current opinion of all Vers'd in Antiquity, that the Homage was due, which appear'd by that Princes Letter to the Pope, Asserting his Superiority, wherein the Authorities are Collected, out of the most Ancient English Historians, and the Chronicles of several Abbies;[2] of which more afterward: But:

TO return a little to Doctor Drake: From what's said, It's evident how far /111/ his performance falls short of an Impartial History, and we may see, there was no Reason to Answer the false passages, in relation to the Homage, When there was no voucher, but a ryming Scribler; And it was most just to condemn a Book stuff'd with so many lyes and calumnies, to the Flames. And it may be presum'd, that his intelligent country-men will think it deserves the like fate in England, for ranking the most Scandalous and Infamous Harding among the best of their Historians.

TO change hands with the Doctor & to turn Physician for a moment, I will lend him a wholesome Recipe, that for preservation of the credit of any part of his impartial performance, he will be pleas'd to throw the Margins of it over board, lest the counter-band Harding confiscat the whole; and for his Friend the Roving Tale-teller, he himself has prescribed the fittest apartment and furniture for these of his temper,[1] But lest the Doctor think, that I officiously lend, I will civilly borrow from him, his prefatory Aphorism concerning this Book, that he knows of no piece that's so great a help to these who are studious /112/ of the knowledg of the Interchangable Rights and Pretensions of the two Crowns upon each other; Now it being clear, that all the Homages related in this non-such Treatise, which are said to be Testified by the Charters and Seal of our King (one of King William's which was Extorted when he was in captivity being excepted) are notorious Forgeries;

P.109 (3) p. 201.
P.110 (1) ibid. (2) p. 7.
P.111 (1) *Select Fables* p. 43.

And the Authors commonplace Book being Harding, who had his hand so deep in the py; I return the Doctor his Aphorism, with a *probatum est:* That no Book gives greater light to the injuries done us, by a number of scandalous Forgeries hatcht to support the Claim of an imaginary Homage: Only when the Doctor's Impartial History is prescribed or used, as a Catholicon, for the interchangable Rights of the two Crowns. It seems convenient as a Gentle and useful Corrective to add a small quantity of the true History of the Actings of his darling Voucher Harding.

THUS I have Essay'd to make good the proposition, That to favour this Claim, our Ancient Imperial and Independent Crown and Kingdom has been abus'd and injur'd, by a Tract, of notorious and unparallel'd Forgeries, of the Charters and Seals of several of our Kings.

/113/ THE next thing which may seem to give any colour to the Homage, are the Laws ascribed to William the Conqueror; as published by Mr. Lambard in his *Archaionomia,* wherein are some things very favourable to the dominion, of the King of England over Scotland.

THESE Laws are scattered in Mr. Atwoods Treatise, wherefore I shall rank them, as they stand in Mr. Lambards Edition in the year 1598, and shortly recapitulat any Paragraphs, from which the Homage may be inferr'd.

THE first, is in the very entry to the Laws of King William the Conqueror, wherein this King with his Nobles, appoint Peace, Concord, Judgment and Justice to be kept, among the English and Normans, also between the French and the Britains of Wales and Cornwall, and the Picts and Scots of Albany; and between the Inhabitants of all the Isles, and Provinces pertaining to the Crown, Honour and dignity of the King, and among all the Subjects through the whole Monarchy of Britain; So that none injure or wrong one another, under the Penalty of the Kings unlaw or fine, /114/ which is termed *foris-factura,*[1] Here the Scots are comprehended in the Monarchy, and subjected to the Laws of the King of England: and Mr. Atwood illustrats this Law, with a Variorum of his own, making England the head of the Monarchy, and says the full forfeitures of all the Subjects of Scotland were not due to their immediat Prince, but did fall to the King of England, as the head of the Monarchy:[2] It seems he had read Lambards Laws, with a large thumb upon the Margin, for there the words *plena Foris-factura* (which he dully Translates Full Forfeiture) are explained by the word *Mulcta;* But Forfeiture looks Big: O happy plantation, that was blest with a Chief Justice, who makes no distinction between a Forfeiture, and a Fine.

THE next Law favouring the Homage, is the 17 Law of Edward the Confessor, confirm'd by the Conqueror, where its said that Eleutherius the Pope in the year 67, in a Letter to King Lucius, made the limits of the Monarchy of old called Britain, then called the Kingdom of England, to be all the continent /115/ and the Isles, as far as Norway and Denmark.[1]

P.114 (1) *Arch. Lamb.* fol. 124 (2) p. 234.
P.115 (1) Lamb. *Arch.* fol. 130.

THE third evidence of the Dominion arising from these Laws, is in some sections of the 35 Law of this Edward the Confessor, wherein, the English, Danes, Welsh, Albanians and Islanders are declared lyable and subject to the same punishment for encroaching upon the Kings forrests:[2] Here also have we the pleasant Story of Ina King of the English, being chosen by an Angel, and that he was the first Monarch after the coming of the English to Britain, and the first Crown'd King of the English & Britons living together in Britain, after the Saxons came from Germany:[3] Here likewise is an Enumeration of some of the large conquests of the Famous King Arthur, That he subdued Scantia, now called Norway and many other Isles beyond Scantia to witt, Island, Grenland, Snechorda, Irland, Gutland, Dacia, Semeland, Winland, Curland, Roe, Femeland, Wireland, Flanderland, Cherreland, Lapland and all the other Lands and Isles of the East Sea even to Russia, and that this valiant /116/ Arthur made Easter Lapland the boundary of the Kingdom of Britain:[1] After this comes the notable Evidence of the Homage, in the account given of our Queen Margaret, That after the decease of her Brother Edgar Atheling she was the true Heir to Edward the Confessor of the Crown of England, And that the Prince of Albany by a fortuitous chance married her; Then follows, The Picts were so called, from Pictus their Leader, and the Scots from Scottus their Leader, for Albany is a part of the Monarchy of England, which of old was called the Kingdom of Britain.[2] Here Albany or Scotland is comprehended under the Monarchy or Dominion of England.

WITHOUT entering upon the Exceptions hinted at by the Learn'd Bishop of Carlile against Mr. Lambard's Edition of the ancient Laws of England, and the account given by his Lordship of the Corrections and Emendations by the Learn'd Junius and Somner;[3] It seems no candid part in Mr. Atwood to obtrude these Paragraphs as Evidences of the Superiority: /117/ For honest Mr. Lambard prefixes to the Laws of Edward the Confessor, and William the Conquerour, a very ingenuous Advertisement, to this purpose, Least any should think these Laws were the product of his own brain, he fairly tells, that he did transcribe them from two Copies, one of which was more ancient, and the other later, and that there were several things in the late Copy, which were not in the ancient one, and that for Distinction he had caused Print these things which are to be attributed to the latter Copy in a lesser Character;[1] This Caveat Mr. Atwood or any who have perused this Book, could not probably slide over without some observance, And all these Paragraphs pointing at the Superiority and Dominion of England over Scotland, are Printed in the lesser Character; which shows that they are not in the ancient Copy, But the confus'd Zelot notices, neither Advertisement nor Marginal Note.

TO Confirm this, There is to be seen a Copy of these Laws in Hoveden,[2] which agrees with the ancient Copy used by Mr. Lambard; and a

P.115 (2) ibid. fol. 139. (3) ibid. fol. 137.
P.116 (1) Lamb. *Arch*. fol. 137. (2) Ibid. fol. 139. (3) *Engl. Hist. Libr*. tom. 1. p. 111.
P.117 (1) fol. 124. (2) *inter quinque Scrip. post Bedam*. p. 600.

/118/ true Master of Antiquity, the very Learn'd and candid Sir Henry Spelman has published the Ecclesiastick Laws of Edward the Confessor, taken from his Secular Laws,[1] where, by way of Introduction, he tells us, He follow'd an old Copy belonging to himself, agreeing with Hoveden, and that it was written in some ancient time, when the Additions that are to be found in Lambard were not known: And in the close of the 15 Law, he remarks, That what follows in Lambard is neither in his Copy nor in Hoveden,[2] which clearly shews, what thoughts this judicious Knight had of these Paragraphs: These grounds of Suspicion, are supported by the Copies, of these Laws in the Chronicles of Litchfield and Leicester; which tho they have not all the Laws in Hoveden, yet they have none but what are to be found in him:[3] But the Falsehood and patching up of these Paragraphs, seems to be clear by the Copy of the Laws of the Confessor, and confirmed by the Conqueror, carried from his Court by /119/ Ingulfus to Croyland, published by Selden,[1] and added to the new Edition of Ingulfus,[2] and transcribed by Sir Henry Spelman, so far as they relate to the Church:[3] In all which Copies there is not a Sillable insinuating or importing the Homage; Nor is there any thing in Bromton (who is thought the most exact in Collecting the English Laws) concerning the Laws of the Conquerour to that purpose.

IF We descend a little into the consideration of what is related in these Paragraphs; They will evidently appear, to be a spurious After-growth, And

FIRST, That William the Conqueror was King or Monarch of Britain, is without any Foundation; For in his Charters and Letters, he designed himself *Rex Anglorum*. And it's known that Malcolm Canmoir, who was the only Cotemporary King of Scotland with him, did once and again take Arms against him, which ended in a League between them at Abernethy settling the Limits of their Kingdoms; /120/ And however some of the English Historians tell us, That at this place, Malcolm payed Homage to the Conquerour,[1] & which is the first time, we find any of their Historians, name Homage or Homager, And by saying, That he did Homage in General, they have left the Expression open to a Fallacy Yet the Import and Extent of the Homage then payed, is very quickly after clear'd by the same Historians when they relate the Rencounter between the same Malcolm, and William the Second called Rufus, the Son and Successor of the Conqueror, where upon the Heads of their Armies, by the Interposition of Edgar Atheling and Earl Robert Brother to William Rufus, There was an Agreement made between the two Kings, by the which William was to give Malcolm Twelve Towns,* (* *Villas*) that he had under his Father with twelve Merks of Gold yearly; By this Addition we see who made Concessions; and Malcolm was to pay the like Homage to him as he had done to his Father the Conqueror,[2] which clearly /121/ evinces, for what this Homage was due.

P.118 (1) *Concil.* tom. 1 p. 619. (2) ibid. p. 622. (3) Seldeni *Not. ad Eadmer.* p. 171.
P.119 (1) Ibid. p. 173. (2) Oxon. 1684. *inter Vet. Scrip. Britan.* p.88. (3) *Concil.* tom. 1. p. 624.
P.120 (1) Flor. Wigorn. & Sim. Dunel. *inter X Script. ad annum* 1072. (2) *ad annum* 1091.

THE English Historians inform us, that about two years thereafter, Malcolm did meet William at Glocester, as had been previously concerted by their Ambassadors: which interview some of the Nobles of England thought, was in order to the establishing of a firm Peace and Friendship between these two Princes, But it turn'd otherwise, both of them having departed displeas'd; For these Historians tell us, That their King's behaviour was proud and haughty, and how he would have forc'd our King Malcolm to do him Homage, in his own Court; But that Malcolm stood upon his honour; and wou'd upon no terms do any such thing, unless in the Marches of the two Kingdoms, where the Kings of Scotland, were in use to make their acknowledgment to the Kings of England, according to the sentiment of the Nobles of both Kingdoms.[1]

THIS plainly shews, That any Homage by the Kings of Scotland, to the King of England, was not for their Kingdom; but only for some Counties /122/ on the borders of England; For if the Homage had been due for Scotland, the Court of the King of England was a very suitable place of performance; and we see our King's refusal was not unjust, nor did it proceed from any resentment he had of the proud behaviour of the King of England; But was mature and deliberat, For our King's deportment, and answer to the surprising demand of King William Rufus, was justified by the Nobles of both Kingdoms.

HENCE it may be observed, That any Homage, which was thereafter made by any of our Kings, to the Kings of England, for what they possest in that Kingdom, was rather complaisance, than right or ancient custom.

IT may also be remarked in this passage, That our King Malcolm went to meet King William Rufus at Glocester, upon peaceable designs, and upon concert by their Ambassadors, to conclude a firm and lasting peace; but a secret design was lodg'd in the heart of the haughty William, that was soon discoverd by an unexpected demand, which was positively refus'd by our brave King who wou'd do nothing that was unusual or unbecoming, & in every respect /123/ acted as a Soveraign Prince, and the true Father of a free people.

BY this passage we may also understand, That any Homage payed by this our King Malcolm, to William the Conqueror, was only for what he possest in England.

THAT the peace between Malcolm Canmoir and the Conqueror, was concluded as between equal forces, so upon equal conditions, we have the plain opinion and authority of the famous Sir William Temple, who for his Learning, Noble thoughts, and charming expressions, is justly ranked among the greatest Men of his age; He with his accustom'd Elegancy, in his *introduction to the History of England,* relates the Motives, Conditions and Articles of this Treaty,[1] In all which there's not the least appearance of Homage; which is the more observable, because the learn'd Knight in this

---

P.121 (1) Flor. Wigorn. Sim. Dunelm. Hoveden *et alii ad annum* 1093.
P.123 (1) p. 220, 1, 2 & 3.

Treatise takes particular nottice of the Homages made by the King of Wales,[2] and by the Men of Kent[3] to the Conqueror.

HERE I cannot pass by a gross blunder and malicious mistake, in the Declaration of War, by /124/ Henry the 8th, where it's said, that Malcolm Canmoir was for his offences deposed, and his Son substitute in his place, who likewise failing in his duty, Edgar was made King by William Rufus; It being known that this King Malcolm was treacherously kill'd at Anwick in Northumberland, where his eldest Son suffer'd the same fate; But the zealous Homage-mongers startle at no mistakes which serve their purpose.

THIS mistake is still the more manifest, because Edgar tho' he was the next heir by right of blood to the Crown, after the Death of his Father and his eldest Brother; yet both our own and the English Historians relate, That Donald and Duncan, Successivly stept in before him, and assumed the Government and Title of King; and Edgar is generally reckon'd the third King after his Father.

SOME wrangler may from this pretend, That Edgar was the true King of Scotland upon his Father and Brother's death, and tho' he was for some time debarr'd from the possession of his Crown and Kingdom; yet he might have used the Title, and made Grants and Homages; and so hammer out an evasion of the pregnant Argument /125/ of the falshood of Edgars Charters of Homage, and of William Rufus's confirmations of them; from their being granted to William Bishop of Durham, who was dead before Edgar was King; by a notion that these deeds were granted, when Edgar had the Right, tho' not the Possession of the Crown of Scotland: And in that vieu they might very well be granted to Bishop William: But any such pretence in this case is wholly silenced and obviated, by the supposed deed it self, wherein our Edgar owns that he was in the Possession of the Kingdom of Scotland, by the Gift of William King of England;[1] So notwithstanding of what's asserted in the Declaration of War of King Henry the 8th, and of what may be pretended, for the right of Blood of Edgar to be King after his Father, yet still the Arguments offered to disprove the Charters of Homage made by him, stand good and firm: And it's observable that even in them, William Rufus is not designed King of Britain, but only King of England.

ALL those things concur, to discredit the empty notion of William the /126/ Conqueror's being Monarch or King of Britain: and as he did take no other designation of King, but of England; so his Successors continued the same Title: wherefore it's charity to think, That the Inscription of William the third by the Grace of GOD, King of Great-Britain, &c[1] upon several Millions of English Money Coin'd in the late Reign, was rather a mistake than any design to insinuat the Homage, there never being another William who was design'd King of Britain, for William the Conqueror, & his son William Rufus, who were the first & second Williams of England, never design'd themselves in their Charters, Letters, Seals, or Coins, by Britain: And the Title

---

P.123 (2) ibid. p. 283. (3) ibid. p. 123.
P.125 (1) *Vid.* Append. Numb. 4.
P.126 (1) *Gulielmus III Dei Gra. Mag. Brit. &c Rex.*

of Great Britain, I presume was not heard of until the Reign of our James
the sixth after his accession to the Crown of England: But true Medals and
Coins, being repute the great lights and sure Vouchers of History, It was fit
to notice this escape, to prevent all wrangling and amusing inferences,
which hereafter might be drawn from it.

THE nixt particular in the suppos'd /127/ Paragraphs of the Laws,
favouring the Homage, Is the Letter or rather Sentence of Eleutherius the
Pope, making the limits of the Monarchy of Britain and England, to be all
the continent and the Isles, as far as Norway: and in the same Paragraph is
the copy of a Letter, from this Pope, to King Lucius,[1] which is meer stuff; for
the Sentence is said to be in the year 67, and the Letter in 169, both by one
Pope, which is very disagreeable, unless we allow ourselfs to believe, that
this Pope lived 140 or 150 years.

THIS Letter is disproved as Spurious, by the Learn'd Sir Henry Spelman,
by many unanswerable Arguments propounded with his accustom'd Candor
and Modesty, such as, That there be words in this Letter not known in the
days of Eleutherius; that the places of Scripture cited in it are taken from the
Translation of St. Jerom, who lived two hundred years after this Pope; and
that this Letter was not heard of for a thousand years after the death of
Eleutherius.[2] And the Ingenious Mr. Tyrrel very frankly owns this Letter
/128/ to be an Imposture.[1]

THE third Evidence of the Dominion, arising from these Laws,[2] contains
a Cluster of ridiculous Absurdities; and first, allowing the Confessor had
made a Law, that any Scots or Albanians should incur the same punishment
with the English if they incroached upon his Forrests: yet this is nothing to
the purpose, for it was a trespass, for which he might chastise any offender.
Secondly, as to the story of Ina's being chosen by an Angel, & of his being
the first Monarch of Britain; nothing can be more vain and extravagant, It
even staggers Mr. Atwood's wide Belief, who, tho' he has no eyes to discover an Advertisement or Marginal Note; yet finds a Typographical Error,
and pretends that *electus per Angelum* should be *per Angliam*, But pray
who gave him Commission to turn Law-Tinker or Statute-Bungler? If in any
measure he has recovered his sight, yet he seems to have lost his Memory:
For he might have remembred, that the Learn'd Mr. Petyt in his *Treatise of
the Rights of the Commons of England asserted*, makes special /129/ use of
this very Paragraph.[1] But the learn'd and ingenious Mr. Tyrrel, who has
shown himself a zealous Friend and Asserter of the Right of the Commons,[2]
takes nottice of this Paragraph concerning Ina, as a notorious Falsehood
inserted by some ignorant trifling Monk among the Laws of Edward the
Confessor,[3] For Ina was never King of Britain, being only King of the West-
Saxons, which is evident from his Laws,[4] and Charters.[5]

P.127 (1) Lambard's *Archaion*. fol. 130 & 131. (2) *Tom. 1. Concil* p. 35.
P.128 (1) *Gen. Hist. of Eng.* tom. I. p. 17. (2) Lamb. *Archaion*. fol. 136 & 137.
P.129 (1) Preface p. 8. (2) Appendix to the 3d Vol. of the *Hist. of England*. (3) Ead.
    Hist. Vol. 1 p. 220. (4) Lamb. *Archaion*. Fol. 1. (4) Spelm. *Concil. tom*. 1. p.
    186. (5) Ibid. p. 227.

THIS Blunder is noticed by Dr. Brady in his Answer to Mr. Petyt,[6] which our Author could not well forget, he having engaged as second to Mr. Petyt, by publishing a Treatise entitled *Jani Anglorum facies nova:* Upon this Book Dr. Brady has made Animadversions, wherein he has outthrown me by far, in a Character of Mr. Atwood; the Drs. Words are[7] This new Face-maker, new Government /130/ maker, and Parliament-maker, hath observed no Order or Method, and his work being as wild extravagant and confused, as his Notion I can only pitch upon some parts of his Treatise, and those the most material which are intelligible, and pass by his impertinent and unintelligible Vagaries, until such time as (if he can) he makes them to be better understood by explaining his meaning; Thus our Author is Characterized by his own Countrey-man, when he had medled in a more suteable Subject than the Homage.

IT is unpleasant to me to be giving disadvantageous Characters of any, but one who sets up for an Incendiary and Fire-brand, by doing what in him lyes to embroil two Protestant Kingdoms, ought to be painted in his true Colours, and the more, when he persists in that abominable office: for I'm credibly informed, he is quickly to publish another unworthy Treatise, under this or the like Title; *The Nullity of the Scots Act of Security demonstrated;* But his Writings are already become so very contemptible, that nothing from him is to be reguarded. If he had not produced Charters and Laws, which speak for themselves, his confused Arguments for the /131/ Homage, wou'd not been worth notice; and if he in this new Treatise or any other, shall justify the Charters forged by Harding, he will merit no answer, unless he Prints them at length with their Seals, that they may appear in their native Colours, and also have some Persons of Credit to joyn with him; For these Deeds are repute Forged by the Learn'd Historiographer of England and the ingenious Mr. Tyrrel,[1] and our Author's own Credit is prostitut and Bankrupt, by advancing empty Notions and Paradoxes in relation to the Homage; whereof I have mention'd some, and in the detail others will occur.

AS to the Victories of Arthur related in the old Laws,[2] nothing could render them more ridiculous; For if Mr. Atwood or any other use this Paragraph, they by a necessar consequence bring in the Laws of England, to vouch the lying and fabulous Tales of Jeffrey of Monmouth.

THAT Scotland had it's name from one *Scottus* our Leader[3] is a mere Whim; For I presume this General /132/ will not be found in any History, but in those Legendary Paragraphs hatcht by the Juggling Monks, who spared not to vitiat their Laws by patching up Paragraphs when they served to colour a pretence to bring Scotland under the Dominion of England.

I HAVE taken the more nottice of the Falsehood of these Paragraphs of Laws, because some learn'd Authors have quoted some of them, among whom our Learn'd Craig has stumbled in this point.

P.129 (6) *Introd. to the old English Hist.* p. 4 & 5. (7) Ibid. p. 165.
P.131 (1) *Gen. Hist of Engl.* Vol. 3. Introduct. p. 10. (2) Lamb. *Arch.* fol. 137. (3) Ibid. fol. 139.

MR. Atwood thinks it not sufficient to adduce some patcht up
Paragraphs of the Laws of England; to support the imaginary Claim of
Homage: but he wou'd even turn our own Laws upon us, by a pretence,
That the Laws of England, since the time of Henry the second, were the
Rule of Government in Scotland: and for proof of this, says, That the Body
of Laws then composed by chief Justice Glanvil, was taken as a Rule for
Judgment and Decision here, and that the *Regiam Majestatem,* which con-
tains our old Laws, is taken from Glanvil, for which he cites our Learn'd
Craig.[1]

/133/ ALLOWING our *Regiam Majestatem,* to be form'd and modell'd
from Glanvil, yet it will not thence follow, That we are subject to England:
For most Nations had their Laws from Rome, there being nothing more ordinary, than for Neighbours to borrow from one anothers Customs and Laws,
and it's known that the Conqueror introduced Laws and Customs from
France and other Nations, yet it were most absurd, from this to infer any
Subjection of England.

IT is indeed generally agreed, That the Affinity between our *Regiam
Majestatem,* and the English Glanvil is such, that the one has been a Model
for the other,; And if there be any Prize or Benefit, by being the model, we
may perhaps bid fair for it.

HERE I shall not incroach upon or anticipate, what with more knowledg and light may be said on this subject, by the Honourable and Learned
Gentlemen, the Lord Pitmedden and Sir James Dalrymple, but shall only
with the utmost Submission offer some few things in relation to this Matter.

IT will easily be made appear, and is acknowledged by the most
Famous /134/ Learn'd Lawyers and Antiquaries of both Kingdoms, That
their Laws and Forms of Writs in many Things agree, especially in the more
ancient Times.

TO put this Matter in its due Light, It may be considered, what is vari-
ously said and asserted, and with what Proof and Authority.

SOME affirm, That the *Regiam Majestatem,* was written in the Reign of
King David the first, called St. David, who reign'd from the Year 1124 to
1153: Others say, it was written some time after, and was for the most part
borrow'd from Glanvil; and others will have it to be composed in the Reign
of King David the second, the Son and Successor of King Robert the Bruce,
who began to Reign in the year 1330, and our Author brings it down to the
days of our James the First.

GLANVIL is said to have been composed about the year 1188, in the
Reign of King Henry the Second of England, and some think it was written
in the Reign of Henry the third, who began to Reign in the Year 1216.
Others think, That Glanvil is only a borrow'd Name, and that the Book was
truly composed by King Henry the /135/ second of England; But none pretend That it was written sooner, than in one or other of these two Reigns.

P.132 (1) p. 296 and 298.

WHENCE it clearly follows, That if it can be made appear, That our *Regiam Majestatem* was composed in the Reign of King David the First, Then without all Peradventure, it turns the Scale, and is the Original, and Glanvil is only the Copy.

OUR Learn'd Countrey-men Skene and Craig, differ on this point. Skene is of Opinion, That *Regiam Majestatem* was collected in the Reign of King David the first,[1] and so before Glanvil: Craig thinks these Books are no part of our Law, but taken from Glanvil, and wrongously imposed upon us:[2] Whose Authority wou'd doubtless be of great weight, if he and Skene had had alike Opportunities of being inform'd in this matter; But it may be presumed, That Skene had moe and better Occasions to know this Affair; for he was a Person of great Learning, was well versed in Antiquity, and was by his /136/ merit (the best Title to a publick Office) advanced to be Clerk Register, whereby he had the Use and Custody of the Records, and was imployed to publish the *Regiam Majestatem* both in Latine and English. He by his frequent Quotations of Glanvil, and of the Statutes of England, shews himself to have been conversant in the Laws of that Kingdom; Whereas Craig wrote his Learn'd Treatise of Feus some years, and deceast a year before Skene published the *Regiam Majestatem,* with the Arguments of its Antiquity; yea Craig's Opinion in his own time was overruled by an Act of Parliament in 1607, among the unprinted Acts, and to be seen in our Records, wherein the *Regiam Majestatem* is declared to be our old Laws, and the People are appointed to be Ruled, Governed and Judged by them: There is also an Act to the same purpose, among the unprinted Acts of the Parliament 1633. It is very frequent among Learn'd men to differ in some Points, and our Learned Neighbours have various Sentiments about their Glanvil, but still Reason and proof is to take place.

THE Opinion of Skene, That *Regiam Majestatem* /137/ was composed in the Reign of our King David the first is very probable, For this King was a liberal Benefactor and Founder of Religious Houses, and a great Encourager of the Clergy, who were then the most Learn'd and best Vers'd in the Law. It's also very agreeable to think, That a Prince so singularly Religious and Just, as both our own and the English Historians reckon him, and who was at so much Pains and Expense to promote what he thought was the Interest of the Church, and who frequently in Person judged the Causes of the Poor, and of Widows and Orphants;[1] wou'd also be very concern'd to have the Laws for the Administration of Justice orderly Digested, for the good of his subjects. This Thought is supported and confirmed by the Chronicle of the Abby of Kinloss[2] founded by this King David, where it's said, that this King employed several of his Nobles to make a Collection of the Laws of their own Countrey, and also of the most laudable Customs and Laws, which /138/ in their Travels they had observed Abroad: This being done, he called a general Council from all the Corners of the Kingdom, to digest these Laws

---

P.135 (1) *Annot. in prefat. lib. 1. Reg. Maj.* (2) *Lib. feud dieg.* 8 p. 38 & 39.
P.137 (1) Boeth: *Hist. Scot: ad Reg.* 91. (2) *Penes* D.R. Sibbald. [i.e. Dr Sibbald]

for the Rule of Judgment in time coming, and by the general Consent of all present, there was from these Collections picked out, That System of our Municipal Law, commonly called *Regiam Majestatem.*

THE Learn'd Skene maintains his Opinion by the tenth Paragraph of the Preface to the *Majesty,* where the Composer says, he digested these Laws by Order of King *David cum sano concilio totius Regni sui tam populi quam Cleri.* Besides in his Annotations upon the Preface, he evinceth that the Majesty contain'd the Laws of King David the first, by two irrefragable Proofs, from the Statutes of King William the Grand-child of this David, and of King Alexander the second his Great-grand-child.

THE first proof is drawn from the first Statute of King William who began to reign in the year 1165, twelve years after the death of David, (having succeeded to his elder Brother Malcolm the fourth commonly called the Maiden) by which it is appointed, /139/ That, If *any be challenged for Theft, the Custom and Statute of King David shall be observed:* which Statute we have set down in the 16 Chapter of the first Book of the *Regiam Majestatem.*

THE next Proof arises from the 12 Chap. of the Statuts of King Alexander the Son of King William, Whereby it is statute, *That all stoln Goods shall be brought to the places appointed by King David;* Which places are particularized in the 20th Chap. of the first Book of *Regiam Majestatem.*

BY these two Laws of King William and King Alexander which are so expressly relative to the Laws contain'd in the *Regiam Majestatem,* it is evident, this collection was made before the Reign of these two Kings in the Reign of King David. This serves also to cancel the Suggestion offered by the Learn'd Duck,[1] That the *Regiam Majestatem* was composed in the reign of our King David the second, For which he adduces the Authority of Sir Henry Spelman in his Glossary at the Words *Lex Scotorum,* but with how little ground shall be shown.

/140/ TO illustrate this matter, and confirm the Opinion of Skene and of several others of our Lawyers, The Sentiments of the Learn'd Antiquaries of England may be considered.

THE ever Memorable and Judicious Sir Henry Spelman in his *Glossary* where he touches the Law of Scotland,[2] mentions the *Regiam Majestatem,* as composed in the Reign of King David the first, and tells that Glanvil was not chief Justice until the year 1180; without moving any Objection against the Antiquity of the *Majesty,* and says, This Book and Glanvil were much the same, which he elegantly expresses thus in Latine, *In prefatione dispositione Canone verborum integrorumque capitulorum textu, adeo inter se passim consentiunt (mutatis & ascriptis quae utriusque gentis postulat ratio) ut alter ex altero manifeste cognoscatur desumptus;* And concludes with a Modesty, suteable to his great Judgment, *Sed an nos e Scotia justitiam nostram reportaverimus alii judicent:* Here this Learn'd Gentleman raises no ground of

---

P.139 (1) *De usu & Auth. Juris Civilis lib.* 2. cap. 10 S. 14.
P.140 (2) *Lex Scotorum.*

doubt, and civilly waves the Decision of this Question; So that Duck has escap'd in /141/ quoting this *Glossary* for what is not to be found in it.

IT may be thought Duck might have produced a more apposite Citation from Sir Henry Spelmans Learn'd and curious Treatise of Feuds and Tenures, wherein this accomplished Gentleman with very much Civility and Respect to our Nation, doth occasionally question our having Feus in the time of Malcolm the second, according to the Laws of that King prefixt to the *Regiam Majestatem,* and by a modest way of proposing of Queries, brings some very pungent Arguments to perswade, that the Laws ascribed to Malcolm the second, are truly the Laws of Malcolm the third: And by the bye discoursing of the *Regiam Majestatem,* says, upon better Examination David the first, may be mistaken for David the Second.[1]

IT were unbecoming in me to enter the Lists with this Hero in matters of Antiquity, especially when the questions are Forreign to my purpose, for the Laws ascribed to Malcolm the second, and the *Regiam Majestatem* are distinct Treatises, and the falling of the one, doth not sink the other; Beside to /142/ support the Laws of Malcolm the second, and in some measure to balance the Gentlemanlie questions of this Learn'd enquirer, we have the positive Judgment and Sentiment of the Justices of Ireland, in a most solemn case and decision.[1] But without dipping farther in that matter, I make bold to think, That by what's already said concerning the statutes of our Kings William and Alexander (which were never called in question, and have been of late cited by two Eminent and Learn'd English Antiquaries Mr. Petyt,[2] and Doctor Brady)[3] there is no place left for any insinuation of David the firsts being mistaken for David the second: I'm moreover credibly informed, there is yet extant a Copy of the *Regiam Majestatem* transcribed in the days of King Robert Bruce, Father to David the second, whose Laws with his Fathers are subjoyn'd to the *Regiam Majestatem,* and I presume I'm enabled to give some light in this matter, and confirm the opinion of /143/ Skene, by some other writings of the Learn'd Sir Henry Spelman.

IN his Treatise of the probat of Wills and Testaments, speaking of their cognisance in ancient times as belonging to the Clergy, he acknowledges, That a manifest proof thereof cannot be had in these Ancient days of the Conqueror and of his Sons from English Authors, but then, he proceeds and gives his Sentiment of our Laws in these words: We must therefore discover as we can, and very material in my understanding as to that purpose, is the Testimony which I find in the ancient Laws of Scotland, composed by the Commandment of David their King, who lived long in the time of King Henry the first, Son of the Conqueror, and of King Stephen the Conquerors Grand-Son, for these laws have that similitude with ours of that time delivered by Glanvil, as that in effect, they be much the same *mutatis mutandis,* and very often *totidem verbis,* with Glanvil.[1]

P.141 (1) *Reliquiae Spelmanianae* p. 28.
P.142 (1) Ibid. p. 27. (2) *Right of the Comm. asserted* p. 83. (3) *Introduct. to the old Engl. Hist.* p. 96 & 97.
P.143 (1) *Reliquiae Spelman.* p. 131.

IN the close of the same Treatise this worthy Knight says, that Wills and Testaments belonged to the Ecclesiastical Jurisdiction, according to /144/ the Scottish Law, in the time of Henry the first who was Co-temporary with our David the first, and for this cites the second Chapter of the first Book of the Regiam Majestatem, whereof the Paragraph is *Placitum de Dotibus & Testamentis ad forum Ecclesiasticum pertinent*, That is, all Pleas concerning Dowries and Testments belong to the Ecclesiastical Court. Immediatly after this, He with the same breath, cites Glanvil to prove, that Testaments belonged to the Ecclesiastical Jurisdiction, in the time of Henry the second of England, who was after our David the first: Then he cites Bracton for their being so, in the Reign of Henry the third,[1] which seems to be a clear concession and proof, That our old Laws called *Regiam Majestatem,* were collected and digested in the Reign of King David the first, and so by a necessar consequence before Glanvil.

THE Sentiment of another very Learn'd English Lawyer and Antiquary, the great Selden is worthy of Remark: He in his *Treatise of the Original of Eclesiastical Jurisdiction of Testaments,* /145/ when bringing proofs for clearing the intrinsecal Jurisdiction to have been in the church, and the extrinsecal Jurisdiction in the Kings Court, he cites the 38 Chapter of the second Book of the *Majesty,* which is very distinct in this point; And says, the Regiam Majestatem of Scotland published by Command of David the first, in the time of Henry the first, hath for the most part, the same Sillables with the suppos'd Glanvil,[1] and this Glanvil he says was Chief Justice under Henry the second;[2] And in several places of his Writings, he questions very much his being Author of the Book, which passes under his Name. It's remarkable, that in the same Paragraph, in which he mentions the *Majesty* to have been published by order of King David, he tells, That Glanvil by severals has been thought to be anothers Work, and of a latter Time, and waves the giving his Opinion; But Nathanial Bacon in his *History of the Laws and Government of England,* taken from Selden's Notes, says, The Book of the Laws of England was composed by Henry the second, and was /146/ put furth under the Name of Glanvil his Chief Justice.[1] This Suggestion gives a considerable lustre to our *Regiam Majestatem,* if it has been used as a Pattern by a Royal Author. From the Learn'd Chief Justice Coke we're ascertain'd, this Prince wrote a Book of the Common Laws of England.[2] Nor are such Borrowings singular; For the *Custumier de Normandy* has several Paragraphs translated from Glanvil. But whether these Laws were digested by King Henry the second, or by Glanvil; it is still after the Reign of Our David the first, and so posterior to our *Regiam Majestatem.* For this Assertion, we may lay Claim to the joynt Sentiments and Authority of the Great Spelman and Selden.

P.144 (1) Ibid. p. 132.
P.145 (1) Selden's *tracts, jurisdict. of Testaments* p. 7. (2) Ibid p. 6.
P.146 (1) p. 105. Edit. 1689. (2) *Proem* 3. Vol. *Reports.*

IT's well known our Countrey has produced men of great Learning, and that the study of the Civil Law, is more pursued with us than with our Neighbours.[3] That our old Laws, are very agreeable to the Civil Law, is evident from Skene's Learn'd Notes upon the *Regiam Majestatem,* which shew that in a great part, It's founded upon the Civil Law, whence the compilers /147/ seem to have taken their model; For it begins like to the *Institutes of Justinian,* and is divided in four Books, according to the Division of the Institutes in the like number: Besides I presume it will not be deny'd, and is of late vouched by the Learn'd Puffendorff (who is not very favourable to us) That when all liberal Sciences were suppress'd in Europe, by a long Barbarism, the same were kept up in Scotland, which did furnish several other Nations with Learn'd Men, who instructed them in these Sciences.[1]

WITH these Authorities may be join'd an Authentick Memorandum sign'd by Edward the first of the Writs left by him in our Archives that were deliver'd to Baliol after he had made him King of Scotland; Among which, there is a Roll Entitled, *Unus Rotulus de statutis Regis Malcolm & Regis David.* This strongly supports both the Antiquity and Authority of the *Regiam Majestatem,* which contains the Laws of King David. So that we seem to have probable Grounds to conceive and affirm, That our *Regiam Majestatem* is the Original, and that Glanvil has /148/ borrowed and copied from us, and not we from him.

BUT whatever may be in these things; It is nevertheless evident that the Paragraphs in the old English Laws published by Lambard, insinuating the Dominion of England over Scotland are notorious falsehoods.

THUS having insisted at some length upon the falshood of the Charters and Laws favouring the Homage; which so far as I know, have not hitherto been handled in that Argument; I shall proceed to the consideration of the two other unbecoming Artifices of Fabulous Tales, and Extorted Acknowledgments used in the claim of Homage, Wherein I shall be the more brief; Because sundry things in Relation to these matters, have with much Learning and Judgment been noticed by our Learn'd Countrey-men, Mr. George Buchanan in his History, Sir Thomas Craig, in the *Soveraignty of Scotland Asserted,* Sir George Mackenzie in his *Precedency and Herauldry,* and Sir Robert Sibbald in his *Treatise of the Liberty and Independency of the Kingdom and Church of Scotland:* Wherefore I shall touch but very little of what has been already offer'd by those worthy Patriots: My /149/ main design being to hint some few things that are new, and to exhibit the Copies of some unquestionable deeds, that give light to our Ancient Liberties, which I presume will be the more acceptable, because most of them are not known among us. And with our Independency, they discover some vestiges of our Ancient Constitution, and may contribute to illustrat some parts of our History.

SUNDRY Fabulous Stories have been invented by the Ancient English Historians, and transcribed by some Moderns, to make the World believe,

---

P.146 (3) Duck *de usu jur. civil. lib.* 2 Cap. 10.
P.147 (1) *Introd. to the History of Europe,* p. 166.

the Dominion of England over Scotland, and are compris'd in a Letter of King Edward the first of England to the Pope, to justifie his claim of the Superiority of Scotland.

I SHALL not trouble the Reader with a Recapitulation of these Fables, and of the Authors who relate them; but refer him to the Appendix,[1] where he will find them in a Translation of a part of this letter. In it after an amazing Introduction, of that King's calling the Great GOD the searcher of hearts to bear Witness, That he was fully perswaded of the truth of what he Writes to the Pope; He rehearses some very Romantick /150/ and Incredible Stories, as evidences of the Superiority and Dominion in ancient times.

TO prevent the swelling of the Appendix to the length of this Letter, there's only published a part of it, For what else is in it worth notice, either is already, or shall be toucht in this Treatise: And any who please may see it at length in Matthew of Westminster,[1] Knyghton,[2] Walsingham,[3] Ryley,[4] and Pryn,[5] and in Transcripts of the Process, which goes under the name of *Processus Baldredi.*

IT'S needless to insist upon the disproof of the idle Stories, implying the Homage in the remote ages; when they are so gross of themselves, and rejected as Fabulous by some of our knowing Neighbours: But they being so solemnly voucht by an English King, who occasion'd a deluge of Blood in this quarrel; And when this Letter is ingrossed in so many Books, and used by our Author as a Text for the Claim of Homage, and much valued by /151/ all who favour that Claim; It was fit to take some notice of the Fables, which are the suteable ground work of the imaginary Homage.

DOUBTLES the Publishers and Abettors of such glittering proofs, think they do service to their Countrey; But when duely consider'd, they only serve to proclaim and display the extravagancies and foulest of play practised in this matter.

I AM fully perswaded, That this Letter will make the Claim of Homage nauseous to all Men of candor and ingenuity in England; And that they will be astonished to see it established upon such a scandalous Foundation, as that of a great King's calling GOD to Witness, of the belief of Fables, which in our times, old Women wou'd be asham'd to tell.

WE'RE almost bound to believe, That these Stories were justified by an English Parliament. Westminster and Walsingham,[1] say that King Edward wrote this Letter to the Pope, by advice of a Parliament Summoned for this effect: This also seems to be plainly implyed in that Parliaments Letter /152/ to the Pope, when they tell him; It was well known throughout England, That the Sovereignty and Dominion of Scotland had been enjoy'd by the Kings of England, both in the times of the Britains and of the English:[1] And

---

P.149 (1) Numb. xxiii.
P.150 (1) Edit. 1601. p. 439. (2) *Inter X Script.* p. 484. (3) *Inter. His. Angl. Norman. &c.* p. 81. (4) Append. *ad placiti Parliament.* p. 596. (5) *Hist. of Edward I.* p. 887.
P.151 (1) Loc. citat.
P.152 (1) Ibid.

it's not to be supposed, but that their Arguments and Evidences for this Assertion were the same with those of their King.

NOT only Mr. Atwood,[2] but also the Great Collector of the Records of this King's Reign, Mr. Pryn, a Zealous promoter of the Homage, and very positive in this matter. Mr. Pryn says, That both these Letters were unanimously agreed and sent to the Pope in a full and famous Parliament, specially Summoned for this occasion, as remarkable evidences of the King of England's Ancient undoubted Right of Scotland.[3] For the truth of this, he produces from the Records a Copy of the special Clause insert in the Writs of Summonds to the Members. He also tells us, That this King did moreover issue special Writs to several Deans, Arch-Deacons, and other Learn'd Men, to appear at this Parliament, to advise with the Lawyers and others of the /153/ Council concerning his ancient Title to Scotland, nor did the King rest here, but likeways sent Writs to the two Universities, that each of them might send four or five of their best Scholars in the written Law; And further, he issued Writs to the Abbots, Priors, Deans and Chapters, to search out and send all their chronicles to this Parliament.[1]

THESE things, at first view, make a mighty Dash and Appearance for the Homage: But it's a strange Infatuation in the Homage-mongers, to be so fond of a Letter, and of late to publish it, so frequently; That in the first Arguments & Evidences which it brings to prove the Homage evidently shows, That Reason was abandoned to gratify a prevailing Itch of Dominion over a free people.

SUCH was the Credit K. Edward gave to these Stories, and his concern to have them believed by others, that he beseeches the Pope to despise all that can be said against them as artificial and lying Tales.

NOR was this Letter sent to the Pope to serve a Turn, by entertaining /154/ the Holy Father with amusing Pretences in behalf of the Superiority. King Edward was resolved to have them also transmitted to Posterity: For besides this Letter, there's yet extant in the Tower of London an Instrument made by this King's special Command written by two sworn Notaries, approved by the Pope, in sundry large Rolls of Parchment, which Mr. Pryn gives at length, and asserts it to be the most compleat and uncontrolable Evidence of the Dominion.[1] In this Record, all the Arguments and Evidences for the Homage are ingrosst, with the names of several Historians from whence some of them are collected. Here the fabulous Stories are placed at large, and one of them with some comical Circumstances not mentioned in the Letter,[2] and how others of the Evidences contained, both in this Record and Letter, are mangled and disguised by K. Edward, will easily be made appear.

ALL who favour the Homage extoll this Prince to the Skies, and others who go not that length, reckon him a brave Prince, and regrate that his /155/ Achievements in Scotland are not recorded by some person of

P.152 (2) p. 101. (3) *Hist. Edw. I.* p. 893.
P.153 (1) Ibid. p. 883, 884 & 885.
P.154 (1) Ibid. p. 487. (2) Ibid. p. 495 & 496.

Abilities, suitable to do so Noble an Undertaking. Respect is due to the
Memory of Crown'd Heads; But the Image and Superscription of Cesar hin-
ders not an enquiry into the Mettal of the Coin. It can scarce be thought that
any Scots-man will entertain a kindly Remembrance of a Prince, who
endeavour'd to sink our Liberties, and destroy'd or carried off our ancient
Records and Monuments; Yet I shall lay nothing to his charge but what's
voucht by English History or unquestionable Records.

HOW big and glorious soever the Actions of Edward the first may
appear to some of our Neighbours, yet when duely considered, they'll be
found to have been levell'd against the Liberties of England, as well as the
Liberties of Scotland: Which is evident from the account of this Kings
Government, given by one of the most impartial English Historians: The
notable Nathaniel Bacon in his valuable *History of the Laws and
Government* of England taken from the notes /156/ of the Learn'd Selden.[1]
This Author plainly unfolds the Arbitrary Designs and Projects of this King.
That under the Colour of the Welsh War he maintained an Army in the field,
that he might the more bow his Subjects to his own bent. That however
Debonair this King seemed to be, yet his Lords trusted him no farther than
needs must, for whether they served in the Council or in the field, still they
were armed. And that by irregular Preparations by War, by summonding his
Vassals, and Taxes imposed by an arbitrary way, he increased the Rancor of
his people into a kind of Statescoul, little better than a Quarrel, for appeas-
ing whereof, he granted many Confirmations of the Grand-charter, but
alwise with Stings in their Tail. Thus the Candid Mr. Bacon Represents the
Actings of Edward the first toward his own people; Then he intermixes this
Prince's Concerns with us, which are with much plainness and significancy
exprest in his own excellent Words: He says, That this Kings last Statute,
confirming the *magna charta*, became like a *hocus pocus*, a thing to still the
people for the present and serve the Kings /157/ turn, that he might more
freely intend the Conquest of the Scots; which once done, he might, if he
would, try Masteries with England. But GOD would not have it so; The King
in Scotland had power to take, but could not overtake; and the Scots like
Birds of the Prey, had Wit enough to fly away, and courage enough to
return upon Advantages: and so the King was left to hunt the Wind; which
made him to return.

HE might now expect the Applause of his people for his good Success,
and the Terrour of those that had stopped the broad way of his extravagant
Prerogative; and therefore, looks big, rubs up old Sores, and (having his
Army yet in the field) sends for those Lords that would not follow him in his
Wars in Flanders. All come and submit, and as it were in so many Words let
the King know, That all England is now Tame, and like to be ridden at his
Discretion. And now there's nothing in the way but the fatal Execration,
which he feared, not in relation to God's anger, but rather to the exasperate
Clergy, and the dread of the Popes direful Thunder-bolt. To avoid this
Storm, he procures a Dispensation from Rome, To Perjure and Oppress

---

P.156 (1) p. 133, 134 & 135.

without sin, a trick that he learn'd of his Father, and /158/ hid it within his Breast, till about two years before his end, he brings it furth to tell all the World that hitherto he had been just against his will. But having obtained his purpose, he, nevertheless, misseth of his end, for a new King of Scots (our old good Enemies) by divine Providence suddenly crossed his way before him, and now it boots not to contend for Arbitrary Rule in England, and lose the Crown of Scotland, which he once thought he had sure; he faces about therefore, and having spoken fair to his People, for Scotland he goes. Thus if all were not in a parenthesis, the King intended a good Period; but GOD only knows what his furthest reach would have been if he had returned; for he was taken out of this World in Scotland, and so left this his Government somewhat like an imperfect Sentence.

I HOPE none will think it forreign to the Purpose to give this Hint of the Government and Projects of this King, who was the Champion of the Homage; from a Treatise so universally and justly valued by all Our Neighbours who regard their Priviledges.

FROM what's said by Mr. Bacon, It's plain that the Liberties of Scotland were the Blind; But the *Magna Charta* /159/ of England was the mark, which this Prince aimed at. His picking Quarrels with us, by a Claim of Superiority, and prescribing us a King upon his own Terms, served as a plausible pretext, to keep up a standing Army that overaw'd his own Subjects; and the more he succeeded in depressing our Liberties, the more was his power in England put beyond controul. And the diversion we gave him in defending our Liberties, was what stopt the Career of his Arbitrary Practices and Designs at Home, and warded the fatal blow, which he designed for the Grand-Charter. To the Reader I leave to Judge, what we might expect from a King, who to bereave his own people of their Birthrights, procured a Dispensation TO PERJURE AND OPPRESS WITHOUT SIN.

IT'S already hinted, how for Evidences of the unjust Claim of Dominion, this King made use of fabulous Stories: And more of his Arguments and Practices in that matter, will hereafter fall in our way.

IF any desire to be farther satisfyed concerning the ridiculous Stories of Brutus and of his Sons & of Arthur & of Athelstan /160/ &c. They may consult Buchanan, Sir Thomas Craig & Sir George Mackenzie in the Treatises I have mention'd. What is most regarded by the Moderns, of that ancient Stuff, is the Story of Edgar of England his having so many Kings under his Dominion, which I have already disproved, and Sir George Mackenzie has evinced the Falsehood of it from Chronology. Now whether we look into the English Historians, or into the Letter of King Edward the first to the Pope, or into the Instrument made by the two Notaries at his Command; It is very manifest that fabulous Stories have been used as pregnant Evidences of the Homage.

IN the next place come to be considered the Acknowledgments made by some of our Kings, Nobles, and Clergy, of the Superiority and direct

Dominion of the Kings of England over Scotland; which I presume will be found to be notorious Extortions, and Acts of Oppression.

THE first plain and positive acknowledgment of the Superiority, was in the Reign of William King of Scotland, and of Henry the second King of England. This King Henry before he came to the Throne, was most kindly /161/ and civilly entertain'd and assisted by King David, Grand-father to King William, and according to the Custom of those Days, he was knighted by him. At this Solemnity Henry did publickly Swear, That if ever he came to be King of England, he wou'd give David New-castle and all Northumberland, and that he and his Heirs shou'd for ever possess all the Lands from Tweed to Tyne, peaceably without any Molestation.[1] Nevertheless, as soon as he came to the Crown of England, he took advantage of the Youth and easie Temper of our King Malcolm the fourth, commonly called the Maiden, the Grand-child and Successor of King David, and contrair to his Oath resum'd all former Grants made by his Predecessors to the Kings of Scotland of the County of Northumberland.[2] And our own Historians tell, That Malcolm's Subjects were so dissatisfied with his suffering himself to be abused by Henry of England, That they besieg'd Perth, where Malcolm /162/ kep't his court, and with much Difficulty were reconciled to him.

THIS Malcolm dying without Issue, William his Brother another Grandchild of King David succeeded him, who immediately upon his Accession to the Crown, demanded of King Henry of England the County of Northumberland as his by Right.[1]

THE King of England knowing how much King William's Grand-father had contribute to the Settlement of the Crown upon him (which is even own'd by Mr. Atwood)[2] and that he had Sworn to maintain him and his, in the right of Northumberland, did put him off for some time by civil Excuses, But King William finding himself eluded by fair pretences, He at length raises an Army to vindicat his Right by the Sword, which he cou'd not obtain by a friendly Treaty. Upon this the Bishop of Durham in name of the King of England, by giving King William in the mean time three hundred Merks of the Rents of Northumberland, procured a Truce for some time;[3] which /163/ being expired, King William enters Northumberland, where he had the Misfortune to be taken Prisoner, by surprise at Anwick; and was in a rude and barbarous manner carried to the King of England, who made him a close Prisoner in Richmond Castle,[1] Thereafter he carried him over to France, where he was again imprisoned first in Caen, and afterwards in Falaise.[2]

WHEN King William was in such Circumstances as to be intirely in the power of the King of England, rudely used and toss'd from Prison to Prison; The King of England extorted from him a Deed bearing date at Falaise.

P.161 (1) Hoveden p. 490. (2) Rad. de diceto *inter X Script.* Matth. Paris, & Mat: Westm. *ad annum* 1157 & Tyrrels *Hist.* Vol.2 p. 303.
P.162 (1) Holinshed *Hist. of Scotland* p. 187. (2) p. 262. (3) Hoveden p. 537.
P.163 (1) Tyrrels *Hist* Vol.2 p. 386. (2) Hoveden p. 540.

BY this extorted Deed our King became Liege-man of the King of England for Scotland and for all his other Lands; and payed Homage to him and his Son, whom he had caused Crown as King. Our King did also undertake, that his Bishops and Nobles shou'd do Homage to the King of England, as his other Liegemen use to do, and that his and their Heirs shou'd do Homage to the Heirs of the Kings of England. /164/ King William likewise granted, That the Church of Scotland shou'd be in such Subjection to the Church of England, as was due and accustomed in the time of Henrys Predecessors Kings of England: And it was agreed, that neither of the two Kings, nor their Subjects shou'd harbour Felons who shou'd flee from the one Kingdom to the other.

FOR Performance of this Agreement, the King of Scotland gave several of his Nobles as Hostages, and delivered up to the King of England the Castles of Roxburgh, Berwick, Jedburgh, Edinburgh and Stirling, as Cautionary Forts, and assign'd a part of his Revenue for the maintaining of these Castles.

THESE be the material Articles of this Agreement, which is to be found at length in Hoveden,[1] Brompton,[2] Pryn,[3] and Dr. Brady.[4] Mr. Rymer has also published it,[5] and Mr. Atwood presents us with a Translation of it.[6]

/165/ IT may be thought needless to bring Arguments to evince the Nullity of Deeds extorted in imprisonment; Or to adduce instances of the like or greater Misfortunes in some Princes, whose surrender of their Soveraignty, was never thought to entail any Servitude upon their Successors and People.

NONE have less Reason to plead any Right or Dominion upon such Deeds than our Neighbours. For Richard the first when he was the Emperours Prisoner, subjected England to the Emperour, and received Investiture from him of that Kingdom, to hold it of him, for payment of a yearly Tribute.[1] King John did yet worse, for when his Brother Richard was in captivity, it's said he aim'd at the Crown by the Assistance of the King of France, of whom he was willing to hold England.[2] Afterwards when this John succeeded as King, by the death of his Brother Richard, he with consent of his Barons made England Feudatory and Subject to the Pope by a most solemn voluntary Deed, made and Sworn to, in presence of his Bishops and /166/ Nobles.[1] Yea, Matthew Paris the Historiographer to Henry the 3d his Son, tells us a long and circumstantiat story, How King John by a solemn Embassy, offered to hold his Crown of a Mahumetan Prince, who was a Negro, and that he was willing to abandon Christianity, and turn Musleman.[2] And King Henry his Son payed Homage to the Pope for England.[3] Yet I presume it wou'd be reckon'd Injurious in the Emperour or Pope to lay claim to England.

P.164 (1) p. 545. (2) *Inter X Script.* p. 1103. (3) *Hist. Edw. I* p. 492. (4) Appendix to the *Hist. of England.* Numb. 67. (5) *Foedera Angliae* tom. 1. p. 39. (6) p. 263.
P.165 (1) Hoveden, p. 724. (2) Id. Ibid.
P.166 (1) Math: Paris *ad annum* 1213 & Rymer *foedera Angliae* p. 176. (2) Math. Paris *ad ann:* 1213. (3) Id. *ad ann* 1216.

THE Novelty of the superiority of England over Scotland is clearly implyed in the before mentioned Deed of King William, seing it does not mention, That any Homage was formerly done or payed for this Kingdom, which certainly wou'd have been exprest if any such thing cou'd have been alledged; For in this Deed, There's a Retrospect as to the Subjection of the Church of Scotland to the Church of England; because from some of the English Historians, we understand that there were Struggles and contests about this Subjection of the Church, which /167/ was claim'd by the English and refused by the Scots; So from hence, it is evident, that there was no former Claim of Dominion and Superiority over the Temporality of Scotland.

BY so many Hostages and Castles being put in the hands of King Henry the second of England, He enjoyed this Superiority and Dominion during the rest of his Reign: But within a little time after his death, his Son and Successor King Richard the first, a brave Prince, being convinced of the Injury done by his Father, to the King and People of Scotland, did by his Charter Restore to our King William such Castles in Scotland as were then in the Possession of the English, as being his own by right of Inheritance, and did acquit him from all Agreements which his Father Henry EXTORTED from him by New Charters and his Imprisonment. By the same Deed King Richard Declares that King William of Scotland did pay Homage to him only for these Lands which his Predecessors held of the Kings of England, As may be seen in this Charter and Renunciation placed in the Appendix.[1]

THAT the Lands for which William /168/ King of Scotland did Homage to Richard King of England were in England, is very clear from this Renunciation, and is fully testified by Hoveden,[1] Matthew Paris and Westminster.[2] In Hoveden the account of this Matter is very particular and distinct, which is the more remarkable, because, as shall hereafter be made appear, it is strongly disguised and mis-represented by King Edward the first. This Historian tells us, That in November 1189 Geoffrey Elect Archbishop of York, with the Barons of York-shire, and Sheriff of York, by Order* (*Per mandatum) of the King of England went to the River of Tweed, and received William King of Scots, to whom they gave all due Honour, and safely conducted him to King Richard at Canterbury, where in December King William did Homage to him for his Dignities in England, as his Brother Malcolm had them: and King Richard restored to him the Castles of Roxburgh and Berwick. and did acquit and free him and his Heirs for ever, from all Allegiance and Subjection for the Kingdom of Scotland, to himself and to his Successors Kings of England. King /169/ William for this Restitution of his Castles, and for the Release of the Fealty and Allegeance for the Kingdom of Scotland, and for a Charter to be granted by Richard thereupon, gave to Richard King of England Ten Thousand Merks Sterling, whereof Richard gave to him a Charter in this Form. Then Hoveden sets down the Charter at full length.[1] The same Hoveden explains the Homage

P.167 (1) Numb. 8.
P.168 (1) p. 662. (2) *Ambo ad annum* 1189.
P.169 (1) Hoveden p. 662.

done by King Malcolm William's Brother, by telling us, That Malcolm met Henry the second at Chester, and payed Homage to him in the same manner as his Grandfather payed to Henry the first, Saving all his Dignities,[2] which *Salvo* must be in Relation to his Royalty of Scotland since he had no other.

ALL which make it as clear as possible, That before this time, there was no Homage known to be due by the Kings of Scotland to the kings of England, but only for such Lands and Honours as they enjoy'd in England: Which evidently demonstrats all Charters of Homage said to be made by any former Kings of Scotland to be /170/ notorious Forgeries, and discovers all the Evidences brought from History for the Homage, in the remote Ages, to be meer Dreams and Imaginations.

SURE none will be so partial to lay the Stories and idle Tales of any Monkish Historians in the Ballance with the Assertion of a brave and famous English King, testified under the Great Seal of England in presence of three Arch-bishops, five Bishops and of several Nobles, and many others.

WERE nothing else known in History or Record, but this Charter of Richard, It is of it self an absolute Condemnation of the Claim of Homage as Unjust, and an unanswerable Evidence of Our Independency, voucht by a King of England, whose Father having invaded Our Liberties, He justly restored them, and in our Vindication by a most solemn Deed, did in plain Terms, Imprint EXTORTION upon the Memory of a King and of a Parent: To which nothing but the force of Truth can be suppos'd to have induced him.

THE Reality of this Deed is acknowledged, being transcribed at full length in Hoveden,[1] Westminster,[2] and /171/ Dr. Brady's *History of England*;[1] and it's mentioned by the Historians, who treat of those Times: Beside we now know, That the Original is yet extant among the Archives of England, and from thence the learn'd Historiographer, has within these few Months published it.[2]

DOUBTLES Edward the first carried off this Deed, with others of our ancient Records and Monuments, That no Vestiges might remain of our Liberties; But Providence, which favours injur'd Innocence, has preserved and discover'd this Charter with the Seal intire,[3] as a visible Mark of the bad Usage we had from this King.

IT seems very odd in this King to recite in his Letter to the Pope the Substance of the Deed, whereby Our William while he was a Prisoner, subjected his Kingdom to England, And to insert this Deed at full length, as a mighty Evidence of the Dominion, in the notorial Instrument depositat in the Tower of London, when by an Original Acquittance taken by him from our Archives, the Deed of Subjection /172/ was releas'd and made void, as being extorted by new Charters from a Prisoner.

P.169 (2) Ibid. p. 492.
P.170 (1) p. 662. (2) *ad ann.* 1189.
P.171 (1) Append. Num. 68. (2) *Foedera Angliae* p. 64. (3) Ibid. p. 66.

NOR can any thing exeem this King Edward, from having his Memory charged with the guilt of shedding Rivers of Innocent Blood, by his making War upon the Scots, in pursuance of a claim of ancient Dominion over Scotland, which was so clearly disproved by Richard's Charter, industriously suppressed by him.

THAT this King did not boggle at such Practices is manifest from a parallel Case, transmitted by his own special Order to Posterity. In the aforesaid Instrument lying in the Tower of London, composed by Direction of the King, and transcribed by Pryn, There is a Citation from Hoveden to prove, that King William payed Homage to Richard the first of England, to this purpose. It is (says the Instrument) to be found in the Chronicles of Roger Hoveden, That in the year 1189 Richard the Son of Henry King of England succeeded to his Father; In the which year in the Moneth of December, William met Richard at Canterbury, and there he did Homage to him. Then the Instrument proceeds to Evidences of /173/ the Homage, in the Reign of King John who succeeded Richard.[1]

THIS plainly displays the most unbecoming Disguise and Misrepresentation that is to be found in History. For I have recited this Passage from Hoveden in his own Words, which is so far from giving any colour to the Homage for Scotland, That it evidently shews, that the Homage was only paid for Lands in England, and to this Passage is subjoyn'd Richard's Charter, which evinces our Independency.

IT was a strange Assurance in King Edward to publish to the World the half of a Sentence, when the rest of it wholly overturned his Claim. What wou'd he not say when he used such shifts? Will any man of Candor or Modesty give Credit to Evidences of Homage, or can he think that they are not one way or other disguised and mangled: when we find such abominable Blunders, in the Proofs digested and composed by Authority and Order of a King.

HENCE we may clearly see, That Edward the first, both knew of, and suppressed the Charter of Richard the I.

/174/ FOR illustration of the Matter, I have placed in the Margin, the words of the Letter to the Pope, and of the Instrument in the Tower, and the Words of Hoveden in their Original.*

-----

* The words of the Letter to the Pope, concerning King Williams Homage to King Richard the First.

> Et idem Rex Scottorum Willelmus post decessum Regis Henrici, veniens Cantuariam Richardo Regi Angliae filio et heredi dicti Henrici fecit Homagium. Quo Richardo viam universae carnis ingresso, &c.

The words of the Instrument in the Tower of London.

> In Chronicis Rogeri de Hoveden invenitur, Quod anno Domini 1189, dicto Regi Anglie Henrico Successit Richardus filius ejus; Quo

-----

P.173 (1) Pryn Hist. Edw. I p. 494.

anno mense Decembris venit Cantuariam idem Willelmus Rex
Scottorum ad ipsum Regem Richardum, et homagium sibi fecit, cujus
tempore Scotti non rebellaverunt, &c.

Then it proceeds to the time of King John.

Hoveden's words are:

Eodem anno (viz 1189) mense Novembris Gaufridus Eboracensis
electus una cum baronibus Eboracensis scyrae et Vice-comite Eboraci
per mandatum Domini Regis perrexit usque ad aquam de Tweed, et
ibi recepit Willelmum Regem Scottorum, et exhibuit ei honorem debi-
tum et securum conductum usque ad Regem Angliae. Venit igitur
Cantuariam Willelmus Rex Scottorum mense Decembris ad Regem
Anglie, Et fecit Homagium pro dignitatibus suis habendis in Anglia
sicut Malcolmus Frater suus habuit Et Richardus Rex Angliae reddidit
ei Castellum de Rokesburh, et Castellum de Berewic, libera et quieta,
Et eum et omnes heredes suos clamavit liberos et quietos ab ipso et
regibus Anglie in perpetuum de omni ligantia et subjectione de Regno
Scotiae, Et pro hac redditione Castellorum suorum, et pro quieta cla-
mantia fidelitatis, et ligantiae de Regno Scotiae, et pro charta
Richardi Regis Angliae inde habenda Willelmus Rex Scottorum dedit
Richardo Regi Angliae decem millia mercarum Esterlingorum. Unde
Richardus Rex Angliae fecit ei Chartam suam in hac forma.
Richardus dei Gratia Rex Angliae, &c.

/175/ PERHAPS Edward thought, That Hoveden wou'd for ever continue in the hands of Friends of the Homage, but the Invention of Printing
has made it more publick, and the zealous Pryn, who publishes this famous
Instrument, as an uncontrollable Evidence of the Dominion, has the singular
Boldness to set in his Margin the 662 Page of Hoveden, where the mon-
strous Disingenuity will stare the Reader broad in the Face.

RICHARD'S Charter is a strong Argument for our Independency, and a
convincing one against the Claim of Homage. It hath so puzzled the Zealots
of that Claim, that in their Evasions, they directly clash against one another.

SOME pretend, That it was granted in consideration of a Sum of Money
which the Scots will never be able to prove was paid. To this Our Learned
Craig makes Answer, That it cannot indeed be easily proved at such an
Interval of time, yet the Prescription of so many Ages, takes away all Right
of Demand, and the Restitution of the Castles, which were laid in pledg give
ground to presume that the Debt was payd.[1] This is sufficient /176/ to
remove that weak Objection. But farther, Hoveden who lived in these times
being Chaplain to King Richard's Father,[1] and other English Historians tell
the Money was paid: Besides, there's a Charter granted by King William to
the Monks of the Cistertian Order, published in the Appendix, from the
Original,[2] in the hands of a Noble and ancient Scots Peer: in the which this
King tells, That himself and his Kingdom being under Servitude to Henry
late King of England, he behoved to pay Money to Richard his Son and
Successor for redeeming of his own freedom, and for restoring his Kingdom
to its ancient Liberty, and says, That this event never before happened, and

---

P.175 (1) *Scotlands Soveraignty* p. 304.
P.176 (1) *Hist. Library of England* tom. 1. p. 160. (2) Numb. XXI.

trusts in God the like shall never occur. This Charter plainly shews that the Money was payed, as likewise that any ancient Claim of Homage was unknown to us.

MR. Atwood turns the Tables, and admits the Money to be payed, but pretends, That it was a private Deed of King Richard, for the sake of a little money, /177/ when he was intent upon the Holy War.[1]

ANY who look upon this Deed, and consider either the number or Quality of the Witnesses, will not readily think it a privat Deed. If it had been such, it's very probable it wou'd have been better known in the days of Edward the first, when it had been more honourable to disprove it upon any plausible ground, than basely to suppress it.

OUR Author farther pretends, That the Words of Richard's Charter are ambiguous, except as to the restoring of the Castles, and the rest was only a Feather in the Scotch Kings Cap.[2]

HE who thinks Extortion and new Charters ambiguous Words, both which are to be found in Richard's Charter, may say what he pleases: But to justify his Pretence, he says, The Acquittance was made with a Proviso, That the King of Scotland perform intirely and fully to King Richard, whatever King Malcolm his Brother did, or of Right, was obliged to do to Richard's Predecessors. From thence he subsumes, That if the Kings of Scotland had been obliged to /178/ do Homage for their Kingdom to the King of England, that Obligation was not intended to be lessen'd by this Charter.[1]

IT seems Mr. Atwood will still be Mr. Atwood: If the Kings of Scotland were Liegemen for their Kingdom to the Kings of England, before the Grant of Subjection, which was extorted from King William: Then there was no use of a Renunciation and Acquittance: And our Author, instead of making this deed a Feather in the Scots Kings Cap, shou'd have given him Hood and Bells, for asking any such Thing; and much more for giving a considerable Sum (in those days) for it. And King Henry of England may be thought to have deserved the like, for demanding an acknowledgment of Subjection from a Prisoner, which was before due to him.

BUT the King of Scotland his becoming Liege-man to an English King, when he was in the dismal Circumstances of an harass'd Prisoner, & the Acquittance of this Subjection, bearing in express Terms, That the Grant was New and Extorted; plainly demonstrat, That the Superiority and Dominion of /179/ England over Scotland was then a Novelty.

THE English Historian William of Newburgh, who lived about those Days, did reckon it a Novelty: For he says, That Henry the 2d was the first of the English Kings, who had dominion over Scotland.[1] The like is said by Henry Knighton a friend to the Homage,[2] and from whom probably Our Author glean'd the Subterfuge of Richard's granting this Charter, for the sake of Money, when he was intent upon the Holy War.

P.177 (1) p. 222. (2) p. 223.
P.178 (1) Ibid.
P.179 (1) Lib. 2. Cap. 4. (2) *Inter X Script* p. 2392.

TO Confirm, if it were needful, this Charter, it may be considered, That by it, King Richard, conform to ancient Custom, was bound to give safe Conduct and suitable Allowances, To King William and his Successors, when they came to the Court of the King of England, as shou'd be regulate by some Nobles to be delegate by the two Kings.

NO sooner was Richard releas'd from his Captivity, and return'd to England; but this matter was settled by a Grant of King Richard delivered /180/ to our King William,[1] whereof the Copy is placed in the Appendix.[2] By it the Bishops, Sheriffs and Barons of the Counties throw which he passed, were appointed to attend him; and the Allowances given to him were great and Noble with respect to those times.

ROYAL Interviews were then frequent; The King of England went sometimes to the Court of France, he having Possessions holding of that Crown. The ground of our Kings having Attendants and Allowances when they went to the Court of England, is explained by the Learn'd Sir Thomas Craig from the Civil Law.[3] By the Collections of the Learned Historiographer of England, We find, That the two Kings met frequently to confer about the Affairs of both Kingdoms at York, being near the Center between the two Royal Seats, and sometimes the Kings of England have come the length of New-castle, Berwick, and Norham for interview, or Treaty.

NOW it cannot be imagined, That if either the Money was not payed to Richard for granting the Acquittance, /181/ Or if he had taken it from a Fondness to go to the Holy War, he who for his Bravery, had the Title given him of *The Lyon's Heart* wou'd have afterward granted any Deed in pursuance of that Acquittance.

THIS last Grant of Richard, bearing such Noble and large Concessions to our King, made Edward the first carry it off with the Acquittance, and other Deeds implying our Independency:[1] But this Deed is yet extant in the Archives of Westminster, and is of late published by Mr. Rymer from the Original.[2]

LEST any shou'd be amused or stumble at these Words in Richard's last Charter, *Postquam Rex Scotiae de Mandato nostro transierit fines Regni sui,* As if our Kings had been under the Command of the King of England; It may be thought fit to notice, That the word *Mandatum* (a Mandat) does not referr to our King, but is a Law Term,[3] and by it here is meant a /182/ Writ direct to them who were to attend our King, when he came to England, without which they were not bound to Attendance. This is evident by the Passage already mentioned in Hoveden, where we find, when William met Richard at Canterbury, There was a Mandat direct to the Bishop and Sheriff of York to attend him. Of such Mandats many are to be seen in Mr. Rymers Collections of Treaties, &c. directed to the Officers of the King of England, (bearing expresly the Title *Mandatum*) for receiving our King upon the

---

P.180 (1) Hoveden p. 738. (2) Numb. XV (3) *Scotl. Soveraig.* p. 305.
P.181 (1) Append. Num. XXVI. (2) *Foedera Angliae* Tom 1. p. 87. (3) Cowells *Interpreter* and Blunts *Law Dictionary.*

Frontiers of that Kingdom, and Conducting him with all Honour to the English Court.

THUS I hope it's evident, That the first Acknowledgment, and Homage made by our King to the King of England for Scotland, was a Manifest Extortion, and Act of Oppression.

THE next Acknowledgments of the Superiority of England over Scotland, are these that were made to Edward the first of England, which shall be demonstrat to have been also Extorted.

TO make these Extortions the more manifest; It seems fit to touch some Historical Passages, from the time of King Richard's granting the Renunciation, /183/ which evinces our Independency, to the Days of this Edward the first; Which will farther clear our Independency, and remove some Arguments and Insinuations offer'd by Mr. Atwood and others, in behalf of the Homage.

IN the Days of King Richard, we find little else did pass between King William and him, beside what is already told, save that William in April 1194 demanded of him the Counties of Northumberland, Cumberland, Westmorland and Lancaster in the Right of his Ancestors. About which demand, Richard having consulted his Nobles, he demurr'd upon a Grant of Northumberland for reasons of State.[1] Thereafter our King renew'd his demand of Northumberland, with an offer of 15000 Merks; Which the King of England was willing to accept of for Northumberland, excepting the Castles: but without them our King wou'd not take it.[2]

AS soon as John Succeeded his Brother Richard in the Crown of England, our King William sent two /184/ Priors, and William Hay, as his Ambassadours, to require of King John, Northumberland and Cumberland, and offer'd for them to Swear Fealty to him. John, being then in Normandy, his Ministers pray'd the Scots Ambassadours, to have a little patience till the Kings return. With this King John being acquainted, he sent his Son in Law Eustach de Vesci to King William, To assure him, That when he came to England, he shou'd give him all satisfaction in his demands.[1]

WHEN King John return'd from Normandy, the Scots Ambassadours made the demand to him, and certified him, That if it was refused, their King wou'd do his utmost to recover his Right. To it King John gave this soft Answer, That when his dear Cusin the King of Scots came to him, he wou'd do him Justice in that and in his other demands. And in Testimony of his Sincerity, he sent the Bishop of Durham to meet our King, and King John went to Nottingham, where he stay'd some Days expecting him: But our King positively refused and renew'd the demand, and Certification made /185/ by his Ambassadours: Only he agreed to a Truce of Fourty Days, that he might have an Answer from King John.[1]

THEREAFTER King John went to York, in hopes that King William shou'd meet him there, which he wou'd not do: But in a little time after, he

---

P.183 (1) Hoveden p. 737 & 738. (2) Ibid. p. 739.
P.184 (1) Ibid. p. 793.
P.185 (1) Ibid. p. 797.

was prevail'd with to come to England: Whereupon King John gave him and his Retinue Letters of Safe Conduct, and sent to the Borders a very Noble and numerous Attendance to conduct him. At Lincoln they met, and in an Interview upon a Hill by that place, Our King, in presence of his Brother David Earl of Huntington, and many other Noble Persons, did Homage to King John, with a *Salvo* of his own Right.[2] Upon doing of this Homage, he required of King John, Northumberland, Cumberland, and Westmorland as his Right and Inheritance: But after much Discourse, the two Kings not agreeing, The King of England desired time of the King of Scots, to deliberat upon it till the ensuing Whitsunday, /186/ which was at his desire Prorogat until Michaelmass.

HERE the Learn'd Mr. Tyrrel Charges Our Buchanan with Vanity, for making this Homage to be paid only for Lands in England; Because after it was made, William demanded the Northern Counties of John: So that it cou'd not be for them. Nor yet could it be for Huntington, because That Estate and Title was then vested in the Person of King William's Brother David, wherefore Mr. Tyrrel concludes it was for Lothian, and some parts of Scotland.[1]

WHATSOEVER is advanced by that worthy Gentleman in this Argument merits Consideration. For tho', as I have observed in the entry of this Essay, he has given a severe, and in appearance, a general Censure of Sir Thomas Craig's Treatise of the Homage, Yet I wou'd fain Hope he did it only upon the Account of Sir Thomas's Suggestion, That there were no English Annals from Bede to the Reign of Henry the first: Seing Mr. Tyrrel shows a dislike of most of the Monkish Stories produced for the Claim of /187/ Homage; Nor hath he conceal'd or disguis'd some great Abuses done to us in that Claim, for which Mr. Atwood has sallied upon him.

BUT to remove the Insinuation made by this Ingenious Person, Of King William's paying Homage to King John for Lothian, It may be considered: That first, It is a Novelty, there being no former instance of any such Homage. If the Passage in Mathew Paris of Alexander the Third's doing Homage for *Laudiana,* which Mr. Tyrrel calls Lothian,[1] has given any Encouragement to this Thought, The Fallacy of that Passage will be hereafter discovered.

NEXT, It's not to be imagined, when Our King was so Zealous in his Demands, as he wou'd not meet the King of England, unless he did him Right, and when that King was so Complaisant, That ever King William wou'd do him Homage, without some previous Concert in relation to the Northern Counties, which tho' not such a Concert, as to give him immediatly Possession, Yet according to the custom of these Days, might be a /188/ sufficient Ground for doing of Homage. Thus we find Alexander the 2d. of Scotland payed Homage to Henry the 3d. of England, by an

---

P.185 (2) Ibid. p. 811.
P.186 (1) *Hist.* Vol. 2 p. 712.
P.187 (1) Ibid. p. 955.

Agreement for some Lands in these Counties, of which he did not get Possession till some Years after the Agreement.[1]

BUT admitting, That this Homage was not for the Northern Counties, yet it might have been very well for Huntington, notwithstanding of the reason offer'd by Mr. Tyrrel in the contrair. For the understanding of which, It is to be considered, That tho' now with Us, Acknowledgments are only made to the Superior, upon the Death of the Vassal, Yet of Old they were also renew'd upon the Death of the Superior. Now by Richard's Charter, we find William did pay Homage to him for Huntington; So that the Right of Huntington was vested in his Person: Wherefore any Transmission or Conveyance of Right in Favour of his Brother David, was in Subjection and Vassalage to him, and not to the King of England: For, from that same Charter of Richard's, /189/ placed in the Appendix,[1] We understand that Sub-feus were then usual.

IT was an ancient Custom in Scotland, that all younger Brethren and Cadets, did hold their Patrimonial Lands of the Chief of the Family; And there was more Reason, that the Brother of our King should hold, and be dependent upon him. So that David having Huntington under his Brother the King of Scotland, there was Homage due for it by our King, to the King of England.

OF this we have an Example and Parallel, in Henry the Father of King William, and the son of King David, who had both the Title and Possession of the County of Northumberland; Yet the English Historians tells us, that the Grant was made to King David, and that King William his Grand-child, demanded that County, not in the Right of his Father Henry, but of his Grand-father King David. The Right of Huntington did also continue in the two succeeding Kings of Scotland, Alexander the 2d, and 3d. For according to Mr. Tyrrel, Alexander the 2d. did Homage for it to the King of /190/ England.[1] And Mathew Paris tells us That Alexander the 3d. had a Charter of it from Henry the Third.[2] Of this we are further ascertain'd by Mr. Tyrrel, when he relates, That Alexander the 2d. went to London upon sundry Affairs, whereof one was to appear and act as Earl of Huntington.[3] All which concur to overturn the Suggestion of that Gentleman, and to acquit Buchanan of Error or Vanity in this Matter.

ABOUT nine years after the Interview of the two Kings at Lincoln, Mathew Paris recites a Quarrel between them, and how John came to Norham, with an Army, where a Peace was concluded; that Hostages were given for Observance of it, and Eleven thousand Merks payed to King John for Damages.[4]

THAT any Sum was payed for Damages, is not probable; For, by a Deed published in Mr. Rymer's Collection of Treatises (which is so very useful for giving Light in many things not known, or disguised) /191/ we

---

P.188 (1) Rymers *Foedera Anglie* p. 372.
P.189 (1) Numb. 8.
P.190 (1) *Hist.* Vol. 2. p. 836. (2) *Ad Ann.* 1259. (3) *Hist.* V. 2. p. 1000. (4) *Ad Ann.* 1209.

find, that there was a Peace made, and Hostages given; But that the sum to be payed was 15000 Merks, not in consideration of Damages, but of some Stipulations between the two Kings;[1] which it seems were not perform'd on the part of the King of England, As appears by a Complaint made by our King to the Pope;[2] As also by a Passage in Matthew Paris,[3] and especially by the Agreement made between Alexander the 2d, and Henry the 3d.[4]

THUS stood matters between the two Kings when William of Scotland Died, to whom Succeeded his Son Alexander the Second.

IN a little time thereafter, a misunderstanding arose between King John and his Barons, who to pacifie them, Granted the *Magna Charta* of their priviledges: But King John having prevail'd with the Pope to Anul and Void that Charter, The Barons of England did Confederat to maintain their Liberties. With them Alexander King of Scots did chearfully /192/ joyn in defence of the Grand Charter against King John, who had made a base and voluntar surrender of his Kingdoms of England and Ireland, To be Holden of the Pope: For which the Holy Father was so exasperat against OUR King, that he caused Excommunicat him, and put his Kingdom under an Interdict.

AT this time, The Barons of England courted our Kings Friendship, and fully Recognized and Establish'd his Right of the Northern Counties, which was Confirm'd to him by Prince Lewis the Eldest Son of the King of France, whom the Barons called in to be their King, As is acknowleged by the English Historians, and may be known by the Titles of some Deeds placed in the Appendix.[1]

THE Barons did solemnly Swear, and Engage, That they should not conclude a Peace with King John, without the Consent of the King of Scotland; But to this Oath, saith Mr. Tyrrel, They were no Slaves.[2] The Confederacies between Our King and the Barons of England; and /193/ the charters made by them and Prince Lewis to him, yea some Bulls which evinced, that our King suffer'd Excommunication for assisting the Barons of England,[1] were carried off, by Edward the First, to obliterat any Deeds which might raise a grateful Remembrance in his Subjects, of the kind Offices done by the King of Scotland, in support of their Grand Charter: For it's well known, that our King raised a powerful Army, which was the Sanctuary and Protection of the Barons of York-Shire and Northumberland, from the cruel and bloody Mercenary Troops of King John, who retired upon the approach of the King of Scotland's Army:[2] And had he either assisted King John, or stood Neuter; It is hard to know, what had been the Fate of the Barons and their Priviledges.

KING John as is said, having fail'd in performance of his part of the Agreement with King William, Alexander his Son complains to the Pope, and prays him either to Confirm or to /194/ void it. Upon which in 1219, the Pope directs a Bull to Pandulf his Legat, impowering him to consider the

---

P.191 (1) *Foedera Angliae* p. 155. (2) Ibid. p. 235. (3) *Ad Ann.* 1236. (4) Rymers *Foedera Angl.* p. 375.
P.192 (1) Numb. XXVI. (2) *Hist.* Vol. 2 p. 801.
P.193 (1) Append. Num. XXVI. (2) Tyrrel. *Hist.* Vol. 2. p. 789.

Agreement, And without Appellation to Confirm or Annul it. In consequence of which Delegation, there was Compearance for both Kings before
the Legat: Who waved the giving a Decision in Law for some time, that he
might negotiat a Peace between them.[1]

IN the Year following, There was a Treaty of Marriage between our
King, and the King of England for his Sister,[2] Which was afterwards solem-
nized, and a Dowry settled upon her.[3]

FOR some Years thereafter, there appears to have been a good
Understanding between the two Kings by the repeated Interviews, until, The
King of England approved of an Appeal, which the Arch-Bishop of York
was to make for the Right of that King, as well as for his own, That the King
of Scots cou'd not be Crown'd in prejudice of the Royal /195/ Dignity of the
King of England, and of the Liberty of this Arch-Bishop and his See.[1]

TO Colour this Appeal, There was a Representation made by Henry the
3d King of England, to Pope Gregory, Reciting the extorted Agreement of
Subjection made by King William to King Henry the 2d; And disguising the
Matter so far, as to pretend, That King John was joyn'd in that Agreement
with his Father Henry the 2d: Yea falsly asserting, That in pursuance of that
Extorted Deed, King William paid Homage to King John, And that
Alexander the 2d had done the like to that King, and to King Henry the
Third. Whereupon the Pope sent a Bull to the King of Scotland, Exhorting
him for Peace's sake to the Observance of that Agreement. He also sent
another Bull to the Bishops of York and Carlile to the same purpose.[2] Which
Bulls were used by Edward the First as evidences to enforce the Homage:
And are Ingrost in the Record kept in the Tower of London, Publish'd by
Pryn.[3]

/196/ THE strain of these Bulls do fully discover that they were
Impetrat from the Pope by Suggestions of the King of England. In them
some things are disguised to the Pope, and other things asserted to him,
which I presume, have no Foundation in Record or History: For in the
extorted Deed of Homage by King William to Henry the 2d, there neither is,
nor properly cou'd be any mention of John, who was at that time only
Henry's second Son. Nor was it ever pretended, That there was any
Agreement to that purpose between William and John; For the Agreement
between them, was in relation to other matters, and not in relation to any
Homage for Scotland, else it's not presumable, That his Son Alexander King
of Scotland wou'd have so eagerly pursued the Performance, and made
Complaint to the Pope for the Failure of the King of England.

WHEN Our King complain'd to the Pope of the King of England, for
not Observing of an Agreement, He sent an attested Copy of it to the Pope,[1]
To shew that the Complaint /197/ was Just. But here the King of England
did not send to the Pope a Copy of the Agreement, By which he claim'd the
Homage; And the reason is obvious, Because he had not the Original to

---

P.194 (1) Rymer's *Foedera Angliae*. p. 235. (2) Ibid. p. 240. (3) Ibid. p. 252.
P.195 (1) Ibid. p. 328. (2) Ibid. p. 334 & 335. (3) *Hist. Edw. I.* p. 495.
P.196 (1) *Foed. Angl.* p. 235.

vouch a Copy, it being long before released and delivered up to Our King, yea any Copy wou'd have display'd the disguise, there being nothing in it concerning John. So that the Representation made in the Name of the King of England to the Pope, was only a vain and empty amusement; Nor had Our King any regard to the Bull, For it did rather sharpen than soften him in his Demands and Claims against the King of England; Since we find him in a little time after, boldly demanding from the King of England, Northumberland, as belonging to him by Charters, and the Testimony of many great Men, and expostulating with him in an Assembly of his Nobles at York for the Violation of Paction:[1] But in the Year following, all Disputs between the two Kings were composed and settled before Otto the Pope's /198/ Legat by a solemn Covenant and Agreement in Writing.

THE King of Scotland's part of this Agreement was carried off from our Records by Edward the First. But this Composition between the two Kings is lately Published by the Learn'd and Industrious Mr. Rymer from the English Records,[1] By which we know the Matters that were then in dispute between the two Kings: As also we Understand, for what Lands our King payed Homage to the King of England.

BY this Agreement, We find the King of Scotland demanded from the King of England the Counties of Northumberland, Cumberland and Westmorland, as his Inheritance. He also Claims Satisfaction for 15000 Merks payed by his Father King William to King John, in Consideration of some Conditions which were not performed by John. He likewise complains for the breach of some Agreements, by which the King of England and his Brother Richard were bound to Marry the Sisters of the King of Scotland. Of all /199/ which and of all other Pleas and Demands, which the King of Scotland for himself and his Ancestors had against the King of England, He acquitts and releases Him and his Heirs.

FOR this Acquittance the King of England gave to the King of Scotland, and to his Heirs Kings thereof, Two Hundred Pound Lands* (*Du-centas Libratas Terrae) within Northumberland and Cumberland, without Castles; And if any part was deficient, it was to be supplyed in places adjacent to these Counties.

THESE Lands were to hold of the Kings of England by a yearly Reddendo of a Falcon at Carlile, with many ample Priviledges and Immunities to the King of Scotland. For these Lands the King of Scotland did Homage to the King of England, and swear Fealty to him.

TO the Observance of this Deed, both Kings made Oath, which is witnessed by many Noble Persons Scots and English; But the King of England did not give Possession and Investiture to the King of Scotland of the Lands granted to him, till five Years thereafter, That he did Commissionat the Bishop of Durham to assign Lands /200/ conform to the Agreement,[1] and then he granted a Charter in which they are particularly enumerat.[2]

P.197 (1) Math. Paris *ad Ann.* 1236
P.198 (1) *Foedera Angliae.* p. 374, 375, 376 & 377.
P.200 (1) *Foed. Angl.* p. 400. (2) *Copia penes Auth.*

MATHEW PARIS, who was Historiographer of England, when this
Agreement was made between the two Kings, has subjoyned to his Account
of it, a Passage very remarkable, How the Legat, who was Mediator of this
Peace and Agreement, signified his Inclinations to go to Scotland, to man-
nage the Ecclesiastick Affairs there as he had done in England: Upon which
the King of Scotland very briskly told the Legat, That in his time there had
been no Legat in his Kingdom, nor was there need of any, all things there
being well: Nor yet had any Legat been admitted in the time of his Father,
or of any of his Ancestors; And that so long as he had the Exercise of his
Reason, he would not suffer any Legat to enter his Dominions. He farder
assur'd the Legat, That if he shou'd adventure to enter Scotland, he was in
great Danger from a fierce People, from whose Insults he was not able to
protect him.[3] Upon this /201/ Passage the ingenious Mr. Tyrrel, makes a
very agreeable Reflection of the different Tempers of the Kings of Scotland
and England; That the one was doing all he cou'd to enslave his Kingdom
to the Pope, and the other to keep it free.[1]

ABOUT seven years after the foresaid Agreement, a War broke out
between the two Kingdoms, and each of them rais'd great Armies: But by
the good Offices of the Nobles of both Kingdoms, a Peace was concluded a
Newcastle upon Tyne: Upon which King Alexander gave to the King of
England a Charter, wherein he calls him His Leige Lord, He also engages in
a constant Bond of Frienship with him, and he and sundry of his Bishops
and Nobles swear to observe it, which is to be seen at full length in Mathew
Paris,[2] Mr. Rymer[3] and our Author.[4]

MR. Atwood imagining, That this Agreement and Charter were mighty
proofs of the Homage, He gets upon his Tiptoes, and Charges Sir Thomas
/202/ Craig with unfairness, and the Moderns with oversight, for not attending to demonstrative Evidences in Mathew Paris, with whom every body
that pretends to know any thing of English History must needs be conversant.

MATHEW PARIS having told, That in the Year before the Agreement,
King Alexander claim'd Northumberland as given to him by King John when
he married his Daughter: Our Author from thence pretends, That
Northumberland was not claim'd upon any ancienter Title than the Gift of
John.[2] This shews his profound knowledg of Mathew Paris and other
English Historians, who tell, That King David the Great-Grand-Father of this
King Alexander had that County, and that William his Father demanded it
frequently as his Inheritance; And by the foresaid Agreement, his Son
Alexander also claim'd it as his Inheritance, which was nowise inconsistent
with any Claim to this County by another Title; since a Person may have different Titles to the same Subject, and may use them joyntly or separatly
without derogating from any of them.

***

P.200 (3) Math. Paris *ad Ann*. 1237.
P.201 (1) *Hist.* Vol. 2. p. 898. (2) *Ad Ann.* 1244. (3) *Foedera Angl*. p. 428. (4) p. 273.
P.202 (1) p. 271. (2) p. 272.

/203/ AS to a Remark made by our Author upon the before-mentioned Agreement, That the doing of Homage was without respect to any particular Lands held in England: If Mr. Atwood had only lookt upon Mathew Paris who minces the matter, he might plead some Excuse for this Remark, But the Remark is very odd, when we find our Author in the second and third following Pages of his Book, giving the substance of that Agreement from the Patent Rolls, where it is ingross'd, and from whence Mr. Rymer had lately Published it; In the which Agreement, It is very plainly said, That the King of Scotland did Homage to Henry King of England for the 200 Pound Lands granted to him by that Agreement.[1] Yea so little regard has our Author to Inconsistencies, and to contradict himself, That he afterwards owns, That the Homage by that Agreement was for these Lands, which he calls, Ten Knights Fees:[2] But to soften the matter, he says, That there was then only an Expectation, but no Investiture till afterwards. This is a /204/ strange shift, to make the King of England's positive Grant for a valuable Consideration, to be only a matter of Expectation. It is true, The Investiture was put off for some Years by the King of England; But to bring this wrong as an Evidence or Insinuation of the Homage is a strange way of arguing.

THESE are slender escapes in Mr. Atwood, if compared with what follows. He says, That the foresaid Agreement between Alexander the Second King of Scotland, and Henry the Third of England, was made in the 21 Year of the Reign of this Henry: That it was not Executed (by which I suppose he meant, That actual Possession of the things contained in it was not obtain'd) till the 26 Year of that Kings Reign, and yet he says, That in the 24 Year of his Reign the King of Scots Executed the Charter before-mentioned.[1] In which He calls the King of England, His Liege Lord, Promises Fealty and Love to him, and never to enter into any League with his Enemies: Or to procure or make War to the prejudice of him, Or /205/ of his Kingdoms of England and Ireland: Unless the King of England oppress'd him. And our Author, when he gives a Copy of this Charter, places in the Margin of his Book,[1] Ann. 1240. 24. Hen. 3.

FROM this Charter, He subsumes, That the King of Scotland, and his Nobles recognized Liege Homage and Fealty, (which he erroneously calls Allegiance) to be due to the King of England, That the Liege-man shou'd not joyn with his Prince's Enemies. And all this being without regard to any Lands Holden in England makes it evident, that was Liege Homage for the Kingdom of Scotland.[2] Thus far Mr. Atwood.

IT is astonishing to see so open and so avow'd a belying of the Records and History of England, when it is evident the contrary of what Mr. Atwood saith is Truth; For he says, The Charter was granted two Years before the Agreement was executed,[3] whereas the Charter was granted two Years after the Agreement was executed. /206/ This is manifest by his own Voucher Mathew Paris, and by Deeds taken from the English Records by Mr. Rymer

---

P.203 (1) *Foed. Angl.* p. 376.
P.204 (1) p. 272.
P.205 (1) p. 273. (2) p. 274. (3) p. 272.

Historiographer of England, to be found in the before-mentioned excellent Collection, Intituled, *Foedera &c. Angliae,* Published at the Command, and upon the Expenses of Her Majesty.

BY them it is very plain, That the Agreement, that was between the two Kings, was in the 21 of Henry the 3d. which was in the Year 1237,[1] That this Agreement was Execute, and Investiture given in the 26 of his Reign, being in the Year 1242,[2] which is own'd by Mr. Atwood:[3] And that the Charter granted by the King of Scotland to Henry the Third, calling him Liege Lord, (which Mr. Atwood says was in the 24th of his Reign and in the Year 1240) was in the 28th of his Reign, and in the Year 1244:[4] This seems to be an affronted boldness, /207/ To arraign Her Majesties Soveraignty as QUEEN of Scotland; And at the same time, so grossly to belye the Records of Her Kingdom of England.

NONE can be amus'd with the King of Scotland's owning the King of England as Liege Lord, when it is considered, That he had then both the Right and Possession of Lands in England, Holden of that King.

NOR was his Engaging, That he shou'd not make War upon the King of England, nor joyn with his Enemies, Any Evidence of Homage for Scotland, if we consider the History of that Affair. By the account of it, as given us by Mathew Paris, (who has minced it as well as the History of the former Agreement) we understand, that the King of Scotland was about to Conferedat with France, being then Married to a Lady of that Kingdom, And that he had Countenanced and Protected some of the King of England's Enemies;[1] Yea, Mr. Tyrrel says, That our King publickly declared, That he wou'd not Hold the least piece of Earth of the King /208/ of England.[1] So high rose the Quarrel between these two Princes, That Ours wou'd not so much as acknowledg the King of England for the Lands he had in that Kingdom: For the two Kings were so enraged against one another, That they brought all their Vassals and Followers to the Field, to decide the Quarrel by the Sword; But by the Mediation of Earl Richard, Brother of the King of England, and of other great Men of both Kingdoms, as is said, a Peace was made between the two Kings.[2]

BESIDES, any such Engagement was very Reasonable, since at the same time, The King of England made the like Engagement to the King of Scotland, That he shou'd neither War upon him, nor Confederat with his Enemies, As appears by the Title of a Deed carried off by Edward the First, mentioned in the Appendix,[3] which Mathew Paris is not so Just as to notice, when he recites the Charter containing Engagements by our King. And we are ascertain'd by a Deed published by Mr. Rymer, subjoyn'd to the foresaid /209/ Charter, That at the time when it was granted, There was also a Paction and Engagements upon the part of the King of England: For

---

P.206 (1) Math. Paris *ad Ann*. 1237, & *Foed. Angl*. p. 374. (2) Ibid. p. 400. (3) p. 272.
P.207 (1) *Ad Ann*. 1244.
P.208 (1) *Hist*. Vol. 2 p. 929. (2) Ibid. p. 930. (3) Numb. XXVI.

Observation of which, Earl Richard had given his Oath.[1] So the Stipulation in this Point being mutual, there can be no Argument for the Homage drawn from it.

NOR can any Insinuation of Homage be inferr'd from the King of Scotland's calling the King of England, Liege Lord, without the Enumeration of particular Lands for which Homage was due; For Reason would say, That if Homage had been due, or acknowledged for the Kingdom of Scotland, it wou'd have been exprest: And that the King of England wou'd not have left it open to a Cavil. Nay Mathew Paris and Westminster,[2] and other English Historians, tell us, That our King had a very numerous and strong Army, viz a thousand Horsemen in Armour, and about an hundred thousand Foot, who had all confess'd themselves, and were willing to die in Defence of their Liberties. Now it's against /210/ Sense to think, That so many brave and resolute Men wou'd have subjected themselves peaceably without a Battle. And tho' Mathew Paris has suppress'd some matters of Fact in this Affair, yet he gives our King Alexander the Second a large Character; That he was a Good, Just, Pious and Bountiful Prince, deservedly beloved by the English, as by his own People. Besides, in all the forged and extorted Deeds, the Homage and Subjection for Scotland is plainly and distinctly expressed.

FROM the Year 1244, wherein this Peace was made, to the Year 1249, when Alexander the Second died, we find nothing but Peace and Concord between the two Kings; But he leaving his only Son, Alexander the Third, a young Boy, Tho' the King of England was in a League of Friendship with him, and that this young prince was contracted in Marriage with that Kings Daughter, yet, He supplicated the Pope, to prohibite the Anointing and Crowning the King of Scotland without his Consent, because he was his Leige-man: which the Pope refused, as being a thing derogatory to Royal Dignity. At the same time, the King of England petition'd the Pope for a /211/ Grant of the *Decima,* or Tenth of the Church Revenues in Scotland, which he also refused, as being a Singularity to Grant that to any King in the Kingdom of another. These things are manifest by the Popes Bull in the Year 1251, yet extant in the Archives of England, and Published by Mr. Rymer:[1] Which clearly evinces, That the Crown and Kingdom of Scotland was Soveraign and Independent according to the Judgment of the Court of Rome.

IN the Year following, when Alexander the 3d. came to York, to Marry the King of England's Daughter, That King design'd some Advantage of a young Prince and Bridegroom, As appears by a Passage related by Mathew Paris to this purpose.[2] "The King of Scots at his Marriage did Homage to the King of England, upon the account of the Tenement which he held of his

---

P.209 (1) *Foed. Angl.* p. 429. (2) *Ad Ann.* 1244.

P.211 (1) *Foed. Angl.* p. 463. (2) *Ad Ann.* 1252. *Fecit igitur Rex Scotiae Regi Anglorum Homagium ratione Tenementi, quod tenet de Domino Rege Anglorum, de Regno scilicet Angliae, Laudiano videlicet & terris reliquis, &c.*

Lord the King of England, That is to say, in the Kingdom /212/ of England,
to wit, *Laudiana* and other Lands". And when, beside this, It was desired of
the King of Scotland, That he shou'd pay Homage to the King of England
for the Kingdom of Scotland, He refused to comply, and gave a sweet and
pithy Answer.

THE Learned Sir Thomas Craig having adduced this Passage as an evidence of Our Independency, Mr. Atwood accuses him, Of a Habit of
Triumphing with Authorities point blank against him;[1] And amongst such,
he reckons this passage in Mathew Paris: Because, as he thinks, It demonstrates, That the King of Scotland did Homage to the King of England for
Lodoney or Lothian, which is a considerable part of Scotland. He also
charges Sir Thomas with adding to the Text of Paris, when he makes it to
run, That the Homage was paid for Laudon or Leuden, which is a Tenement
of Northumberland; This last Sentence not being in Paris:[2] And our Author
attacks his Candor for giving such cramp Names as Laudon or Leuden, to
that which is truly Lodoney /213/ or Lothian; That he might shun so plain
an Argument for the Homage.[1]

THERE is indeed here an Error in the Learn'd Treatise, of Sir Thomas
Craig concerning the Homage,[2] which is not to be ascribed to the ingenious
Translator, since he has followed the Latin Original, and even there the
Mistake is excusable, being probably only in Pointing: For placing the
Sentence that is quarrel'd *in Parenthesi*, which by the reading, it appears
should be, all Mr. Atwood's Charge evanishes. In a far greater Mistake falls
he himself in the first Approaches of this Attack upon our Learn'd Craig;
when he says, That the Marriage of the King of Scot's Son, to Henry the
Third's Daughter, was part of the Agreement at York in the 21st of Henry
the Third.[3] Which was in the year 1237: Whereas the Convention about that
Marriage was in the year 1242:[4] Nor cou'd it be in 1237, as Mr. Atwood fancies; For the Son, for whom our King contracted Marriage, was not /214/
Born; nor was his Father then Married to the French Lady, who was afterwards his Mother: Yea, it's well known he was married at that time to the
King of England's Sister, who died shortly after without Issue.

BUT to return. The foresaid Passage in Mathew Paris may at first view
prove stumbling, and occasion a Thought, That the *Laudiana* or
Laudianum mentioned by him, is Lodeney or Lothian, being generally so
render'd; And in that Sense, this Passage is the most powerful Historical
Evidence, That Homage was voluntarily paid for any Lands upon this side of
Tweed: wherefore I shall take the more Notice of that Passage, and endeavour to clear it.

IN the first place, It might be contended, That no Evidence from
English Historians shou'd be received for England against Scotland, They
being domestick Testimonies, under the suspicion of Partiality: And it were
easy to make appear, That this Author doth not plainly and fully rehearse
some Passages concerning the Homage, and other Transactions between

P.212 (1) p. 275. (2) p. 278.
P.213 (1) Ibid. (2) p. 344. (3) p. 275. (4) Math. Paris *ad Ann*, 1242.

these two Kingdoms. For Instance, besides what I have already /215/ hinted; He says, That when King William was taken Prisoner by the English near to Anwick in Northumberland, There was such a Slaughter of Scots, whom in contempt he calls *Formicae,* as was never known:[1] Whereas some who are more Ingenuous in the account of that Rencounter, tell, That our King was taken in Surprise, when there was only about sixty Horse with him; That he behaved Gallantly and resisted until his Horse was killed under him, and that upon the News of his being Prisoner, the rest of his Army retired. By this we may plainly see Mathew Paris's partiality in his Accounts of what concern'd the Affairs of Scotland with relation to England.

OF the same Temper are most of the Ancient English Historians, in expressing bitter Invectives against us; Which makes any Passages in them favouring the Homage the less to be credited, and makes any Evidences brought from them for our Independency the more strong and convincing; Since they are not to be suspected of Truth, in what they say to the /216/ advantage of them, who commonly were the Subject of their reproachful Expressions.

IN the next place, It might be pretended, That it was customary in these Days to disguise the Homage made by our Kings; For Edward the First was about Thirteen Years of Age, when this Homage was done to his Father Henry the 3d, and probably was present at the Ceremony, being perform'd at his Sister's Wedding; Yet in his Letter to the Pope, he says, That this Alexander the 3d paid Homage to his Father for Scotland: Whereas this Historian tells, That there was no Homage paid for it. If then a King cou'd so invert the Homage, as when it was only made for some particular Lands, to take a Kingdom to it, The Historian may pass for modest, if he only tackt Lothian to it.

BUT Admitting this Historian to relate true matter of Fact, nevertheless Lodoney or Lothian will not be found to be amongst the Lands for which this Homage was paid: For Mr. Atwood who Challenges others for abusing Mathew Paris's Text, wou'd himself confound it by a pretence, That the /217/ Words, *Fecit Rex Scotiae Regi Anglorum Homagium Ratione Tenementi quod tenet de Domino Rege Anglorum, de regno scilicet Angliae Laudiano videlicet & reliquis terris,* are not aright Translated; The King of Scotland did Homage to the King of England for the Tenement which he held of his Lord the King of England, That is to say, In the Kingdom of England, viz. Laudiana and other Lands; But that they shou'd be Translated to this purpose, That he did Homage for the Tenement, which he held of the King of England, that is to say, Of the Kingdom of England, &c.[1]

IT may be thought, That all who understand any thing of Latin, or who notice the turn of this Sentence, will agree, That by the Words, *De Regno Angliae,* is here plainly meant, In the Kingdom of England; The Preposition

---

P.215 (1) *Ad Ann.* 1174.
P.217 (1) p. 277.

De being frequently Synonimous with the Proeposition *In:* Nor can *De* be otherways Translated in this place, without a manifest Tautology.

TO Remove any thing that may be amusing in this Passage, It may be considered, That at the time when /218/ this Homage was paid, The River of Tweed was the Boundary of the Two Kingdoms, as may be gathered from Deeds under the Seals of the Two Kings, Alexander the 3d. and Henry the 3d.[1]

BESIDES, Long before that time, Tweed was reckon'd the Boundiary. William of Newburgh is very plain in it:[2] And other English Historians[3] say; That when the English passed Tweed, they came into Scotland.

LEST any incline to think, That Lodoney or Lothian was of old reckon'd to be in England, Because in a Passage of the Saxon Chronicle,[4] It is said, That Malcolm Canmoir with his Army met King William Rufus in Lodene in England; Which by the Learn'd Editor is explain'd in the Margin by *Provincia Loidis* from Florence of Worcester, and Simeon of Durham: And by *Provincia Loudicensis,* from Bromton; And in the Exposition of names of Places subjoyn'd to that Chronicle, These words are Exponed, Louthane a Province of Scotland:[5] I shall endeavour to make it appear /219/ That neither the *Laudanium* mention'd by Paris; Nor yet this Lodene, *Provincia Loidis,* or *Loudicensis,* are the Lothian in Scotland, but places in England.

TO clear this matter; Let it be considered, That the Northern Counties of England to wit, Northumberland, Cumberland, and Westmorland were called, and did pass under the Name of *Comitatus Laudonensis,* or *Lodonensis;* For when Newburgh,[1] Wicks,[2] and Hemmingford,[3] of the more ancient Historians, and Mr. Tyrrel,[4] and other Moderns, relate the Story of Henry the Second's taking the Northern Counties from Malcolm the Fourth, They call them Northumberland, Cumberland, and Westmorland; But when Mathew Paris,[5] the User of the Word *Laudanium,* Ralf de Diceto,[6] *The Annals of Weverley,*[7] and Mathew of Westminster,[8] relate the same Story, They express these Counties by the Name of *Comitatus Laudonensis,* or /220/ *Lodonensis:* So that probably *Laudanium* was some place in these Counties, or was the common Name of our Kings Possessions in them.

NOR was Lothian in Scotland, a part of that *Comitatus Laudonensis,* since it was not claim'd by Henry the Second; And further by the same Authors,[1] we find, That when King William who succeeded Malcolm, did demand back these Northern Counties, and enter'd them with an Army, Lothian was reckon'd in Scotland, as distinct from these Counties: And Mathew Paris gives it another Name than *Laudiana,* viz. *Laudonesium.* The like may be said of the *Provincia Loidis,* for Simeon of Durham; As when he tells, That Malcolm Canmoir gave to Earl Gospatrick, Dumbar in Lothian, He

---

P.218 (1) *Foed. Angl.* p. 565. (2) Lib. 2. cap. 30. (3) *Ad Ann.* 1173. (4) p. 197. (5) p. 36.

P.219 (1) Lib. 2. Cap. 4. (2) *Hist. Angl. Scriptores,* Vol 2. p. 30 (3) Ibid. p. 492. (4) *Hist.* V.2. p. 303. (5) *Ad Ann.* 1157. (6) *Inter X. Script.* p. 531. (7) *Hist. Angl. Script.* V.2. p. 159. (8) *Ad Ann.* 1157.

P.220 (1) *Ad Ann.* 1173.

expresses it by *Lodoneium*.[2] Nor will it be found, That Lothian was design'd by *Provincia;* There's indeed frequently mention'd in the ancient Historians, *provincia Northanhimbrorum,* which with all Submission, I conceive to be the same with the *Provincia Loidis,* and /221/ the *Comitatus Laudonensis,* or *Lodonensis,* because it included Carlile.[1] This is also clear by comparing two Passages in Ralf de Diceto,[2] where the same Lands, which in the one, he calls *Comitatis Lodonensis,* are in the other, said to be in *Provincia Northanimbrorum;* And with the same Breath, he mentions Lothian as being in Scotland, and distinct from that Province or County, and expresses it by a word different from either of them; As also different from the *Provincia Loidis,* which he makes the place of the Rencounter of the two Kings, Malcolm Canmoir and William Rufus.[3] Beside, the English Historians make the *Provincia Loidis* to be without Scotland,[4] and Lothian to be in it,[5] which demonstrates them to be distinct.

THEY who are versed in the antient Topography of England may give more Light in this Matter; since perhaps the Affinity of some Names of Places might occasion Mistakes: But /222/ I hope by these hints it's very presumable, That *Laudianum* and *Provincia Loidis* are in England; At least some Names of Places are so confounded by the English Historians, that no Inference can be drawn from them in favours of the Homage, or for comprehending Lothian under England.

AFTER the Marriage of Alexander the 3d. to the King of England's Daughter, we find much Peace and Friendship between the two Kings. The King of England upon many occasions, gave evident Testimonies, That he wou'd not encroach upon the Liberties of Scotland; And we find our King had a watchful Eye upon him, and a concern for our Liberties: As may be seen by some Deeds placed in the Appendix.

WHEN Henry the 3d. of England went to France; such was his Confidence in our brave King Alexander the 2d. That he committed to his Care, the Northern part of his Dominions:[1] And our King, to shew the like Confidence in that King, recommended the Care of his young and only Son to him, as an Allie, Neighbour, /223/ & design'd Father in Law; And after the Marriage we find him frequently discharging the Office of a true Friend and Allie.

SOME of the Ministers of Alexander the 3d. being uneasy to him and his Queen; The King of England and his Queen came to the Castle of Werk upon the Borders, to Visit them; and he required all his Vassals in England and their followers to attend him:[1] But lest this shou'd have given any Umbrage to the Scots, He publishes a Declaration, In which he testifies That, He had no design to prejudice or infringe the Liberties of Scotland; But to his Power to preserve them according to several Leagues. And because that when Our King was Married to his Daughter at York, He had

---

P.220 (2) *Inter X. Script.* p. 205.
P.221 (1) *Hist. prioris Hagustald. inter X. Script.,* p. 312. (2) Ibid. p. 531 & 573.
    (3) Ibid. p. 490. (4) *Ad Ann.* 1091. (5) *Ad Ann.* 1173.
P.222 (1) Math. Paris, *Ad Ann.* 1242.

recommended some Counsellors and Judges to the young King, He
declared, That what was then done, shou'd be nowise prejudicial to the
Liberties of Scotland.

AT the same time the King of England, as also two of his Brethren, and
several of his Nobles engaged, That the King and Queen of Scotland shou'd
/224/ come and go, to and from the King of England At their pleasure: And,
That he wou'd not do, nor suffer any thing to be done, in prejudice of the
Liberties of Scotland: As appears by two Deeds Published by Mr. Rymer
from the English Records,[1] and to be found in the Appendix.[2]

THE Uneasy Ministers in Scotland were at the Instances of the King of
England removed, and others appointed in their place; But the Deed of our
King in this point is very Cautious; Yea so Circumspect were Our brave
Ancestors in what concern'd their Liberties, That they got from the King of
England a solemn Deed, under his Seal, granted by Advice of his Nobles
and Counsellors, Declaring, That what was done in displacing of some
Counsellors, and appointing others by his Mediation, shou'd not be prejudi-
cial to the King of Scotland and his Heirs, or to the Liberties of that
Kingdom. All which is evident from a Copy of this Deed Published by Mr.
Rymer, and in which the /225/ foresaid Deed of Our King is ingrossed.[1]

THE King of England having undertaken the Crusade, The Pope for his
Encouragement gave him the *Vicesima* or twentieth Penny of the Church
Benefices of Scotland, and appoints John Frusinon his Chaplain in Scotland
to uplift it, but with this Caution, That it shou'd be despositat in some
secure place, so that the Pope might order the expending of it, towards the
Defence of the Holy Land.[2]

NOTWITHSTANDING of this Caution, Lest the King of England might
have improved this Grant to the prejudice of Scotland, our King wou'd give
no Obedience to the Popes Bull, until the King of England by a Deed,
Declared, That it shou'd be of no prejudice thereafter to the King of
Scotland and his Heirs: Which is Published by Mr. Rymer,[3] and to be seen in
the Appendix.[4]

IN the Year 1260, The King of England invited the King of Scotland
/226/ and his Daughter the Queen to his Court, and gave them and their
Retinue safe Conduct, with assurance, That they shou'd not in any wise be
desired to Treat of any Scots matters concerning themselves, their Kingdom,
or Counsellors:[1] Likewise the King of England issued forth Mandats to the
Sheriffs of the Counties, through which they were to pass, To attend them,
and to give them the Use of the Kings Houses, Forrests, and Warranries; As
also to see that all Honours and Courtesies were done to them.[2]

OUR Cautious Ancestors were so very regardful of their Liberties, That
they prudently provided against any thing that might entangle them;
Wherefore at this time, it being suspected, that the Queen of Scotland was

P.224 (1) Ibid. 561 & 562. (2) Numb. XVI, & XVII.
P.225 (1) *Foedera Angliae* p. 565, 566 & 567. (2) Ibid. p. 517. (3) Ibid. p. 582.
    (4) Numb. XVIII.
P.226 (1) *Foed. Angl.* p. 713. (2) Ibid. p. 714.

with Child, and they not knowing what might fall out, while the King and she were in England; Therefore, before they went thither, The King of England Grants and Swears to a Deed, Published by Mr. Rymer,[3] and Transcribed in the Appendix:[4] /227/ By which the King of Scotland was to have full Liberty to carry back his Queen when he pleased, and if she stay'd till her Delivery, He was to dispose of her and the Child as he Will'd; And if he died, The Child was to be at the disposal of the Nobles of Scotland.

THE Queen of Scotland proving to be with Child; The King, Queen, and Nobles of England, dealt with our King to let her stay in England till her Delivery; Which being granted, there was a new Deed made more ample than the former, with this special Caution, That if our King died, The Child was to be delivered without any Dispute or Cavil, to certain Noblemen therein Named, or any three of them having that Deed: Which is Published by Mr. Rymer,[1] and placed in the Appendix.[2]

THIS Deed was very solemn, For it was not only Sworn by the King of England, but also by his Brother the King of the Romans as Guarrantee; As likewise by several Nobles of England: And the King engaged to /228/ cause his eldest Son Prince Edward, and the two Arch-Bishops, and some of his principal Nobles and Ministers who were absent, also to Swear the Observance of it.

BY these Deeds, It's manifest, That the Kings of England had no Claim of Superiority, nor of any Guardianship or Wardship of our Kings.

AFTER this we find little past between two Kings, Alexander the 3d, and Henry the 3d; Save that Henry did mediat a Peace between our King and the King of Norway.

KING Henry died, when his Son and Successor Edward the First was Abroad in the Holy Land; Who as is said, was the Champion of the Claim of Homage; And of all the Kings of England most boldly and plainly asserted it, as due by Right, and pursued that Claim by a long and Bloody War: But with how much Justice, will appear by what follows.

WHEN Edward the First return'd to England, Our King, who was his Brother in Law, went to England to visit him, and was present at his Coronation; But that no Advantage might be taken of his Civility, He had from the King of England, a Deed, bearing /229/ That his presence at that Solemnity shou'd be nowise prejudicial to him and his Kingdom.[1]

AT this time he did Homage to Edward; But this Homage was only for the Lands our King had in England, As appears by the account of it, placed in an Ancient Cartuary of the Monastry of Dunfermline, in the Library of the honourable Faculty of Advocats, and from thence Published by the Learn'd Sir Robert Sibbald;[2] And the like Account I have seen in other Ancient Scots Manuscripts. It is also touched by Matthew Westminster, and Thomas

P.226 (3) Ibid. p. 714. (4) Numb. XIX.
P.227 (1) *Foed. Angl.* p. 715. (2) Numb. XX.
P.229 (1) Append. Numb. XXVI. Walsingham *inter Script. Angl. Hiber. Norm, &c.* p. 80 & Westminster edit. francf. 1601. p. 436. (2) *Independency of Scotl.* p. 5.

Walsingham,[3] the English Historians of these Times: Yea by the Memorandum communicated by the Learn'd Mr. Petyt to Mr. Atwood, and Published by him;[4] It is evident, That Alexander the Third did not Homage to Edward for Scotland; Yet that King in his Letter to the Pope takes the Freedom to assert, That this King Alexander did Homage to him for the Kingdom of Scotland.

/230/ A LITTLE after King Edward arrived in England, He was ingaged in a War against the Prince of Wales; In this War, Our King assisted his Brother in Law the King of England; But was so Cautious to obtain a Deed from him, Testifying, That the assistance given by him in the Welsch War, was not by way of Duty or Service,[1] but as a special Favour.[2] All which concur to Evince, That our King was Independent of the King of England.

THE unlucky and fatal Death of Alexander the Third, King of Scotland, by a fall from his Horse, put the Kingdom in great disorder, until the Community appointed Governours, who had the Management of Affairs for six Years of an Inter-reign.

THIS King left no Descendants of his Body, save Margaret, commonly called the Maid of Norway, His Grand-Child by a Daughter, who was Married to the King of Norway.

IF Scotland had been Dependent upon England, Then the Custody and Wardship of that young Lady, had /231/ belonged to Edward by Right of Seigniorie; But he never demanded any such thing: Yea so far was he from claiming the disposal of this Princess, That he address'd the Governours, and Treated with them, for having her in Marriage to Prince Edward his eldest Son. So that Mr. Atwood shou'd been asham'd to palliat Edward's not claiming the Guardianship of that Lady, with an empty Notion; That it argued no more, Than a Tenderness, and Compliment to the fair Sex, in not obliging her to Travel to the English Court.[1]

DURING the Inter-Reign, The Governours kept a good Correspondence with Edward of England; But still with great Circumspection in what might tend to the least Diminution or Incroachment upon the Liberties of the Kingdom: As appears by a Letter from them to that King, ingrost in the English Records,[2] whereby they Impower Commissioners sent by them, to Treat some matters with the Ambassadors of Norway before the King of England: But with this express Caution; /232/ Saving alwise in and by all things, The liberty and Honour of the Kingdom of Scotland: Which is to be seen at full length in the Appendix.[1]

TO perpetuat the Friendship of the two Nations, There was a Marriage concluded between Edward the eldest Son of the King of England, and Margaret the Maid of Norway, Queen of Scotland: And Articles of Marriage concerted by the Governours of Scotland, and the Commissioners of the King of England, which were afterwards ratified by him.

P.229 (3) Locis citat. (4) p. 80.
P.230 (1) Walsingham, p. 48. (2) Westminster, p. 436.
P.231 (1) p. 97. (2) Pryn's *Edw. I.* p. 392.
P.232 (1) Numb. XXII.

BY these Articles, It was agreed, That if Edward and Margaret shou'd die without Issue, The Crown of Scotland shou'd return free without any Subjection to the next Heir of the Kingdom: It was also stipulated, That the Kingdom shou'd remain separated, divided and free in it self from the Kingdom of England, without any Subjection by its Bounds and Limits, as it had been in times before.

TO this last mentioned Article was added a *Salvo,* which is exprest in too general Terms by Mr. Tyrrel, viz. Saving the King of England's Right /233/ which he had before this.[1] For according to the Transcript of these Articles Published from the English Records by Mr. Pryn,[2] The *Salvo* runs thus, Saving the Right of the King of England, and of any other person, which before these Articles was competent, or at any time thereafter might in Justice be competent to him or them; Of any Lands upon the Borders or elsewhere.

IT'S known, That Edward the First was very dexterous in making of *Salvo's;* For when he confirmed the *Magna Charta* of England, He did it with a Saving of the Right of his Crown:[3] Nevertheless, I presume, None will from thence contend, That thereby the Grand Charter was any-wise lessen'd: So neither by any such *Salvo* cou'd our Independency be infringed, unless Edward had instructed some prior Right; For tho' by a *Salvo,* Liberties may be preserved, yet no Right of Superiority can be constitute by any such *Salvo.*

BUT the *Salvo* adjected to the foresaid Article, was not in relation to the /234/ Kingdom of Scotland; So cou'd be of no Advantage to the King of England, or any wise prejudicial to the Liberties of Scotland; For by the *Salvo* itself, it is manifest, That it was in relation to the Lands, which our King had in England, For Alexander the 3d dyed Vested and Seised, not only in the Lands of Penreth and others in Cumberland, amounting to the 200 Pound Land granted to his Father by Henry the 3d, which were upon the Borders; But also in Lands elsewhere in England; To wit, in the Honour of Huntington and Lands of Tyndale: And Baliol after he had basely subjected Scotland to the King of England, was Cognosced Heir to Alexander the 3d. in these Lands, by an Inquisition made before Sir Thomas Normanvil Escheator beyond Trent.

THIS is evident by an *Inspeximus* or Transcript by King James the Sixth of Scotland, and First of England, under the Great Seal of England; Of this Inquisition and of sundry other Deeds in time of Edward the First, concerning the Scots King's Right to Penreth, Tyndale, and Huntington. In these Deeds is also to be found *Salvo's* by that King of his own Right, or of the /235/ Right of any other Person, in these Lands.

A Copy of this *Inspeximus,* from the Original, was transmitted by the right Reverend and Learn'd Bishop of Carlile, a sincere Lover of Truth and Justice, to the Honourable Sir James Dalrymple, and was communicated by

---

P.233 (1) *Hist.* Vol. 3. p. 60. (2) *Edw. I.* p. 366. (3) Walsingham. p. 76 & Tyrrel's *Hist.*
     Vol. 3. p. 133.

that worthy Gentleman to me. By the bye that *Inspeximus*, as also a Deed Publish'd by Mr. Rymer,[1] convicts Mr. Atwood of an Error, in asserting, That the King of Scot's paying Homage to the King of England for Tyndale and Penreth, was perfectly a new Invention.

BUT to return. The blooming Hopes of a perpetual Cement of the two Nations, were soon defeat by the untimely Death of Margaret the Maid of Norway, after she was Contracted in Marriage with Prince Edward.

UPON her decease, the Kingdom fell into great Convulsions, and Factions by the several Competitors to the Crown. The remote Relation of these pretenders to the Royal Stock, did much contribute to enflame the Divisions; Since none of them has a /236/ Title, which was not the subject of Dispute.

IT will not suit with the brevity I propose to descend into an Enumeration of the Competitors Names, who were not a few; Nor of their respective Claims and Pretensions, which may be seen in Mr. Pryn's Collections, Published from the Records of England.[1] It may suffice to notice, that the two best founded Competitors were Bruce and Baliol; Men of great Families, Estates and Followings, both in Scotland and England. So that the Community of Scotland being divided by the Interests of so many, and some of them very Powerful Rivals; It was difficult for them to determine the right of Preference without imminent hazard of a Civil War.

WHILE the Kingdom of Scotland was thus distracted, Edward the First of England, commonly called Langeshanks, as a Neighbour and Allie, say some, offer'd his Good Offices for a Just and peaceable Settlement of our Crown; Or, as others say, was by the Bishop of St. Andrews, and others /237/ delegat from the Community, desired to be Arbitrator in that weighty matter.

BUT whatsoever was the Motive, To the Borders he goes, well appointed and attended by many of his Nobles and Bishops, and also by the Militia of England, under colour and pretence, That he might the better support the title of the righteous Heir, and suppress any disorders from disappointed Competitors.

THIS seasonable piece of Friendship was kindly taken by the Scots, who did Commissionat some of their Nobles and Wise Men, to Meet and Confer with him: But these Commissioners were much surprized when the King of England demanded as a preliminary, that they should testifie their assent, of his being Umpire among the Competitors, as Superior Lord of Scotland. This demand could not but be very terrible to the Scots, in the dismal Circumstances they were then in, to find a Powerful Prince, who pretended to be a Friendly Mediator and Arbiter, trumping up an unjust Claim of Superiority over them.

NEVERTHELESS, they were very Nice and Bold in what concerned /238/ their Independency; For Walsingham tells us,[1] The Scots answered,

---

P.235 (1) *Foed. Angl.* p. 668.
P.236 (1) *Edw. I.* p. 513.
P.238 (1) p. 56.

"That they knew nothing of any such Superiority belonging to the King of England; Neither cou'd they answer such things without a Head and King, upon whom it was incumbent to understand such a demand; nor did they think, That they were bound at present to give any other answer, by reason of an Oath that they made one to another after the Death of King Alexander: Which Oath they were to observe under the pain of Excommunication". The King of England having taken this Answer into Consideration, He gave to the Scots a Charter, By which he "declared, That the coming of the Scots over Tweed into England shou'd not at another time be prejudicial to their coming again into England": Which was to smooth the demand he had made, that so highly offended them, and to entangle them in a second Conference, by bringing them again into England.

MR. Atwood is agreeable to himself when he pretends, That there was /239/ never any such Deed;[1] But Walsingham, as is said, positively asserts it, and Westminster also mentions it.[2] Our Author might have remember'd, That in the same Chapter of his Book, wherein he Questions that ever there was such a Deed, He calls Walsingham, a most faithful Historian.[3]

BY that Deed Edward designed to elude the Scots, and render them secure, till he try'd what he could do by Address, to gain his end, before he used open Force: And to keep a seeming good Correspondence with them, till his projects were ripe for Execution.

THIS Matter is related more favourably in the Instrument in the Tower of London, which says, That when Edward demanded the Nobles of Scotland to Recognize his Superiority, They desir'd time to Advise with those who were absent, and that as a Favour he allow'd them the next Day, but after prorogued it for three Weeks: This Instrument also says, That Edward offer'd to Instruct his Right of Superiority from the Chronicles of /240/ several Monasteries: And if they had any Muniments to exclude him from that Right, He appointed them to produce them, precisely at the next Meeting, protesting he was willing to do Justice.[1]

ADMITTING this fair fac'd Narration to be True, yet even by the Behaviour of the Scots, and by Edward's offering to prove his Right, It appears, That this Claim was a new thing to the Scots, and was not demanded till there were Intestine Divisions in Scotland, and when there was as many Factions and Parties almost in it, as there were Competitors to the Crown: And if Edward had been a fit Judge, The Scots would soon have exhibit many Evidences of their Independency, which in a few Years there-after they represented to the Pope.

IN the Interval of these Meetings, Edward and his Emissaries were busie in practising some of the Competitors; But their great Work was, in hatching and framing a Writing, by which the Competitors to the Crown were to submit their Claims and Pretensions to the Crown of Scotland, to be deter-mined /241/ by the King of England, as Supreme Lord and Superiour of the Kingdom of Scotland, And to engage to stand by his Decision.

P.239 (1) p. 99. (2) p. 436. (3) after p. 96.
P.240 (1) Pryn, *Edw.I.* p. 489.

THE Scots, in the Faith and Assurance made to them by the forementioned Deed, met Edward upon the day appointed, where, without any regard to these Assurances, He positively demanded the Competitors and Nobles to Recognize his Superiority; But they demurring, He exhibited the forsaid Submission ready fram'd, and by Force and Violence made the Competitors, who were present, sign it, and the other Nobles to Recognize that pretended Right.

THAT these Acknowledgments were extorted by Force and Fear, doth appear from the Accounts given by Westminster,[1] and Walsingham,[2] of what the Pope Wrote to the King of England, upon this Subject. And this Extortion is now evident and put beyond Denial and Question, by the account of this matter, given by the Abingdon Chronicle in the Bodleian Library, and by the Second Part of the Chronicle of Walter Hemmingford, /242/ in the Library of Trinity Colledge in Cambridge, Transcribed by the Learn'd Mr. Tyrrel, who from them says,[1] "That when the Scots seem'd dissatisfied, and not willing to comply with the Kings demands, He was so far incensed, That he Swore by St. Edward (the greatest Oath he ever used) That he would lose his Life in the prosecution of his just Rights; and indeed he had all the Militia of England then ready prepared to have fallen upon and compel them, if they had then denied what he demanded: So that it was no wonder, if not only the Scottish Nobility, but all the Competitors to the Crown either for Hope or Fear, made the above-mentioned Recognition of King Edward's Right to the Superiority over all Scotland".

THESE Things fully demonstrat, That Edward's assuming the Title and Office of Superior Lord of Scotland, was an evident Usurpation; and that the Acknowledgments made by the Scots of this pretended Right, were manifest Extortions, and Acts of /243/ Violence and Oppression; Wherefore not only these Acknowledgments, But also all others made in consequence of them were null and void.

THE Scots being thus under constraint by irresistible Force, They were obliged from time to time to follow such measures as the uncontrollable Will and Power of Edward did prescribe.

BUT he knowing, that this Submission wou'd not be effectual, unles he were also Master of the Kingdom, with the Castles and strong Holds in it; Therefore next day, he under pretence, That he might deliver them to the person who shou'd be found to have right to the Crown, proposed the sequestrating of them in his Hands; And made the Competitors sign another Deed, for his having possession of the Kingdom and Castles of Scotland, as Superior Lord thereof, till their Pretensions to the Crown were determined.

THESE two Deeds are transcribed by Westminster,[1] Walsingham,[2] and Pryn.[3] and by some English Historians.

/244/ WHEN the King of England had thus forced the Scots to recognize his pretended Superiority, and to give him possession of the Kingdom

---

P.241 (1) p. 436. (2) p. 80.
P.242 (1) *Hist.* Vol. 3. p. 65.
P.243 (1) p. 415. (2) p. 56. (3) p. 502 & 504.

and Castles; There wanted nothing in appearance to make his Right and Title perpetual, But a Removal or Destruction of such Deeds as were in our Archives, that evinced our Independency; Wherefore in August 1291, when the Disputes among the Competitors were at the greatest height, He issues forth a Writ impowering the Abbots of Dunfermling and Holy-rood-house, and three English Men therein named, to Review and Examine the Records of Scotland, which were in the Castle of Edinburgh, or elsewhere in that Kingdom; and to depositat them in such Places, as that King shou'd appoint. By this Writ the three English-men had power to proceed in that Affair without the two Scots Abbots.

MR. PRYN has publish'd this Writ from the English Records, to shew the great Esteem and Care King Edward had of the Records of Scotland,[1] But the Design of that King was far otherwise /245/ being either to carry off, or to cause destroy, what was in our Records that wou'd confound his usurp'd Superiority; For this Writ bears Date the 12 of August, and in a few days thereafter on the Eve of St. Bartholemew in the same Month, several Deeds which were clear Evidences of our Independency mentioned in an Inventary signed by the saids Commissioners, were taken by Order of King Edward from the Castle of Edinburgh to Berwick: From an ancient Transcript of which Inventary, and of an Inventary of our Records made in the year 1282, I have placed in the Appendix, a List of some Deeds that were among the Archives of Scotland, and either carried off by King Edward, or destroyed: Which by their very Titles show our Independency.

BESIDES, The Deeds concerning any Transactions between the two Kingdoms published by Mr. Rymer Historiographer of England, do fully manifest, That we have had Deeds in our Archives in relation to our Liberties, that have been either carried off, or destroyed; Since some of them are taken by that Learn'd Person from the Originals, and others from /246/ the Records. Nor can I mention this, without a due acknowledgement of Thanks to that worthy Gentleman; By whose Candor and Industry we are favoured with the Publication of many Deeds that evince our Independency, and illustrat our History.

WITHIN some few Months after these Muniments of our Liberty were carried off, Baliol was made King by Edward, who not only did Homage to him for the Kingdom, but also did acquit him of some Engagements he had made to the Scots after his usurpation of the Superiority.

BUT behold the Fate of Baliol, and in him of all the Betrayers of the Liberties of their Countrey; For no sooner had the King of England gain'd his Purpose by him, but he despised and contemn'd him; First, in the matter of a Complaint by a Burgess of Berwick; and thereafter in an Appeal by Mackduff to the King of England, by which he was toss'd from one Parliament of England to another for some time: Yea when the Cause was try'd, so far was he undervalued, That he was not allow'd Procurators, nor

---

P.244 (1) Ibid. p. 548.

was he permitted to plead his Cause in his Seat, but was made to /247/ rise, and go to the usual place of Pleading.

THESE Affronts rouz'd the Courage even of this easie Man, to assert the Independency of the Kingdom, and to vindicat the Injuries done to the Scots by Edward, in extorting Acknowledgments of Superiority, whereupon a War broke out between the two Nations; But the Scots being so unhappy in having Baliol to their King, and by some fatal Divisions among their Leaders, had not that Success in defending of their Liberties, as they had afterwards, when in much worse Circumstances, under the Conduct of the brave and valiant Robert the Bruce. So that again Baliol submitted to the King of England, and Edward by Force and Violence, and by many Tortures and Threats compell'd most of the Nation to acknowledg and swear to his usurped Right of Superiority. Nevertheless the Scots never gave over to struggle for their Liberties, but upon all occasions exposed themselves to the utmost Dangers in asserting them: For they justly reckon'd, that Engagements extorted by Force, were void and null, and from /248/ them they were absolved by the Pope.

BUT to return, Baliol was for some time a Prisoner in England, but ended his unfortunat days as an Exile in France, being reckon'd by the Scots, the Betrayer of their Kingdom. And tho' Edward Baliol his Son, by the under-hand Dealing at first of Edward the Third, and then by his avow'd Assistance, usurped the Crown of Scotland for a little time: Yet the Scots expell'd him and his Posterity for ever.

IT'S not my Business to relate the many Bloody Battles and Engagements between the two Nations, occasioned by the imaginary Claim of Homage, so zealously pursued by Edward the First; Nor how in the days of his Son Edward the Second, The Scots beat the English out of Scotland, and reduced three of the Northern Counties of England to their Obedience, the King of England having much ado to defend the rest,[1] Nor of the unsuccessful Expedition of Edward the Third against the Scots.

I SHALL only notice, That at length there was a Peace concluded /249/ between King Robert Bruce and Edward the Third: Of which Peace, one Article was, That the King of England should renounce all Claim of Homage to Scotland, and acquit all Deeds of Homage and Subjection, and deliver them up: Which, tho' of no great Consequence, since all these Deeds were extorted, yet shews the great Care of our Ancestors to remove all things that had the least shadow to question their Independency.

OF this Renunciation, I have placed a Copy in the Appendix,[1] taken from two Manuscripts in the Library of the Honourable Faculty of Advocats: There is also a Copy of this Deed ingross'd in the Continuation of Fordon's History, in the Library of the College of Edinburgh, and I have also seen Copies of it in the Records of some Monasteries.

MR. ATWOOD pretends, That this Release was granted by Edward the 3d, while he was under Age, by the Influence of Mortimer; And, That it was

---

P.248 (1) Tyrrel's *Hist*. V. 3. Introd. p. 8.
P.249 (1) Numb. IX.

done without the Consent of the States of the Realm; For among the Articles upon which Mortimer was Impeach'd in /250/ Parliament attainted, and afterwards Executed for high Treason, One was, That he Confederated with the Scots, against the Honour of England; Another, That he caused all the Ancient Records of the Scots Homage, and Obedience to the Kings of England to be delivered to them.[1] To vouch these Articles, Mr. Atwood Quotes in his Margin, The Rolls of Parliament, and with them joyns Grafton, a late Author of a very low Character.

IF Mr. Atwood be not grossly Ignorant of the tenor of this Release, which he undertakes to Impugn, he seems to be pretty bold, To give a Crown'd Head of his own Nation so plainly the Lie; For Edward the 3d, in that Deed, says in express words, That he granted it with the Advice and Consent of his Parliament,[2] and our Author's Most faithful Historian Walsingham confirms this.[3]

HE also seems to belie the Records of the English Parliament, in adducing them to vouch these two Articles of Impeachment against Mortimer; For the Ingenious Mr. Tyrrel has of late /251/ Published the Articles exhibited in Parliament, against Mortimer, from the French Original in the Tower of London,[1] wherein the two Articles mentioned by Mr. Atwood, are not to be found.

THE Tragical History of those times doth fully display the fatal Consequences of the Encroachments made by Edward the First, upon our Liberties, and the various Turns of Fortune in a long and Bloody War, wherein the Scots were in the end Victorious. Nor have some of the English Historians been wanting to make suitable Reflections upon these calamitous times.

AMONG others, The Accomplisht Mr. Daniel has some thoughts worthy of Remark, This Gentleman says,[2] "That upon Edward the first's Claiming the Superiority of Scotland, brake out that mortal Dissention between the two Nations, that consumed more Christian Blood, wrought more Spoil and Destruction, and continued longer than ever Quarrel we read did, between any two People of the World. That all the Successive Kings /252/ of England had their share more or less in this miserable Affliction, both to their great Expense of Treasure, and extreme Hinderance in all other their designs That it doth not now concern to stand upon any points of Honour, whether of the two Nations did the bravest Exploits in these Times, seing who had the better was beaten, neither did the Overcomer Conquer when he had done what he could: That little which was gain'd cost so much more than it was worth, as it had been better not to have been had at all. And if any side had the Honour, It was the invaded Nation; Which being the weaker and smaller, seems never to have been Subdued, tho' often Overcome: Continuing, notwithstanding of all their Miseries, resolute to preserve their Liberties; Which never People of the World more Nobly Defended against so Potent and Rich a Kingdom as England: By the which

---

P.250 (1) p. 316. (2) Append. Numb. IX. (3) p. 128.
P.251 (1) *Hist.* V.3. p. 362. (2) *Hist. of England,* p. 192.

without an admirable Hardiness and Constancy, It had been impossible, but they must have been brought to an utter Consternation."

HAVING now proven our Independency from the English Historians /253/ and Records, I shall take the Liberty to offer a few things from the Fragments left us of our Records, which confirm our Independency, and Illustrat some parts of the History of the Reign of Robert the Bruce, that perhaps are not well known.

IF then, we cast our Eyes upon what is left in Record to us by our brave Ancestors, who lived in the Days of King Robert Bruce, We will find Noble Monuments of our Liberties. The Calamities of Scotland were in those Days many and heavy; But we have some Comfort, for the loss of a valuable Treasure of our Antiquities, That there yet remain Excellent MANIFESTOS of our Independency.

OF these, The first may be reckon'd, A Declaration in Parliament, By the Clergy and Community of Scotland: Whereof I have seen a Copy among the Collections of the Learn'd and Industrious Antiquary Sir James Balfour, unto which is subjoyn'd a Memorandum, That he copied it with his own Hand, from the Treasury of Antiquities, kept by Sir Robert Cotton at Westminster. It is the same Word by Word, with a Declaration by the Clergy of /254/ this Kingdom, met in a National Council, with the Addition only of the Words, And Community, Or, People of Scotland, in such places of it, as mention the Clergy. Of this Parliamentary Declaration, The Conclusion, and date runs, Given in a Parliament, Holden at St. Andrews in Scotland the 17 of March, 1308.

THE Original Declaration by the Clergy in a National Council of Scotland, Holden at Dundee in February 1309, is yet extant, and to be seen among our Records in the Parliament House, from whence I have Published it in the Appendix.[1] I have likewise seen in several Collections of Antiquities, Copies of these Declarations; As also a Copy of a Declaration in the same Terms, by the Bishops, wherein their Names are particularly exprest, which I have subjoyn'd to the Translation of the Clergy's Declaration.[2]

WHAT is contain'd in these Declarations, being done and testified by the Unanimous and joynt Sentiment of a Parliament, and of a National Council, the two Supreme Judicatures /255/ Civil and Ecclesiastick of this Kingdom, is of great Authority; And they indeed contain Matters of great Import, in relation to our Liberties.

FOR the Satisfaction of all, I have Translated this Deed of the Clergy: And also another Evidence of our Independency, The Letter of the Nobility and Community to the Pope:[1] If in any part, the Translations please not, The Appendix presents the reader with them both in their Original Latin.

BEING thus, It's needless to make long Reflections upon these Declarations; Only to pursue the Threed of this Essay, It appears from them, that our Ancestors were very sensible, How much their Calamities, and the

---

P.254 (1) Numb. 12. (2) Numb. 14.
P.255 (1) Append. Numb. 13 & 14.

danger of their Liberties, flow'd from the unhappy competitions and Factions among themselves. They mournfully Reflected upon and bewail'd the doleful Consequences of their Divisions; Which had brought the Kingdom to the brink of perpetual Ruine: And as a warning to Posterity, They tell, That nothing could have /256/ preserved the Kingdom and Government from Perishing, unless by Divine Providence, They had united their Hearts and Counsels for the common Safety. They complain of the King of England's imposing a King upon them: And with all Honour and regard to the Royal Line, They boldly assert their Priviledges in the Settlement of the Crown.

THEY Publish their just Resentment against Baliol, the betrayer of the Kingdom, and express much Gratitude to Robert the Bruce their King, as being under GOD, the Instrument of their Delivery: And, with a becoming Generosity, measure the Obligations they had to their Deliverer, by the Dangers and Evils from which they were rescued. They frankly own'd, That the Kingdom had been several times in Danger of being lost, but was still recover'd by the valour of their Kings. And they publickly proclaim to the World, That any former Deeds, containing the consent of the People and Commonalty, in prejudice of their Liberties, were Extorted by irresistible Force and Violence, and by threats of Torture, and other Terrors, which might distract the /257/ Spirit of the best of Men, and are incident to the most composed Mind.

CAN there be a greater Evidence of the Independency and Freedom of a Nation, Than the Liberties which we find our Ancestors exerted. One remarkable Instance is in a plain and weighty Paragraph of these repeated solemn Declarations by the Clergy and Community of Scotland. In them it is said; That the Right and Title of King Robert the Bruce to the Crown, was declared by the Judgment of the People, That he was assum'd to be King by their Knowledg and Consent, for ends mention'd by them; That being Advanced by their Authority to the Crown, He was thereby Solemnly made King of Scotland. These appear to be Important and Comprehensive Sentences. How far they establish and confirm a Revolution Settlement, as being agreeable to our ancient Constitution; Or how far they discover, That a Claim of Right is no Novelty in Scotland, but was a Principle and Practice of our Fathers: And how far the Title of King Robert Bruce and his Successors, who have sway'd our Scepter, for these four Hundred Years, is settled and Founded in these Principles, /258/ I leave to every Man to Judge: But sure I am, These Declarations plainly evince, That any Homages made by the People of Scotland, to Edward the first, were extorted Acknowledgments.

IN pursuance of their Independency and Freedom, and also for security of the Kingdom, and to shew that England had no Concern in the Settlement of our Crown: There was about four or five years after these Declarations, a most solemn Act entailing our Crown, made at Air in the year 1315, by the King, and Lady Marjory his Daughter, and Lord Edward Bruce his Brother: By the Bishops, Abbots, Priors, Deans, Arch-deacons, and other Prelates: By the Earls, Barons, Knights, and by the remanent of the Community of the Kingdom of Scotland, Clergy and Laity.

BY this Act, they unanimously entail and provide, the CROWN of Scotland, after the decease of King Robert the Bruce, to the Heirs-male of his Body, which failing, to Lord Edward Bruce his Brother, and to the Heirs-male of his Body: Which failing, to Lady Marjory Bruce the Kings Daughter, and failing of her to the nearest Heir /259/ of the Body of King Robert Bruce: With this Condition, that Lady Marjory marry with Consent of her Father; And in the case of his decease, with Consent of the greater part of the Community of Scotland.

BY the same Act, If the Heirs-male of King Robert, or of his Brother Lord Edward were Minors, Thomas Randolf Earl of Moray, was appointed to be Governour of the Heir and Kingdom, until the Heir by the Community or major Part was declared fit for Government. This Earl was also made Governour to the Heir of Lady Marjory, if she died in Widowity, and left her Heir Minor.

BY that Act, it is provided, that if all these Heirs of Entail should fail, the Earl of Moray was to be Governour of the Kingdom, until he cou'd conveniently call a Meeting of the Prelates, Earls, Barons and others of the Community to settle the Succession and Government.

LORD Edward Bruce who was the first presumptive Heir of Entail became King of Ireland, where he died without Issue-male. Likewise Lady Marjory the next presumptive Heir deceased, leaving only a Son.

/260/ KING Robert Bruce having as yet no Heir-male of his Body, There was an Act of Parliament, made in the Year 1318: By the which, The States Swear to stand by the King, in Defence of the Rights and Liberties of the Kingdom against all deadly, under the pain of High Treason. It is also unanimously agreed; That if the King died without Male-Issue, That Robert the Son of the then deceased Lady Marjory his Daughter, by her Husband Walter Stewart of Scotland shou'd succeed as Heir to his Grand-father in the Kingdom; And if he, or any other Heir of the Body of the King, shall be Minor at the King's Death, Thomas Randolf Earl of Moray, and failing him by decease James Lord Douglas, were appointed Regents, until by the States, the Heir was thought fit for Government.

THE States wisely considering, how much some Questions about the Succession had embarass'd the Nation, They by this Act determine the course of Succession, and the Points that had been formerly controverted between Bruce and Baliol.

FOR Satisfaction of the Curious, I have placed in the Appendix, the /261/ Copies of these two Acts of Settlement taken from the collections of a worthy Gentleman long ago deceased, who transcribed them from the Originals. Copies of these Acts are also to be seen in the continuation of Fordon's History in the Library of the Colledge of Edinburgh, fairly written upon Vellum: And in a Collection of Antiquities in the Lawyers Library.

BY these Declarations and Settlements may be seen, the great Care of our Brave and Judicious Ancestors, in some matters of the utmost Concern; and amongst other things, their Concern to declare the Rights of our Kings, in such manner, as shew'd them to be Independent of the King of England, who then claim'd the Superiority.

THE next Monument of our Independency in those days, is the known letter by the Nobility & Community to the Pope in the year 1320. It has been published both in Scotland and England; But some words being wanting, and others mistaken, I have by the Courtesie of the Noble Person in whose Hands there is a fair Original, with most of the Seals intire, given a more exact Copy of it, in the Appendix.

/262/ IN this Letter, we have the Enumeration of some Noble and worthy Patriots, Protectors and Asserters of our Liberty; whose Names will ever live in the lasting Records of Fame, to incite their Noble Successors to due Regards for the Liberties of their Countrie; or to stand as a perpetual Mark of their Degeneracy.

ALBEIT Edward the first in his Letter to the Pope, did plead the Superiority, upon his Predecessors being descended of Brutus, who with others of a Trojan Race, in the days of Eli and Samuel, vanquished Giants; Yet our Nobles wou'd not rencounter that Fable, or defeat the whimsical Story of Albanactus, by such another Tale hammer'd out by our Monks, of our being descended of Scota the Daughter of Pharaoh; But they give a more probable and reasonable Account of their Origin. They glory in their being a free People under the Government of a great Number of KINGS, of an uninterrupted Royal Race: And that they were blest with being among the first who embraced the Christian Faith. Tho' Edward the first did treat them in his Letter with the harsh Names of Perfidious and Rebellious, /263/ yet like Gentlemen and Men of Breeding, They gave him the Title of Magnificent Prince; And with as much Modesty as the Subject would allow, rehearse the Injuries he had done to them, when they were without a Head, and expected no ill at his Hands. They in Terms, like to these contained in the before-mentioned Declarations by the Clergy and Community, acknowledge King Robert as their Deliverer, who by the Divine Providence, by the Right of Succession, and by their Consent, was made their King. And with much Boldness, They declare, That if he subjected the People, or their Kingdom to the English, they would thrust him out, and make another King. That their Plea was not for Glory, Riches, or Honour, But only for LIBERTY, which no good Man loses but with his Life. Being so zealous of their Liberties, they were not asham'd to acknowledge the small Bounds of their Countrey, but rather rejoyced and gloried in their being contented with their own, and that in so little a Spot of Ground, they and their Predecessors had maintained their Independency.

/264/ IN this letter, we find the Number of our Kings exceed what is mentioned in our History; The Learn'd Sir George Mackenzie thinks, they have numbered some Regents and Vice-Roys amongst our Kings.[1] Whatever be in this; It is of no Advantage to the Opposers of our Antiquity, since it doth not diminish the Number of our Princes; And perhaps in these days,

---

P.264 (1) *Preced. & Herauldr.* p. 19.

our ancient History, and the Number of our Princes was better known, than now, when the Annals of some of our Kings may be lost by the Havock of our Records and Monuments made by Edward the First.

BY what is said, It plainly appears, That in the days of King Robert Bruce, Scotland enjoy'd her ancient Liberties, and Independency, and ever since continues in the Possession of them: For whatsoever were the base Surrenders of the *De Facto* Kings, the mean Spirited John Baliol, and his Son Edward of the same temper, yet these can be no infringement of the Soveraignty of our Crown.

THE Forgeries and Falshood of the Evidences of the Homage paid by /265/ King David Bruce, and by King James the First, are already noticed. And tho' amongst the Deeds Forged by Harding, There may be found proofs of the Homage of this David, and also of his Nephew and Successor King Robert the Second, the Grandfather of our King James the First; Yet these Deeds being own'd as notorious Forgeries, by the Learn'd Mr. Rymer Historiographer, and the Ingenious Mr. Tyrel,[1] I shall take no further notice of them.

FROM the Reign of our King James the First, It is universally acknowledged, There was no demand or surmise about the Homage, until King Henry the Eighth (as is said) made a long Narration concerning it, in his Declaration of War against his Nephew King James the Fifth.

WHAT is in that Declaration of War, in behalf of the Homage, is Collected from Records and Proofs already Refuted; There's indeed one singular Article of Indictment against us, by which we are arraign'd, For stealing out of the King of England's Treasury divers Instruments, made and /266/ Sealed with the Seals of our Kings' testifying their Homage, which nevertheless, were afterward recovered again.[1]

IT'S not to be imagined, That under this horrid Charge, are comprehended such Instruments as were voluntarly given up, and released by Richard the First, and Edward the 3d. Of other Deeds made by our Kings importing Homage we have not heard, but of these scandalous Charters that were Forged by Harding, and delivered by him to the Treasurer of King Henry the 6th of England, and depositat in the Chapter House of Westminster; Which I presume are the only Original Instruments with our Kings Seals, testifying the Homage to be found in the Archives of England. This I may with the more boldness say, because I have perused the Repertory or List of the Writs concerning Scotland in that Treasury.

IF then, to protect these abominable Forgeries from an obvious exception, and ground of discovery, by their being so lately depositat in the Treasury of Westminster, a Story was /267/ invented of their being stollen and recovered again, and we publickly arrain'd for the stealth of the Compilers of that Declaration; This still more and more discovers the wicked Injuries done to us in the Claim of Homage.

P.265 (1) *Hist. of Engl.* 3. Vol. Introd. p. 9.
P.266 (1) *Vid.* Copy of this *Declaration* in Holinshed's *Hist. of Scotl.* p. 326.

THE Evidences of Homage contained in the Letter of Bishop Tonstal, in the Reign of King Edward the 6th, are already toucht. In those days, an assuming Lawyer, like my Friend, Published a little Book, Intituled, *The Kynges Title to Scotlande*; Written I suppose, in order to betray the Justice and Innocence of that Good and Religious Prince. In it the Author repeats the common Cant, upon that subject from Brutus. This Treatise is of no use, but only to confirm, That all that has been said in that Argument is stuff'd with blunders and falshood: For besides the usual Topicks, this Author disguises many Historical passages. Amongst others, he, and after him Hollinshed,[1] says, That Robert the 3d King of Scotland, by appointment of Henry the Fourth of England, resigned his Crown, and delivered /268/ his Son James, being then of the Age of 9 Years, to this King Henry to remain in his Custody, and Wardship, as of his Superior Lord, according to the old Laws of King Edward the Confessor.

NOTHING can be more gross; For how this Prince came in the Hands of the King of England, and how Afflicting it was to his Father, who died for Grief, is very well known. And tho' this James, by the happiness of a sweet Temper, and of an undisturbed Education, became one of the best Kings that ever mounted a Throne; Yet the manner of his being taken Prisoner by the English in time of Peace, and his being detain'd so long in England, admitts of no reasonable excuse or pretext.

MR. ATWOOD will not leave the Homage at the Reign of Edward the Sixth, but to distinguish himself by being singular, will hand it forward to the days of Oliver Cromwel. The Metaphisical Gentleman then pretends, That the Subjection was own'd in the Reign of Queen Elizabeth, by telling, As the Declaration of War by Queen Mary of Scots, was contrary to her Duty, who was an Homager to the Crown of /269/ England, the Nobility of Scotland by disbanding the Army then rais'd, disavow'd that Renunciation of Homage, and therein submitted to the Right of the Crown of Scotland.[1]

THIS is a nice Original of Historical Chimistry in our Author, who can extract Homage from the Nobles of Scotland, their Disbanding and Discountenancing an Army, rais'd to the prejudice of the Reformation in both Nations, and for concurring with our Neighbours, in Strengthening that blessed Turn in the Matter of Religion.

BY such Reasonings and Inferences, We may be accounted Homagers, by concurring in the late happy Revolution; Some of our Troops being Disbanded for not being affected to that Interest: But it's to be hoped, Wiser Men will make more suitable and solid Reflections, from the part we acted upon both these Occasion.

OUR Author allows the Homage to have continued in suspence during the Reigns of James and Charles the First; But that soon after the Affairs /270/ of England and Scotland had a new Face. He tells us, That Cromwel and General Monk having subdued Scotland, settled Garisons where they

---

P.267 (1) *Hist.* Vol. 1. p. 127.
P.269 (1) p. 316.

found it requisite to keep them under the Parliament of England, as the part who acted, called themselves.[1] He tells us, That several Acquisitions in the times of the Usurpation, were retain'd by the English, such as Dunkirk and Jamaica:[2] Then if he cannot hit us by the Homage, He would fain throw us in with the Acquisitions by a singular whim; That King Charles the 2d by taking the Solemn League and Covenant, effectually abdicated or renounced, being King of England: And whatever Right over the Scots, was acquired during that Abdication, must needs have been effectual to all Intents and Purposes:[3] To this he adds, That the Power of England had Opportunity to compleat the Reduction of Scotland, while King Charles had abjured the Church of England.[4] Thus by the Courtesie of Mr. Atwood, we're made a subdued Province of England.

/271/ THESE Mystical Schemes are so very Ridiculous, That it may be thought they will for ever be peculiar to our Author.

I MUST own myself to be very little Versed in the Transactions of those times; But by any glimmerings I have of them, I would think, That things of a different nature may be drawn from them.

AFTER the most barbarous Murder of King Charles the First, by the colour of Law and Justice; We having own'd Charles the 2d, his Son, as our King, There was an Army came from England, under the Command of General Cromwel, who defeat the Scots Army at Dumbar; But this defeat was as fatal to England as to Scotland; As will appear by what follows.

IT'S already noticed, That Edward the first of England, endeavoured to be Master of Scotland, to make way for his intended absolute Power of England. What could not be effectuat by the Violence of that War-like Prince, and of his Son, and grand-child, Edward the Second and Third, was wrought by the cunning and address of an Usurper: It being well known, How Cromwel, after the Battle /272/ of Dumbar, insinuated himself upon the Scots, which rais'd a jealousie of his Power in the long Parliament, who were about to remove or retrench him: But he having an English Army in Scotland at his Command (tho' he had his Commission and Instructions from that Parliament) He fairly bad his Constituents defiance, turn'd them disgracefully out of Westminster-Hall, and then discovered his purposes for himself; Who from a General, was rais'd to an Office, in which, tho' he had not the Name, yet enjoy'd all the Powers and Authority of an absolute Soveraign.

THESE things are plainly to be seen in the Annals of those times; And the Foreign Historians who have Written the Life of Oliver Cromwel, take particular notice of the Victory at Dumbar in Scotland, as what laid the foundation of his Usurpation, and uncontrollable Power.[1]

NOR needs Mr. Atwood mention the settling of Garisons here, as /273/ Evidences of our being reduced, since they were chiefly kept to overaw England: And it may be remembred, That as the English Army in Scotland

---

P.270 (1) p. 317. (2) p. 319. (3) p. 320. (4) p. 323.
P.272 (1) Ragunet *Hist. D' Oliv. Cromwel,* Lib.4. p. 236 &c. G. Leti. *Hist. D' Ol. Cr.* 2d Part Lib. 4. p. 191, &c.

did contribute to the rise of Oliver Cromwel; So General Monk by the same Army, in concert with the Scots, did again turn the ballance of Britain at the Restauration

HAD Mr. Atwood, in stead of his empty Treatise about an imaginary Superiority, employ'd his Reading and Thought, to present the World with some Arguments and Instances, to evince, That the Liberties of both Kingdoms are so stated, That the one cannot Suffer, without endangering the other, he had done better Service to both.

A GREAT Statesman, the famous Sir William Temple, has a noble and Remarkable Thought and Reflection, upon the Quarrels between the two Kings, Malcolm Canmoir of Scotland, and William the First of England, which seems to point at somewhat beyond the Illustration of the History of those ancient times. Whatsoever is done by this worthy Gentleman, is so fine, That I presume it will not be /274/ unacceptable to transcribe that notable passage.[1]

"For some days (saith this great Man) the two Armies stood at a Bay, seeming both prepared for a fierce Encounter, and yet both content to delay it, from a mutual respect they had for one anothers Forces and Dispositions. They were indeed not much unequal in Numbers, nor in the Bravery and Order of their Troops; Both Kings were Valiant and Wise, having been train'd up in Arms, inured to Dangers, and much embroil'd at Home in the beginning of their Reigns. They were now animated to a Battle, by their own courage, as well as their Souldiers; But yet both considered the Event, in the uncertainty and the consequence: The loss of a Battle might prove the loss of a Crown, and the Fortune of one day determine the fate of a Kingdom: and they knew very well, that whoever Fights a Battel, with what Number and Forces, what Provisions and Orders or Appearances /275/ soever of Success, yet at the best runs a Venture, and leaves much at the Mercy of Fortune, from Accidents not to be foreseen by any Prudence, or governed by any Conduct or Skill. These Reflections began to dispose both Kings to the Thoughts of ending their quarrel by a Peace, rather than a Battle, and tho' both had the same Inclinations, yet each of them was unwilling first to discover it, lest it might be interpreted to proceed from Apprehensions of Weakness or Fears, and thereby dishearten their own Soldiers, or encourage their Enemies. The Scots at length begun the Overture, which was received by King William, with a shew of indifference, but with a conceal'd Joy, and the more reasonable, as having the greater Stake, the less to win, and the more to lose by the issue of a Battle".

WITH my Heart, I regrate, That ever this Controversie about the Homage shou'd have been again brought into the Field, and not the less, that I am unluckly engaged in it. What I have advanc'd upon that Subject is without any Design to offend: And I hope, I will not be blam'd, so long /276/ as Self-defence is justifiable. I have all due regard for the Noble and Mighty Kingdom of England, and for the Learn'd and Ingenious of that Nation: Wherein I differ from any of them, I have offer'd my Reasons, which

---

P.274 (1) *Introduct. to the Hist. of Engl.* p. 120, 121 & 122.

if Lame, I humbly submit to Correction. And I presume the judicious will consider, under what Disadvantages any person who undertakes this Province is, when our Archives have suffered so many Misfortunes; So that for our Defence, there is now nothing left, but what can be glean'd from the English Historians and Records, and from a few Fragments of our own Records.

HAVING examined the most material Arguments and Proofs, brought by Mr. Atwood, for the Homage, It will be expected, that I shou'd take a little notice of the Scar-crows with which he would frighten Opposers.

BEING possest with an Imagination, That he has demonstrat Scotland to be an Appennage of the English Monarchy, he wou'd bring in all who deny his Doctrine, as guilty of high Treason, by their derogating from the right to the Crown of England ascertain'd /277/ by the Act of Settlement in that Nation.[1] And at best reckons his Opponents to be either such Scots-men as are influenced by French Counsel,[2] or the Non-jurors in both Kingdoms.[3]

WHETHER such Thoughts and Expressions are more Injurious or Insolent, is hard to determine: Cou'd Impudence go higher, than to give to a Statute of his own Countrey, such a scandalous Gloss and Stretch, which was never thought nor designed by the Law-givers? Such a wicked and silly commentary is not to be paralelled. Nor cou'd Malice devise any thing more Calumnious, than to conclude all Scots Men, who will not calmly surrender their Liberties, to be deeply engaged with France:[4] And to reckon all English men, who are not in his ridiculous Sentiments to be Enemies to the Government. These be shrewd Presumptions, that there was great Danger of Life, Fortune, and Reputation, even under the colour of Law, in the District of such a wild Chief Justice. /278/ One who under the Cloak of a Protestant Interest,[1] has so unseasonably, publisht a Book with an Alarming Title, stufft with provoking doctrine and irritating consequences, who justifies Fables, defends Forgeries, and startles at no Absurdities, cannot but be thought a fit Tool for mischievous Purposes.

THE long and Bloody Wars in the Reigns of the first three Edwards, give us a doleful Prospect of the lamentable consequences of this quarrel, which to revive, none will wish or promote, but mercenary Scriblers and Fire-brands that are enemies to both Nations.

IT'S not presumeable, that any Person of Worth or Reason in cool thoughts, and after glancing upon the true State of the Matter, will Support or Countenance any Attempts upon our Independency. Far less can it be supposed, that the wise People of England, who have so much Signalized themselves in behalf of the Protestant Religion, and of the common Liberties of Europe against a Powerful Prince, will ever overturn the /279/ Liberties of a free People, who have chearfully join'd in the common Cause. How much in the late and present Wars, Our Countrey-men in the most Bloody and Desperate Engagements have shown their wonted Bravery, and with

---

P.277 (1) p. 568 & 569. (2) p. 570. (3) p. 573. (4) p. 575.
P.278 (1) p. 569.

what Advantages is sufficiently known; And if Justice be done them, will be recorded in the Annals of this Age

KING William and Queen Mary were cautious as to any thing, that might give the least Umbrage of this Claim; For at the Solemnity of their Coronation in England, Tho' they were both of the Blood Royal of Scotland, and that this Good Queen, as a Daughter of Scotland, might have born the Armorial Ensigns of that Kingdom, yet in this August Appearance, because Our Estates had not then Declared them Our Soveraigns, They did not use these Arms, But Supplied the Quartering of their Royal Atchievements, by a Repetition of the Armorial bearing of Ireland, which is to be seen by the Records of the Herauld-Office in England, and by a Print of the Procession observed at that Solemnity.

IT may be presumed, that it is the /280/ sincere and fervent Wish and Prayer of all Good Men, That upon Just and Equal, and by consequence lasting Terms, a Good Understanding may be Established between two Nations, planted by Nature in one Isle, People of the same Language, linked by frequent Inter-marriages in Affinity and Consanguinity, and by the Blessing of Heaven already Engaged to one another, by the most Endearing Tye of Religion.

THUS, In Duty to my Countrey, and in Self-defence, when without any Provocation attack'd by Mr. Atwood, I with all Submission have offered my Thoughts concerning our Independency, wherein I have been the more full and plain, in Relation to the unbecoming Artifices employ'd to Support the imaginary Claim of Homage, That if possible, the Abettors of that Claim may be Silenced, who, pretend what they will, yet can have no other Design but to Foment and Create Misunderstandings between two Protestant Independent Kingdoms, which I pray GOD may continue in Peace and Amity, while Sun and Moon endure.

FINIS

The Appendix Containing the Copies of several CHARTERS
And other WRITS; With the SEALS of four of them Engraven in
COPPER-PLATE, Which Illustrate some Passages in the
preceding ESSAY.

1. Copy of the Forg'd Charter of Homage by Malcolm Canmoir, King of Scotland with the Seal. Taken from a Copper-plate Copy, the Original being of late casually somewhat defaced.

2. Copies of five Genuine Charters of Edgar King of Scots with his Seal. Taken from the Originals.

3. Copy of the Forg'd Charter of Homage by Edgar King of Scotland with the Seal. Taken from the Original.

4. Copy of the Copy of a Charter said to be granted by Edgar King of Scotland. Taken from the Copy in the *Monasticon anglicanum* and from a Copy at Durham.

5. Copy of the Duplicated Charter by William Rufus king of England. Taken from the Original.

6. Copy of a Charter of Thor Longus with his Seal. Taken from the Original.

7. Copy of the Deed of Pension by Henry the sixth of England to John Harding. Taken from the Records. Rot. pat. 36. H. 6. p. 1. m. 8.

8. Copy of the Renunciation made by Richard the first King of England, Of the Deed of Homage for the Kingdom of Scotland, Extorted by Henry the second his Father from William King of Scotland. Taken from the Original by Mr Rymer the Historiographer of England, and published in the first Tome of the *Foedera &C Angliae.*

9. Copy of the Renunciation by Edward the third King of England of all Claims of Homage from Scotland. Taken from two MSS. in the Library of the Honourable Faculty of Advocats, the one entitled *Tractatus Scotici*, and the other *Extracta de Chronicis Scotiae.*

10. Copy of a Proclamation by QUEEN ELISABETH, declaryng the untrueth of certaine malitious Reportes Devised and Published in the Realme of Scotlande Taken from a Copy Printed by Richard Jugge and John Cawood Printers to this Queen.

11. Copy of a LETTER from the Nobility and Community of SCOTLAND, to the Pope, asserting the Independency of that Kingdom. Taken from an Original, there being one sent to the Pope, and another preserved as an Evidence of our Liberty.

12. Copy of a Manifesto by the Clergy of Scotland, Concerning the Liberties of the Kingdom, and Shewing any Deeds in the contrair to have been extorted by Force, Violence, &c. Taken from the Original.

13. The LETTER from the NOBILITY and Community of SCOTLAND to the POPE. Translated from the Latine. [Also known as the Declaration of Arbroath.]

14. The MANIFESTO or DECLARATION of the Clergy of SCOTLAND. Translated from the Latine.

15. Copy of a Deed by King Richard, the first of England, To William King of Scotland, concerning the Liberties and Rights belonging to the King of Scotland, when he goes to the Court of England. This deed and the other five Deeds following are Published by Mr. Rymer, the Historiographer of England, in his Collection of Treaties &C and are taken from the Originals or Records. From the Original.

16. Copy of a Publication of the Intention of King Henry the third of England, wherein he declares, he had no design to Prejudge or Infringe the Liberties of Scotland, but to his power [sic] to preserve them. Taken from the Records.

17. Copy of the Letters of Safe Conduct by King Henry the third of England, to the King and Queen of Scotland. Taken from the Records.

18. Copy of a Letter by the said King Henry To the King of Scotland concerning a Grant by the Pope. Taken from the Records.

19. Copy of a Deed by the said King Henry the third, Concerning the Queen of Scotland's being with Child and brought to bed in England. Taken from the Records.

20. Copy of a Deed by the same King of England to the like purpose: For observance of which this King and King of the Romans, and several of the English Nobles give their Oaths. Taken from the Records.

21. Copy of a Deed by William King of Scotland, To the monks of the Cestertian order wherein the Ancient liberty of that Kingdom is asserted. Taken from the Original.

22. Copy of a Letter of the Governours of Scotland, To Edward the first King of England. Taken from the English Records by Mr. Rymer.

23. Copy of a part of the Letter of Edward the first King of England, To the Pope Concerning his Right and Title to the Kingdom of Scotland.

24. Copy of a Declaration of the Estates of Scotland, concerning the Settlement of the Crown in the days of King Robert Bruce.

25. Copy of an Act of Parliament in the time of King Robert the Bruce for Security of the Kingdom.

26. List of some of the Writs concerning the Independency of the Kingdom and Church of Scotland, which were amongst the Records of that Kingdom, and were carried off by Edward the first; or destroyed. Listed are twenty-one CHARTAE and ten BULLAE PAPALES.

JOHN SPOTSWOOD, PROFESSOR OF LAW:
A PRELIMINARY SKETCH

By JOHN W. CAIRNS, LL.B., PH.D.,

Department of Scots Law, University of Edinburgh*

In the later seventeenth century, members of the Faculty of Advocates expressed increasing concern about the unavailability of legal education in the Scottish universities and the consequent necessity for study abroad. As Dean of Faculty from 1682 to 1689, Sir George Mackenzie, whose tenure as dean was particularly associated with educational issues, energetically sought finance to establish a chair, but this was not achieved.[1] In the 1690s, the Faculty's attempts to ensure the foundation of a chair in law continued,[2] and, in the context of a general attempt to expand the scope of university education, the University of Edinburgh itself pursued the creation of such a professorship.[3] Adequate funding was still not forthcoming, however, although the influence of the Queensberry family obtained from parliament for Alexander Cunningham a salary and appointment as professor of civil law in 1698. He does not appear ever to have taught.[4]

---

*   I am grateful to the following for their comments on this paper: Roger Emerson, Brian Hillyard, Hector MacQueen, John Robertson, David Sellar and Alan Watson. For David Cook.

1   See J.W. Cairns, 'Sir George Mackenzie, The Faculty of Advocates, and the Advocates' Library' in G. Mackenzie, *Oratio inauguralis in aperienda jurisconsultorum bibliotheca*, edd. J.W. Cairns and A.M. Cain (Edinburgh, 1989), 18–35 at pp. 23 and 33 n.43.

2   See, e.g., *The Minute Book of the Faculty of Advocates. Vol.I. 1661–1712*, ed. J.M. Pinkerton [hereinafter cited as *Minute Book*, i], (Stair Society, 29, Edinburgh, 1976), p. 133 (2 Mar. 1694), p. 140 (18 Jan. 1695), p. 160 (24 Dec. 1695), pp. 189–90 (19 Nov. 1698), p. 191 (1 Dec. 1698) and p. 192 (6 Dec. 1698).

3   See A. Bower, *The History of the University of Edinburgh; chiefly compiled from original papers and records never before published.* 2 vols. (Edinburgh, 1817), i, 328–34 and 344–46.

4   The late John Pinkerton, in *Minute Book*, i, Introduction, p. xix, was surely correct in stating that the provision of adequate funding was the continuing difficulty; but I hope elsewhere to discuss further the background in the seventeenth century to the subsequent founding of professorships in law. On Cunningham's salary and appointment (renewed in 1704), see *A.P.S.*, x, 176 (Act 1698 c. 37) and appendix at pp. 27–28; xi, 203 (Act 1704 c. 9). In 1698, the Town Council of Edinburgh granted Cunningham a licence to teach civil law in the city: W.A. Kelly, The Library of Lord George Douglas (c.1667/8–1693?) (unpublished M.A. thesis, University of Strathclyde, 1975), p. 122. (I am grateful to Dr. Kelly for allowing me to read and cite his thesis). As well as Kelly, op. cit., see on Cunningham, D. Irving, *Lives of Scotish [sic] Writers*. 2 vols. (Edinburgh, 1839), ii, 220–38; R. Feenstra, 'Scottish-Dutch Legal

Over the same period, the Faculty of Advocates regularised its
admission procedures so that, by 1700, there were two clearly defined
modes of entry laid down by acts of sederunt of the Lords of Session and
the acts and practice of the Faculty. The first was by trial on civil law alone.
The applicant presented a petition for his admission to the Lords of Session
who would then refer him to the Dean of the Faculty for private and public
examination in civil law. The private examination took place before a
number of elected examiners and was conducted *viva voce* in Latin. From
1693, for the public examination, the intrant had to print theses and *corol-
laria* on a designated title of civil law which he had to defend publicly in
Latin in a procedure modelled on a university disputation *pro gradu*. He
was then required to read before the Lords of Session a lesson on civil law
on a 'law' assigned by the Dean from the title on which he had written his
theses. After reading this lesson, the intrant took the necessary oaths and
was admitted as an advocate.[5] The second mode of entry was by trial on
Scots law. This applied to candidates admitted 'extraordinarily' upon a bill.
Originally such candidates were admitted by the Lords of Session without
undergoing any trial, but on 5 June 1688, the Faculty of Advocates
appointed a committee, including the Dean, Sir George Mackenzie, 'to give
in overtures to the Lords ... anent the way of entring per bill'.[6] This resulted
on 6 July 1688 in an act of sederunt 'concerneing the Tryall of Advocats,
who enter upon a Bill to the Lords', which, after ratifying the 'ordinary way'
of entry by private and public examination and public lesson, provided that
'in time comeing, when any persones shall apply to the Lords to be entered
advocats, without undergoeing the ordinary tryall, they shall be examined
by the Lords *in praesentia*, concerneing their knowledge of the styles, the
forme of process, and of the principles of our law'.[7] By an act of sederunt of
25 June 1692, the Lords changed the procedure so that henceforth such an
intrant would be 'remitt[ed]... to the Dean and Faculty of Advocates to be
tryed concerning his knowledge of the practique of our law, the styles and
form of process'.[8] On 15 January 1696, the Faculty decided that such intrants
in the future would undergo both a private and public trial on Scots law.[9]
With only minor changes these two alternative modes of entry remained

4...   Relations in the Seventeenth and Eighteenth Centuries' in *Scotland and Europe
        1200–1850*, ed. T.C. Smout (Edinburgh, 1986), 128–42 at pp. 134–36; and
        G.C.J.J. van den Bergh, *The Life and Work of Gerard Noodt (1647–1725):
        Dutch Legal Scholarship between Humanism and Enlightenment* (Oxford,
        1988), pp. 78–79. For an indication that Cunningham did not teach see text
        below at nn. 14–22.
5   See J.W. Cairns, 'The Formation of the Scottish Legal Mind in the Eighteenth
        Century: Themes of Humanism and Enlightenment in the Admission of
        Advocates' in *The Legal Mind: Essays for Tony Honoré*, edd. N. MacCormick
        and P. Birks (Oxford, 1986), 253–77 at pp. 255–56.
6   *Minute Book*, i, 85.
7   *The Acts of Sederunt of the Lords of Council and Session, from the 15th of
        January 1553, to the 11th of July 1790* (Edinburgh, 1790), p. 181.
8   Ibid., p. 200.
9   *Minute Book*, i, 164–65.

possible until 1750.[10] Shaw has pointed out that, in any case, advocates overwhelmingly entered by trial on civil law,[11] and it is worth noting that this was considered the more 'honourable' way to be admitted.[12]

By the end of the seventeenth century, therefore, not only was there pressure to create regular education in law in Scotland, but there was also an admission procedure to the Faculty of Advocates which established for such education a basic curriculum of, first, civil law and, second, Scots law, the latter being further divided into principles or practick, styles, and form of process. Hannay pointed out in 1933 that this situation would 'promote private enterprise in legal education'.[13] In the *Edinburgh Gazette* in April 1699, Alexander Drummond, advocate, advertised instruction 'in the knowledge of the Institutions and Pandects of the Civil Law, and the Laws of this kingdom, or either of the two, or both'.[14] Drummond does not appear to have attracted students of Scots law, for, when he advertised his next session, in September 1699, he only offered civil law.[15] According to John Cuninghame, writing in 1705, Drummond was the first to teach civil law in Scotland,[16] a claim which Drummond himself repeated in 1706.[17] Other than newspaper advertisements, no information is available on Drummond's teaching; given that he petitioned the Faculty for charity in 1709, he may ultimately have been unsuccessful when competition appeared.[18] Indeed, in October 1701, John Spotswood (or Spottiswoode) was apparently unaware of Drummond's classes.[19] Cuninghame stated that Spotswood was the

---

10   See generally Cairns, op. cit., n. 5 above, pp. 264–66.
11   J.S. Shaw, *The Management of Scottish Society 1707–1764: Power, Nobles, Lawyers, Edinburgh Agents and English Influences* (Edinburgh, 1983), p. 27.
12   J. Spottiswoode, *The Form of Process, Before the Lords of Council and Session . . . Written for the Use of the Students in Spotswood's College of Law* (Edinburgh, 1711), p. xxxix; W. Forbes, *A Journal of the Session* (Edinburgh, 1714), p. viii. For the implications of this, see Cairns, op. cit., n. 5 above, pp. 257–61.
13   R.K. Hannay, *The College of Justice: Essays on the Institution and Development of the Court of Session* (Edinburgh and Glasgow, 1933; reprinted Stair Society, Suppl. Vol. 1, Edinburgh, 1990), p. 162.
14   See *Edinburgh Gazette*, 3/6 and 12/14 April 1699; the first advertisement is mentioned in Irving, op. cit. n. 4 above, ii, 220–21 n. 3.
15   *Edinburgh Gazette*, 11/14 and 18/21 Sept. 1699; John Spotswood claimed in 1711 to be the first to have taught Scots law: see, e.g., *Evening-Post, or, The New Edinburgh Gazette*, 3/5 May 1711. If correct, Drummond only ever taught civil law despite his first advertisement.
16   J. Cuninghame, *Oratio inauguralis recitata Edinburgi; cum primum jus civile docere coepit* (Edinburgh, n.d. [1705]), p. 7. For the date 1705, see the advertisement for this work in *Edinburgh Courant*, 24/26 Dec. 1705.
17   *Edinburgh Courant*, 1/3 and 3/6 May 1706.
18   *Minute Book*, i, 278, 279 (18 and 23 Feb. 1709).
19   See N.L.S., MS 2934, fo. 121r, where Spotswood describes himself as 'first professour'. In all quotations from MSS, standard abbreviations are expanded; but spelling and punctuation remain as in the original. Spotswood spelled his name in a variety of ways. I have adopted the simplest, as obviously representing how he pronounced it, although 'Spottiswoode' is now more familiar.

second person in Scotland to give 'colleges' on law.[20] He appears to have been successful, and, though there was at least one significant period when he stopped teaching, he seems to have done much to introduce and develop a European model for legal education in early eighteenth-century Scotland. Cuninghame described himself as the third person in Scotland to teach law.[21] Like Spotswood, he was obviously successful; but, though there is interesting material on which to base a discussion of Cuninghame's classes,[22] I shall here confine myself to consideration of Spotswood, who taught over a much longer period, and was generally a more significant figure in Scottish cultural life. Fuller consideration of the significance of all the early lecturing advocates will be postponed to elsewhere. Since this is a preliminary sketch of Spotswood's life and teaching, the approach will be descriptive rather than analytical.

John Spotswood was born in Edinburgh on 28 November 1667.[23] He was the second son of Alexander Spotswood, advocate, designated 'of Crumstaine' in right of his first wife, the daughter of Sir John Home of Crumstaine in Berwickshire. By this marriage his father already had a son, Alexander, who was to die unmarried. John Spotswood's mother was Helen Trotter, the seventh daughter of John Trotter of Mortonhall. He was the greatgrandson of Archbishop Spotswood, and grandson of Robert Spotswood, Lord Newabbey, a senator, and later president, of the College of Justice, whose practicks he was to edit and publish.[24] In 1710 Spotswood married Helen Arbuthnott, daughter of Viscount Arbuthnott, and widow of John MacFarlane of that Ilk.[25] This made him the step-father of the future distinguished antiquarian, Walter MacFarlane.[26] The family of Spotswood was ancient, though the original family estate of Spotswood in Berwickshire had passed out of their hands; John Spotswood was to reacquire it from the Earl of Lauderdale in February 1700, becoming infeft in the lands and

20   Cuninghame, *Oratio inauguralis*, n.16 above, p. 7.
21   Ibid.
22   See, e.g., ibid.; *A Discourse by Mr. John Cuninghame Advocate, At the Beginning of his Lessons upon the Scots Law* (Edinburgh, 1705); Edinburgh University Library, MS Gen. 1735 (an incomplete set of notes from Cuninghame's 'college' on Scots law, dating from 1709); and N.L.S., MS 3413 (discussed below, n. 123). There also survive student notes of Cuninghame's 'colleges' on civil law.
23   N.L.S., MS 2934, fos. 127r–129v, 'The chief passages of my lyfe' at fo. 127r. (I have retained all dates as either old style or new style as in the original: in letters from the Netherlands, Spotswood himself gives both).
24   *Practicks of the Laws of Scotland, Observed and Collected by Sir Robert Spotiswoode of Pentland, President of the College of Justice, and Secretary of State to K. Charles the I. . . . . Publish'd by John Spotiswoode of That-ilk, Advocate, the Author's Grand-son* (Edinburgh, 1706).
25   For the family, see R. Douglas, *Baronage of Scotland* (Edinburgh, 1798), pp. 446–50; N.L.S., MS 2936, fos. 174v–175r contains a family tree.
26   D. Whyte, *Walter MacFarlane: Clan Chief and Antiquary* (Aberdeen, 1988), p. 4. I am grateful to my friend David Sellar for pointing this out to me.

barony of Spotswood on 25 March 1700.[27] He thereafter designated himself as John Spotswood of that Ilk. This background of minor landowners connected with the professions was not unusual for members of the Faculty of Advocates in this period.[28] Spotswood was active as an elector in Berwickshire by virtue of his barony,[29] and in 1704 was appointed a commissioner of supply for that county.[30] He was a sufficiently important figure in the county for the Earl of Home, who was later to be imprisoned under suspicion, to try to involve him in meetings forming a background to the 1715 rebellion and for the Earl of Marchmont, as sheriff, to write to him warning of the Jacobite invasion.[31] Spotswood sensibly remained uninvolved.

Spotswood described himself as initially schooled in Pilrig in Crumstaine and in Duns. In October 1677, he went to Kelso school where he learned Latin and some Greek.[32] In April 1683, he started in the bajan class at the university of Edinburgh, where he continued with Greek. When he entered the bachelor class in Edinburgh, he studied mathematics under the famous Newtonian, Professor David Gregory, with whom he studied further in 1685 and 1686, while also continuing philosophy under his regent, Herbert Kennedy.[33] Spotswood was to retain a strong interest in mathemat-

---

27   N.L.S., MS 2934, fo. 129r. Archbishop Spotswood had sold the Barony in 1620: Douglas, op. cit., n. 25 above, p. 447.
28   See N.T. Phillipson, 'Lawyers, Landowners, and the Civic Leadership of Post-Union Scotland: An Essay on the Social Role of the Faculty of Advocates in 18th Century Scottish Society', *Jurid. Rev. (N.S.)*, xxi (1976), 97–120; N.T. Phillipson, 'The Social Structure of the Faculty of Advocates in Scotland 1661–1840' in *Law-Making and Law-Makers in British History*, ed. A. Harding (Royal Historical Society, Studies in History, 22, London, 1980), 146–56; Shaw, op. cit., n. 11 above, pp. 18–40; and T.I. Rae, 'The Origins of the Advocates' Library' in *For the Encouragement of Learning: Scotland's National Library 1689–1989*, edd. P. Cadell and A. Matheson (Edinburgh, 1989), 1–22.
29   See [J. Spotswood], *A Speech of one of the Barons of the Shire of B[erwick] at a Meeting of the Barons and Freeholders of that Shire, for Choosing Commissioners to Represent them in the ensuing Parliament, Summoned to Conveen at Edinburgh the 12th day of November 1702* ([Edinburgh], 1702); in N.L.S., MS 2934, fo. 129v he mentions writing this speech in which he raised the issues of an incorporating union with England and the succession to the throne. He returned to both of these in [J. Spotswood], *The Trimmer: Or, Some necessary Cautions, concerning the Union of the Kingdoms of Scotland and England; With an Answer to some of the chief Objections against an Incorporating Union* (Edinburgh, 1706). In N.L.S., MS 10285, fos. 4–5, we find a letter from the Earl of Marchmont, dated 3 Feb. 1715, summoning Spotswood to a meeting to elect the member of parliament for Berwickshire.
30   *A.P.S.*, xi, 140.
31   N.L.S., MS 10285, fos. 6–11 (letters of 7 May, 10 June, and 25 July 1715). In 1717, the Earl of Home wrote to Spotswood asking him to write a letter for Home's friend John Brown (who had been involved in the 1715) recommending him to Governor Spotswood of Virginia, his cousin: ibid., fos. 12–13.
32   N.L.S., MS 2934, fo. 127r.
33   Ibid., fo. 127r–127v.

ics in all its forms,[34] and in June 1701, George Brown, inventor of the Rotula, because of Spotswood's 'skill in *Mathematical* Learning', dedicated to him his treatise on decimal arithmetic.[35] Spotswood was presented by Kennedy for graduation as M.A. in August 1686.[36]

On 15 December 1686, Spotswood, acting with the advice and consent of his mother as his curatrix, apprenticed himself to James Hay of Carriber, Writer to the Signet, whom he later described as 'the ablest Writer and Conveyancer of the last Age', and whose youngest son, Thomas, he was later to instruct in law.[37] Though the indenture was for three years, Spotswood stayed with Hay until 1692.[38] The styles of Scots conveyancing interested Spotswood. When he fell ill in November 1689, he started to collect materials for a style book of Scots law.[39] On 28 November 1689 he

---

34   *A Catalogue of Curious and Valuable Books, Being the Library of Mr. John Spotiswood of that Ilk Advocate, lately deceas'd. To be Sold by Way of Auction in the High Exchange, on Munday [sic] the first Day of July 1728* (Edinburgh, 1728) lists many works on mathematics and related disciplines. In Spotswood's papers and projects there are many allusions to mathematics: see for example N.L.S., MS 658, fo. 25r where (on 1 June 1701) he proposes to study mathematics on Monday, Tuesday and Wednesday afternoons in March; ibid., fo. 28r (25 Mar. 1706) where a programme of personal study includes mathematics; and N.L.S., MS 2937, fo. 4r (where, after setting out a programme of study in Scots and civil law) on 27 Aug. 1705 he sets out proposals to study mathematics.

35   G. Brown, *A Compendious, but a Compleat System of Decimal Arithmetick, Containing more Exact Rules for ordering Infinites, than any hitherto extant* (Edinburgh, 1701), Dedication, sig. *r. Brown was the author of a number of works on arithmetic or which provided tables to facilitate calculations. On the dedication to Spotswood, see N.L.S., MS 2934, fo. 129r. Spotswood was at this time Clerk of the Faculty of Advocates, and may have been instrumental in Brown's presentation to the Faculty of an example of his rotula, a type of calculating machine: *Minute Book*, i, 218 and 220 (28 Feb. and 28 June 1701). I am indebted to Dr. B. Hillyard of the National Library of Scotland for the information that Spotswood's own rotula has survived: it was displayed in the exhibiton '300 Years, 300 Books' (1989). See *An Account of the Rotula Arithmetica Invented by Mr. George Brown, Minister of Kilmaurs* (Edinburgh, 1700). Brown had been minister of Kilmaurs in Ayrshire, presented in 1685, and seemingly 'outed' in 1688: see *Fasti Ecclesiae Scoticanae*, iii, 113–14.

36   *A Catalogue of the Graduates in the Faculties of Arts, Divinity, and Law, of the University of Edinburgh, Since its Foundation* (Edinburgh, 1858), p. 129.

37   N.L.S., Ch. 1566, 'Indenter betwixt James Hay and John Spotswood'. For the comment on Hay, see J. Spotiswood, *An Introduction to the Knowledge of the Stile of Writs, Simple and Compound, Made Use of in Scotland; . . . Written for Use of Students in Spotiswood's Colledge of Law, and now Publish'd for the Common Good* (Edinburgh, 1708), Preface, sig. a2r. Thomas Hay, son of James, studied with Spotswood from May 1710 until early 1712: N.L.S., MS 2937, fos. 35v, 36v and 37r (class lists for colleges beginning 8 May 1710, 10 May 1711, and 5 Nov. 1711). See also ibid., fos. 39r, 41r and 50r for mention of Hay in lists of students.

38   N.L.S., MS 2934, fo. 127v.

39   Ibid., fo. 127v.

headed the collection: 'An essay towards the Digesting and disposing in good order, and to the best advantage the Styles of all the writts evidents and securities made use of in the Scotch law, and practised among the writters to the Signet'.[40] His first plan for teaching law appears to have been to teach the styles of Scots law to writers to the signet and their clerks. He noted this ambition in resolutions drawn up on 12 September 1698, planning to be ready to teach by November 1699.[41] Nothing came of it. On 14 May 1706, however, he did submit a collection of styles to the Writers to the Signet for their approval,[42] and in 1708 he published *An Introduction to the Knowledge of the Stile of Writs*.[43] His larger collection has never been published. Even during his time with Hay, Spotswood seems to have been considering the bar, for in an undated paper from this period, in which he set out his plans and resolutions for the coming winter, expressing worry that studying Scots law might distract him from learning the styles with Hay, he noted that: 'The study of the Scotch law may very fitly be carried along with that of the civil if ever I read it and if it shall be God's will that I do not reach the degree and dignity of an advocat what is more necessary in the first place to be known by a writer or Agent than the Scotch styles and formes of processes ...'.[44]

On 20 August 1692, Spotswood set sail for the Netherlands, and, after a voyage of ten days and spending some time in Rotterdam, he travelled to Leiden,[45] where he matriculated in law on 30 September 1692.[46] There he studied civil law under Professors Vitriarius and Noodt.[47] Both were eminent men, Noodt in particular being an outstanding scholar.[48] Spotswood also attended a class in chemistry with Jacob Le Mort.[49] At his death, Spotswood owned works of all three Leiden teachers.[50] His stay at

---

40 N.L.S., MS 2946, fo. 1r.
41 N.L.S., MS 658, fo. 20r.
42 *A History of the Society of Writers to Her Majesty's Signet With a List of the Members of the Society from 1594 to 1890 and an Abstract of the Minutes* (Edinburgh, 1890), p. xxxv, n. 1 and pp. 373–74.
43 Spotiswood, *Stile of Writs*, n. 37 above.
44 N.L.S., MS 2934, fo. 177r.
45 Ibid., fo. 127v.
46 *Album studiosorum Academiae Lugduno-Batavae MDLXXV – MDCCCLXXV* (The Hague, 1875), col. 724.
47 N.L.S., MS 2934, fo. 127v
48 On Noodt, see now van den Bergh, op. cit., n. 4 above; on Ph.R. Vitriarius, see R. Feenstra and C.J.D. Waal, *Seventeenth-Century Leyden Law Professors and their Influence on the Development of the Civil Law: A Study of Bronchorst, Vinnius and Voet* (Amsterdam and Oxford, 1975), pp. 43–44 and esp. at p. 43 n. 193.
49 N.L.S., MS 2934, fo. 127v. On Le Mort, see J.W. van Spronsen, 'The Beginning of Chemistry' in *Leiden University in the Seventeenth Century: An Exchange of Learning*, edd. Th.H. Lunsingh Schleurleer and G.H.M. Posthumus Meyjes (Leiden, 1975), 329–43 at pp. 338–42.
50 See *A Catalogue of Curious and Valuable Books*, n. 34 above, p. 40: 'Jacobi Le Mort Chymia *Lugd.* 1688', p. 52: 'Vitriarii Universum Jus Civile *Lugd.* 1697', p. 82: 'Vitriarii Institut. Juris Naturae & Gentium *Lugd. Bat.* 1711'; and p. 86:

Leiden was eventful. He organised the funeral and settled the affairs of a friend who died.[51] In the summer of 1693, he made a tour of the Low Countries.[52] Spotswood evidently enjoyed his time at Leiden, despite his doubts about the healthiness of the climate,[53] for in a letter to his mother in August 1693 he indicated his desire to stay on beyond the one year originally planned, though offering to come back should she so wish.[54] Although his sister had recently died, his mother evidently agreed, for he stayed on until December 1693.[55]

On 13 January 1694, Spotswood arrived back in Leith. He was ill until February when he presented his 'bill to be admitted Advocat'.[56] In the course of a journey to court in London about his affairs, between December 1695 and June 1696, Spotswood visited the university of Oxford.[57] He passed June 1696 in studying for his civil law trials.[58] When he underwent the private examination is unknown, but on 19 December 1696 he passed his public examination.[59] His theses were on the title of the Digest *de jure dotium* (D. 23, 3).[60] The Dean of Faculty assigned D. 23, 3, 2 to Spotswood for his lesson, which he delivered before the Lords of Session on 24

50... 'Gerard Noodt Probabilia Juris Civilis, &c. *Lugd.* 1691'. These four works can be identified as: J. Le Mort, *Chymia, rationibus et experimentis auctioribus, iisque demonstrativis superstructa, in qua malevolorum calumniae modeste simul diluuntur* (Leiden, 1688) (not seen); *Universum jus civile privatum ad methodum institutionum Justiniani compositum a Philippo Reinhardo Vitriario jcto & antecessore Lugdunensi. In quo praeter principia, & controversias juris civilis, indicantur fontes juris naturae & gentium, unde illa deducta esse videntur* (Leiden, 1697) (the copy in the N.L.S. (pressmark Nha. 1162) has on the title page the name Duncan Forbes – presumably Spotswood's pupil, the future Lord President); Ph.R. Vitriarius, *Institutiones juris naturae et gentium ad methodum H. Grotii conscriptae et auctae a JJ. Vitriario. Accedit I.F. Buddei historia juris naturalis et gentium; ut et synopsis juris naturalis et gentium, juxta disciplinam Ebraeorum* (Leiden, 1711) (this edition not seen); G. Noodt, *Probabilium juris civilis libri quatuor. Quibus accedunt de jurisdictione et imperio libri duo. & ad legem Aquiliam liber singularis* (Leiden, 1691) (this edition not seen).

51   N.L.S., Adv. MS 82.2.6, fo. 83v.
52   N.L.S., MS 2934, fos. 127v–128r; and see also the copy of a letter to his mother in August 1693 describing the tour, N.L.S., MS 2933, fos. 37v–38v.
53   See the copy letter in N.L.S., MS 2933, fo. 36r–36v at 36v.
54   See ibid., fo. 38r (copy of letter to mother of August 1693).
55   On the death of his sister, see the copy letter of June 12/2 1693 in ibid., fos. 39v–40v, resuming at 42r; on his staying till December, see N.L.S., MS 2934, fo. 128r.
56   N.L.S., MS 2934, fo. 128r; see the draft copy of such a petition in N.L.S., MS 658, fo. 3r.
57   N.L.S., MS 2934, fo. 128v.
58   Ibid.
59   *Minute Book,* i, 173.
60   N.L.S., MS 2228 contains his (printed) *Disputatio juridica inauguralis, de jure dotium* (Edinburgh, 1696).

December 1696, and was duly admitted.[61] In one of his account books he noted: 'I enter'd advocat upon the 24th. December. 1696. and gott no consultations till January'.[62] Through the 1690s, his earnings suggest a steady progress in his career.[63]

At the same time, Spotswood was active in the affairs of the Faculty of Advocates. On 3 July 1697 he took on the work of Clerk to the Faculty in the absence of Andrew Rule.[64] He continued as Clerk until 6 January 1702.[65] This involved him in a great deal of work on the Dean's council and as a regular appointee to committees dealing with a variety of business, including, notably, the dispensing of the Faculty's charity.[66] Though no longer Clerk, he continued on the committee which dispensed charity to the poor, and on 6 January 1702 was also appointed a private examiner for that year.[67] This was a duty he took seriously, for, on 15 March 1702, he approved a scheme of study which he had already set out for himself on 1 June 1701 (encompassing civil law, Scots law, philosophy, languages, medicine, mathematics, astronomy, geography, chronology, history, ancient and modern literature, feudal and canon law, and, on Sunday, theology), but added: 'I make this alteration, To read with all expedition and every day Civil Law, to enable my self the better to discharge the office of an private Examinator'.[68]

On 8 July 1702, because of the illness of James Stevenson, Keeper of the Library, Spotswood was 'unanimously appointed' the 'supervisor of the Library'.[69] He was required to give a receipt for the books in the Library to

61   S.R.O., Books of Sederunt of the Lords of Council and Session, CS 1/9, fos. 135v–136r; see also N.L.S., MS 2934, fo. 128v. For the text of Spotswood's lesson, see N.L.S., MS 2228 where he wrote it out on the fly leaves of his *Disputatio*.
62   N.L.S., MS 10283, fo. 11v.
63   Ibid. Further account books may be found in N.L.S., MS 2937, fos. 6r–29v and N.L.S., MS 2947. Further study of these should help to illuminate Spotswood's career.
64   *Minute Book*, i, 176.
65   Ibid., 229.
66   See ibid., *passim* between pp. 176–229: Spotswood is sometimes mentioned by name and sometimes just alluded to as the Clerk. Much of his work was taken up with the Faculty's dispensing of charity: e.g. ibid., 188 (18 July 1698), 195 (3 Jan. 1699). He also, as Clerk, was on the committee to consider the Christie Bursary, ibid., 189 (19 Nov. 1698). He was generally kept very busy on Faculty business.
67   See ibid., 236–37 (5 June 1702) for continuance of former committee for the poor including Spotswood; see ibid., 229 (6 Jan. 1702) for his appointment as a private examiner. He was on the list of public examiners on 1 Feb. 1700 (ibid., 208) on 8 Jan. 1711 (ibid., 290) and finally on 7 Jan. 1724: *The Minute Book of the Faculty of Advocates. Vol.2. 1713–1750*, ed. J.M. Pinkerton [hereinafter cited as *Minute Book*, ii], (Stair Society, 32, Edinburgh, 1980), p. 70.
68   N.L.S., MS 658, fo. 25r–25v.
69   *Minute Book*, i, 238; N.L.S., MS 2934, fo. 129r gives the date as 9 July 1702. On the Advocates' Library during Spotswood's Keepership, see B. Hillyard, 'The Formation of the Library, 1682–1728', in *For the Encouragement of Learning*, n. 28 above, 23–66 at pp. 41–57.

the representatives of Stevenson.[70] Although Spotswood was to serve as Keeper until his death on 13 February 1728,[71] it does not appear that his tenure was untroubled. By 30 July 1702, Stevenson was dead, and the Faculty was asked by the Dean whether they wished to continue Spotswood as Keeper; the meeting of the Faculty could not agree.[72] At the next meeting on 31 July, before the Faculty voted on whether to proceed to an election or to delay, Spotswood addressed the Faculty offering to serve without salary or fee, and to write up the pleadings on the interlocutors. After this the meeting broke up without reaching a decision.[73] Spotswood remained Keeper, and on 5 January 1703 was re-elected Clerk to the Faculty.[74] That not all members were happy with Spotswood is again suggested by, on the proposal of some members, the joining of Adam Coult with him as joint Clerk and joint Keeper on 16 January 1703.[75] It is possible, as will be discussed below, that the opposition to Spotswood derived from his private teaching of law.[76] I do not propose to discuss further Spotswood as Keeper; but it is worth noting that on 4 January 1704 some members of Faculty proposed that the office of Keeper should be considered. Spotswood and Coult, however, were ultimately continued as joint Keepers.[77] On 24 November 1705 they were joined as Keepers and Clerks by William Forbes.[78] Spotswood ceased to be Clerk on 1 January 1706,[79] though, as noted, he continued as Keeper until his death, while also serving the Faculty in a variety of other ways, even participating in the heated debate over the Jacobite medal presented by the Duchess of Gordon in 1711.[80]

---

70   *Minute Book*, i, 238; N.L.S., MS 658, fo. 16r contains a draft for this receipt.
71   For the date see S.R.O., Register of Edinburgh Testaments, CC 8/8/93, fo. 86v (31 July 1730); and N.L.S., MS 2936, fos. 174v–175r.
72   *Minute Book*, i, 239–40.
73   Ibid., 240; see also N.L.S., MS 2934, fo. 149v on his resolve, recorded here on 19 Aug. 1702, to keep a journal of the Session pursuant to his undertaking.
74   *Minute Book*, i, 241.
75   Ibid., 242.
76   See text at nn. 136–40 below.
77   *Minute Book*, i, 247–48.
78   Ibid., 261.
79   Ibid., where only Forbes and Coult were named as Clerks. In *Minute Book*, ii, 43 we see him officiating again as Clerk (2 Jan. 1722) in the absence of the ordinary Clerk, Alexander Bruce.
80   See *The Truth at Last; Or, The Whole Affair of the Scotch Medal; set in a true Light in a Letter from Mr. John Sporeswood [sic] Keeper of the Advocates Library at Edinburgh to Mr. James Mackenzie Student at Oxford, Transmitted from thence by the last Post* (1711). The (printed) letter bears the date 4 Aug. 1711. James Mackenzie is not listed in the matriculation album for Oxford: *Alumni Oxonienses: The Members of the University of Oxford, 1500–1714: Their Parentage, Birthplace, and Year of Birth, with a Record of their Degrees*, ed. J. Foster. 4 vols. (Oxford, 1891–92), iii, 957. On the affair of the medal, see *Minute Book*, i, 293–94 (17 and 18 July 1711); I.G. Brown, '"This Old Magazine of Antiquities": The Advocates' Library as National Museum', in *For the Encouragement of Learning*, n. 28 above, 149–85 at p. 162; and A. Murdoch, 'The Advocates, the Law and the Nation in Early Modern Scotland' in *Lawyers in Early Modern Europe and America*, ed. W. Prest (London, 1981), 147–63 at p. 156.

In the address 'To the Reader' with which Spotswood prefaced his edition of Gilmour's and Falconer's decisions,[81] and which was probably written in 1700 or early 1701,[82] he reflected on the current state of legal education in Scotland, contrasting it unfavourably with the past, when 'our Predecessors' were at great pains 'to attain the Knowledge of the Laws, Civil, Feudal, Canon, and Municipal, beside the full Knowledge of History, Politicks, Philology, and Classical learning.' He noted, however, 'That the Encouragement which the professors of the Law then had, and the Respect pay'd them, was greater than it is at present; Places and Preferments were bestowed according to Merit, every Man had an Employment according to his Skill'.[83] The decay of legal science is, of course, a stock theme,[84] and, as noted, Spotswood in 1699 had considered teaching styles to writers and their clerks,[85] despite this lack of encouragement to those who professed law. By 6 October 1701, he had formulated more ambitious plans, which he set out in a paper of that date.[86] He explained that he had been solicited by some gentlemen to instruct them and to let them 'have the liberty of [his] consulting roome'. He had considered mortifying out of his lands of Newabbey (the rights to which had been disponed to him by Alexander, his elder brother) a fee for a professor; but he was not in possession of the lands.[87] '[T]he wellfare of the kingdome', however, had decided him to

---

81   *A Collection of Decisions of the Lords of Council and Session, In Two Parts. . . . Observ'd by Sir John Gilmour of Craigmiller . . . [and] by Sir David Falconer of Newton . . .* (Edinburgh, 1701), pp. [5]–8 (separately paginated). Though Spotswood's name does not appear in the work, he alludes to it as his in his edition of his grandfather's *Practicks*, n. 24 above, sig. b[1]r; and notes his working on it and its publication in N.L.S., MS 2934, fo. 129̊r.

82   I would suspect this because, in N.L.S., MS 2934, fo. 129r, he notes that he worked on the edition in March and August of 1699 and 1700 and that the work was published in June 1701. It was advertised for sale in *The Edinburgh Gazette* of 23/26 June 1701.

83   [Spotswood, ed.] *A Collection of Decisions*, n. 81 above, p. 7 (first sequence of pagination).

84   See van den Bergh, op. cit., n.4 above, p. 161.

85   See text at n.41 above.

86   N.L.S., MS 2934. fos. 121r–122v.

87   Ibid., fo. 121r. On his difficulties with gaining the lands of Newabbey, see N.L.S., MS 2934, fo. 128v; see also the printed broadsheet, *Unto his Grace, His Majesties High Commissioner, and the Honourable Estates of Parliament. The Petitition of John Spotswood Grand-child to Sir Robert Spotswood of Newabbay, sometime President of the Colledge of Justice, and thereafter Secretary of State to King Charles the first* ([Edinburgh, 1695] N.L.S., pressmark, 7.70 (19)) which was presented in parliament in 1695 and referred to the committee for private affairs. Spotswood's grandfather had been compelled to resign the barony of Newabbey in return for a promised £3000 sterling (never paid). The barony was to be used to support the new bishopric of Edinburgh. Parliament found in favour of Spotswood and recommended that the king give him a new signature of entitlement to the lands: *A.P.S.*, ix, 481–85 and appendix, pp. 118 and 124. In December 1695, Spotswood went to London to try to get his right to Newabbey completed, returning to Edinburgh in June 1696. It was on this journey that he visited Oxford (N.L.S., MS 2934, fo. 128v). He was unsuccess-

undertake himself the duty of teaching law, so he was determined 'to begin on that footing both as the founder and first professour, and to take on with such gentlemen as are desireous of [his] direction'.[88] He planned to seek the approval of the Faculty of Advocates and its permission 'to teach and profess', after sounding out 'the most considerable members'. He also was to seek the approval of the Lords of Session and members of the privy council. He would then request the town council as patrons of the University to admit him as a professor with all appropriate privileges. He also aimed to gain a royal patent as regius professor of the laws and the degree of doctor of laws from the University. He proposed to proceed cautiously at first with ten or twelve students.[89]

His initial intention was to teach Justinian's *Institutes*, showing at the end of each title the conformity of the civil with the municipal law. He would teach three times a week in the evening during dates which coincided with the winter and summer sessions of the Court, that is from early June to early August, and early November to early March. He considered that a short style book and an account of the form of process might be prepared to encourage the auditors. The charge would be five guineas. Should more instruction in Scots law be demanded he would teach, firstly, Mackenzie's *Institutions*, adding such titles of law as were missing and a fuller style book and account of conveyancing and a full account of actions, processes, decreets, and of the offices of writer to the signet, advocate, judge and clerk of court. For this he would charge no less than five guineas. He would teach this on the days he did not teach civil law.[90] The programme is obviously derived from the acts of sederunt on the examination of advocates.

In his papers from 1702, we find draft addresses from students requesting instruction in civil and Scots law.[91] He recounted that on 3 July 1702 he 'begun to teach the Scotch law, and dictated to five young gentlemen the forme of Process'.[92] A paper of around August 1702 contains a discussion of schedules for classes on Scots law,[93] while another dated 19 and 31 August 1702 sets out a detailed analysis of lectures on Mackenzie's *Institutions* as far as the fourth title of the second book.[94] A paper of 1 September 1702 discusses the organisation of classes on civil law.[95] He duly noted that in November 1702 he 'begun to teach the Civil law to six young

---

87... ful, which was why he was not in possession in 1701. It was not until 1742 that his son got his right recognised (Douglas, *Baronage*, n. 25 above, p. 450).
88   N.L.S., MS 2934, fo. 121r.
89   Ibid., fos. 121v–122r.
90   Ibid., fo. 122r–122v.
91   Ibid., fo. 149r.
92   Ibid., fo. 129r.
93   Ibid., fo. 149v.
94   Ibid., fo. 126r–126v.
95   Ibid., fo. 150v.

gentlemen; as also I explained McKenzie's institutions and my forme of pro-cess'.[96] In August 1703 he 'begun to dictate [his] stylebook to [his] scholars students in the lawes'.[97] Spotswood thus established the general pattern for his 'colleges' or classes on the basis of his plan of 1701. One variation was that, while in 1701 he had envisaged charging five guineas for each course, he ultimately charged five for both; a student taking only one paid three guineas.[98] He did not achieve his aim of a university appointment.

I hope to analyse Spotswood's colleges in detail elsewhere, but it is appropriate to make a few remarks here. The basic textbook he used for teaching the 'principles' of Scots law (to use the term of the act of sederunt of 1688) was Sir George Mackenzie's *Institutions of the Law of Scotland*, first published in Edinburgh in 1684 with a second edition (by Mackenzie) of 1688, also published in Edinburgh. There were to be many other editions of this work,[99] including one by Spotswood with notes seemingly to some extent based on his lectures.[100] Mackenzie consciously wrote his *Institutions* as an institutional or instructional work,[101] and Spotswood told his students that: 'These Laws are commonly taught by way of Institutions (or Instituts) which are ane Epitome or abridgement of the Cheif [sic] heads and generall terms and principles of Law extracted out of the Law Books of the learned Jurists: Which Institutions are written both by McKenzie and Stair's [sic]. The first whereof serves as a Rudiments, and the second as a Grammar, or (as

---

96   Ibid., fo. 129v.
97   Ibid.
98   See Spotswood's account book, N.L.S., MS 2947 where, at fos. 19v–27r, are listed payments by students over the period 1703–6. To take some examples: ibid., fo. 19v: 'From Baine of Logie for civil Law colledge this year. 3. guineas and thereafter 2 guineas for whole colledges.' (This is the future professor of Scots law in Edinburgh.) Ibid., fo. 20r: 'From John Ker sone to Laird of Cavers for both colledges of Law. 5. guineas.' Ibid: 'From John Scrimzeour for civil law colledges. 3. guineas.' Ibid., fo. 20v: 'From Robert Ker yr. of Cavers for Scots Law colledge. 3. guineas.' The fee for one college remained 3 guineas: see S.R.O., Campbell of Barcaldine Muniments, GD 170/793/3 (letter dated 26 June 1721 from John Campbell to Patrick Campbell of Barcaldine). In N.L.S., MS 2937, fo. 42r there is a list (from Nov. 1710 – Jan. 1711) of students who have paid. Ibid., fo. 42v has a similar list (May – June 1711(?)).
99   See F.S. Ferguson, 'A Bibliography of the Works of Sir George Mackenzie Lord Advocate Founder of the Advocates' Library', *Edinburgh Bibliographical Society Transactions*, i (1935–38), 1–60 at pp. 30–4.
100   *The Institutions of the Law of Scotland. By Sir George Mackenzie of Rosehaugh, Advocate to K. Cha. II. and to K. Ja. VII. The Sixth Edition, Revised, Corrected and Augmented* (Edinburgh, 1723). A paper, probably to be dated to 6 Aug. 1722, contains a draft title page for this work: N.L.S., MS 2934, fo. 182v. It is described as 'reformed and illustrated with notes', 'Made easie and fit for the meanest capacity and even useful to those who are advanced in the study of the law' and also as 'Necessary to all Students of the Law at their first setting out, and even convenient and agreable to those who ar advanced in this study'.
101   G. Mackenzie, *Institutions of the Law of Scotland*, (2nd edn., Edinburgh, 1688), Epistle Dedicatory.

the Civilians term it) Pandects or Digests'.[102] Of Mackenzie's *Institutions* in particular, Spotswood said: 'This book is called Institutions or Instituts as being a Collectione of the most generall and easy terms and principles upon which the Law is founded. This name is of a verry antient Originall, it being made use of in the time of the Roman Common wealth by Justinian and others and is the most generall and easy way of teaching any art Science or language'.[103] Spotswood in 1701 had proposed to add to his classes on Mackenzie's *Institutions* such titles of law as were missing.[104] He appears to have done so, for in 1710 he published a treatise on elections from Scotland to parliament based on lectures given to students.[105] Furthermore, in a newspaper advertisement in the same year, he described this part of his lectures as on 'The Institutions of the Laws of Scotland, and other Subject[s] relating thereto'.[106] Spotswood explained procedure in the Court of Session, the second requirement under the act of sederunt, by expounding to students his treatise on the form of process,[107] which he was to publish in 1711.[108] The third requirement under the act of sederunt of 1688 was examination in 'styles'. Spotswood described thus his instruction in this: 'I shall explain a brief Treatise concerning the Stile of Securities ... and shall shew the essential Clauses in Writs, that most frequently occur, and the various Expressions and Forms, according to Circumstances us'd by Writers'.[109] He was to publish this treatise in 1708.[110]

---

102   N.L.S., MS 3412, 'Observations upon Sir George Mckenzies Institutions of the Law of Scotland Delivered by Mr. John Spotiswood of that Ilk Advocate etc. To the Students in thier [sic] Colledges. Collected by some of their Students. Dumfries. Written in Anno 1717', fo. iv verso (I have deleted the copyist's eccentric use of the apostrophe 's').

103   Ibid., 1. On institutional literature as a genre, see J.W. Cairns, 'Institutional Writings in Scotland Reconsidered', *Jour. Leg. Hist.*, iv (1983), 76–117; 'Blackstone, an English Institutist: Legal Literature and the Rise of the Nation State', *Oxf. Jour. Leg. Stud.*, iv (1984), 318–60; 'Eighteenth Century Professorial Classification of English Common Law', *McGill Law Journal*, xxxiii (1987), 225–44.

104   See text at n. 90 above.

105   J. Spotswood, *The Law Concerning Election of Members for Scotland, To Sit and Vote in the Parliament of Great-Britain* (Edinburgh, 1710). In his preface (ibid., sig. A2r), he points out his duty in teaching 'to study the several Parts and Titles' of Scots law, and to reduce his observations on them to a suitable scheme for instruction, remarking that friends thought he should not confine his essay on elections 'to private Students'.

106   *Scots Courant*, 1/3 and 3/5 May 1710: he goes on to mention the other two parts of his classes on the form of process and on styles.

107   See J. Spotiswood, *A Discourse Shewing the Necessary Qualifications of a Student of the Laws: And what is Propos'd in the Colleges of Law, History & Philology, Establish'd at Edinburgh. Deliver'd at the Commencement of the College of Law. VI. November MDCCIV* [hereinafter cited as Spotiswood, *Discourse*], p. 11.

108   Spotiswood, *Form of Process*, n. 12 above.

109   Spotiswood, *Discourse*, n. 107 above, p. 11.

110   Spotiswood, *Stile of Writs*, n. 37 above.

Less information is available on Spotswood's lectures on civil law, and no student notes from the class have been discovered. He seems only to have lectured on Justinian's *Institutes*,[111] using as his textbook Böckelmann's compend,[112] one of the most successful student texts of the period, described by Robert Feenstra, as a 'hit' ('succesnummer').[113] It was with this work that Böckelmann had revolutionised the teaching of civil law in the Netherlands by introducing the *methodus compendiaria*, which he had already used at Heidelberg, whereby the professor taught on the basis of a manual rather than the actual Justinianic texts of the Roman law.[114] Though Spotswood's teacher, Noodt, strongly disapproved of the *methodus compendiaria*, it is easy to understand its attraction to Spotswood who was aiming to deal with Roman law in seventy-five days.[115] Hints at the material Spotswood drew on in his colleges in civil law may be gathered from reading programmes he set out, probably for himself, and notes he made on the method of studying civil law. Provisional study of these suggests that he did not have a deep scholarly interest in civil law; but I shall pursue this elsewhere.[116] Though we have no direct evidence, it is fair to assume that, while he taught Scots law in English, he lectured in Latin on civil law.

Spotswood did not confine his students' studies to Scots and civil law in a narrow sense. He expected them to be proficient in languages and to be 'skillfull in *Grammar, Rhetorick*, and *Logick*'.[117] Furthermore, at one stage, he provided for them two teachers of, respectively, history and philol-

---

111 See *Edinburgh Gazette*, 8/11 November 1703, where, for teaching civil law, he only mentions '*The Institutions of the* Roman *or* Civil Law'. See further below.

112 J.F. Böckelmann, *Compendium Institutionum Justiniani sive elementa juris civilis* (1st edn. Leiden, 1679 and many subsequent). At his death, Spotswood owned two editions of this work, both Leiden, 1681 and 1685 respectively: see *A Catalogue of Curious and Valuable Books*, n. 34 above, p. 50 (no. 927) and p. 82 (no. 1550). For Spotswood's use of Böckelmann's textbook, see N.L.S., MS 2934, fo. 150v.

113 R. Feenstra, 'Johann Friedrich Böckelmann (1632–1681): Een markant Leids hoogleraar in de rechten' in *Bestuurders en Geleerden: Opstellen over onderwerpen uit de Nederlandse geschiedenis van de zestiende, zeventiende en achtiende eeuw, aangeboden aan Prof. Dr. J.J. Woltjer bij zijn afschied als hoogleraar van de Rijksuniversiteit te Leiden*, edd. S. Groenveld, M.E.H.N. Mout and I. Schöffer (Amsterdam and Dieren, 1985), 137–50 at p. 141. For editions of the *Compendium*, see M. Ahsmann and R. Feenstra, *Bibliographie van hoogleraren in de rechten aan de Leidense Universiteit tot 1811* (Amsterdam, Oxford and New York, 1984), pp. 61–64 (nos. 32–44).

114 Feenstra, 'Johann Friederich Böckelmann', n. 113 above, p. 142; Feenstra and Waal, op. cit., n. 48 above, pp. 36–37.

115 In N.L.S., MS 2934, fo. 150v, Spotswood wrote (on 1 Sept. 1702): 'By explaining in Böckelm: Instit. 4. pages per diem twice a week. the whole may be finished in 75. dayes. which is the winter and summer session.' On Noodt's attitude to *compendia*, see van den Bergh, op. cit., n. 4 above, pp. 31, 164–66 and 301.

116 See N.L.S., MS 658, fos. 25r and 25v (1 June 1701), 27r (10 Nov. 1705) and 28r (25 Mar. 1706); and MS 2937, fo. 3v (27 Aug. 1705).

117 Spotiswood, *Discourse*, n. 107 above, p. 10.

ogy, because, as lawyers, they required a knowledge of history and, secondly, because they required 'to be made Partakers of the *Grecian* and *Roman* Wit and Prudence'.[118] While this may well reflect Spotswood's experience in Leiden, where his teacher Noodt was noted for his elegant learning, being described by the Utrecht historian, Graevius, as the only Dutch law professor not unschooled in 'our' letters,[119] such views were conventional. In 1695, when members of the Faculty of Advocates had sought from parliament funding for a chair in law, they had noted that '[t]he professione [i.e. professorship] of the laws carys necessarly with it all the belles Letres and the knowledge of ancient and modern history'.[120] In his *Oration* of 1689, presumably delivered on the formal inauguration of the Advocates Library, Sir George Mackenzie had made similar remarks.[121] Spotswood thus sought to achieve the desiderata for legal education he had established in the prefatory address in 1701 to his edition of the *Decisions* of Gilmour and Falconer.[122]

Though we only have student notes for Spotswood's lectures on Mackenzie's *Institutions*,[123] it is possible to give an account of his instructional methods in all of his classes. He taught in two separate sessions each year: the summer session running from early May to early August and the winter from early November to early March.[124] Schedules for his classes in Scots law show that he moved methodically through Mackenzie's *Institutions*, typically starting a class with an examination of the students on

---

118   Ibid.
119   See van den Bergh, op. cit., n. 4 above, p. 46.
120   *Minute Book*, i, 160 (24 Dec. 1695).
121   See G. Mackenzie, *Oratio inauguralis in aperienda jurisconsultorum bibliotheca*, n. 1 above, pp. 58–59 and 73.
122   See quotations in text above at nn. 82–83.
123   N.L.S., MS 3412, n. 102 above; N.L.S., MS 3413 'Observations Upon Sir George McKenzie's Institutions of the Law of Scotland. The First Two Books Delivered By Mr. John Cunningham Advocat. And the Last Two Books By Mr. John Spotiswood of that Ilk Advocat. To The Students in their College. Drumfries [sic] Written Anno Domini 1717.' This latter MS also contains Spotswood's introductory account of the books and sources of Scots law and concludes with his guidance on vacation reading. It is presumably based on notes dating from 1710, when Spotswood took over Cuninghame's Scots law class in May 1710: *Scots Courant*, 1/3 and 3/5 May 1710. From the wording of Cuninghame's advertisements, it appears that in his summer session he was *continuing* his lectures on Scots law, and so in May he would only have completed the first two books of Mackenzie's *Institutions*: see *Edinburgh Courant*, 24/26 Mar. 1708; and 13/15 Mar. 1710. His schedule was rather different from Spotswood's.
124   See, e.g., *Edinburgh Courant*, 4/6 June 1705; *Scots Courant*, 1/3 May 1710, 16/18 Oct. 1710, and 25/27 April 1711; *Evening Post, or, the New Edinburgh Gazette*, 10/13 Mar. and 3/5 May 1711, and 6/8 Sept. 1711; *Scots Courant*, 18/21 Apr. 1712, 20/22 Oct. 1712, and 20/22 Apr. 1713. In the *Edinburgh Gazette*, 8/11 Nov. 1703, Spotswood indicated he would teach civil law from 15 Nov. and Scots law from 1 Dec.; but all the other advertisements conform to the pattern I have indicated.

the subject of the previous lecture.[125] In his *Discourse*, he stated that this
would allow the students to demonstrate their 'Application and Profit in
Study'.[126] He appears to have woven his account of the form of process into
his lectures on Mackenzie's *Institutions*.[127] He also examined his students
daily on the form of process.[128] In the *Discourse* he stated that he would test
the students' 'Understanding' of the form of process by making them answer
'Questions about Form'.[129] For his classes on styles, he said to his students
that: '[I shall] try your Skill in That, by making you compose according to
Notes, which I shall give you, some Security or other, which is to be
impugn'd and defended'.[130] Though the evidence is less full, it is nonetheless conclusive that he started his class on civil law with an examination of
the students on the subject matter of previous classes.[131] He kept examination rolls naming the students examined on each day,[132] and lists survive
which may indicate assessment of the students' performance.[133] Spotswood
expected students in a second course of study with him to argue for or
against particular cases put to them and to judge the arguments made.[134]
This suggests the common practice of disputation *exercitii gratia*. In the
vacation, students in Scots law were expected to engage in extensive private
study for which Spotswood gave them detailed guidance on reading.[135]
Though there is no evidence, it is likely that he gave a similar list of vacation reading to those studying civil law. This whole programme of instruction was obviously intended to give the students a thorough grounding in
law.

    Spotswood initially proposed to proceed cautiously, and he obviously
feared opposition to the establishment of his 'colleges' in civil and Scots
law. In the preface to his edition of Gilmour's and Falconer's *Decisions*, he
had regretted the lack of encouragement given to professors of law.[136] He
reflected this in his proposals of October 1701, when he wrote: 'I thought to

125 See N.L.S., MS 2937, fos. 51r–52v; and 55r–55v. Ibid., fo. 48v at the foot gives a
schedule of classes on Scots law, which is possibly an examination schedule
given it follows an examination schedule on civil law; see also fo. 49v.
126 Spotiswood, *Discourse*, n. 107 above, p. 11.
127 See N.L.S., MS 2937, fos. 53r–54v for his classes over the winter session from
November 1711 to March 1712.
128 See ibid., fo. 50v for a list of examination of students on the form of process:
the names of the students set down for examination on particular days (and
see also fo. 50r), when compared with dated lists (see ibid., fos. 39r, 44r, and
35v), suggest this paper dates from 1710.
129 Spotiswood, *Discourse*, n. 107 above, p. 11.
130 Ibid.
131 See N.L.S., MS 2937, fo. 48v.
132 See ibid., fo. 44r for November 1710 and fo. 50r and fo. 50v (probably also of
1710 – see n. 128 above).
133 See ibid., fo. 48r (on civil law); fo. 49r (on Scots law); and fo. 50r (perhaps on
the form of process given the examination roll on fo. 50v).
134 Spotiswood, *Discourse*, n. 107 above, pp. 11–12.
135 N.L.S. MS 3412, n. 102 above, pp. 478–80; MS 3413, n. 123 above, pp. 385–87.
136 See quotation in text above at n. 83.

have undertaken the publick profession of the lawes, had I mett with that encouragement I demanded of some great men, which is necessary to support me against the calumnies and reproaches, which I may meet with'.[137] This was no doubt why he decided to seek the approval of the Faculty, the Lords of Session, and the privy council.[138] Such opposition may have materialised, perhaps related to Alexander Cunningham's parliamentary appointment, for in a paper dated 17 September 1702, written shortly after Spotswood had started his first class in Scots law and shortly before he started his first in civil law, he confessed he was 'tossed among divers doutes' and he alluded to his 'fear to disoblige great men solliciting my complyance with their recommendation, and a fearfulnes to swerve from my own inclinations'. Honour and his duty to his country dissuaded him from complying with the 'great men', but he noted that following his own inclination was 'full of danger' for it would make 'these great men [his] enemies, who acted with a spirit of revenge shall embrace every occasion of marring [his] interest'. He prayed for God's guidance that he should neither depart from his duty nor make enemies.[139] If these fears related to his colleges, and it is not entirely certain that they did, it may explain the apparent opposition to him as Keeper which appeared on 30 July 1702, shortly after he had started to teach on the third of that month.[140]

If he did face opposition, his colleges seem quickly to have been a success. Surviving class lists show a decent number of students.[141] Some of them can be identified as the sons of distinguished men and as future judges: three sons of Robert Dundas of Arniston, senator of the College of Justice;[142] Alexander Bayne, the future professor of Scots law in Edinburgh;[143] and Duncan Forbes of Culloden,[144] to name but a few. The

---

137   N.L.S., MS 2934, fo. 121r.
138   Ibid., fo. 121v.
139   Ibid., fo. 151v.
140   See text above at nn. 71–78 and 91–97. *Minute Book*, i, 306 (6 Dec. 1712) contains a tantalising but obscure reference to a committee 'appointed for Mr. Spotiswoods affairs'. Perhaps the opposition was also linked to his political endeavours; but his Berwickshire Speech, n. 29 above, was published *after* the opposition to him emerged, and he had expressed obvious doubts about the colleges.
141   N.L.S., MS 2937, fos. 33r–34r (Nov. and Dec. 1703: 37 students); fo. 35v (May 1710, Scots law: 19 students); fo. 36r (Nov. 1710: 22 students); fo. 36v (May 1711: 14 students); fo. 37r. (Nov. 1711: 15 students); fo. 37v. (May 1712: 7 students); and fo. 38r (Nov. 1712: 7 students).
142   See ibid., fo. 33r: 'James Dundas, yr of Arniston' and 'Robert Dundas sone to Lord Arniston' (Nov. 1703); fo. 47v (undated paper but names from same class of 1703–4). The latter was the future Lord Advocate and Lord President. Ibid, fo. 38r: 'Dundas third son of The Lord Arniston' (Nov. 1712).
143   Ibid., fo. 33r (Nov. 1703); and fo. 48r (examination roll of 1704?). See also n. 98 above for his payment for both colleges.
144   See G. Menary, *The Life and Letters of Duncan Forbes of Culloden Lord President of the Court of Session 1685–1747* (London, 1936), p. 6. He is the 'D. Forbes' noted on what are probably assessments of examinations dating from ca. 1704: N.L.S., MS. 2937, fos. 48r and 49r.

last wrote on 17 November 1704 to his brother, requesting five guineas for the fee, because their uncle, Sir David Forbes, was 'very positive anent my ... going to Mr Spotswood's Colledges of Law'.[145] Some of his students stayed for three sessions.[146] Obviously they found the classes worthwhile.

This sketch of Spotswood's life and career as a professor has scarcely touched upon the intellectual influences on him and their effect on his teaching, nor has it sought to place him in his wider Scottish milieu. His political views remain as yet enigmatic, though there are possible hints of Jacobite sympathies. It is worth noting, however, that Spotswood was, at least at one time, obviously intimate with James Anderson, the historian and antiquary.[147] Thus, when Anderson was in Durham collating manuscripts and copying records on behalf of Sir Robert Sibbald,[148] it was Spotswood who wrote to him asking him to return because his wife was ill, while Spotswood's sister later asked Anderson to buy her a fashionable scarf and hood.[149] This suggests Spotswood's connection with the circle of those interested in Scottish history which Sibbald had collected around himself, and in which Thomas Ruddiman, with whom Spotswood must have had a close relationship in the Advocates Library, played such a notable part.[150] In Spotswood's papers we find proposals in 1702 for the creation of a society to promote knowledge of history and collect historical documents, and the establishment of a professor of Scottish history, and in 1709 again for the foundation of a historical society.[151] He obviously shared the historical concerns of Scottish virtuosi of this period.

His formal education must also have exerted influence. In Leiden, Noodt was an outstanding critical and historical scholar of Roman law.[152] It seems unlikely, however, that Spotswood was strongly interested in this type of work, though he did own a copy of his teacher's *Probabilia* and a

---

145 See *More Culloden Papers*, ed. D. Warrand. 5 vols. (Inverness, 1923–30), ii, 1–2.

146 See N.L.S., MS 2937, fo. 36v listing 'Tertians' in May 1711; and fo. 37r for 'Tertians & ultra' in November 1710.

147 Anderson was the author of *An Historical Essay showing that the Crown and Kingdom of Scotland is Imperial and Independent* (Edinburgh, 1705), which is reprinted in this volume, and *Selectus diplomatum et numismatum Scotiae thesaurus* (Edinbugh, 1739). On him, see D. Duncan, *Thomas Ruddiman: a Study in Scottish Scholarship of the Early Eighteenth Century* (Edinburgh and London, 1965), pp. 123–25 and 129–35; Hillyard, op. cit. n. 69 above, pp. 53–55; and W. Ferguson's introduction to the reprint of the *Historical Essay*, pp.1ff above.

148 See Duncan, op. cit., n. 147 above, p. 124; on Sibbald, see R.L. Emerson, 'Sir Robert Sibbald, Kt, the Royal Society of Scotland and the Origins of the Scottish Enlightenment', *Annals of Science*, xlv (1988), 41–72.

149 N.L.S., Adv. MS 29.3.4, fo. 22r; N.L.S., Adv. MS 29.1.2 (vi), fo. 231r. See also N.L.S., Adv. MS 29.1.2 (viii), fo. 41 for a discharge between Spotswood and Anderson of 1697 (wrongly dated 1695 in *Catalogue*).

150 Duncan, op. cit., n. 147 above. See generally, H. Ouston, 'Cultural Life from the Restoration to the Union' in *The History of Scottish Literature. Volume 2. 1660–1800*, ed. A. Hook (Aberdeen, 1987), 11–31.

151 N.L.S., MS 2934, fos. 125r–125v and 137r.

152 See van den Bergh, op. cit., n. 4 above, pp. 321–33.

number of other humanist and elegant works on Roman law;[153] but it is difficult to put great significance on this given the size and scope of Spotswood's library, which, when auctioned, contained nearly 3,000 titles.[154] Spotswood expressed the desire '[t]hat the Students of the Laws would apply themselves to a more Assiduous Study of the Law of their own Countrey',[155] though he was clearly far from denying the importance to lawyers of Roman law and elegant learning.[156] Nonetheless, pure scholarship in Roman law does not seem to have interested him, and it may be significant that, when, in 1699, he listed a number of books he was considering buying, that by Noodt was his treatise *De foenore et usuris*, which related to contemporary debates as well as being an elegant piece of fine humanist scholarship. (He presumably decided not to buy it, since he also noted that there was a copy in the Advocates Library).[157] More intriguing is the possible influence on Spotswood of Noodt's interest in natural law. As van den Bergh has pointed out, Noodt, in his inaugural address at Franeker, called for the teaching of natural law, and he was later in Leiden to teach a *Collegium Grotianum*.[158] We can be certain in this respect of the influence on Spotswood of his other professor, Vitriarius, who, from 1682, had taught a course on natural law,[159] since, of the two works of his which Spotswood owned at his death, one constantly alludes to the foundation of civil law in natural law, and the other is specifically on natural law; moreover, on 27 August 1705, in a scheme of study of civil law, Spotswood proposed to read Voet's compend of the Digest '*secundum tit[ulos] parallelos ex Vitrario*'.[160] (Spotswood must have bought both these works of Vitrarius after returning from Leiden to Scotland.) The catalogue of his library lists many works on Grotian natural law.[161] Furthermore, his method of studying civil law included the works on

---

153   On Spotswood's copy of the *Probabilia*, see n. 50 above: van den Bergh describes this work as 'typically humanistic', op. cit., n. 4 above, p. 141. For humanistic works in Spotswood's library, see, e.g. *A Catalogue of Curious and Valuable Books*, n.34 above, p. 5 (no. 11): 'Alciati opera omnia in 4 Vols. *Basil.* 1582'; p. 26 (no. 203): 'Budeus de Asse et partibus ejus 1514'; p. 26 (no. 213): 'Cujacii Opera omnia 2 Vols. *Lugd.* 1614'; p. 27 (no. 246): 'Budaei Comment. in Pandectas [*Basil.*] 1557'; p. 43 (no. 346): 'Corpus Juris Civilis notis Gothofredi *Amst.* 1663'; p. 62 (no. 393): 'Codex Theodosianus Gothofredi 6 Vols. *Lugd.* 1665'; p. 62 (no. 405): 'Alciati Opera 4 Vols. [*Fran.*] 1617'. I have not sought to verify these titles and editions.

154   *A Catalogue of Curious and Valuable Books*, n. 34 above, which lists 1,840 titles in octavo & infra, 741 in quarto, and 401 in folio, in total: 2,982. The legal component of this collection is considerable.

155   See his address to the reader in *A Collection of Decisions*, n. 81 above, p. 6.

156   See ibid., p. 7; and text above at nn. 117–22.

157   See N.L.S., MS 2934, fos. 97v–98r. On Noodt's *De foenore et usuris libri tres* (Leiden, 1698), see van den Bergh, op. cit., n. 4 above, pp. 181–91.

158   Van den Bergh, op. cit., n. 4 above, p. 283.

159   Ibid., p. 271.

160   N.L.S., MS 2937, fo. 3v; see n. 50 above for the works of Vitriarius which he owned.

161   See, e.g., *A Catalogue of Curious and Valuable Books*, n. 34 above, p. 45 (no. 760): 'Grotius de Principiis Juris Naturalis *Cantab.* 1673', p. 47 (no. 807):

natural law of Grotius and Pufendorf.[162] This raises tantalising (but possibly unanswerable) questions about Spotswood's views on the origin of law and the source of its authority. Eighteenth-century Scottish philosophy and social thought both drew on and reacted against the theories of Grotius and Pufendorf.[163] Finally on Spotswood's experiences in Leiden, it may be noted that his programme of study for his students – civil law, municipal law, history and philology, with the expectation that students would have a knowledge of the classical languages, grammar, rhetoric and logic[164] – reflects to some extent the curriculum at that university;[165] but the exact import of this is hard to determine, since this was generally the contemporary view of the ideal in legal studies.[166]

We have seen that Spotswood had a continuing interest in mathematics, and his professor of that subject in Edinburgh, David Gregory, is famous as a follower of Newton. Christina Eagles has demonstrated, however, that Gregory did not introduce Newtonian philosophy into his classes except in some lectures written in or after 1687,[167] by which time Spotswood had graduated. Eric Forbes has pointed out that Herbert Kennedy, Spotswood's

---

161... 'Ofiandri Observationes in Grotium de Jure Belli ac pacis *Tubingae* 1671'; p. 56 (no. 1021): 'Defensio Dissertationes de Origine Juris Naturalis *Utrajecti* 1687'; p. 74 (no. 1370): 'Les Devoirs de l'Homme par Puffendorf *Amst.* 1715'; p. 74 (no. 1378): 'Belthemi Introduct. ad Opus Grotii de Jure Belli ac pacis *Jenae* 1676'; p. 76 (no. 613): 'Puffendorf de Jure naturae & Gentium *Lond.* 1662'; p. 79 (no. 1449): 'Ziegleri Notae, &c. in Grotium de Jure Belli ac pacis *Fran.* 1686'; p. 79 (no. 1459): 'Puffendorf Elementa Juris prudentiae *Cantab.* 1672'; p. 80 (no. 1494): 'Grotius Erotematicus a Geo. Simone *Lipsiae* 1687'; p. 82 (no. 1541): 'Grotius de Jure Belli ac Pacis Notis Gronovii *Amster.* 1689'; p. 82 (no. 1542): 'Wolfgangi Jageri Observat. in Grotium de Jure Belli ac Pacis *Tubing.* 1710'; p. 82 (no. 1544): 'Jo. a Felden Annot. in Grotium de Juri [sic] Belli ac Pacis, &c. *Amster* 1653'. I have not sought to verify the existence of these works or editions, though one entry (p. 76, no. 613) is evidently faulty, since Pufendorf's *De jure naturae et gentium libri octo* was not published until 1672.

162   See N.L.S., MS 658, fo. 25v: 'The order of reading the civil Law in special parts, is to begin with the books written by Grotius and Puffendorf on the laws of nature.' It is worth noting that Spotswood's library did not contain any works by Cumberland, on whom see M. Forsyth, 'The Place of Richard Cumberland in the History of Natural Law Doctrine', *Journal of the History of Philosophy*, xx (1982), 23–42.

163   See, e.g., P. Stein, 'Legal Thought in Eighteenth-Century Scotland', *Jurid. Rev. (N.S.)*, ii (1957), 1–20; P. Stein, 'Law and Society in Eighteenth-Century Scottish Thought' in *Scotland in the Age of Improvement: Essays in Scottish History in the Eighteenth Century*, edd. N.T. Phillipson and R. Mitchison (Edinburgh, 1970), 148–68; and P. Stein, *Legal Evolution: The Story of an Idea* (Cambridge, 1980), pp. 3–8.

164   See text above at nn. 81–83 and 117–118.

165   See van den Bergh, op. cit., n. 4 above, pp. 271–74.

166   See text above at nn. 119–22.

167   C.M. Eagles, 'David Gregory and Newtonian Science', *British Journal for the History of Science*, x (1977), 216–25 esp. at p. 221.

regent in Edinburgh, was also aware of Newton's work;[168] but it must be left
an open question whether or not Spotswood was made aware of the new
science through his teachers. Though the influence of these teachers is
incalculable, it may be pointed out that his published works betray a concern with structure and method, even if this is indeed common at this
period. In his *Stile of Writs*, he explained that his purpose 'was in a
Scientifick and Rational way to teach' the writing of deeds and he commented on his 'boldness in venturing to reduce into Rules, and in
Fashioning into a scientifick Form, what was look'd on hitherto to be inca-
pable of Rule, and only acquirable as a mechanical Art, by Practice'.[169] He
planned a further *Analytical and Nomological Treatise of Obligations,
Securities and Conveyances*,[170] and he commented that an analysis of styles
'is as useful to a Writer, as a Sceleton and Anatomy Tables and Carts, is to a
Student of Medicine', so he pointed out to students 'the essential and accidental Clauses of the several sort of Writs and Conveyances'.[171] In his *Law
Concerning Election*, he said that he endeavoured 'to explain the divers
Matters of Law, in a scientifick Method'.[172] The significance of this must
remain undecided; but it does suggest Spotswood's background in Grotian
natural law and modern science.[173]

As noted, Spotswood started to teach the Scots law and civil law in 1702,
advertising his colleges on both in newspapers in November 1703 and June
1705.[174] He obviously taught both courses in his usual two sessions through
1702 to 1705.[175] No advertisements survive after June 1705 until Spotswood
described himself as 'to resume the Teaching of the Law' in May 1710.[176]

---

168   E. Forbes, 'Philosophy and Science Teaching in the Seventeenth Century' in
      Four Centuries: Edinburgh University Life 1583–1983, ed. G. Donaldson
      (Edinburgh, 1983), 28–37 esp. at p. 34.
169   Spotiswood, *Stile of Writs*, n. 37 above, sig. a2v.
170   Ibid., 222. If ever written, this treatise does not seem to have survived. From a
      letter he wrote on 20 December 1712, if we can identify 'the second tome of
      [his] styles' with this work, he had planned to start writing it over the court
      vacation from December 1712 to January 1713: N.L.S., Adv. MS 29.1.1(ii), fo.
      65r.
171   Spotiswood, *Stile of Writs*, n. 37 above, sig. [a3]r.
172   Spotiswood, *Law Concerning Election*, n. 105 above, sig. A2r.
173   On the relationship between natural and moral philosophy at this period, see
      now R.L. Emerson, 'Science and Moral Philosophy in the Scottish
      Enlightenment' in *Studies in the Philosophy of the Scottish Enlightenment*, ed.
      M.A. Stewart (Oxford Studies in the History of Philosophy, 1, Oxford, 1990),
      11–36, at pp. 11–25.
174   See text above at nn. 91–98; *Edinburgh Gazette*, 8/11 Nov. 1703; *Edinburgh
      Courant*, 4/6 June 1705.
175   The lack of advertisements may relate to the irregular survival of copies of the
      Edinburgh Gazette. The evidence of Duncan Forbes indicates Spotswood was
      teaching in 1704: see text above at nn. 144–145; as does Spotiswood,
      Discourse, n.107 above.
176   *Scots Courant*, 1/3 May 1710.

Copies exist of the *Edinburgh Courant* from June 1705 through to September 1706; but there are no advertisements by Spotswood. Yet he seems still to have been teaching, as, in a paper dated 10 November 1705, around when he would have started his winter session, he noted a project to be carried out after revising 'for the colledges of law at 2'.[177] This means he must have taught the winter session through to March 1706. In an account book, he also noted receipts for the colleges through November 1705 to January 1706.[178] A paper dated 25 March 1706, after Spotswood would have finished the winter session, sets out a method of study, including Böckelmann's compend (and other similar works) and Mackenzie's *Institutions*.[179] This could suggest preparation for the summer session. Whether the summer session materialised is unclear. He did not advertise one in the *Edinburgh Courant*; though he could have advertised in the *Edinburgh Gazette*, which has not survived for this period except in the most fragmentary way.[180] From September 1706 to March 1708, the *Edinburgh Courant* also survives only in isolated issues; but it seems clear that Spotswood had stopped teaching by 1708, since, in that year, in the preface to his *Stile of Writs*, he described the collection as intended '[f]or the Use of the Gentlemen, I some time ago Directed in the Study of the *Scots-Law*'.[181] If the class of the winter session 1705–6 was not his last, it was certainly very nearly so.

Why did Spotswood stop teaching? It may provisionally be suggested that he did so because of the success of John Cuninghame who, as we have seen, started to teach in 1705, and who taught not only Scots law and Justinian's *Institutes* but also Justinian's *Digest*.[182] If Spotswood's account book over 1705 to 1706 is an accurate guide, he may have had a significant falling away of pupils.[183] Certainly Cuninghame seems to have monopolised law teaching in Edinburgh from 1708 until his death in 1710.[184]

---

177   N.L.S., MS 658, fo. 27r.

178   N.L.S., MS 2947, fos. 25r, 27r.

179   N.L.S., MS 658, fo. 28r.

180   For information about Edinburgh newspapers, I have relied on the invaluable J.P.S. Ferguson, *Directory of Scottish Newspapers* (Edinburgh, 1984) consulting the actual library when a fairly long but broken run is indicated.

181   Spotiswood, *Stile of Writs*, n. 37 above, sig. a2r.

182   See the advertisements of Cuninghame in the *Edinburgh Courant* of, e.g., 24/26 Mar. 1708, 29 Sept./1 Oct. 1708, 11/14 Mar. 1709, 30 Sept./3 Oct. 1709, 13/15 Mar. 1710; *Scots Courant*, 20/22 Mar. 1710. These advertisements are all repeated in several subsequent issues. In Cuninghame's 1705 and 1706 advertisements (*Edinburgh Gazette*, 3 Aug. 1705; *Edinburgh Courant*, 25 June/8 Oct. 1705, 6/8 May 1706) civil law and Scots law are just mentioned generally; but in at least his first year of teaching he taught only the *Institutes*: Cuninghame, *Oratio inauguralis*, n. 16 above, p. 7.

183   N.L.S., MS 2947, fos. 25r, 27r (this account book may be unreliable, however, as an indicator of the number of pupils).

184   See the advertisements over 1708 to 1710 listed in n. 182 above. No-one else advertised in this period.

In March 1710, Cuninghame advertised his lessons on the *Institutes* of Justinian as beginning again on 13 April, those on the *Digest* as continuing from that date, and those on Scots law as continuing from 5 June.[185] Shortly thereafter he died. On 3 May 1710, Spotswood announced his intention '[a]t the Request of several Gentlemen, and Students of the Law' to resume teaching on 8 May, continuing Cuninghame's colleges, not only on Scots law, but also on Justinian's *Institutes* and *Digest*.[186] On 10 May, however, Spotswood announced the continuation of only his colleges on Scots law.[187] It is unclear whether no students came forward for civil law or whether Spotswood decided not to teach the subject, perhaps because he was not deeply interested in it. However this may be, the probable cause of either was James Craig's advertisement on 5 May of his continuation of Cuninghame's classes on civil law.[188] Other advocates also attempted to seize the opportunity provided by Cuninghame's death, and what may be described as an advertising war broke out between them. Most, if by no means all, of these competitors were interested in the presumably lucrative classes (given the advocates' examinations) on the *Institutes* and *Digest*.[189] Spotswood may have felt it was sensible to concentrate on Scots law, referring in his advertisements to the fact that he had been the first to teach it, his publications in the field, and the necessity of knowledge of styles of securities and conveyances to those in the chambers of writers to the signet.[190]

From advertisements, Spotswood can be traced as teaching his classes on Scots law from 1710 through to his summer session in 1713.[191] This raises two possibilities: first, did he stop teaching again with the summer session in 1713? Or, second, did he stop advertising? In favour of

---

185 *Edinburgh Courant*, 13/15, 15/17, 17/20 Mar. 1710; *Scots Courant*, 20/22 Mar. 1710.
186 *Scots Courant*, 1/3 May 1710 see also 3/5 May.
187 Ibid. 8/10 May 1710.
188 Ibid. 3/5 and 5/8 May 1710.
189 As a sample of advertisements: Sir Archibald Sinclair (*Scots Post Man or the New Edinburgh Gazette*, 25/27 May 1710 and many subsequent); James Lesly (*Scots Courant*, 12/15 May 1710 and many subsequent); Robert Craigie (*Scots Courant*, 17/19 May 1710 and many subsequent); Malcolm Gregory (or McGregory) (*Scots Courant*, 14/16 June 1710; *Scots Post Man or the New Edinburgh Gazette*, 4/6 Nov. 1710); see also the advertisements by John McDowall (*Evening-Post, or, the New Edinburgh Gazette*, 26/28 Dec. 1710; *Scots Courant*, 1/3 Jan. 1711 and many subsequent) who offered courses in classics and history to supplement civil law studies. McDowall was not an advocate. I hope elsewhere to examine in detail this development and the alternative strategies developed by these men to attract students.
190 See, e.g., the advertisements in *Scots Courant*, 8/10 May and 16/18 Oct. 1710 and 25/27 April and 11/14 May 1711; and *Evening-Post, or, the New Edinburgh Gazette*, 3/5 May and 6/8 Sept. 1711.
191 See, e.g., *Scots Courant*, 1/3 May, 8/10 May, and 16/18 Oct. 1710, 25/27 Apr. and 11/14 May 1711; *Evening-Post, or, the New Edinburgh Gazette*, 10/13 March, 3/5 May and 6/8 Sept. 1711; *Scots Courant*, 18/21 Apr. and 20/22 Oct. 1712, and 20/22 Apr. 1713.

the former possibility is one of Spotswood's manuscript class lists which covers his colleges from 8 May 1710, listing students from the summer session of that date when he took over Cuninghame's Scots law class, for every session through to the winter session starting in November 1712. The paper finishes with two headings ('May. 1713' and 'Novr. 1713') each followed by a blank space. Conceivably he attracted no students for his summer and winter sessions in 1713, and in 1712 the numbers of his students had certainly halved (and indeed had been dropping since 1710).[192] In favour of the second possibility is the statement in the preface to the second edition of his *Stile of Writs* (1715) that the collection was made '[f]or the use of the Gentlemen, I Direct in the Study of the *Scots* Law'.[193] This could represent hope rather than reality, and certainly, in the second edition of the *Form of Process* (1718), Spotswood made no allusion to his colleges in the preface, in this differing from the preface to the first edition of 1711;[194] but this is inconclusive. There is, moreover, the equivocal evidence of a set of student notes copied out in 1717. The dictates on the first two books of Mackenzie's *Institutions* derive from Cuninghame's lectures, while those on the last two derive from those of Spotswood. This shows that the original set of notes on which the fair copy is based must have been made in 1710 when Spotswood took over Cuninghame's class of Scots law.[195] In a discussion of the literature on Scots law, however, the notes mention the 1715 edition of Spotswood's *Stile of Writs*.[196] Either the copyist in 1717 updated the reference, or, more likely, he attended a course of lectures delivered by Spotswood between 1715 and 1717, having already obtained (as was not uncommon) an earlier set of notes to aid his attendance at Spotswood's classes. If this is correct, then Spotswood must have been teaching at least sometimes between 1715 and 1717. On balance, it seems likely that, even if Spotswood did not teach every session between 1713 and 1717 (for example, correspondence directed to him at his estate in the summer of 1715 might possibly suggest he did not teach that session,[197] he at least taught for some of them.

---

192 N.L.S., MS 2937, fos. 35r–38v ('Names of the Gentlemen who have been Students In the Colledge of Scotch Law'). For the drop in numbers, see n. 141 above.

193 J. Spotiswood, *An Introduction to the Knowledge of the Stile of Writs, Simple and Compound, made use of in Scotland; . . . Written for the Use of the Students in Spotiswood's Colledge of Law, and now Publish'd for the Common Good. The Second Edition with Additions* (Edinburgh, 1715), sig.*[1]r.

194 J. Spotiswood, *The Form of Process Before the Lords of Council and Session . . . The whole revised, corrected, and very much Augmented in this Second Edition. Written for the Use of the Students in Spotiswood's College of Law* (Edinburgh, 1718), 'To the Reader': compare, *Form of Process*, n. 12 above, 'To the Reader'.

195 N.L.S., MS 3413. See on this MS, n.123 above.

196 N.L.S., MS 3413, XXIV.

197 See the letters from the Earl of Home dated 7 May and 10 June 1715 and from the Earl of Marchmont dated 25 July 1715 in N.L.S., MS 10285, fos. 6–11, which are not addressed to him at Edinburgh, but as 'of that Ilk' or at Spotswood.

Whether or not Spotswood ceased to teach in or after 1713, in October 1719, he again advertised colleges of Scots law to start on 10 November.[198] There is no further information on this college which would have run through to March 1720. In 1721 he was still teaching, as in a letter of 26 June of that year, John Campbell wrote to his father, Patrick Campbell of Barcaldine, explaining that he had decided to wait for Spotswood's winter session of that year rather than attend the summer session.[199] It is probably Spotswood's winter session of this year which is advertised (without the professor being named) in October.[200] If this took place, it would have run through to March 1722.

After this date, no mention of Spotswood's lectures on Scots law can be traced. No arguments can be drawn from his publication in 1723 of an annotated edition of Mackenzie's *Institutions*, his main text book for Scots law;[201] and, indeed, at his death he was putting another elementary text through the press.[202] By this date he had certainly ceased to teach, for, in the third edition of his *Stile of Writs* (1727), he described his collection of styles as intended '[f]or the Use of the Gentlemen, I some Years since directed in the Study of the *Scots* Law'.[203] A plausible hypothesis is that the appointment of Alexander Bayne in 1722 as professor of Scots law in the university of Edinburgh led Spotswood to discontinue his lectures, possibly because Bayne drew away his students.[204] This would fit with his not teach-

198 *Edinburgh Evening Courant*, 29 Sept./1 Oct. 1719.
199 S.R.O., Campbell of Barcaldine Muniments, GD 170/793/3.
200 *Edinburgh Evening Courant*, 27/30 Oct. 1721; *Caledonian Mercury*, 27 Oct. 1721.
201 See n.100 above.
202 *Practical Observations Upon divers Titles of the Law of Scotland, Commonly called Hope's Minor Practicks. Written by Sir Thomas Hope of Craighall, some-time Advocate to King Charles I. . . . To which is subjoined, An Account of all the Religious Houses that were in Scotland at the Time of the Reformation. By the late John Spotiswood of that Ilk, Advocate* (Edinburgh, 1734). In the preface, Spotswood's son alludes at p. iv to the printing being half finished when his father died. (In ibid., p. iv, Spotswood alludes to his father's Scots law lexicon – this cannot refer to N.L.S., MSS 2944–2945 (incomplete) which contain references to matters and statutes years after Spotswood's death.)
203 J. Spotiswood, *An Introduction to the Knowledge of the Stile of Writs, Simple and Compound, Made use of in Scotland . . . Written for the Use of the Students in Spotiswood's College of Law, and now publish'd for the common Good. The Third Edition with Additions* (Edinburgh, 1727), sig. a4r.
204 See A. Grant, *The Story of the University of Edinburgh During its First Three Hundred Years.* 2 vols. (London, 1884), i, 288. In *The Law Concerning Election of Members for Scotland, To Sit and Vote in the Parliament of Great-Britain . . . The Second Edition Corrected and Augmented with several Acts and Statutes relative to Elections* (Edinburgh, 1722), Spotswood omitted from his Preface the first paragraph – alluding to the problems of structuring material for students – which was found in the first edition, n. 105 above, sig. A2r; but, since he was still teaching in 1721, it is difficult to draw any significance from this, and he did mention the view of 'some Friends' that the essay 'ought not to be confin'd to private students' (though this is alluding to the 1710 edition).

ing civil law in 1710 after James Craig (and others) also advertised lectures, especially when, later in 1710, Craig was appointed first professor of civil law in the university of Edinburgh.[205] Bayne, like his teacher, Spotswood, also taught Scots law on the basis of Mackenzie's *Institutions.*[206] Though he was by no means elderly, infirmity may also have influenced Spotswood. Duncan has pointed out that Spotswood took little part in running the Advocates Library for some years before his death.[207]

By the 1720s, the position of legal education in Scotland had changed. In 1707 the regius chair of public law and the law of nature and nations was established in the university of Edinburgh, to be followed by the two other professorships already mentioned.[208] In 1719, in the same university, a chair of universal history was created which largely dealt with the needs of law students.[209] A regius professor of law was appointed in 1714 in the university of Glasgow, with the professor's duties limited to civil, feudal, canon, and Scots law.[210] By the date of Spotswood's death, the need for legal education which he had met privately was largely being provided for by these two universities, even though private teachers can still be traced subsequently.[211]

The subjects covered by the four Edinburgh chairs associated with legal studies followed the curriculum established as desirable by Spotswood as early as 1701 (supposing the students came to them after their basic courses in arts).[212] It is less easy to infer an influence on the development of legal education in Glasgow, given that there was only one chair in law in that university; but it is worth noting that, from 1692, there was in Glasgow a lectureship in civil history, and in 1722, the professor of ecclesiastical history, William Anderson, advertised classes on universal history.[213]

205 Grant, op. cit., n. 204 above, i, 284–85.
206 See A. Bayne, *Notes, for the Use of the Students of the Municipal Law in the University of Edinburgh: Being a Supplement to Sir George Mackenzie's Institutions* (Edinburgh, 1731). For use of the *Institutions* in law teaching, see J.W. Cairns, 'John Millar's Lectures on Scots Criminal Law', *Oxf. Jour. Leg. Stud.*, viii (1988), 364–400 at pp. 382–89.
207 Duncan, op. cit., n. 147 above, p. 29; I am grateful to Dr. B. Hillyard for confirming this to me from his study of the records of the Library in this period.
208 Grant, op. cit., n. 204 above, i, 232–33 and 283.
209 Ibid., at i, 285–88; see also L.W. Sharp, 'Charles Mackie, the First Professor of History at Edinburgh University', *Sc. Hist. Rev.*, xli (1962), 23–45. In the 1750s and 1760s the Faculty of Advocates encouraged intrants to attend the lectures given by the holder of this chair: Cairns, 'Formation of the Scottish Legal Mind', n.5 above, pp. 265–66.
210 J. Coutts, *A History of the University of Glasgow From its Foundation in 1451 to 1909* (Glasgow, 1909), pp. 193–94; *Munimenta alme Universitatis Glasguensis: Records of the University of Glasgow from its foundation till 1727*, ed. C. Innes. 4 vols. (Maitland Club, Glasgow, 1854), ii, 411.
211 See, e.g., the advertisement by John Lookup, advocate, in *Edinburgh Evening Courant*, 12/16 Oct. 1732.
212 See quotation in text above at nn. 82–83.
213 Coutts, op. cit., n.210 above, p. 170; *Edinburgh Evening Courant*, 11/15 Oct. 1722. Anderson described himself as 'Professor of History' in this advertisement.

Furthermore, in 1723, the professor of humanity in Glasgow advertised private classes on Roman books for, among others, law students.[214] Natural jurisprudence would have been taught by the regents in philosophy, and the most noted of them of this period, Gershom Carmichael, first professor of moral philosophy after Glasgow gave up the regenting system in 1727,[215] published an annotated text of Pufendorf's treatise *De officio hominis et civis* as a student manual.[216] While the classes in history and natural jurisprudence in Glasgow were perhaps connected more with general instruction in arts rather than with the requirements of legal education, the faculty had certainly envisaged in 1714 the possibility that law students would also need to take classes from professors other than that of law.[217] It is clear, however, that the curriculum in law was to broaden under John Millar, professor in Glasgow from 1761 to 1801.[218] At a different level, one may infer the influence of Spotswood's views on legal education from his nomination in 1724 to the committee of the Faculty of Advocates appointed to consider the proposed examination in Scots law of all intrants.[219]

While the conception of legal studies as consisting of civil law (encompassing in this Grotian natural jurisprudence), municipal law, history and philology (taking the last two in a wide sense) was scarcely original, being ultimately of humanist origin, Spotswood, perhaps drawing on his experiences in Leiden, and taking into account the two modes of qualifying for the Scots bar, shaped into a settled curriculum the inchoate expressions

---

214 See *Edinburgh Evening Courant*, 10/14, 17/21, and 21/22 Oct. 1723. See Coutts, op. cit., n. 210 above, p. 188.

215 Coutts, op. cit., n. 210 above, pp. 207–8.

216 *S. Puffendorfii de officio hominis et civis, juxta legem naturalem, libri duo. Editio nova, aucta observationibus & supplementis, academicae institutionis causa adjectis A Gerschomo Carmichael philosophiae in academia Glasguensi professore* (Glasgow, 1718); (other editions: Edinburgh, 1724; 2 vols., Leiden, 1769 (not seen)). It is the 1724 edition which contains Carmichael's extensive annotations and commentary. On Carmichael, the teacher of Francis Hutcheson, see J. Moore and M. Silverthorne, 'Gershom Carmichael and the Natural Jurisprudence Tradition in Eighteenth-Century Scotland' in *Wealth and Virtue: The Shaping of Political Economy in the Scottish Enlightenment*, edd. I. Hont and M. Ignatieff (Cambridge, 1983), 73–87.

217 *Munimenta alme Universitatis Glasguensis*, n.210 above, ii, 411.

218 See J.W. Cairns, 'John Millar and Innovation in Law Teaching', unpublished paper delivered to the Scottish Legal History Group, October 1988, abstract in *Jour. Leg. Hist.*, x (1989), 394–95.

219 See *Minute Book*, ii, 74 (15 Feb. 1724); he was not at the meeting of the committee, however, which drafted the crucial report: ibid., 74–75 (22 Feb. 1724). The presence on the committee of Alexander Bayne, professor of Scots law in Edinburgh, and Spotswood's pupil, suggests Spotswood's appointment to it was based on his experience in legal education. On the curious parallelism of Spotswood's and Bayne's careers, see W. Menzies, 'Alexander Bayne of Rires, Advocate', *Jurid. Rev.*, xxxvi (1924), 60–70 at pp. 63–64. Menzies's article is out-dated in some respects, but there is greater evidence of Bayne 'understudying' Spotswood than he perceptively suggests: notably Bayne achieved Spotswood's desire of a university appointment.

of desire on legal education found, for example, in the Faculty's views in 1695.[220] And although some of the details of instruction were to vary, and later in the century there was to be significant change,[221] Spotswood established a basic pattern for legal education in eighteenth-century Scotland, whereby Scots law was taught using Mackenzie's *Institutions*, and civil law by using a compend, with joined to both a study of history, classical culture, and natural jurisprudence. This was to be an important legacy.

---

220 See text above at nn. 117–22.
221 I have explored some of the later developments in J.W. Cairns, 'John Millar's Lectures on Scots Criminal Law', n. 206 above; in 'Rhetoric, Language and Roman Law: Legal Education and Improvement in Eighteenth-Century Scotland', *Law and History Review*, ix (1991), 31–58; and in two conference papers: 'Mackenzie's *Institutions* and law teaching in eighteenth century Scotland', unpublished paper delivered to the Scottish Legal History Group, October 1984, abstract in *Jour. Leg. Hist.*, vii (1986), 86–87; and 'John Millar and Innovation in Law Teaching', n. 218 above.

LORD GEORGE DOUGLAS (1667/1668?–1693?) AND HIS LIBRARY

By W.A. KELLY, M.A., PH.D., F.L.A.,

National Library of Scotland

The library of Lord George Douglas was one of the earliest donations to the Advocates Library. The high regard in which it was held in the early years of the Library's existence contrasts with the oblivion into which it fell later. My investigation of the library was based on the manuscript catalogue and other documents now in the possession of the Faculty of Advocates and the origins were elucidated by the letters written by Douglas and his tutor to the former's father.[1]

Lord George Douglas was born in 1667 or 1668, the third and youngest son of William, first duke of Queensberry. After schooling possibly in Dalkeith and certainly in Haddington he matriculated on 1 December 1682 in the fourth class at Glasgow University, into which most students were admitted until the humanity class was revived in 1683.[2] The detailed picture given us by Coutts of the arts course at the university in the 1650s was in large measure applicable in Lord George's day. Accordingly he and his contemporaries in the fifth and fourth classes, the most junior ones, were drilled mostly in Latin and Greek, with some introduction to Hebrew later. One of Lord George's classmates was Archibald Campbell, the eldest son of Lord Neil Campbell of Ardmaddie, who was later to achieve an equivocal fame as a non-juring bishop, and a more respectable, if less public, one as a book collector.[3] The mention of Lord George, the Hon. Archibald Campbell and other sons of noble Scottish houses in the matriculation lists is evidence of the University's ability at that time to attract students from the higher reaches of society.[4] What little evidence we have of Lord George's undergraduate career comes from two lists of books which had been bought for him in the autumn of 1683.[5] The contents of the first list, which are mostly in Latin and are concerned largely with religion and philosophy, have come down to us virtually intact, while the fate of those in the second, all in English and mostly historical, is unknown. Of those books which have survived many bear on the flyleaf Lord George's signature and

1   The Library of Lord George Douglas (*c.*1667/8–1693?) (M.A. thesis, Department of Librarianship, University of Strathclyde, 1975), hereafter 'Kelly'. I am grateful to the Faculty of Advocates and to the Duke of Buccleuch and Queensberry for access to these materials.

2   *Munimenta Almae Universitatis Glasguensis*, ed. C. Innes. 4 vols. (Maitland Club, 72, Glasgow, 1854), iii, 140; J. Coutts, *A History of the University of Glasgow* (Glasgow, 1909), pp. 108 ff. and p. 155; J.D. Mackie, *The University of Glasgow, 1451–1951* (Glasgow, 1954), p.127.

3   *D.N.B.*, iii, pp. 791–92.

4   Mackie, op. cit., p. 127.

5   Kelly, pp. 414–18.

the date 1685. The purchase some two years before their use of Derodon's *Opera philosophica*, More's *Enchiridion ethicum*, and of Descartes' *Epistolae, Meditationes de prima philosophia, Passiones animae, Principia philosophiae* and *Specimina philosophiae* would suggest that, his intellectual promise having been recognised not long after the start of his university career, his father wished to provide him with more than the basic requirements of the philosophy part of the arts curriculum. Besides a good knowledge of the theories of Descartes and also of Antoine Le Grand he seems to have been acquainted already with Thomas Burnet's theory of the origins of the universe, which had been greatly influenced by Newtonian philosophy.

The religious works owned by Lord George at this time and later provide us with an excellent insight into his spiritual views. His collection of Bibles reflects not only his own scholarly tastes, but also those of his countrymen. Though Scots such as Henryson, Scrimgeour and Buchanan were widely recognised in their own day and later for their classical scholarship, their countrymen in general had contributed very little to a scholarly study of the languages in which the Bible had been transmitted to post-Reformation Europe; thus Scottish Protestants still had to rely on foreign productions, both Protestant and Roman Catholic. The only Latin translation of the entire Bible in Lord George's library, that containing the work of Tremellius and Junius on the Old Testament and that of Beza on the New Testament, and the translation of the New Testament by Castellio, were standard Protestant works, while the Greek texts represented both parties. On the Romanist side stood the translation of the Old Testament issued on the authority of Pope Sixtus V, and on the Protestant the editions of the New Testament produced by Estienne, Froben and Episcopius, and an edition in Hellenistic and modern Greek with a preface by Cyril Lucaris, the Protestantising Patriarch of Constantinople. A noticeable feature of the religious works owned by Lord George was the number of translations. From his days at university, when he was reading *The whole duty of man*, usually attributed to Richard Allestree, in the Latin translation prepared for Westminster School, to the time of his Continental tour, when he was acquiring not only translations of the Bible, or of parts of it, into Italian, Dutch, French and even Romansch, but also Richard Lucas's *Practical Christianity* in French and Calvin's *Institutes of the Christian Religion* in Spanish, he seems deliberately to have used devotional works as an aid to learning foreign languages.

There is no evidence that Lord George graduated before leaving Glasgow University, at the end of March 1686 to judge from his accounts, but to one of his social position the general education offered by a university was more important than a degree. Despite the disfavour which was felt in some quarters towards the custom of sending young men abroad as a means of preparing them for a learned profession or public service, the Duke seems to have entertained no doubts about its value to his youngest son's prospects.[6]

---

6   J. Howell, *Instructions for Foreign Travel*, ed. E. Arber (English Reprints, 16, London, 1869), p. 11; R. Lassels, *The Voyage of Italy* (Paris, 1670), p.[12]; [R.

As the youngest son of a duke, with almost no hope of succeeding to the title, Lord George was faced with the necessity of making his own way in the world. However, in the hope that he would follow in the family's tradition of public service, he was to receive a thorough grounding in law and allied subjects.[7] To this end the Duke chose as tutor a trained lawyer and classical scholar, Alexander Cunningham, who had obtained his M.A. at Edinburgh University.[8] After a brief stop in Rotterdam Lord George and Cunningham settled into lodgings in Utrecht in mid-July 1686. The choice of Utrecht was influenced as much by the Duke's concern for his youngest son's somewhat delicate health as by his desire to protect his own position. Having been stripped of his public offices, he would be open to the slightest suspicion of disaffection towards King James. It is therefore understandable that he should forbid his son, whose rank was to be kept secret, to associate in any way with English or Scots, especially Scottish army officers and refugees of either nationality, or to visit the court of William of Orange, who was deeply distrusted by his father-in-law, King James.[9]

For the first six months in Utrecht Lord George received most of his introduction to Roman law from Cunningham. Both reported in the letters to the Duke that the university term was so far advanced by the time of their arrival that it would be best for Lord George, who had no previous knowledge of the subject, not to attend too many public lectures on it. Cunningham informed the Duke that his practice was to go over with his charge the material covered in the public lectures. This method is confirmed by numerous marginal notes in their hands in a copy of Vinnius's edition of Justinian's *Institutes* published at Leyden in 1646, which is now among the Advocates' Manuscripts on deposit in the National Library of Scotland. In the published catalogue only Cunningham's hand was recognised in this copy, and the notes were dated to the early years of the eighteenth century, some

6...   Hurd], *Dialogues on the Uses of Foreign Travel*, (2nd edn. London, 1764), pp. 8, 104, 129; V. Knox, *Liberal Education* (London, 1781), p. 333; J. Milton, *A Tractate of Education* (Berwick upon Tweed, 1753), pp. 29–30.

7   Kelly, p. 63.

8   *D.N.B.*, v, 306; T.B. Smith, 'Scots Law and Roman-Dutch law: A Shared Tradition' in *Studies Critical and Comparative* (Edinburgh, 1962), p. 51; R. Feenstra and C.J.D. Waal, *Seventeenth-century Leyden Law Professors and their Influence on the Development of Civil Law: A Study of Bronchorst, Vinnius and Voet* (Amsterdam, 1975), pp. 86–87; R. Feenstra, 'Scottish-Dutch Legal Relations in the Seventeenth and Eighteenth Centuries' in *Scotland and Europe: 1200–1850*, ed. T.C. Smout (Edinburgh, 1986), 135–36; G.C.J.J. van den Bergh, *The Life and Work of Gerard Noodt (1647–1725): Dutch Legal Scholarship between Humanism and Enlightenment* (Oxford, 1988), pp. 78–79. Van den Bergh is no doubt correct in drawing attention to Cunningham's having studied at Utrecht as a possible reason for its choice as Lord George's first stop in his Continental tour. However, in describing my speculations for the choice as superfluous he has failed, I believe, to appreciate the delicacy of Queensberry's position in wishing his son to avoid the company of Scottish and English exiles.

9   Kelly, p. 64.

twenty years too late.[10] He also told the Duke that, not long after settling at Utrecht, he had started to show Douglas round the bookshops in order to acquaint him with the best editions of legal, historical and classical texts and their prices. He did not hesitate to report later that he had helped Douglas to acquire many of these works by guiding his purchases at second-hand dealers and auctions; nor was he slow to point out, with Lord George's support, that by doing so he had saved the Duke a great deal of money. Both his knowledge of books and his expertise in Roman law, which he so freely put at Lord George's service, gained him the younger man's unstinted admiration. The money spent on books both in Utrecht and elsewhere on the tour was to prove a source of friction between the Duke and the two travellers. The Duke, who was neither a miser nor a philistine, but was in fact in danger of bankrupting himself throughout this period as a result of stretching his resources in the construction of Drumlanrig Castle, was eager to have less money spent on clothes, as well as on books. Lord George and Cunningham, to judge from references in their letters and accounts, seem genuinely to have spent very little on clothes, often to the surprise of many of those with whom they came in contact later in Germany. Knowing Lord George's rank, they found it hard to believe that a nobleman could dress so simply. As to the books, they alternated between pleas that those they bought could be obtained in few other places, and had moreover been acquired at very reasonable prices, and confessions that they had perhaps been a little extravagant, and intended to buy no more, a promise for the breaking of which they usually found a good excuse.

In the latter half of April 1687 they moved to Heidelberg, where Lord George began a course of lectures on Grotius's *De jure belli* and on natural law, as well as continuing to receive private tutoring from Cunningham. Consideration of the next stage of their tour had to begin towards the end of the summer of that year, when Cunningham announced that Lord George, through no fault of his own, had become well known to many prominent people in the town. The next town decided on was Strassburg, to which they moved at the beginning of April 1688. There they lodged with the professor of Eloquence and dined with one of the professors of Law. The mornings were taken up with instruction in Roman law from Cunningham and the afternoons with lectures on Canon law and European history from the time of Charlemagne. These lectures he attended only because they were given by his landlords, though he felt that he could have spent the time to greater profit under Cunningham's tutelage. Though Lord George's impression of the Rhineland town was a favourable one, they only remained there until the end of August, moving on to Basle, where they found lodgings with Buxtorf, the professor of Hebrew, who also acted as university librarian. With his help Lord George gained access to the university library's holdings of manuscripts and medals; a knowledge of these and subjects such as inscriptions and ancient geography, Lord George assured

---

10   N.L.S., *A Summary Catalogue of the Advocates' Manuscripts* (Edinburgh, 1971), item 838, p. 68.

his father, were very necessary preparations for his tour of Italy. His legal studies, which he forecast would of necessity be interrupted by these other studies, were further curtailed by his Italian lessons. In these his prodigious progress can be estimated by his remark to his father a month or so later that he had already read Sarpi's history of the Council of Trent and Machiavelli's works.[11] If he did not spend as much time as formerly on law, his buying of books continued unabated. The Duke of course jibbed at the expense involved, but was met with a number of spirited replies from Lord George, who, while remaining outwardly deferential towards his father, was showing definite signs of that independence of mind so characteristic of the Queensberry Douglases.[12] In an impressive defence, which proved how much he had benefitted from Cunningham's lessons on legal, classical and historical bibliography, he pointed out that many of the volumes which he had bought were not in the university library at Basle, and that certain other libraries, including the Advocates Library, had been prepared to pay very highly for some which he had acquired quite inexpensively.[13]

The long awaited Italian part of the tour began in mid-September 1689 when they arrived in Milan, where they spent much of the time in the Ambrosian Library. From there they moved to Florence in mid-October, where they visited the Grand Duke's Library. Although the Grand Duke and his librarian were highly impressed by Lord George's learning, a more exacting critic, Gottfried Leibnitz, who met him and his tutor during his own tour in Italy, was not unnaturally more impressed by Cunningham, whose legal acumen he never ceased to admire.[14] In spite of Leibnitz's objective appraisal favouring Cunningham, Lord George, drawing on his earlier study of manuscripts, gave a good account of himself in reading the Florentine Pandects.[15] Pleasant as was the stay in these towns, it was merely a preliminary to the visit to Rome, where Lord George and Cunningham arrived on 14 December 1689. As if to impress on the Duke that Lord George would probably not study as much in Rome as in other places Cunningham wrote to point out that, if his charge lived as retired a life there as elsewhere, he would lose the benefit of the conversation of the learned. Though he certainly spent more time on cultivating the society of such people both there and elsewhere for the remainder of his tour, he did not neglect the opportunities offered to him for intellectual stimulation in the Italian capital. Armed with such aids as the *Guida angelica per visitar le chiese ... di Roma* (Rome, 1681), he saw all the sights as well as managing to improve greatly his knowledge of Italian by reading with a hired teacher a number of poets. Indeed such was his preoccupation with Italian literature that Cunningham, by way of excuse, assured the Duke that, although it was a delight rather than instructive, Lord George would make good use of it. Though Lord George's legal studies had been neglected somewhat since his arrival in

11   Kelly, p. 43.
12   C.T. Ramage, *Drumlanrig Castle and the Douglases* (Dumfries, 1876), p. 36.
13   Kelly, p. 44.
14   G.W. von Leibnitz, *Opera omnia.* 6 vols. (Genevae, 1768), v, 571.
15   Kelly, p. 45.

Italy, his grasp of the subject was such that he could, according to Cunningham, recover his detailed knowledge in a few months. The possibility that Cunningham's assertion might be put to the test was mentioned obliquely in the first letter sent from Venice on 15 February, when he referred to a plan of the Duke that Lord George should leave Italy and study law at some unspecified place in Germany.[16] In opposition Cunningham asserted that his charge, besides being able to learn more by private study than he could under any professor, either in Italy or in Germany, would be better advised to study politics, diplomatic history, and the law of nature and of nations. Such a course of study would be, in Cunningham's opinion, of far greater value to an aspiring diplomat such as Lord George than an exact knowledge of law. Apart from the Duke's later, rather half-hearted suggestion that his son should take a doctorate in law at Padua University there was no further exhortation to him to occupy his time in serious study of any kind.

By the beginning of April 1692 Lord George and Cunningham had moved to Germany, and from that point on until his return to London the former led the life of a cultured sightseer, moving in circles which few grand tourists of a later age were able to enter for all their financial resources. For the rest of his stay on the Continent Lord George's letters, though still of interest, tend to be taken up with lists of the people he had met and with information about exchange rates. Various German cities were visited, including Leipzig, Dresden and Berlin, before they moved briefly to Poland, where Lord George was entertained by a number of Scots merchants resident there. The latter country was visited as an alternative to a visit to Scandinavia, to which the Duke made some unknown objection.

Within a few days of their arriving in London at the end of November 1692 Lord George was presented to the King, who asked him for an account of his travels, and he was invited to join the Royal Society. Although there had been speculation in the latter part of his tour of an offer of an embassy to Lord George, Cunningham was able to report to the Duke by the end of the year that he confidently expected the King to offer Lord George the choice of a post in Sweden, Denmark or Brandenburg. If any of these were selected, the Duke would have to let his decision be known quickly to his son, who was in favour of accepting. As late as the middle of January 1693 the Earl of Nottingham was able to tell Lord George that the King was prepared to give him another three or four weeks to come to a decision. It is a matter of some surprise that the Duke, who since the mid 1680s at least had hoped that his son would follow a public career, and who had known for some weeks of the necessity for a quick decision, should have delayed. His silence meant that Lord George and Cunningham, who had reported before a definite offer of a post had been made that for health reasons he could not travel north before the spring, had to undertake the journey to Scotland during a frosty spell. They arrived in Edinburgh on the afternoon of 27 January and planned to leave for Sanquhar within a few days. At this point

---

16   Ibid, p. 50.

our information on Lord George ends. Although the date of his death is unknown, it is generally accepted that it occurred some time in July 1693.[17] The only certain fact is that he was buried in the family's vault at Durrisdeer Parish Church, which lies in the barony of Drumlanrig.[18]

Lord George's library comprises over eight hundred titles, of which the legal texts are the most important section. Extensive though this collection was, it is by no means complete. It would be difficult to imagine that anyone, even one endowed with Lord George's advantages of wealth, position and first-class bibliographical advice from Cunningham, could have acquired all published legal materials of importance before his twenty-eighth birthday.

The earliest text of Roman law represented in Lord George's library is the Basle 1528 edition of Theodosius II's *Codex*, followed by the Nuremberg 1530 edition of Justinian's *Codex repetitae praelectionis* and the editions by Scrimgeour and Pacius of the *Novels*. Although there is no copy in his library of Dionysius Gothofredus's 1583 edition of the *Corpus iuris civilis*, which has been claimed as making the first use of the fuller term in the title, the text was represented by the two-volume Paris 1628 edition. If that term had in fact been used first by Gothofredus, it was a coinage for which the path had been prepared by earlier publications such as the 1570 edition of Haloander, of which Lord George owned a copy.

It should not surprise us that he owned a copy of the commentaries of Bartolus, in the four-volume Venice edition of 1570 – indeed it would be a major and most alarming lacuna if he had not owned an edition. In view of the continued reputation of the commentators in Spain and Germany it is also natural that he should have owned editions of Didacus Covarruvias's *Opera* (Frankfurt, 1573) and Benedikt Carpzov's *Commentarius in legem regiam Germanorum* (Frankfurt, 1677) and *Practica nova imperialis Saxonica rerum criminalium* (Wittenberg, 1652). Besides his copy of the former's works the other works on Canon law in Lord George's library were the three-volume edition by Perrinus and Fontanus of the *Decretum* of Gratian and the *Decretals* of Pope Gregory IX, Agustín's two-volume summary of earlier ecclesiastical law, *Iuris pontifici veteris epitome*, Lancellotti's *Institutionum ad universum ius pontificium, sive canonicum, libri quatuor* (Basle, 1566) and Corvinus's *Jus canonicum per aphorismos strictim explicatum* (Amsterdam, 1657).

Considerable though the influence of the commentators had been on legal development in Europe, the scholasticism of its chief representatives was challenged and eventually overthrown by champions of the revival of classical learning which manifested itself in Italy in the mid-fifteenth century. An idea of the comprehensive education which humanists expected a student of law to possess can be seen in Jan van der Linden's belief that the preparatory studies necessary for the training of a lawyer are

17   Sir J.B. Paul, *The Scots Peerage*. 9 vols. (Edinburgh, 1904–14), vii, 140.
18   Ramage, op. cit. n. 12 above, pp. 381–83.

1. A thorough knowledge of Latin ...
2. A knowledge of Greek ...
3. A knowledge of Roman history and antiquities ...
4. A knowledge of the history of Roman law ...
5. A general knowledge of philosophy ... principally logic ... mathematics ... and ethics ...
6. Some acquaintance with modern or living languages.[19]

It is to Lord George's credit that he could have placed a tick against each of these requirements. The first goal of the French humanists was to reconstruct the texts of Roman law by means of such tools as philology, history, numismatics and inscriptions. One of the main obstacles to any previous attempt to produce an accurate text of Justinian's *Digest* was the restricted access to the principal manuscript, which from 1406 to the end of the eighteenth century was kept in an iron-gilt chest at the Palazzo Vecchio in Florence. If a bare inspection of the manuscript, such as that accorded to Lord George, was allowed only under ceremonial safeguards, permission to collate it was an honour very sparingly granted, and one to which the favoured few naturally raised no objection. Reprehensible as is the use, particularly without acknowledgment, of a secondary source by an editor when a primary one is available, much more damning is the representation of readings from a transcript as those of the original manuscript. This was the case with the copy of the Florentine Pandects which Bolognini left to the Benedictines of Bologna on condition that they imposed on its accessibility restrictions similar to those imposed on the original. In fact he went further and stipulated that, if anything were copied from it, the Benedictines would forfeit it. Two scholars, Alciati and Haloander, who were allowed not only to see the transcript but also to publish their readings – and both works found their way into Lord George's library – were hardly in a position to reveal the breaking of the donor's injunction, or so their apologist, Agustín, argued.[20] The consequence of their enforced silence was that for more than a generation readings from the transcript had borne the authority of a primary source. Among the editions of the *Corpus iuris civilis* produced in furtherance of the humanists' first goal, a goal given substantial aid by the published works of Cujas, were those of Charondas, Gothofredus and Pacius.

The humanists' second goal, consequent upon the first, was to show the original significance of Roman law and to what extent their synthesis of it was applicable to their own age. The humanists' very real sense of revolt from the medieval lawyers' reluctance, indeed failure, to go back to the sources of Roman law was closely linked to their belief that the judicial

---

19   J. van der Linden, *Institutes of Holland, or Manual of Law, Practice, and Mercantile Law* ... Trans. Sir Henry Juta (5th edn., Capetown, 1906), pp. xxxiii–xxxv. Quoted in A.A. Roberts, *A South African Legal Bibliography* (Pretoria, 1942), p. 12; see also J.W. Cairns, 'John Spotswood, Professor of Law: A Preliminary Sketch', above at pp. 145–46.
20   F. de Zulueta, *Don Antonio Agustín* (David Murray Lectures, 8, Glasgow, 1939), p. 43.

abuses prevalent in their own day could be reformed by the introduction of Roman concepts and principles. However, this approach, which dealt first with general principles and only then moved on to specific details, was one to which the *Corpus* was unfortunately unsuited. In an attempt to resolve this difficulty they were compelled to embark on a complete reconstitution of the content of the *Corpus*. One of the first to tackle this problem was Franciscus Duarenus, of whose works, all written in an elegant classical style, Lord George owned one, the Frankfurt 1607 edition of his *Commentarii in Digesta*. It was left to one of Duarenus's pupils, Hugo Donellus, to effect the wholesale reworking of the established legal system, a process which is represented in Lord George's library by three works of his, including the eight-volume Frankfurt 1596 edition of his *Commentaria in jus civile*. Despite the great reputation which Donellus's work acquired in Germany, where it was regarded as a model of the systematic approach to law, his work, like that of his fellow systematists, worked rather to lessen the authority of Roman law. Although Donellus insisted against his critics' charge of seeking to overthrow the authority of the *Corpus* that it could be saved only by a rearrangement of its parts, his accusation that Justinian's jurists were ignorant of jurisprudence made it difficult to accept like the systematists that the fragments of the *Corpus* could be reduced to a system.

The demand for a system of law reorganised on new principles was started in France, where a respect was also growing for customary law among legal thinkers, particularly Hotman, Bodin and Balduinus. A considerable intellectual authority had always been accorded in France to Roman law, the progress of which in the later Middle Ages had been aided there by a chaos of conflicting local customs, but it had never been accepted fully as the common law. However from the middle of the fifteenth century the reception of Roman law in France had suffered a major and irreversible setback when a beginning was made on editing local customs, albeit with the assistance of Roman legal ideas.[21] This process of comparison and synthesis was seen as a possible basis for a new legal code by Charles Du Moulin, whose *Commentarii in Parisienses totius Galliae supremi parliamenti consuetudines* (Bern, 1603) was owned by Lord George.

A much more developed comparative approach was carried out by Bodin, whose appeal to history was combined with a rejection of a solely Romanist jurisprudence. Though he is often assumed to have been a neo-Bartolist, the review of Roman jurisprudence prefixed to his *Methodus ad facilem historiarum cognitionem*, which Lord George owned in the Heidelberg 1591 edition, shows that he was a humanist. His allegiance to his early training at Toulouse University is shown further by his fourfold classification of contemporary jurists. The first and worst is the cloistered academic, of whom Cujas is held up as the standard offender, while mere empiricists, who have picked up prudence from the law courts, are lumped in the second class with the barest of mentions. Only when one considers

---

21   J.H. Franklin, *Jean Bodin and the Sixteenth Century Revolution in the Methodology of Law and History* (New York, 1963), p. 37.

the third class, that is those in whom practice was combined with precepts, does one find something of value. This class contains all of Bodin's favourite contemporaries, among whom are Baron, Connan and Du Moulin. All of those in this class are represented in Lord George's library. However the highest class – of whom Bodin seems to be the only member – comprises those jurists in whom philosophy and literary culture are joined to precepts and experience.[22]

That the humanist theorists nevertheless failed to carry all before them can be seen in the figure of Albericus Gentili, who raised a powerful voice in defence of Bartolist methods from his exile in England. In keeping with his realistic attitude towards legal education he took a keen interest in all the legal, political and moral questions of his day, as he exhibited in his *Prima commentatio de iure belli*, of which Lord George owned the Hanau 1598 edition. In approaching the subject from a non-military standpoint Gentili can fairly be regarded as the real founder of modern international law. In his work he struck out on a new path by rejecting both the theological assumptions and the abstract, metaphysical speculations which characterised the work of his predecessors such as Suarez. These he rejected because to his mind they envisaged an ideal system of law which was divorced from the real world with which lawyers had to deal. Although he was out of step with his new countrymen in his anti-humanist views, he was able to exert a strong influence on later English-born writers on international law, particularly John Selden and Richard Zouche. The latter has been credited with being the second father of the law of nations, perhaps because he introduced the term *ius inter gentes* in place of the older less exact *ius gentium*.[23] However his use of this phrase has been described by one critic as the only noteworthy feature of his *Iuris et iudicii fecialis, sive, iuris inter gentes, et quaestionum de eodem explicatio*, a copy of the Oxford 1650 edition of which was in Lord George's library.[24] In his work Zouche was more concerned with citing examples and precedents than with working out a system of law. He was at one in this with other English writers, who adopted a practical attitude to their subject. This can be seen in Selden's *Mare clausum*, but also in Hobbes's *Elementa philosophica de cive*, which were both owned by Lord George, as well as in the philosophical writings of Bacon and Locke. Gentili's complaint about previous writers having mingled natural law, divine law, the law of nations, civil law and canon law was reiterated by Grotius in the introduction to his *De jure belli et pacis*, of which Lord George owned a copy of the Hague 1680 edition.

Important as the last-named writer was in the development of the law of nations, he is much more important for his contribution to the theory of natural law. Though himself a Protestant, he was at pains to rebut the neo-

---

22   Ibid, pp. 66–67.
23   [C. Phillipson], 'Richard Zouche' in *Great Jurists of the World*, edd. Sir J. Macdonnell and E. Manson (London, 1913), p. 22.
24   H. Wheaton, *History of the Law of Nations in Europe and America* (New York, 1845), p. 101.

Aristotelian belief of many contemporary Protestant writers in the state as ultimately based upon the will of God. This rebuttal, he realised, could be achieved only by constructing a theory of natural law on a scientifically sound basis. His influence in this respect is seen in the works of later writers such as Regnerus ab Oosterga, Bachov ab Echt and Huber, each of whom was represented in Lord George's library.

In the search for a scientific basis for his system of jurisprudence the analogy with mathematics suggested itself to Grotius, but it was left to a later writer, Pufendorf, to develop it. The son of a clergyman and himself destined for the church, Pufendorf was sent to Leipzig University, but, finding the teaching of the theological faculty too narrow and dogmatic, he moved in 1656 to Jena University. There he formed a close friendship with the mathematician, Erhard Weigel, who introduced him to the philosophy of Descartes and demonstrative methods of reasoning.[25] Weigel's teaching is seen most clearly in Pufendorf's *Elementa jurisprudentiae universalis*, of which Lord George bought a copy of the Jena 1669 edition in Utrecht. It was not until 1672 that his most famous work, *Juris naturae et gentium libri octo*, which Lord George owned in the second, revised Frankfurt edition of 1684, appeared. In this he presented an entire system of jurisprudence, private, public and international, based on the concept of natural law.

It is possible that Pufendorf's work was already known to Stair when he was preparing his *Institutions of the Law of Scotland.*[26] This possible familiarity with Pufendorf's work, however, does not imply that he was closely influenced in his thinking by the German writer. Though a convinced Presbyterian, he did not hold the extreme voluntarist views of his co-religionists; neither did he go to the opposite extreme with Pufendorf when the latter argued that God, having once created man as a rational being, could not possibly constitute an irrational law for him.[27] Like his fellow lawyers in Scotland, however, Stair was greatly influenced both in his professional duties and in his own writings by Continental jurists, mainly Dutch, German and French. Many authors are quoted by Stair as well as in the decisions of the Court of Session collected by Fountainhall.[28] It is a mark of the richness of Lord George's library that he owned the published works of many of these selfsame authorities: Bechmann, Böckelmann, Brandmüller, Clarus, Gaill, Giphanius, Gothofredus, Gudelin, Huber, Matthaeus, Panciroli, Petitus, Someren, Wesenbeck and Wissenbach.

Lord George was fortunate in being able to entrust the shipping of his books home to a Scottish banker resident in Rotterdam, James Gordon. Though this arrangement ensured that the books were safely packed, it

25   H. Schüling, *Erhard Weigel (1625–1699): Materialien zur Erforschung seines Wirkens* (Berichte und Arbeiten aus der Universitätsbibliothek Giessen, 18, Giessen, 1970).

26   A.H. Campbell, *The Structure of Stair's Institutions* (David Murray Lectures, 21, Glasgow, 1954), p. 23.

27   Ibid., p.28

28   Sir J. Lauder, Lord Fountainhall, *The Decisions of the Lords of Council and Session, from June 6th, 1678, to July 30th, 1712* (Edinburgh, 1759–61).

could not avoid the hazards of sea travel or delays caused by bad weather.
Soon after his arrival in London Lord George informed his father that
Gordon still had in store books bought nearly five years earlier in Strassburg
which might better be left with him until the spring.[29] If this advice was followed, it seems possible that the entire library was assembled at Sanquhar
Castle, the Duke's residence, only a month or so before Lord George's
death. The presence of the Queensberry arms, often accompanied by the
Duke's initials, W.D., on the boards of many of Lord George's volumes suggests that the Duke had at one time intended keeping his son's library.
Some time later, however, he apparently changed his mind, for at a meeting
of the Faculty of Advocates on 1 March 1694/95 the dean, Hugh Dalrymple,
announced that the Duke intended to donate the collection to the Faculty,
in response to which the members decided to have the books set up in distinct presses surmounted by a suitable inscription.[30] One authority speaks of
this decision as if it had actually been carried out, although there is no mention in the Faculty's records of the work having been done.[31] Moreover
when the English bibliophile, the Rev. T.F. Dibdin, visited the library in 1838
he made no reference to Douglas's books, which he probably would have
done, had they been specially designated.[32] A possible answer to the problem is to be found in the fire which befell the Advocates Library in early
February 1699/1700. In the Faculty's minutes for 26 July 1701 there is a list
of books from the Library's general collections lost in the fire, followed by a
separate list of twelve items from Lord George's library which had
perished.[33] In the need to provide new accommodation and fittings for the
Library the Advocates may well have had to postpone any plans for provid-
ing special shelves for Lord George's books. This would seem to be corroborated by the changes of pressmarks recorded in his books.

Lord George's books were formally handed over to the Faculty by
Alexander Cunningham on the Duke's behalf. After their transfer a
manuscript catalogue, fifty three pages in length, was drawn up by the
Keeper of the Library, James Stevenson, in which the books were listed by
size, beginning with folios and ending with octavos and smaller formats,
with copies of the Faculty minutes relating to the donation appended. It
would appear that this catalogue was intended as a receipt for the Duke,
for, besides the Queensberry arms stamped on its boards, it bears a
Queensberry library pressmark. The volume was offered as item 4429 in the
auction of the books of James, second Duke, which was held between 18

29   Kelly, p. 119.
30   *The Minute Book of the Faculty of Advocates, Volume 1. 1661–1712*, ed. J.M.
      Pinkerton (Stair Society, 29, Edinburgh 1976), p. 153.
31   Ramage, op. cit., n. 12 above, pp. 381–82.
32   T.F. Dibdin, *A Bibliographical, Antiquarian and Picturesque Tour in the
      Northern Counties of England, and in Scotland.* 2 vols. (London, 1838), ii, pp.
      591–604.
33   *Minute Book of the Faculty of Advocates*, n. 30 above, p. 225.

November and 29 December 1813.[34] Whether by purchase or by donation it returned to the Faculty, where it still is.

Though only two of the twelve volumes from Lord George's library listed as missing after the fire in February 1699/1700 were actually destroyed, the fact that the collection was distinguished in this way from the general stock shows the respect in which it was held. Continuing evidence of this high regard is reflected in the catalogue of the Library's holdings which Thomas Ruddiman signed on taking over as Keeper in 1730. The general 'Catalogue of the Books in the Bibliotheck pertaining to the Faculty of Advocates at Edinburgh' was followed by 'A Catalogue of Lord George Douglas his Books, which his Father William Duke of Queensberry (after his decease) gave in to the Faculty of Advocates'. Such a high opinion, however, contrasts all the more with the oblivion into which Lord George and his library fell in later times, as can be seen in the report published by the Faculty on its legal collections in the early 1950s. In commenting on volumes donated to the Library by members of the Faculty, the author, D.M. Walker, erroneously included George Douglas, but about him he knew no more than that his *floruit* was about 1686.[35]

---

34   *Catalogue of a Valuable Collection of Books, including ... [those] of James, the Second Duke of Queensberry ... which will be sold by auction ... by J. Ballantyne* (Edinburgh, 1813), p. 167.

35   [D.M. Walker], Report to the Dean of Faculty on books in the Advocates' Library presently housed in Room 'J'. [Typescript] [Edinburgh, 1952], p. 7. Quoted with the permission of the Clerk to the Faculty of Advocates.

STAIR'S LATER REPUTATION AS A JURIST: THE CONTRIBUTION OF WILLIAM FORBES

By HECTOR L MacQUEEN, LL.B., PH.D.[1]

Department of Scots Law, University of Edinburgh

The tercentenary of the publication of Stair's *Institutions* in 1681 prompted the appearance of several re-evaluations of the work and the place in Scottish legal history of its author, the eponym of this Society. Perhaps the fullest discussion has concerned the problem of the institutional writers of Scots law, those authors some of whose works (often entitled *Institutes* or *Institutions*) are treated as formal sources of law possessed of a particularly high authority. Amongst them, it is now generally agreed, Stair stands pre-eminent in the field of civil (as distinct from criminal) law. The historical questions, however, are when, how and why the category of institutional writers, and Stair's leading position within it, came into existence. John Blackie's contribution to the *Stair Tercentenary Studies* published in 1981 suggested that Stair's work was not immediately accorded the supreme status amongst Scottish law books that it later enjoyed. Rather this, along with the whole concept of the 'institutional writers', was a development of the early nineteenth century.[2] Never clearly and definitively rationalised or, indeed, articulated, the category remains an amorphous one to the present day, as John Cairns has pointed out.[3]

Institutes or institutions of law are found not just in early modern Scotland but throughout contemporary Europe, including England.[4] They were, however, typically introductory works divided into four books on the model of Justinian's *Institutes* and they were usually intended for use in

---

1   This paper was first presented at a meeting of the Legal History Discussion Group, Faculty of Law, University of Edinburgh, where I received many helpful comments. I am further indebted to my colleagues, Dr. J.W. Cairns and Mr. W.D.H. Sellar, and to Professor W.M. Gordon, for valuable comment on a revised version.

2   J.W.G. Blackie, 'Stair's Later Reputation as a Jurist' in *Stair Tercentenary Studies*, ed. D.M. Walker (Stair Society, 33, Edinburgh, 1981), 207–27.

3   J.W. Cairns, 'Institutional Writings in Scotland Reconsidered', *Jour. Legal History*, iv (1983), 76*–117*, reprinted in *New Perspectives in Scottish Legal History*, edd. A. Kiralfy and H.L. MacQueen (London, 1984), 76–117. See especially pp. 98–104.

4   K. Luig, 'The Institutes of National Law in the Seventeenth and Eighteenth Centuries', *Jurid. Rev.*, xvii (1972), 193–226; A. Watson, *The Making of the Civil Law* (Harvard, 1981), pp. 62–82; idem, 'Justinian's *Institutes* and Some English Counterparts', in *Studies in Justinian's Institutes in Memory of J.A.C. Thomas*, edd. P.G. Stein and A.D.E. Lewis (London, 1983), 181; idem, 'The Structure of Blackstone's *Commentaries*', *Yale Law Jour.*, xcvii (1988), 795–821; Cairns, 'Institutional Writings', pp. 78–88; idem, 'Blackstone, an English Institutist', *Oxf. Jour. Leg. Stud.*, iv (1984), 318–60.

legal education. The genre is best represented in Scotland, not by the massive works of Stair, Lord Bankton, John Erskine or the *Commentaries* of George Joseph Bell, but by the much smaller texts of Sir George Mackenzie and William Forbes, and the *Principles* of Erskine and Bell.[5] Although Stair seems to have been the first in Scotland to make use of the title *Institutions*, his work does not altogether conform to the European institutional pattern, a fact which may have prompted the publication of Mackenzie's *Institutions* only three years later. Certainly it is possible to see some implied criticism of Stair's work in Mackenzie's comment that 'the natural and easie way of writing [Institutions] is by going from the first principle to a second and from that to a third, the admired method of Euclid in his elements, though much neglected by all who have written Institutions of Law'.[6] It is surely significant that Stair only adopted the Justinianic structure of four books in his second edition, published in 1693, following its employment by Mackenzie in his work. It has also been pointed out that Stair's views on the sources of Scots law were not consistent with those of Mackenzie, whose opinions on this subject were more in line with the earlier orthodoxies of Balfour, Skene, Craig and Hope, and continued to be upheld by most Scottish jurists in the eighteenth century.[7] Alan Watson has gone so far as to argue that Mackenzie's *Institutions* were written 'in response to, in emulation of, and with some irritation at, Stair's *Institutions*'.[8] Whether or not this is accepted, it seems clear that the *Institutions* of Stair were not wholly free from contemporary criticism.

Contemporary evaluations of Stair's achievements are also likely to have been coloured by the political controversies which surrounded his career. He was a figure much more in the public eye for political reasons than would be expected of a judge today. When Stair died in 1695, it was a sufficiently noteworthy event for a litigious minor landowner in Berwickshire, George Home of Kimmerghame, to record the fact in his private diary: 'Sunday December 1st. At Church I heard the Vicount Stair dyed on munday of a strangury or as some say ane Ulcer in his bladder. He was 77 years old'.[9] Amongst various actions which led to fierce criticism during his lifetime were acceptance of appointment as a judge during the Cromwellian Commonwealth; his qualified declaration against leagues and covenants in 1664 which allowed him to retain his seat on the bench; his relationship with the Duke of Lauderdale, who held sway over Scotland from the Restoration until 1681, was responsible for a policy of brutal repression against the Covenanters, and was frequently accused of corruption and partiality in his administration; his appointment as Lord President

---

5   Cairns, 'Institutional Writings', pp. 90–94.
6   Mackenzie, *Institutions*, Dedication.
7   H.L. MacQueen, 'Mackenzie's *Institutions* in Scottish Legal History', *Jour. Law Society of Scotland*, xxix (1984), 498–501.
8   A. Watson, 'Some Notes on Mackenzie's *Institutions* and the European Legal Tradition', *Ius Commune*, xvi (1989), 303 at p. 310.
9   *An Album of Scottish Families 1694–96*, edd. H. and K. Kelsall (Aberdeen, 1990), p. 101.

under Lauderdale's patronage in 1671; his role in the disbarment of the advocates in 1674; his refusal in 1681 to take the Test against leagues and covenants opposing the king, leading to his exile to Holland in 1682; and his return to Scotland and restoration to the Presidency by King William following the Glorious Revolution.[10] It is difficult, if not impossible, to determine the extent to which criticism of Stair's actions was justified; but the legal and constitutional theory which seems to inform the *Institutions* clearly had a political edge which many in seventeenth-century Scotland must have found hard to accept, and which may have accordingly detracted from the status to be accorded to the work. Even his judicial conduct was not above reproach: Dr Cairns has drawn attention to the criticisms of Stair by his contemporary, John Lauder of Fountainhall, suggesting that his decisions were influenced by his family and political friends.[11] Thus in one case in 1677 Stair's court reversed four previous decisions that a particular ship was the subject of prize and held it free; 'some thought Lauderdale influenced this change', comments Fountainhall.[12] He also noted of a decision in 1672 that it was 'shaking the very foundations of law and leiving nothing certaine',[13] while another in 1676 'took back with the on [*sic*] hand what it gave with the other'.[14] During his second term as President, Stair was sued by one Duncan Robertson and his spouse, who alleged buying of pleas and abuse of process in a complex executry matter.[15]

In his recently published *Scottish Jurists*, David Walker has come to the defence of Stair's character and argued for an immediate contemporary recognition of the pre-eminence of his work. He is able to point to praise of Stair by contemporaries and near-contemporaries, and gives particular prominence to some observations about him made by William Forbes, Regius Professor of Law at Glasgow University 1714–45.[16] These views (which Professor Blackie characterises as being possessed of 'some hyper-

---

10   For accounts of Stair's life see A.J.G. Mackay, *Memoir of James Dalrymple, First Viscount Stair* (Edinburgh, 1873); J.L. Duncan, 'The Life and Times of Viscount Stair', *Jurid. Rev.*, xlvi (1934), 103; G.M. Hutton, 'Stair's Public Career', in *Stair Tercentenary Studies*, cit. sup. n. 2, p. 1; D.M. Walker, *The Scottish Jurists* (Edinburgh, 1985), pp. 106–18.
11   J.W. Cairns, Book Review, *North. Ire. Leg. Quart.*, xxxvii (1986) at p. 405.
12   *Historical Notices of Scotch Affairs selected from the MSS. of Sir John Lauder of Fountainhall.* 2 vols. (Bannatyne Club, 1848), i, 132.
13   Ibid., i, 40.
14   Ibid., i, 116.
15   *Information for Mr. Duncan Robertson and his Spouse against the Viscount of Stair, Lord President of the Session, and Mr. Patrick Smith and his Spouse* (Edinburgh, 1695); *Information for the Viscount of Stair, Lord President of the Session, to vindicate him from the calumnies contained in the petition of Mr. Duncan Robertson* (Edinburgh, 1695).
16   Walker, *Scottish Jurists*, pp. 120–22. On Forbes see also ibid., pp. 185–94 and D.M. Walker, *A History of the School of Law: the University of Glasgow* (Glasgow, 1990), pp. 23–24, both of which should be read in the light of J.W. Cairns, 'The Origins of the Glasgow Law School: the Professors of Civil Law 1714–1761', in *The Life of the Law: Select Proceedings of the Tenth British Legal History Conference*, ed. p. Birks, forthcoming.

bole'[17]) are found in the preface to Forbes's *Journal of the Session*, a collection of the decisions of the Lords of Session published in 1714. They are quoted in *extenso* by Professor Walker, who also comments in a note that 'there must have been many lawyers alive in 1714 who remembered Stair, so that Forbes's estimate is probably substantially accurate'.[18] The relevant passage certainly gives a glowing view of Stair and his work, as can again be seen from its reproduction here:[19]

> During the long Time he was a Judge, none could ever stain him with the least Malversation or Insolence in his great Trust, at a Time when it would have been thought obliging and good Service to Men of Power, who wanted nothing more than the least Ground to call him in Question. He could not indure to be solicited, or impertinently addressed to in Matters of Justice. The Memory of the many good Regulations in the Form of Process before the Session owing to his Lordship will never be obliterated. He had a stiff Aversion from being concerned in Criminal Matters, either as a Judge or a Lawyer. In the Matter of Civil Government, he was always for sober Measures. He thought it neither the Interest nor Duty of Kings to rule arbitrarily: Both King and People have their Titles and Rights by Law; and an equal Ballance of Prerogative and Liberty being necessary to the Happiness of a Common-wealth. His Judgment never led him to use or approve Severity against those, who being sound in the Fundamentals of Religion, differ'd only in Circumstantials. When he sat in the Privy Council, he always interpos'd so far as he could with Safety, to rescue the suffering Presbyterians from suffering the sharp Edge of penal Laws, to which they lay obnoxious in the Reign of King Charles the II and suffered often publick Reproach for his so doing. Where he gave it as his Opinion, that the Privy-Council, to whom the Government and Policy of the Nation was committed, ought to be equally prudent and just in applying the Severity of the Laws: albeit Judges in other Courts are to walk by the Letter of the Law, however rigorous and hard. He was a devout Christian, a sincere Protestant, and a true son of the Presbyterian Church of Scotland, tho' prudence allowed him not at all Times to make a Noise. He approv'd himself to be of steddy Principles, in thrice forsaking his honourable and profitable Station, rather than comply with the Corruption of the Time. 1. He refused absolutely to take the Usurper's Tender, and contentedly sat down with the Loss of a beneficial Imployment as an Advocate, till it was dispens'd with. 2. He risked his Place of an ordinary Lord of Session,

---

17   Blackie, 'Stair's Later Reputation', n. 2 above, p. 221.
18   Walker, *Scottish Jurists*, p. 152 n. 91.
19   W. Forbes, *A Journal of the Session Containing the Decisions of the Lords of Council and Session in the Most Important Cases Heard and Determin'd From February 1705 till November 1713* (Edinburgh, 1714), pp. xxxviii–xl.

in the Year 1664, before he would sign, without a Commentary, the Declaration then imposed on all in Publick Trust. And 3. exposed himself to be shuffled out of his Presidency (as he was) in the Year 1681, by his boldly standing up in Defence of the Protestant Interest. In the midst of the Multiplicity of Civil Business, which his Imployment and Character brought upon him, he always found some Time for the Study of Divinity, wherein he arriv'd to a deep Pitch of Knowledge and directed every Thing else to it. In short he was indefatigable in Business, even when he might have used the Privilege of his Age to ly by and withdraw from it. He knew not what it was to be idle, and took a strict account of his Time: Dividing himself between the Duties of Religion, and the Studies of his Profession, which he minded the more than the raising a great Fortune. He was sober, temperate and mighty regular. He duly prayed always and read a Chapter of the Bible to his Family before they sat down to Dinner, and performed the like divine Service after supper: Which he would not interrupt upon any Consideration of Business, how important soever. He had a great Spirit, and equal Temper in the harshest Passages of his Life: By the constant Bent of his Thoughts to what was serious or profitable, he knew how to divert them from any uneasy Impression of Sorrow. He was apt to forget, at least not to resent Injuries done to him, when it was in his Power to requite them.

His excellent Writings will carry down his Memory to the latest Posterity. His *Institutions of the Law of Scotland*, wherein that is compared with the Canon and the Civil laws, and the Customs of neighbouring Nations, are so useful, that few considerable Families in Scotland, not to mention professed Lawyers, do want them. He hath therein so cleared up the Springs and Grounds of our Law, that had been damm'd up from ordinary Observation by Rust and Rubbish, and reduc'd it into a sound and solid Body (for which he deserves to be reckon'd a Founder and Restorer of our Law) that if it were lost, it might be retrieved, and the tenor on't made up out of his excellent *Institutions*. He hath judiciously observed the Decisions of the Session from the Restauration of the Sovereignty, and Re-establishment of the College of Justice to it's ancient Constitution and Splendor, till August 1681: In which he hath not omitted any Case of Difficulty or Importance determined when he was present on the Bench; without expressing his own Opinion when different from that of the Plurality of the Lords, out of Modesty and Deference to their Judgment. He wrote them *de die in diem*, commonly before Dinner when fresh in his Memory: And was the more fitted to do it, that he was not a Day absent during that Period of 20 Years, except the Time of the Summer-Session 1679 when he attended the King by his Majesty's special Order. I have seen his *Philosophia Nova Experimentalis*. He wrote a Treatise concerning the Royal Prerogative and the Rights and Privileges of the Subject, and some Sheets in Vindication of the Church Government: But I don't remember to have seen either of these in Print. He wrote also *A Vindication of the Divine Perfections*, which was published at London in the Year 1695, with a Preface by Doctors W. Bates and J. Howe; wherein these learned divines give this character of the book: *The Clearness and Vigour of the noble Author's Spirit are illustriously visible in managing a Subject so deep and difficult. And in his unfolding the glorious and amiable Excellencies of the Blessed God, there is joined with the Strength of Argument, that Beauty of Expression, as may engage all Readers, to be happy in the entire Choice of God for their everlasting Portion. Which Performance shews it to be a Thing not impracticable, as it is most praiseworthy, amidst the greatest secular employment, to find Vacancy and a Disposition of Spirit to look with a very inquisitive Eye into the deep Things of God: Which (if it were the Author's Pleasure to be known) would let it be seen, the Statesman and the Divine are not Inconsistencies to a great and comprehensive Mind.*

Professor Walker notes that this estimate of Stair 'never appears to have been challenged'.[20] There is a difficulty, however, in regarding it as a wholly detached and objective assessment of Stair. This is because it can be shown to be derived almost entirely from Stair's own defence of his career and work, *An Apology for Sir James Dalrymple of Stair, President of the Session, by Himself*, published in 1690 in response to a pamphlet attack against him launched the previous year.[21] The attack was contained in an anonymous pamphlet entitled *The Late Proceedings and Votes of the Parliament of Scotland contained in an Address Delivered to the King, Signed by the Plurality of the Members thereof, Stated and Vindicated* usually attributed to Robert Ferguson, a non-conforming minister nicknamed 'the Plotter'. The parliament of 1689 had come into conflict with King William and his advisers (including Stair) over whether judicial appointments pertained to the royal prerogative or to parliament. Stair's reappointment as President of the Session was made by virtue of the prerogative. Ferguson's pamphlet is a sustained polemic against the king's advisers who, he argues, are overthrowing the laws of Scotland and enabling the reassertion of arbitrary and despotic power. Stair's appointment to the Presidency is a particular target. The passage which forced Stair into a public defence is an extra-ordinary piece of sustained invective:[22]

Staires [*sic*] assuming the Office of President, upon the illegal Choice of the forementioned King, was both an Affronting and

---

20   Walker, *Scottish Jurists*, p. 152 n. 91.
21   I have used the original eight page edition. The text was reprinted as *Dalrymple's Apology* by the Bannatyne Club in 1825 and again in More's edition of Stair's *Institutions* (Edinburgh, 1832).
22   (Glasgow, 1689), pp. 32–33.

Betraying of the known Laws of the Kingdom; so his whole behaviour in that Station was of one piece and complexion with his entering upon it, being a continued series of Oppression and Treachery to his Country. For besides that all his Verdicts between Subject and Subject, were more Ambiguous than the Delphick Oracles, and the occasion of the Commencement of innumerable Suits in place of the determinating of any, he was the principal Minister of all Lauderdale's Arbitrariness, and of King Charles's Usurpations. Nor was there a Rapine or Murder committed in the Kingdom under the countenance of Royal Authority, but what he was either the Author of, the Assister in, or ready to justify. And from his having been a Military Commander, for asserting and vindicating the Laws, Rights and Liberties of the Kingdom against the little pretended Invasions of Charles I, he came to overthrow and trample upon them all in the quality of a Civil Officer under Charles II. Nor is their [sic] a Man in the whole Kingdom of Scotland, who hath been more accessary to the Robberies and Spoils, and who is more stained and dyed with the Bloody Measures of the Times than this Lord Staires [sic], whom, his Majesty hath been impos'd upon to constitute again President of the Colledge of Justice. And as an aggravation of his Crimes he hath perpetrated them under the vail of Religion, and by forms of Law: Which is the bringing in the Holy and Righteous God to be an Authorizer and Approver of his Villanies, and the making the Shield of our Protection to be the Sword of our Ruin. But there being some hopes that the world will be speedily furnished with the History of his Life, I shall say no more of him, but shall leave him unto the expectation and dread of what the famous Mr Robert Dowglass foretold would befal him in his Person and Family, and of which having tasted the first Fruits in so many astonishing Instances, he may the more assuredly reckon upon the full Harvest of it. And the method he hath lately begun to steer is the most likely way imaginable to hasten upon him and his, what that Holy, and I might say, Prophetical Man denounced against them. For whereas the Nation would have been willing upon his meer withdrawing from Business, and not provoking their Justice by crouding into the Place in which he had so heinously Offended: To have left him to stand or fall at the great Tribunal, and to have indemnify'd him as to Life, Honour and Fortune here, upon the consideration of his having co-operated in the late Revolution, and of his having attended upon his Majesty in his coming over to rescue and deliver the Kingdoms from Popery and Slavery: He seems resolved to hasten his own Fate, and through putting himself by new Crimes out of the capacity of Mercy, to force the Estates of the Kingdom to a punishing of him, both for them and the old.

Stair's reply is usually known as *Dalrymple's Apology*, and is so referred to here, because it was published just before he was elevated to his viscountcy in May 1690. In addition to the passages about to be quoted, Stair sought to refute the claim that appointment to the Presidency of the Session did not fall within the royal prerogative, and denied that Mr Robert Douglas (a moderate Presbyterian minister) had ever prophesied the doom of his family.[23] Our concern is not with these arguments, however, but to show the way in which Forbes used *Dalrymple's Apology* in composing his panegyric on Stair's character, career and achievement. Forbes also made use of Stair's own preface to the first volume of his *Decisions*, published in 1683 and a work with which Forbes's *Journal* has other significant links, as will be shown later. These borrowings by Forbes from Stair's own writing do not account for everything found in the passage from the *Journal* quoted by Professor Walker, however; nonetheless there is an argument, to be set out more fully below, that those sentences not dependent on Stair should also be treated with care before they are accepted as evidence of any general early eighteenth century assessment of the value of his work.

The first task is to show the extent of Forbes's dependence on Stair's own words in the *Journal* preface. This is done here by means of parallel passages, taking Forbes's words sentence by sentence, except where there is a block of connected sentences related by their reference to a particular topic or issue. For convenience of later reference, each section thus treated has been numbered. The page references are to the original edition of *Dalrymple's Apology*:

1. *Forbes:*

   During the long Time he was a Judge, none could ever stain him with the least Malversation or Insolence in his great Trust, at a Time when it would have been thought obliging and good Service to Men of Power, who wanted nothing more than the least Ground to call him in Question.

   Dalrymple's Apology:

   All his malice hath not prevailed with him, to asperse me with any thing that concerns my special Trust, as Senator of the Colledge of Justice... or as President of it ... (p 2). No man was found to witness the least Malversation or Baseness by indirect interest in any Cause, by taking any Bribe or Reward, by Partiality or Insolency, though nothing would have been more acceptable to the Court than by one blow against my Fortune and Fame, to have ruined me, upon Malversation in my trust as a Judge. (p 3).

---

23   The Douglas story is probably to be related to the well-known series of misfortunes which befell Stair's family, for which see Mackay, *Memoir*, n. 10 above, pp. 81–88.

2. *Forbes:*
He could not indure to be solicited, or impertinently addressed to in Matters of Justice.

Dalrymple's Apology:
When my Sons came to the House, I did most strictly Prohibite them to Solicite me in any Case, which they did exactly Observe. (p 3)[24]

3. *Forbes:*
The Memory of the many good Regulations in the Form of Process before the Session owing to his Lordship will never be obliterated.

Dalrymple's Apology:
I was also the first Author, and prime promoter of that Order of bringing in Processes, for every person, without exception, as they were ready, that the greatest man of the Nation could not have preference before the meanest, and that all might be free of uncertain attendance; Whereas before, all depended upon the Arbitrary Calling of the Lords, as they pleased; so that every Judge might call his own Friends, in his own Week. (p 6)

4. *Forbes:*
He had a stiff Aversion from being concerned in Criminal Matters, either as a Judge or a Lawyer.

Dalrymple's Apology:
I did never medle in any Criminal Court, nor was I ever Judge, Pleader, Juror or Witness therein. (p 3)

5. *Forbes:*
In the Matter of Civil Government, he was always for sober Measures. He thought it neither the Interest nor Duty of Kings to rule arbitrarily: Both King and People have their Titles and Rights by Law; and an equal Ballance of Prerogative and Liberty being necessary to the Happiness of a Common-wealth.

Dalrymple's Apology:
As to the matter of Civil Government, since I was capable to consider the same; I have ever been perswaded, that it was both against the Interest and Duty of Kings, to use Arbitrary Government; that both Kings and Subjects had their titles and rights by Law; and that an equall ballance of Prerogative and Liberty was necessar for the happiness of a Common-wealth. (p 4)

---

24   But cf. Fountainhall's comment of one case that Stair had been solicited by his wife and that his son had 'agented shamefully' for a party (*Historical Notices*, i, 37). During Stair's Presidency, however, there were at least three Acts of Sederunt against solicitation of the judges: Mackay, *Memoir*, pp. 136–37, 267–69.

6. *Forbes:*

His Judgment never led him to use or approve Severity against those, who being sound in the Fundamentals of Religion, differ'd only in Circumstantials. When he sat in the Privy Council, he always interpos'd so far as he could with Safety, to rescue the suffering Presbyterians from suffering the sharp Edge of penal Laws, to which they lay obnoxious in the Reign of King Charles the II and suffered often publick Reproach for his so doing. Where he gave it as his Opinion, that the Privy-Council, to whom the Government and Policy of the Nation was committed, ought to be equally prudent and just in applying the Severity of the Laws: albeit Judges in other Courts are to walk by the Letter of the Law, however rigorous and hard.

Dalrymple's Apology:

But my Judgment and Inclination never led me to use or approve severity against these, who suffered for serving God in the way they were perswaded, without Idolatry or overturning the Principles of Religion, necessar for holiness and happiness, so far I was from being the Author, or justifier of the severities used against those of my own Perswasion, of whom many are my witnesses, that I did what I durst to save them, and I was always so esteem'd, and often publicly reproacht in Council for so doing...[25] and in the Council I did frequently declare my Judgment, that though in other Courts the Judges were oblidged to follow the Law, although rigorous; yet the Council, to whom the Policy and Government of the Nation is committed by the King, was not bound so to apply the severities of the Law, but as they judged it as well prudent as just. (p 3)

7. *Forbes:*

He was a devout Christian, a sincere Protestant, and a true son of the Presbyterian Church of Scotland, tho' prudence allowed him not at all Times to make a Noise.

Dalrymple's Apology:

I was ever fully perswaded (since I came to ripeness of Age) of the Truth of the Protestant Religion, and of the Constitution and Government of my Mother Church, and Prelacy reformed from Popery, though Prudence allowed me not at all times to make noise. (p 3)

8. *Forbes:*

He approv'd himself to be of steddy Principles, in thrice forsaking his honourable and profitable Station, rather than comply

Dalrymple's Apology:

Let my enemies then, show how many they can instance in the Nation, that did thrice forsake their station, though both Honourable

25   Some support for this contention of Stair may be found in Fountainhall, *Historical Notices*, i, 235 and 273 and Mackay, *Memoir*, pp. 133–34.

with the Corruption of the Time. 1. He refused absolutely to take the Usurper's Tender, and contentedly sat down with the Loss of a beneficial Imployment as an Advocate, till it was dispens'd with. 2. He risked his Place of an ordinary Lord of Session, in the Year 1664, before he would sign, without a Commentary, the Declaration then imposed on all in Publick Trust. And 3. exposed himself to be shuffled out of his Presidency (as he was) in the Year 1681, by his boldly standing up in Defence of the Protestant Interest.

and Lucrative, rather than comply with the Corruption of the time. (p 5) To shew how little I have been a Changeling, or Time-server, it is commonly known, and there are hundreds can witness, that I was excluded from the Bar, for not taking the Usurper's Tender, engaging to be faithful to the Commonwealth of England without King or House of Lords, and never appeared again, till that Tender was laid aside. (p 4) But when the Declaration was enacted by Parliament, required of all in Publick Trust, I did rather renounce my place than take it, and did retire unto the Countrey, where I lived a Year, privatly and quietly, but, without my desire or expectation, K[ing] Ch[arles] called me to London, and desired me to return to my Station in the Session, and when I told him, I could not sign the Declaration, unless it were so explicat and restricted, that by the general Terms expressed in it, I did declare against no more than what was opposite to his Majesties just Right and Prerogative, and that I should have these terms from his Majesty in Writing, which he granted, and I have yet to shew, which the Act of Sederunt at my Restitution doth import. And in the third place, when the late Test was enacted in the Parliament 1681, though I was well pleased with the first part of it, which was the safest Hedge against Papists, that ever I saw, yet I could not sign the latter part of it ... I did therefore go up to the King, to shew him, that I could not take that Test, to desire Liberty, with his favour to retire, but, before I came, the new Commission for the Session, wherein I was left out, was past, so that I had no further to say; and therefore I neither did resign, nor was excluded by the Act of the Test, seing the day was not come, but by meer Arbitrary Power. (pp 4–5)

[No parallel in *Dalrymple's Apology*.]

9. *Forbes:*
In the midst of the Multiplicity of Civil Business, which his Imployment and Character brought upon him, he always found some Time for the Study of Divinity, wherein he arriv'd to a deep Pitch of Knowledge and directed every Thing else to it. In short he was indefatigable in Business, even when he might have used the Privilege of his Age to ly by and withdraw from it. He knew not what it was to be idle, and took a strict account of his Time: Dividing himself between the Duties of Religion, and the Studies of his Profession, which he minded the more than the raising a great Fortune. He was sober, temperate and mighty regular. He duly prayed always and read a Chapter of the Bible to his Family before they sat down to Dinner, and performed the like divine Service after supper: Which he would not interrupt upon any Consideration of Business, how important soever. He had a great Spirit, and equal Temper in the harshest Passages of his Life: By the constant Bent of his Thoughts to what was serious or profitable, he knew how to divert them from any uneasy Impression of Sorrow. He was apt to forget, at least not to resent Injuries done to him, when it was in his Power to requite them.

10. *Forbes:*

His excellent Writings will carry down his Memory to the latest Posterity. His *Institutions of the Law of Scotland*, wherein that is compared with the Canon and the Civil laws, and the Customs of neighbouring Nations, are so useful, that few considerable Families in Scotland, not to mention professed Lawyers, do want them.

Dalrymple's Apology:

I may say without vanity, that no man did so much, to make the Law of this Kingdom known and constant, as I have done, that not only bred Lawers, but generally, the Nobility and Gentry of the Nation might know their Rights. And I did Write the Institutions of the Law of Scotland, and did derive it from that Common Law that Rules the World, and compared it with the Laws Civil and Canon, and with the Custom of the Neighbouring Nations; which hath been so acceptable, that few considerable Families of the Nation want the same, and I have seen them a-vending both in England and Holland. (p 6)

11. *Forbes:*

He hath therein so cleared up the Springs and Grounds of our Law, that had been damm'd up from ordinary Observation by Rust and Rubbish, and reduc'd it into a sound and solid Body (for which he deserves to be reckon'd a Founder and Restorer of our Law) that if it were lost, it might be retrieved, and the tenor on't made up out of his excellent *Institutions.*

[No parallel in *Dalrymple's Apology.*]

12. *Forbes:*

He hath judiciously observed the Decisions of the Session from the Restauration of the Sovereignty, and Re-establishment of the College of Justice to it's ancient Constitution and Splendor, till August 1681: In which he hath not omitted any Case of Difficulty or Importance determined when he was present on the Bench; without expressing his own

Dalrymple's Apology:

I did carefully and faithfully observe the Debates and Decisions of the Lords of Session, during all the time I was in it, expressing mainly the Reasons that the Lords laid hold on, in all important Cases, which were not come to be incontroverted, as a beaten Path, or were obvious to common capacities, and I did seldom eat or drink and scarcely

Opinion when different from that of the Plurality of the Lords, out of Modesty and Deference to their Judgment. He wrote them *de die in diem*, commonly before Dinner when fresh in his Memory: And was the more fitted to do it, that he was not a Day absent during that Period of 20 Years, except the Time of the Summer-Session 1679 when he attended the King by his Majesty's special Order.

ever sleept, before I perused the Informations that past every Sederunt day, and set down Decisions of the Lords, (though, sometimes, not in the same Terms as they were marked by the Clerks; for at that time the Interlocutors were all upon their Trust, without being Revised and Signed by the President, as now they are) while they were fresh in my memory. (p 6)

Stair's Decisions:
Our sacred Sovereign who now reigns did restore the Colledge of Justice to its ancient constitution and splendor ... It was very necessary that their decisions should be observed which induced me ... to undertake that task, which I did constantly follow, making up this Journal of all the decisions that had any thing of difficulty or importance in them ... I did not pick out such decisions as I liked best, leaving out others which might have shown contrariety; nor did I express my opinion when different from the plurality, but I ever had that deference to your judgment that I did not omit any thing that was said for it, much less did I magnifie my own opinion against it, though I cannot say that I did oft differ from it. I did form this Breviat of these decisions, in fresh and recent memory, *de die in diem* as they were pronounced; I seldom eat, before I observed the Interlocutors I judged of difficulty that past that day, and when I was hindered by any extraordinary occasion, I delayed no longer than that was over ... I had the best opportunity to make these Observations, being scarce a day absent in any of these Sessions wherein I have marked them from the first of June 1661 until the first of August 1681. And I was not one day absent from the thirteenth of January 1671 when it pleased his Majesty to appoint me to be constant President of the Session ... except the Summer Session 1679 when I attended his Majesty by his own command.[26]

13. *Forbes:*
I have seen his *Philosophia Nova Experimentalis.*

[No parallel in *Dalrymple's Apology.*]

---

26   Observe how both Stair and Forbes refer to 'the Session' rather than 'the Court of Session'. The latter description of the court seems to be first found in Article XIX of the Treaty of Union and was certainly not Scottish usage until some time after 1707.

14. *Forbes:*

He wrote a Treatise concerning the Royal Prerogative and the Rights and Privileges of the Subject, and some Sheets in Vindication of the Church Government: But I don't remember to have seen either of these in Print.

15. *Forbes:*

He wrote also *A Vindication of the Divine Perfections,* which was published at London in the Year 1695, with a Preface by Doctors W. Bates and J. Howe; wherein these learned divines give this character of the book: *The Clearness and Vigour of the noble Author's Spirit are illustriously visible in managing a Subject so deep and difficult. And in his unfolding the glorious and amiable Excellencies of the Blessed God, there is joined with the Strength of Argument, that Beauty of Expression, as may engage all Readers, to be happy in the entire Choice of God for their everlasting Portion. Which Performance shews it to be a Thing not impracticable, as it is most praiseworthy, amidst the greatest secular employment, to find Vacancy and a Disposition of Spirit to look with a very inquisitive Eye into the deep Things of God: Which (if it were the Author's Pleasure to be known) would let it be seen, the Statesman and the Divine are not Inconsistencies to a great and comprehensive Mind.*

Dalrymple's Apology:

As to the matter of Civil Government ... I have fully exprest my judgment therein, in a Treatise, (when published which) [*sic*] I hope will not be unacceptable to so Gracious and Moderat a PRINCE as we now have, nor to the People. (p 4)

[No parallel in *Dalrymple's Apology.*]

These parallel passages make it plain that as Forbes wrote the preface to the *Journal* he had a copy of *Dalrymple's Apology* close to hand. At one level, this was of course a perfectly sensible thing, for clearly the *Apology* is a very important source for Stair's life and public career. Where by modern standards at least Forbes slips over from summarising or drawing upon his main source into merely copying it down with trivial adjustments so that it appears to be his own is, however, very plain. There are all manner of turns of phrase and ordering of words which move straight from the *Apology* – and in the case of No. 12, from the *Decisions* also – into the *Journal*, without any indication of their origins. There is a contrast with No. 15, where Forbes indicates that he is quoting from the preface to the *Vindication of the Divine Perfections*.

Forbes's use of the *Apology* in the *Journal* preface is not confined to the passages which have been the subject of discussion so far. The passage is the conclusion of a biography of Stair, which is included along with those of others who had compiled decisions of the Session before Forbes himself. The biography of Stair is by far the longest, and much of it comes from the *Apology*. A particularly striking example is Forbes's account of the advocates' 'strike' in 1674, one of the many events in which Stair played a controversial role.[27] This is how Forbes describes it:[28]

> The Lord Stair was quarrelled as the author of the Privy Council's banishing the greatest part of the advocates from Edinburgh in the Harvest-Vacation *anno* 1674; albeit he was altogether free from that imputation, being in the country when the thing was done. And the truth is, he never seem'd to have pleasure in the affairs then most agitated in Council.

The description is a bare editing of Stair's own account:[29]

> I have been quarrelled for being the Author of the Banishing of the Advocats from Edinburgh, in the year 1674, in the Harvest Vaccance, which is taken notice of, in the Grievances, as an incroachment upon them, done by the then Privy Council, whereof I was altogether free; for it was done in the Vacant time, when I was in the Countrey, and the inspection of the Sederunts of the Council will demonstrat, that in that whole Vaccance I was not present, yea, seldom was I present in any Vaccance, and ofttimes absent in Session-time, especially when the Affairs of the Session required afternoon Meetings. God knows, I had no pleasure in the affairs that were then most agitated in Council.

Other striking instances where Forbes is heavily dependent on Stair's interpretation of events are in his accounts of Stair's relationship with the

---

27   For a modern account see J.M. Simpson, 'The Advocates as Scottish Trade Union Pioneers' in *The Scottish Tradition*, ed. G.W.S. Barrow (Edinburgh, 1974), 164–77. Note also the doubts cast on Stair's account by Mackay, *Memoir*, pp. 118–19.
28   Forbes, *Journal*, n. 19 above, p. xxxiv.
29   *Dalrymple's Apology*, n. 19 above, p. 6.

Duke of Lauderdale,[30] Stair's role in the 1681 parliament,[31] and circumstances surrounding and following Stair's deposition as Lord President in the same year.[32]

There are, however, four passages where Forbes does not appear to have relied much if to any extent upon Stair's own writings – numbers 9, 11, 13 and 15. In the last of these, as already noted, Forbes makes it clear that he is quoting from the preface to the *Divine Perfections*, written by Bates and Howe. No. 13 merely records the fact that Stair published a work entitled *Physiologia Nova Experimentalis*, and Forbes's failure even to give the title correctly suggests that he had not looked deeply into it. No. 9 gives a good deal of personal detail, some of which may have come from the *Apology*. The reference to Stair continuing to work 'even when he might have used the privilege of his age to lie by and withdraw from it' faintly echoes a comment in the *Apology* concerning his return to Scotland and the Presidency of the Session in 1689 – 'I had chearfully adventured, not only my Life and Fortune, but the Ruine of my Children, with the King in His Expedition to Britain, in the Winter Season, in the Seventieth Year of my Age, with all the chearfulness imaginable'[33] – as well as the story recorded in Crawfurd's *Peerage*, attributed by Aeneas Mackay to the Dalrymple family, that when told by William of Orange of his intention to go to England, Stair pulled off his wig, pointed to his bare head, and declared, 'Though I be now in the seventieth year of my age I am willing to venture that, my own and my children's fortunes in such an undertaking'.[34] Similarly the statement that Stair was more mindful of religion and law than the raising of a great fortune may owe something to comments in the *Apology* that 'it is a further Evidence of my Integrity, that though I have been Fourty Years, in Publick Imployment, yet I have not Bought an Hundred Pound Sterling of Rent more than I have Sold', and that his 'pension' as President was half that of Sir George Lockhart, who held the office between Stair's two terms therein.[35] Yet another sentence – 'he was apt to forget, at least not to resent injuries done to him' – is reminiscent of a comment made of Stair in Mackenzie's *Memoirs of the Affairs of Scotland*: 'that which I admired most in him was that in ten years' intimacy I never heard him speak unkindly of those who had injured him'.[36] *The Memoirs* were still in manuscript in 1714, and were to remain unpublished for another century and more, but their existence was sufficiently well-known at the time (a proposal was current for their publication in the then-forthcoming *Works* of

---

30   Compare Forbes, *Journal*, pp. xxxiv–v with *Dalrymple's Apology*, pp. 5–6
31   Compare Forbes, *Journal*, p. xxxv with *Dalrymple's Apology*, pp. 2–3.
32   Compare Forbes, *Journal*, pp. xxxvi–vii with *Dalrymple's Apology*, pp. 2,4 and 5.
33   *Dalrymple's Apology*, p. 3.
34   G. Crawfurd, *The Peerage of Scotland* (Edinburgh, 1716), p. 451; Mackay, *Memoir*, p. 213.
35   *Dalrymple's Apology*, p. 3.
36   G. Mackenzie, *Memoirs of the Affairs of Scotland*, ed. T. Thomson (Edinburgh, 1821), p. 215.

Mackenzie but proved abortive[37]) to make it quite conceivable that Forbes had access to this source as well. On this occasion, however, the source is one independent of Stair himself and is written by one with no particular reason to flatter the subject.

I have not identified a source for the other observations in No. 9. The knowledge and study of divinity would be a reasonable conclusion from Stair's publications on the subject, however. The remainder of the passage deals with Stair's personal habits, and the likeliest source for these – in particular the custom of reading a chapter of the Bible to his family before dinner[38] – is identified at the very end of Forbes' preface, when he acknowledges the assistance of, amongst others, three of Stair's sons: Sir Hew Dalrymple of North Berwick, Lord President of the Court of Session, Sir David Dalrymple of Hailes, Dean of the Faculty of Advocates, and Sir James Dalrymple of Borthwick, advocate. An indirect hint of Forbes' desire to please the Dalrymples may be seen in No. 2, where he edits Stair's words so as to leave out the reference to even the possibility of the sons having solicited their father in the discharge of his judicial duties. The three eminent sons may also account for No. 11, the final passage in Forbes's preface for which no direct source is identifiable in Stair's writings. This is a particularly interesting passage, for in it we see for the first time the idea of Stair as the 'founder' of Scots law which still lies at the root of his pre-eminence amongst the institutional writers. It was an idea which would doubtless have been very gratifying to the great man's distinguished and influential offspring. Forbes wrote as he took up his appointment as first holder of the chair of Civil Law at Glasgow. Pleasing those in high places who were and had been important supporters of other of his endeavours cannot have been far from his mind. As early as 1705 he had dedicated his *Treatise of Churchlands and Tithes* to Sir Hew Dalrymple, acknowledging 'the learned and useful advice I received from your Lordship in some points handled in this treatise'. The compilation and publication of the *Journal of the Session* had been made possible by both the Dean and Faculty of Advocates, and the Lords of Session, whose respective roles are made clear on the title page. In this the Dalrymples must have had a considerable influence, in particular the Lord President whose own reports of the decisions of his court from 1698 to 1720 were to be posthumously published in 1758. Stair himself had been the first to publish decisions; Forbes's *Journal* was the first publication since then of cases decided after Stair's time.[39] He may therefore have been seen as following the trail first blazed by Stair, and declaring the value which that trail had.

---

37   See the preface to the *Memoirs*, pp. iv–v.
38   Stair was a busy man before his meals since by his own account (see No. 12) he wrote up the day's decisions at that time as well.
39   *Durie's Decisions*, covering the period 1621–42, had been published in 1690, possibly thanks to Stair, if we may judge from a dedication to him and the other Lords of Session. In 1701 John Spotswood published decisions reported by Lord President Gilmour and Lord President Falconer covering the period 1661–86.

Forbes's imagery in No. 11, showing Stair removing obscurity and making the law clear is interesting. It was not the first time that metaphors conveying the idea of the single jurist heroically clarifying a previously uncertain law had been used in Scotland. William Drummond of Hawthornden had addressed a sonnet to Sir John Skene in praise of his edition of *Regiam Majestatem* (1609), making use of images of cobwebs and darkness to evoke the state of the law before Skene's work:[40]

> *To the honourable author, Sir John Skene*
> All lawes but cob-webes are, but none such right
> Had to this title as these lawes of ours,
> Ere that they were from their Cimmerian Bowres
> By thy ingenious labours brought to light.
> Our statutes senslesse statues did remaine,
> Till thou (a new Prometheus) gave them breath,
> Or like ag'd Æsons bodye courb'd to death,
> When thou young bloud infus'd in evrye veine.
> Thrice-happye Ghosts! which after-worlds shall wow, [*scil.*, vow]
> That first tam'd barbarisme by your swords,
> Then knew to keepe it fast in net of words,
> Hindring what men not suffer would to doe;
> To Jove the making of the World is due,
> But that it turnes not chaos, is to you.

Again, Robert Burnet had remarked in the preface to his edition of Thomas Craig's *Jus Feudale*, published in 1655, that 'our author arose, like another Justinian, and extracted light from darkness'.[41] The ultimate source of such images is, of course, Justinian's *Institutes*, where the Emperor's legislation is said to have 'brought light to areas darkened by disuse'.[42] Elsewhere Justinian provides a variation on the theme, when the *Institutes* are described as 'shaped from almost the whole body of ancient Institutes and channeled from all their muddy sources into one pure reservoir by the agency of Tribonian, that glorious man'.[43] Forbes's readers, in particular the Dalrymples, would certainly have had little difficulty in recognising that he was comparing the work of Stair with that of Justinian and Tribonian, upon which later knowledge of the law of Rome depended. In any event, Forbes was employing a conventional method of describing the achievement of individual jurists, and there is no more reason to accept uncritically his characterisation of Stair's work than there is to do likewise with Drummond's eulogy of Skene or Burnet's praise of Craig.

In conclusion, it is suggested that our judgement of the value and significance of Forbes's remarks about Stair must be tinged with more caution than deemed necessary by Professor Walker. Forbes's employment of

---

40   Found quoted in J. MacQueen, *Progress and Poetry* (Edinburgh, 1982), p. 27.
41   Published London and Edinburgh, 1655.
42   Justinian, *Institutes*, proemium.
43   *Constitutio Tanta* (16 Dec. 533); Pennsylvania *Digest* translation, ed. A. Watson. 4 vols. (Philadelphia, 1985), i, p. li.

Stair's own view of the controversies in his career looks designed to retain
the goodwill of the influential Dalrymple family, and must create doubt as
to whether the few independent passages really represent a detached and
objective view of Stair and his work as it seemed twenty years after his
death.[44] This need not mean that Forbes did not truly admire Stair; fulsome
tributes in some of his other books compare Stair with Azo and Baldus, two
great medieval jurists,[45] and there is no reason to doubt the genuineness of
his enthusiasm. But the view expressed in the *Journal* is essentially Stair's
own verdict on his career. Forbes was not wholly impartial or writing without a view to his own interests when he exalted Stair's character and juristic
achievement.

This paper has stressed the negative view of Stair in his own lifetime
in order to highlight some of the background against which the words ultimately employed by Forbes must be understood. It is only fair to draw
attention also to the better reputation which he held in other quarters.
Perhaps the most balanced judgment is that of his rival Mackenzie:[46]

> Nor did any suffer so much as the Lord Stairs, President of the
> Session; who, because of his great affection to Lauderdale... suf-
> fered severely, though formerly he had been admired for his
> sweet temper and strong parts. And by him our countrymen may
> learn, that such as would be esteemed excellent judges must live
> abstracted from the court *[that is, the king's court]*; and I have
> heard the President himself assert that no judge should be either
> member of Council or Exchequer, for these courts did learn men
> to be less exact justiciars than was requisite.

This might be read as implying that Stair was not 'esteemed an excellent judge', as a result of his activities in the Privy Council and government
of Scotland; certainly the view attributed to him as to the exactness required
for the administration of law there as opposed to the courts of justice paral-
lels the opinion on the same subject given in *Dalrymple's Apology* (see No. 6
above). But Mackenzie seems also to be saying that the popular view of
Stair was mistaken, when he suggests that Stair had 'suffered severely'. We
may also note another, better-known, comment of Mackenzie, to support
this contention, the opening words of which suggest that he was going
against a more commonly-held view:[47]

> And really Stair was a gentleman of excellent parts, of an equal
> wit and universal learning, but most remarkable from being so
> free from passion that most men thought this equality of spirit a
> mere hypocrisy in him. This meekness fitted him extremely to be

---

44   For further discussion of the patronage of Forbes by the Dalrymple family see
      J.W. Cairns, 'Origins of the Glasgow Law School', n. 16 above.
45   See his *Treatise of Church-lands and Tithes* (Edinburgh, 1705), preface (Azo);
      A Methodical Treatise Concerning Bills of Exchange (2nd edn., Edinburgh,
      1718), preface, p. ix (Baldus).
46   Mackenzie, *Memoirs*, n. 36 above, p. 241.
47   Mackenzie, *Memoirs*, p. 214.

a president, for he thereby received calmly all men's information, and by it he was capable to hear without disorder or confusion what the advocates represented.

In other words, he was a good judge from the point of view of the bar. Further, the originality of Stair's thought in the field of unjustified enrichment has been recently highlighted,[48] while he could also dissent from Grotius on whether acceptance was required to make a promise binding.[49] What is badly needed is a full-length critical study, setting Stair in the context of his own times, and against a deeper background of Scottish and European legal development; only this will enable us to make judgements which are not dependent on a received tradition which is at best of suspect origin.

Nor should we think any the less of Forbes, a jurist who has not yet received the attention he deserves in his own right, because he has been detected in relatively minor and harmless plagiarism. The idea that copying another person's work is a wrong is a comparatively recent one, and in many cultures even today it is perceived as an honour to the author thus dealt with. The modern law of copyright was in its infancy in Forbes's day, and was primarily concerned with the rights of publishers rather than those of authors. In his recent interesting and entertaining book, *Stolen Words*, Thomas Mallon suggests that the idea of plagiarism as a wrong really only took root in Britain in the seventeenth century, becoming well-developed in the eighteenth.[50] Forbes may therefore not have been conscious of any real wrongdoing, especially if he was working under the eyes of the Dalrymple family in which any rights in the matter, legal or otherwise, would presumably have vested. His greatest offence in contemporary eyes may have lain in his not making clear that he was using Stair's own account, which, given that it had only been published in pamphlet form nearly quarter of a century before, may not have been especially well known outside the Dalrymple circle. Others might then have suspected more strongly that a principal motive in Forbes's work was the promotion of the reputation of the Dalrymple family. In any event, as Brian Simpson has remarked, 'at least in the Western European legal tradition of private law successful creative work consists in a combination between intelligent plagiarism and systematisation of what is lifted from others'.[51] In legal writing there is always difficulty in combining accuracy with original forms of expression.

---

48   P. Birks and G. McLeod, 'The Implied Contract Theory of Quasi-Contract: Civilian Opinion Current in the Century before Blackstone', *Oxf. Jour. Leg. Stud.*, vi (1986), 46 at pp. 56–58.
49   Stair, *Institutions*, I, x, 4.
50   T. Mallon, *Stolen Words: Forays into the Origins and Ravages of Plagiarism* (New York, 1989), pp. 4–8. Note, however, the story of the denunciation of St. Columba following his copying of another monk's MS. (F. Kelly, *A Guide to Early Irish Law* (Dublin, 1988), pp. 239–40) and Craig's condemnation of the compiler of *Regiam Majestatem* as a thief (*Jus Feudale*, I, viii, 11).
51   A.W.B. Simpson, *Legal Theory and Legal History* (London and Ronceverte, 1987), p. 178.

Plagiarism has played its part at different times in the legal history of Scotland, and on a much more significant scale than in Forbes's borrowings from Stair. The classic example is the appropriation of much of the English text *Glanvill* by the compiler of *Regiam Majestatem*. Stair himself may have steered close to plagiarism of Grotius, Gudelinus, Vinnius and Thomas Craig, as Bill Gordon has pointed out.[52] But it would be unwise to assume that the views expressed by Forbes and drawn from Stair were universally held in the Scottish legal world early in the eighteenth century, or, indeed, at the time of their first publication quarter of a century earlier.

---

52   W.M. Gordon, 'Stair, Grotius and the Sources of Stair's *Institutions*' in *Satura Roberto Feenstra Oblata*, edd. J.A. Ankum, J.E. Spruit and F.B.J. Wubbe (Fribourg, 1985), 571. A minor example of Stair following Craig and evidently not checking his sources is where he states that *Glanvill* is in thirteen books; in fact it is in fourteen. Compare Craig, *Jus Feudale*, I, viii, 11 with Stair, *Institutions*, I, i, 16. On Stair's dependence on Craig in his *Institutions* see also J.M. Halliday, 'Feudal Law as a Source' in *Stair Tercentenary Studies*, 136–40.

Causa.

Item is ane pece Lend callit the ten pund Land of [...] of the said ten pund, the
Lend fiue pund Land and be a Lend or sum be y generale dominit b is apperit as
pius dissignat in speciale b thair effect confirme b ane decreit of nonentres and
liquidation, yett decreit is asua generalie gebin and broim na certaine of y
divis. And inlikewayis thair is sum gentilmen infeft halduand immediatlie of o
soueraine lord Dromy the sull zeris of the nonentres quhoim the said decreit
is past in ane speciale part of ye said ten pund Land extending to ane fiue pund
Land thairof gett is separathe becaus debitis and bonds be for bouand sper
uenu and desigria in quhoim na decret of nonentres is gebin in speciale thes
being entes sull bot broim ye said put of the sull ten pund Land are indivisit
coperand b mak stop b the said persuing allegis yt the mynest out and sekis
tenes b the said decreit and deminitratioun, temporiss me fiue pund Land and
Land or sibe m generale out of ye said ten pund Land bot senidie yf te
gentilmans infstruct halduand vmediatlie of o soueraine lord Dromy the sull
of nonentres, the said fiue pund Land of the said ten seueralie bomdit m sic ms
fice the best and y the said mynest sull expriss generalie it the said soy
thair it puendge no is said is y abbe infestment broim the said speciale so
and gif thay mand no the said persoum Protesht be mesull etro

Quæstio

Ingadebow yf the mynest wmitto wasfull etro yf tey mak no the said
the persund infestment being segaltoy b thems of the said speciale yt m me
persund or not

Responsio

Is ansor affirmatine be the Lacours vndeuttm that tey wmith ivfefin
etro yf tey mak no the said persoum m ye altes

[...] mstop yf y[...]
[...] sum to be the quhilk sull all y[...]
[...] of y[...] tenie
Sot vulebm xm ea que expondit Alex manchan   Ita mihi
                                                  [...] shang
                                                  vnd of
                                                  m R [...]

Sic sensit Mr Henricj Makcalzane
[...] bonle mgr senum tune   m David mchffil

i Bd Henryson   m Edmond [...]

m thomas crosbey   m Iohne fundes
sic subt
m henry balf   m [...] mackorbauffy

A SIXTEENTH CENTURY LEGAL OPINION

By DAVID B. SMITH, M.A., LL.B., F.S.A.SCOT.,

Sheriff of North Strathclyde at Kilmarnock

If a person wishes at the present day to obtain the opinion of counsel his law agent sets forth the facts of the case along with the specific questions to which the answer is sought in a document known as a memorial for the opinion of counsel. The advocate either appends his answers briefly to the memorial or puts them down in a separate document. The document which is printed below may be an interesting and early example of a memorial and opinion of counsel. Unlike a modern memorial it is framed as an academic problem, although it is clear from its form that the problem was an actuality. Professor W.M. Gordon has suggested that it might be an advisory opinion from experts, such as was regularly obtained by courts using the Romano-canonical procedure and this suggestion is supported by Dr. John Durkan. The document comes from a miscellaneous collection of letters, some legal, in the National Library of Scotland, NLS MS 3998, fo. 1.

From the Act 1469 until the Adjudication Act 1672 an important part of the law of diligence against a debtor who had no moveable estate to arrest or poind was the process of apprising, or comprising. The opinion printed relates to an apprising of 1574. In an apprising the creditor obtained letters from the Court of Session charging his debtor to compear before a messenger or other person (who was made judge and sheriff in that part) and to hear the lands specified in the letters apprised by an inquest of fifteen sworn men and declared to belong to the creditor for payment of his debt. The messenger denounced the lands to be apprised on the ground of the lands and at the market cross of the sheriffdom, stewartry or regality in which the lands lay. On the day fixed for compearance the judge chose an assize of fifteen or thirteen men who valued or apprised the lands to be worth so much, or that such a portion of the lands was worth the sum in the decree. Whether the assize or inquest merely performed a formal function or not is not clear as Balfour records it as having been decided that 'ilk twentie schilling land of auld extent sould be comprisit to twentie markis'.[1] The lands, or part thereof, were thereupon offered by the judge to the debtor on payment of the sum in the decree; and if the debtor failed to pay, the lands were decerned by the verdict of the assize to belong to the creditor.[2]

---

1   *The Practicks of Sir James Balfour of Pittendreich*, ed. P.G.B. McNeill. 2 vols. (Stair Society, 21 and 22, Edinburgh, 1962 and 1963), ii, 401–3.

2   For discussion of apprising see Balfour, loc. cit.; H. Bissett, *Rolment of Courtis*, i, 246; Stair, III, 2, 14; G. Mackenzie, *Observations on the Acts of Parliament* (Edinburgh, 1686), pp. 70–74; *Introduction to Scottish Legal History* (Stair Society, 20, Edinburgh, 1958), pp. 33, 48, 229 and 235; I.D. Willock, *The Origins and Development of the Jury in Scotland* (Stair Society, 23, Edinburgh, 1966), pp. 137–38.

There are several printed examples of such processes.[3]

Although, according to Craig, 'it not infrequently happens that the debtor astutely avoids any appearance in the proceedings for apprising' the matter was not always a formality: the assize in the apprising recorded in the Regality of Dunfermline Court Book 'wald nocht as this day deliver nowther affirmative nor negative and sa departit and refusit to do the samyn allegeand thai var simpell men chosin heyr on and the actione intentit grit and aganis ane grit and noble man and thai culd nocht gudly decern heyrintill quhill thai var reconsilat with vtheris hewand vnderstandyng heyrintill and thair efter thai vald serve this process efter thair cunnyng and knawleg'.[4] The process thereafter duly ran its course to decree.

Craig goes on to say, 'that sometimes a third party who in good faith claims to have a real right in the subject of the apprising, and apprehends prejudice to his interests, appears to oppose them ... The keenest controversy often arises in the circumstances between the pursuer in the apprising and such third parties upon the written titles produced by the latter ... The tendency of our judges is favourable to the admission of a compearance, if the right alleged by the would-be compearer is founded on any kind of title, even a presumptive one'.[5] The mere production of a title was not sufficient unless it was supported by possession on the part of the third party. If there was no possession it was Craig's opinion that the judge of the apprising 'will not err if he disregards the title proponed and proceeds in the apprising'.[6]

It appears then that the present document was intended for use by a third party infeft in a specific, or 'speciale', part of larger lands which have been denounced for apprising and that it was intended for production in the process of apprising to support his title and proof of possession: it is averred in the narrative part of the document that the 'gentleman' was 'infeft haldand immediatlie of our souerane lord during the haill zeiris of the nonentrie ... in ane speciale part of the said ten pund land extending to ane four pund land thairof quhilk is separatlie knawin devidit and brukit be him berand speciale name and designation the samyn being ever full ... ' From the terms of the document it appears that the 'gentleman' had appeared in the apprising to stop it and submitted that the assize should apprise gener-

3   E.g. *St. Andrews Formulare 1514–1546, Vol. II*, ed. G. Donaldson (Stair Society, 9, Edinburgh, 1944), p. 274; Historical Manuscripts Commission, 9th Report, App. ii, p. 189; *The Scotts of Buccleuch*, ed. W. Fraser. 2 vols. (Edinburgh, 1878), ii, No. 102; *Memorials of the Family of Wemyss of Wemyss*, ed. W. Fraser. 2 vols. (Edinburgh, 1888), ii, No. 81; *Regality of Dunfermline Court Book*, edd. J.M. Webster and A.A.M. Duncan (Dunfermline, 1953), pp. 62, 66, 75, 77 and 82; *Records of the Sheriff Court of Aberdeenshire*, ed. D. Littlejohn. 3 vols. (New Spalding Club, Aberdeen, 1904–7), i, 80; *Formulary of Old Scots Legal Documents*, compiled by P. Gouldesbrough (Stair Society, 36, Edinburgh, 1985), chap. 17.

4   *Regality of Dunfermline Court Book*, above n. 3, p. 63.

5   Craig, *Jus Feudale*, (Lord President Clyde's translation, Edinburgh and London, 1934), III, 2, 9.

6   Ibid, III, 2, 10.

ally, but with the proviso that it should not prejudice his infeftment, and had protested for wilful error if the assize did not make the said provision.

That the document was actually used is shown by the docquet on the backing which records that it was produced on 19 July 1574. Unfortunately, the place where it was produced is not recorded, nor has it been possible to assign an identity to the clerk who appended his signature to the docquet.

Having narrated the problem in such terms as to make it clear that it was an actual problem and that the above course of action had been followed, a question is put as to whether the assize commit wilful error if they do not make the provision once the infeftment has been shown to them. The opinion – entitled 'Responsio' – is written below, in the same hand as the rest of the document, and obviously *unico contextu* with what had gone before. The opinion was in the affirmative. There follow the signatures of thirteen advocates. All were in practice and of considerable experience; some were eminent, or were to achieve eminence. Henry Kinross was procurator-fiscal in the Commissary Court of Edinburgh from 1564; Edward Henryson, one of the original four commissaries of Edinburgh, had been professor of law at Bourges, and an extraordinary lord of session in 1566.[7] David McGill became King's Advocate on 12 June 1582 and later that same month, 27 June, a lord of session.[8]

I have been unable to find any similar document. The conclusion to which I have come is that this document was a joint opinion of thirteen advocates, obtained by 'the gentleman ... haldand immediatlie of our souerane lord', for use in the process of apprising and used by him in it. Curious as it may appear to modern ideas of propriety that a litigant should seek to influence a court by producing to it an opinion of counsel the practice was by no means uncommon. Indeed it appears that litigants had even resorted to obtaining opinions for this purpose from lords of session for there appears in the MS Books of Sederunt a hitherto unpublished act of sederunt dated 29 May 1584 which prohibited the lords from subscribing questions put to them by parties 'quha hes actioun dependand befoir diuerss vtheris Juges ... '[9]

---

7   He was professor of civil law in the university of Bourges in 1554. In 1556 he returned to Scotland to lecture publicly on Greek and law in Edinburgh. In 1564 he was appointed one of the first four commissaries of Edinburgh. In 1566 he became an extraordinary lord of session in place of Secretary Lethington but in 1567 he was removed 'off the Sessioun' because he was one of the King's Counsel (Pitmedden MS). In 1566 he was licensed to print Acts of Parliament and the Auld Lawes (*R.S.S.*, v, no. 2869). The Black Acts were the result. In 1567 he was appointed an advocate for the poor before the Lords (*R.S.S.*, v, no. 69).

8   The biographical notes on the advocate signatories given here and in the notes to the document are taken from *The Faculty of Advocates in Scotland, 1532–1943, with Genealogical Notes*, ed. Sir Francis J. Grant (Scottish Record Society, 145, Edinburgh, 1944).

9   MS Books of Sederunt, vol. III, fo. 229 (S.R.O. CS 1/3/2).

CAUSIS

Thair is ane peice Land callit the ten pund land of   of the quhilk
ten pund, thair is/ ane four pund land and vijs land or thairby in generale
denuncit to be apprysit na/ part designit in speciale to that effect conforme
to ane decreit of nonentrie and/ liquidatioun, quhilk decreit is alsua generalie gevin and vpoun na certane part pro/ diuiso. And inlikwyiss thair is ane
gentleman infeft haldand immediatlie of our/ souerane lord during the haill
zeiris of the nonentrie quhairvpoun the said decreit/ is past in ane speciale
part of the said ten pund land extending to ane four pund/ land thairof
quhilk is separatlie knawin devidit and brukit be him berand speciale/ name
and designatioun quhairvpoun na decreit of nonentrie is gevin in speciale
the samyn/ being euer full bot vpoun the said part of the haill ten pund
land pro indiuiso. Quha/ comperand to make stop to the said comprysing
Allegis that the inqueist aucht and suld Con/forme to the said decreit and
denunciatioun compryiss ane four pund land and vijs/ land or thairby in
generale out of the saidis ten pund landis but preiudice of the/ gentleman-
nis infeftment haldand immediatlie of our souerane lord during the haill
zeiris/ of nonentrie, the said four pund land of the said ten seueralie
boundit in his infeftment/ fra the rest And that the said inqueist suld compryiss generalie with the said provisioun/ that it preiudge nocht as said is
the vther infeftment vpoun the said speciale part/ And gif thay maid nocht
the said provisioun Protestit for wilful errour

QUESTIO
Quhidder gif [sic] the inqueist committis wilful errour gif thay mak nocht the
said provisioun/ the foirsaid infeftment being schawin to thaim of the said
speciale part in maner/ foirsaid or not

RESPONSIO
It is anserrit affirmatiue be the Lawaris vnderwrittin that thay committ wil-
full/ errour gif thay mak nocht the said provisioun in thair retour

        Ita sentit Johannes moscrop[1] gif the/
        the foure 1 be schawin full all the/
        tyme of the nonentrie

    Sic videtur secundum ea que proponuntur Alexandro mauchan[2]
                                        Ita mihi magistro
                                        Roberto Strang[3]
                                        videtur
                                        M R Strang

---

1   Moscrop, John, of Casselton, (? – 1600); admitted 1554
2   Mauchan, Alexander, of Overbarnton, (? – ?); admitted 23 June 1564.
3   Strang, Richard, (? – ?); admitted 13 November 1555.

Sic sentit Magister henricus Makcalzane[4]
Ita Sentit magister henricus kinross[5]   Magister david makgyl[6]
ita Eduardus Henryson[7]   Magister Edmond hay[8]
Magister Thomas Westoun[9]   Magister Johnne frude[10]
sic sentit
Magister henry balfour[11]   Ita sentit Magister Thomas harvy[12]
                    Magister Johannes Marioribankis[13]

Verso

Productum xix Julij
   anno 1574
   J Craig
   N P

---

4   Makcalzane, Henry, (? – ?).
5   Kinross, Henry, (? – 1578); admitted 8 July 1561.
6   McGill, David, of Nisbet, (? – 1596); admitted 13 November 1555.
7   Henryson, Edward, (? – 1585); admitted 22 February 1557.
8   Hay, Edmond, (? – 1589); admitted 1553.
9   Weston, Thomas, (? – ?); admitted 9 December 1562.
10   Frude, John, (? – ? 1586); admitted ? 1572.
11   Balfour, Henry, (? – ?); admitted 12 March 1570; commissary of Peebles, 6 November 1609.
12   Harvy, Thomas, (? – 1589); admitted 1553.
13   Marjoribanks, John, (? – ?); admitted 13 November 1555.

A MEMORIAL AND OPINION OF 1762 GIVEN BY ROBERT McQUEEN, LATER LORD BRAXFIELD

By ANGUS STEWART, Q.C., M.A., LL.B.,

Advocate of the Scottish Bar

The documents reproduced come from a bundle of ninety-one unsorted items in the Barcaldine muniments relating to the sequestration of Dougal Stewart X of Appin.[1] The principal creditor was Duncan Campbell of the Barcaldine-Glenure family.

On 29 July 1745 Dougal Stewart was restored to the lands held of the Duke of Argyll forfeited by his father under the Clan Act 1715. Was the timing pure chance, or was it policy? In any event, the young chief took no active part in the Rising of 1745. The Appin Regiment fought for the Prince under the command of Charles Stewart head of the senior cadet branch of Ardsheal.[2] Ardsheal was forfeited.

As Crown factor on the annexed estate of Ardsheal, Colin Campbell of Glenure initiated a policy – unique in the history of the forfeitures – of replacing the pro-Jacobite tenants. At the same time the pasture lands of Ardsheal were dissociated from the traditional economy and absorbed into the regional grazing system of the Campbell lairds.[3] The first act was the removal from the Glenduror grazings in 1751 of James Stewart in Auchindarroch, Ardsheal's half brother. The eviction of the small tenants was fixed for 15 May 1752. On the afternoon of 14 May Glenure was shot dead as he entered the Ardsheal estate.

Allan Breck Stewart was the prime suspect, but escaped. James Stewart was found guilty of murder art and part. He was hanged on the knoll at Ballachulish and his remains kept wired up on the gibbet for years afterwards – until secretly removed for burial.

---

1   S.R.O. GD 170/428. Most of the material for this introduction comes from these items. For details of the Appin Murder and subsequent trial reference is made to D.N. Mackay, *Trial of James Stewart* (Notable British Trials, Edinburgh and Glasgow, 1931) and Sir W. MacArthur, *The Appin Murder* (London, 1960).

2   The usual explanation for Dougal's non-participation in the Rising of 1745 is that he was too young. This seems to be incorrect. Dougal's date of birth is unknown but his parents married about 1710 (Sasine on marriage contract, S.R.O., RS 10/8/470). He appears subscribing a deed on his own behalf in 1733 (ibid., RS 10/7/24); he had succeeded to the title by 1741 (ibid., RS 10/7/194); and he married in 1742 (Discharge and renunciation, 5 April 1759 infra).

3   A.G. MacPherson, 'The Annexed Estate of Ardsheal' in *The Stewarts*, (Edinburgh, 1956), vol. X, 2, 94

The thing that damned James Stewart was evidence of malice, probably perjured, given by John Dow Breck MacColl, Appin's bowman[4] in Caolisnacoan, Glencoe. The prosecution also founded on a remark made by James to the effect that if Glenure wasn't stopped at the rate he was going he would soon be 'the Laird of Appin'. Glenure's transactions on the Ardsheal estate are well enough known: but what dealings did he have with Appin?

By 1751 Glenure had acquired two of Appin's farms and got tacks of two others including the key holding of Lagnaha which lay between Auchindarroch and Ardsheal Mains. Together with the tacks granted by Glenure as factor on Ardsheal (one of which was to himself) this created a solid belt of Campbell possessions right across the middle of the Stewart clan's territory. But what really put Appin in Glenure's power was a series of loans amounting by 1752 to £2,000 Sterling largely secured over some of his debtor's best properties.[5] Interest on the total was running at 5% p.a. – while the cash rental of the whole estate was about £170.

Duncan Campbell, Colin's brother and successor, continued to make funds available.[6] In 1753 he had conveyed to him outright four of the security subjects including Lagnaha. The new laird of Glenure then set about trying to acquire the whole estate. The stage of draft missives was reached. But from Martinmas 1755 interest fell into arrears and the other creditors lost patience. In April 1756 Appin put the keys of his Edinburgh residence in the hands of his agent and left Scotland to escape his difficulties.[7]

A ranking and sale was raised in the Court of Session. Inhibitions had been used and on 1 March 1757 decree of declarator and adjudication was pronounced in favour of Glenure and his step-brother John Campbell of Barcaldine whereby they were found entitled as adjudgers to the reversion of *inter alia* the twenty merkland of Glencoe[8] The creditors were on the point of agreeing a distribution when Appin's wife entered the process with a claim against the factor[9] for her 'jointure'. Glenure sent his brother Robert

---

4   Bowman: stock manager. The bowman's full appellation is given in James Stewart's speech from the scaffold.

5   According to an account of the much disputed conversation between James Stewart and Rob Roy's son James More which took place at Edinburgh in April 1752, Stewart railed against Appin as 'a scoundrel' and 'a base fool'; he complained that Appin had given Glenure one farm in exchange for £500; and he prophesied that Glenure would soon get Lettershuna (the small classical mansion-house of Appin built by Appin's father about 1725). (S.R.O. GD 50/166). This particular conversation was not formally put in evidence at the trial.

6   See also letter Appin to Glenure April 1753, S.R.O. GD 170/1423.

7   *Appine's Creditors*, 1760 Fac. Coll. ii, 471, No. 256.

8   The twenty merkland of Glencoe comprised nine farms. Appin feued Carnoch/Polveig and Laroch to the Macdonald chief, and Achtriachtan to a Macdonald cadet.

9   The factor was Alexander Stewart head of the cadet branch of Invernahyle, brother-in-law of Appin and cousin of Glenure. He was wounded at Culloden and spared from execution in romantic circumstances. Scott, who became a friend, described him as 'A noble specimen of the old Highlander – gallant, courteous and brave even to chivalry'. Appin had left Invernahyle to manage his affairs in Argyll. Invernahyle was appointed factor by the court at the instance of the creditors on 2 February 1758.

to London to negotiate a settlement with the Laird of Appin and his lady. On 27 March 1759 Robert reported:–

> ... This job has given me such a Specimen of the said Laird and Lady that I hope never to see there fface on Business again. you are well quitt of them. you are more oblidged to there distress than the Justness of your Cause ...

Lady Appin formally discharged and renounced her claim – in so far as it attached to the lands in which Glenure was interested – on 5 April 1759.

The delay brought to the fore the problem of Appin's wadset[10] properties. In 1749 Appin had raised cash by wadsetting two of the Glencoe farms, Brecklet and Achnacoan.[11] The charters provided for redemption on forty days notice at any term of Whitsunday up to 1761 by repaying the purchase price between the hours of ten a.m. and twelve noon at 'the Parish Church of Appin'. It became apparent that the sequestration was unlikely to be complete before the deadline for redemption and that, unless steps were taken, the full value of the farms would be lost to the estate. Anxious queries were put to counsel:[12] who had title to operate the redemptions – the factor or the adjudgers; did payment have to be made in gold or silver coin or would Edinburgh bank notes do; and where should payment be made – properly speaking there was no 'Parish Church of Appin' since the parish of Appin was united with that of Lismore and the minister of the united parish lived on Lismore and preached at the church there?[13] Counsel advised that the adjudgers should proceed by way of court action with an offer to pay at the bar. As the Memorial reproduced narrates, this course, combined with proceedings for removing, was successfully followed through to decree on 2 March 1762.

The wadsetter of Achnacoan was Duncan Stewart of the Ballachulish family (another cadet branch of Appin). He was probably a nephew of the laird of Ballachulish, one of those wounded at Culloden. By 1762 Duncan had been succeeded by his son, also Duncan. (Glenure initially forgot to tell his agent[14] of the change and so the summons anent redemption had to be rewritten).

---

10   Wadset: sale under reversion, in terms of which there was reserved to the seller a right exercisable within a limited time to re-acquire the subjects by paying back the purchase price.

11   The hamlet of Brecklet is signposted at East Laroch, Ballachulish. Achnacoan (not to be confused with Achnacone in the Strath of Appin) is now the mountain rescue centre which can be seen beside the A84 two miles south of the turn off for Glencoe village. Achnacoan had already figured in history: it was here that Macdonald of Achtriachtan and others including a five-year-old boy were massacred in 1692. The Stewarts acquired Glencoe in the 1680s. P. Hopkins, *Glencoe and the End of the Highland War* (Edinburgh, 1986).

12   James Ferguson was consulted twice on this matter.

13   The parishes were re-united in 1661. The minister in 1762 was the Rev. John MacAulay, grandfather of the historian, fervent Whig who was lectured at by Dr. Johnson at Inveraray in 1773.

14   David Campbell, W.S., a nephew of Glenure.

The wadsetter of Brecklet was John Stewart younger of Ballachulish. His brother Alexander had been killed at Culloden. In the events of 1752 young Ballachulish, then aged twenty-six, had shown ability and resolution: he had been chosen to assist the tenants at the Ardsheal evictions; and, despite Barcaldine's threats, he had persisted in seeking legal representation for James Stewart. It was he who at length succeeded in giving a decent burial to James's remains. John Stewart remained an object of Campbell suspicion – suspicion which appeared to be given substance in 1758 when it was reported that Allan Breck was back in Appin, lurking at Ballachulish.[15]

It is easy to imagine that there was more than the usual animus between litigants. The wadsetters did not mean to yield easily: and Glenure was intent on pursuing them with a variety of claims and on putting in his own tenants.

It was in this context that Glenure's agent framed the Memorial of 1762 for the Opinion[16] of Counsel. Apart from the context, the interest of the Opinion lies in its treatment of custom and in the identity of the author, Robert McQueen, afterwards Lord Justice-Clerk Braxfield, then making a name for himself as an advocate advising on difficult questions of land law relative to the forfeitures. The style – trenchant and unencumbered by reference to precedent – gives a foretaste of the forthright delivery which characterised McQueen's pronouncements from the bench.

The Opinion was signed at Edinburgh on 5 August 1762 and the client's copy reproduced was soon in Glenure's hands. On 30 August Glenure's petition was presented to the Sheriff-Substitute at Banavie (near Fort William) with claims for dilapidations, fodder and teinds. On the same day the Sheriff-Substitute ordered service with answers to be lodged by 15 September; 'before answer' appointed a comprisement to be made by the birleymen of the parish;[17] and allowed the petitioners proof of their averments of custom, assigning 15 September as the diet. It seems that fifteen witnesses were carefully precognosced of whom eight were led – including the same John Dow Breck MacColl ('formerly in Caolisnacoan') who had testified against James Stewart ten years before.

But answers were put in and the proof was contested. The matter must have given Sheriff-Substitute MacVicar some difficulty for he took the

---

15   S.R.O., GD 170/3321, 3322.
16   The documents reproduced are the copy Memorial and Opinion made for the client at a cost of sixpence per page. The entry for this particular opinion in the agent's account has not been traced but from other entries for 'advising with Counsel' it seems that the going rate was three guineas with additional payments to counsel's clerk and footman.
17   Birleymen or byrlawmen: tenants sworn to act as valuers and arbiters in neighbourhood disputes. (In 1750 Colin Campbell had agreed to James Stewart swearing in 'two discreet honest men' as 'burliemen'). The official comprisement or valuation was made in this case by John Livingstone, John McCombich and John McIntyre on 5 and 6 September 1762. Each was paid a shilling a day. The bill of comprisement showed tenants in nine separate holdings on Brecklet and in five on Achnacoan. The dilapidations of the 'beggings' (buildings) amounted to £42 in total.

precaution of remitting the process to the Sheriff for *avizandum*. Glenure, professing only concern for the plight of the new tenants, drafted a private letter to the Sheriff reminding him of the issues. If sent, the letter did not have altogether the desired effect. On 29 December 1762 at Banavie the Sheriff-Substitute issued his judgement finding the wadsetters liable for half the straw of the last oat crop and for the teinds of 1762, but not liable for dilapidations which constituted the major part of the claim. Glenure's local agent presented him with a bill of £34. Glenure then got into a dispute with the other creditors over the cost of the whole exercise in Edinburgh and Argyll.[18]

Dougal Stewart was the last chief of Appin in the main line. He died in March 1764[19] survived by a daughter Anna. She challenged the transactions of Glenure and the other creditors on the ground of fraud but without success. The title passed to the Ardsheal branch. The mansion house of Appin and other remnants of the estate including the twenty merkland of Glencoe, were acquired by the Duke of Argyll who, on 3 May 1769, sold the property on to Hugh Seton of Touch.[20]

The original pagination of the documents reproduced is indicated thus /2/. Words inserted or substituted to clarify the sense of the original are shown in square brackets. The word 'authouse' which appears twice at the end of the Opinion is taken to stand for 'authorise'.

---

18   Alexander Campbell, writer, Killin acted for Glenure in the proceedings before the sheriff substitute. One item claimed by Glenure was £25 plus interest for coming to Edinburgh to pay the wadset money ('14 days from home'), obtaining specie and attending the consignation.

19   Service of heirs of special provision, 19 July 1802 (S.R.O. C22/95/244).

20   S.R.O., RS 3/274/252. I am indebted to Mr.John Mayer for tracing this transaction. The usual account, namely that Appin finding himself without male heirs sold the estate to Seton in 1765 or 1766, appears to be incorrect. The Setons were Jacobites. On 6 April 1752 James Stewart had conferred with Seton at Touch about how to prevent the Ardsheal removings. Once installed at Appin, Seton campaigned, in the event with success, for the restoration of the Ardsheal family.

MEMORIAL & QUERRIES
FOR DUNCAN CAMPBELL OF GLENURE &TC
CREDITORS ADJUDGERS OF THE ESTATE
OF APPINE

11th April
1749

Of this date Dougal Stewart of Appine executed two severall Charters the one of the lands of Brecklet in favour of John Stewart of Balechish and the other of the lands of Achnacoan in favour of Duncan Stewart then possessor thereof; whereby in consideration of the sum of £324 advanced by the said John and £405 advanced by Duncan Stewart Appine Dispones the respective Lands abovementioned but seeing the above sums were greatly below the reale value of the lands they are declared redeemable at any term of Whitsunday within twelve years from Whits. 1749 in manner mentioned in the said Charters.

Appine having thereafter become bankrupt a Ranking and Sale of his Estate was brought which is now depending before the Court of Session – In this process John and Duncan Stewarts were called, and they accordingly appeared and produced their Interests in the ranking and deponed thereon, and the State having been made up they were preferred to the property of these Lands during the not redemption.

/2/ The memorialist at first expected that the Ranking and Sale might have been finished before the term of Whits. 1761 which is the term limited for the expiry of the reversion in the above wadsett right in which case the purchaser would have redeemed the Wadsett.

But finding that this could not possibly be done they thought it advisable to take measures for keeping open the right of Reversion – which if allowed to Expire would be a Loss to them of £400 or £500 Sterling.

The State of the ranking having been made up and allowed to be seen it was objected thereto 'That as the said John and 'Duncan Stewarts had produced their rights in the Ranking the 'same should be held as equal to an order of Redemption so as 'to Barr any claim they might make to the Absolute property by 'the Lapse of the 12 years within which by their rights the 'same could only be redeemed and they should therefore be 'only ranked upon the price of the Lands for the above sums 'respectively advanced by them to Appine and to the continu-'ance of their possession till paid out of the proceeds of the 'said Lands when sold and that altho the same /3/ should not 'happen on or before the term of Whits. 1761 years –'

Tho the memorialists apprehended they might have relyed upon the above Step as sufficient to keep open the right of Redemption they did not stop there, for to take away all pretence of cavelling from the wadsetters, the memorialists resolved to interpose their Credite for procuring money to redeem the Wadsetts for the Benefite of the whole agt. the term of Whits. 1761 which in virtue of their adjudications they were Impowered to do, and having advised with Councill with what manner or form this redemption should be followed out, they were directed to bring a process before the term to have it Found and Declared that the Lands were redeemable, and that the Wadsetters should be bound to denude thereof upon payment of the wadsettsums and that this process if brought in proper time, they were advised would Supercede the necessity of using an order of Redemption which upon account of the many Formalities attending it was a troublesome method –

22d & 23d
Jany 1761

Accordingly of these dates the Memorialist /4/ Executed Summonses of Reduction and Declarator agt. John and Duncan Stewarts concluding Inter alia 'That it should be found and 'Declared that the citations to be given and the said 'Summonses should be held equall to a premonition and in all 'respects the same as if the haile Order of Redemption sett 'furth in the Charter had been used and that the Offer of pay-'ment of the wadsett sums at the Barr of the Court of Session 'should be held equivalent to a consignation thereof'.

As a Messenger could not be Immediately had to Execute the Summonses they did not return in time to have any procedure had upon them in the winter of 1760/61 and the Memorialists therefore used an order of Redemption and Consigned the money in terms of the Clause of reversion in the wadsett rights and upon the order of Redemption, Summonses of Declarator and removing were raised and Executed which were called remitted & conjoined to the Reduction above mentioned, upon which Conjoined processes they at last obtained the Following Interloqr.–

'Edr 2d March 1762 The Lord Ordinary /5/ having considered 'what is above represented of new Finds and Declares the 'lands lybelled to be lawfully redeemed from and after 'Whitsunday next and ordains the defenders to Cede the pos-'session to Glenure at the said term, and to convey their rights 'in favours of him with warrandice from fact and deed and the 'redeemers to be at the expense of making out the 'Conveyances redeemable upon payment of the sums 'advanced to Appine to pay the said Wadsetters and Expence 'he has been put to in using and following furth the redemp-'tion and that upon the pursuer paying to the Defenders or in

'case of their Absence lodging the forementd. Sum in the hands
'of the cashier of the royall Bank and decerns in the Declarator
'of Redemption and Removing accordingly'.

In consequence of this Interlocutor the memorialist Glenure
paid of the said wadsetters in the term of Whitsunday last and
took Conveyances to the Wadsett rights of the Lands Wadsett to
them. But as Duncan Stewart had notwithstanding the Decision
of the Court of Session Laboured and sowed his farm, he
Insisted that the Disposition to be granted by him should /6/
Bear the memorialists entry to the arable land not to commence till the Separation of the crops from the Ground –

There is no such stipulation in the conveyance granted by
Ballachulish, and the memorialist was advised that as Duncan
Stewart had already laboured and sowed the Ground, it was
better for him to End matters in the way he did, than enter into
a fresh Litigation as the Consequence thereof would be the
Entire disappointment of the people to whom in Expectation of
Duncan Stewart removing the memorialist had sett the farm,
Especially as the Court would find Duncan Stewart lyable in
any Damage that arose from not getting possession of the
arrable land for so long a time after the term.

The Beggings upon both farms particularly those upon
Brecklet are quite ruinous and no ways habitable. The
Memorialist has caused them to be comprised by the sworn
Birleymen of the Bounds and the Bill of Comprisement for
both ammounts to above £40 Sterling of which there is about
£29 for the deficiency of /7/ the houses, Corn dykes etc. upon
Brecklet.

The Memorialist is informed by the tennants upon the farm
that they got no Comprisement for their Beggings at their Entry
and that it is not the Custom of that part of the Country to
Comprise the Beggings either at Entry or removeale of the
Tennants the only comprisement in use in that Country being
that of Corn dykes, the Comprisement of which in the present
case being but a Trifle.

The Memorialist is also Informed that it is the Custom of
that part of the Country that the removing Tennant leaves to
the incoming one the half of the whole fodder of that Crop and
a tenth part of said Crop and Straw for the Teinds due out of
the possession in regard the Incoming Tennant is Lyable to pay
same to the Minister or Titular – In other parts of the Country it
is Customary for the outgoing Tennant to leave the whole
fodder and it is a proper custom as that is the only thing the
Incoming Tennant has for furnishing him that /8/ years manure
– These things premised the Memorialist would be advised –

1mo.   As the Interlocutor finding the Lands redeemable was pronounced upon 3d of March last before the Labouring com-
menced was not the Wadsetters in male fide to Labour and
sow the Grounds – and therefore does not the Crop upon the
Grounds belong to the Memorialist upon paying the seed and
the Labour – And

2do.   As Duncan Stewart Laboured and sowed the Ground before
granting the conveyance and therefore refused to grant the
conveyance unless it contained a clause bearing that the
Memorialist possession to the arable Ground was not to commence till after the Separation of the Crop from the Ground,
can any Benefite arise to him therefrom, as the Memorialist had
no choice left but Either to Comply with that demand; or not
only to disapoint the Tennants to whom he had set the farm
for that year but also Enter into a new Litigation with Stewart
thereannent.

3tio.   If it is thought this Clause in Duncan Stewarts Conveyance
to the Memorialist gives /9/ him a right to reap his Crop, is he
not lyable in the rent of the arable Ground as he got payment
of his money at the term.

4to.   If it is thought that the memorialist has a right to the Crop
upon paying the seed and Labour can he not Intromitt therewith as soon as it is fitt for Cutting down, or what steps must
be taken – thereanent – and if Duncan Stewart can only be
made lyable for the rent of the arable ground cannot the
Memorialist cause sequestrate as much of the Crop as will
answer payment thereof, as the same shall be Comprised by
the Birleymen of the Bounds –

5to.   Are not the Wadsetters obliged to leave their houses in a
Sufficient habitable Condition as Comprised by the sworn
Birleymen of the Bounds, if they are cannot the Memorialist
retain the ammount of the Bill of Comprisement out of the
price of the seed and Labour of the Crop, if found to belong to
him as above – or if it is thought that the Memorialist has no
right to the Crop has he notwithstanding /10/ thereof a right to
retain as much thereof as will pay the ammount of the said Bill
of Comprisement as the same shall be ascertained by
Birleymen; which is the universale Custom of that part of the
Country in cases where the Comprised sums are not immediately paid down –

6to.   If it is thought that the memorialist has no right to keep the
crop as above – Has he not a right to the fodder at least to the
half of it which is the universale practice of the Countrey, and
is in this case highly reasonable, where there was a mala fides
in sowing, and depriving the incoming Tennant of having a
Crop and fodder of his own –

As these Questions will probably occurr betwixt the Memorialist and the purchaser of these Lands at the Sale he wants to be advised what steps are proper for him to take thereannent viz as to the reparation of Houses Dykes etc, in case the wadsetters are not thought obliged to leave /11/ the same in a habitable Tennantable Condition that he may act in such a way as to give no handle for any Disputes or after Canglings Either with Appines Creditors or those who may purchase his Estate at the Judicialle Sale.

Edr. 5th. Augt 1762

This is the Memoriall and Queries to which my opinion of this date does referr.

signed Robt. McQueen

ANSWERS to the MEMORIALE &
QUERIES for DUNCAN CAMPBELL
of GLENURE and Others CREDITORS
adjudgers of the ESTATE of APPINE

I have considered the foresaid memoriale and Queries which are on paper a part and in answer to the first and second Queries I am humbly of opinion That the wadsetters will be Entitled to the Crop presently upon the Grounds – they are by Decreet of the Court ordained to remove only at the term of Whitsunday 1762 and the Lands are declared to be redeemed as at that period and therefore it falls to be considered as if a year had been added to the term fixed [for] the redemption [of] the wadsetts –

In this view of the Case I think the reaping of the Crop that was sown by them before the term of their removeale is no more than what they in Justice and Equity were Entitled to – As by their wadsett rights their Entry was at Whitsunday so they could not get the Corn Crops of that year and so if they don't reap /2/ the Crops the year of their Removale they had not been thirteen years full possession of the lands which they are certainly Entitled to, and as I Incline to think that this will hold as to both wadsetters multo magis must it hold as to Duncan Stewart who made it a Condition in the Conveyance that he granted of the Lands that the Memorialists possession to the arrable Lands was not to Commence till after the separation of the Crops from the Ground and indeed I think that this Stipulation was no more than he was in Justice intitled to demand since he was allowed to possess to Whits. 1762.

The Third Queerie is in Effect already mentioned I think the memorialist is Entitled to no rent for the arrable Grounds since without reaping the
Crops for the year 1762 the wadsetters possession would not have been
compleat.

The Fourth Querie is already answered at the same time upon the
supposition that the Memorialist was Entitled to the Crops I have no doubt
that he could Intromit therewith whenever he thought /3/ fit, and that without any order of Law, as the wadsetters were to all Intents and purposes out
of the possession at Whits. 1762 and the Memorialist had then assumed the
full possession of the lands, for altho the wadsetters may have a right to
Cutt down the Crops yet they cannot be said to be in possession of any part
of the Lands and upon the Supposition that the wadsetters were liable for
rent for the arrable lands the Memorialist might no doubt sequestrate part of
the Crops untill the Wadsetters should find Caution for payment of what
should be afterwards ascertained to be the rent of the arrable Lands which
behooved to be ascertained in a Court of Law if the parties could not agree
among themselves – But as I have already observed I dont think there is at
present room for the Question.

As to the Fifth and Sixth Queries I think what is therein stated will be
Entirely regulated by the Custom of the Country – where a Custom is any-
howe Generall it must regulate the Contracts /4/ and agreements of parties
where the contrary is not Expressly stipulated – The Generall Custom of a
Country is understood to be under the view of parties at the time of
Entering into the Contract and to be an Implied Condition in it unless where
there are Express Provisions to the Contrary –

As to the last Query as the memorialists redeeming of the lands was a
Beneficiale act to the whole Creditors it is therefore most Equitable that he
should not lose one pennie by his Interfeiring in that matter – whatever
money he shall Expend in making proper and necessary repairs of the
houses and other Beggings on the lands he will be Entitled to state to the
Creditors when they come to redeem the Subjects from him and that there
may lie no after Question betwixt the Memorialist and the Creditors as to
the propriety of any repairs that may be made I think they ought to be
made by the Authority of a Court of /5/ Justice after having ordered a previous visitation of the Subjects by a Tradesman or other persons skilled in
these matters.

If the lands in Question were under Sequestration, the repairs
behooved to be made by authority of the Court of Session, if the Factor on
the Estate immagined that he in virtue of his Factory had not proper powers
to do so of himself – But as it occurrs to me the presents Subjects do not fall
under the Sequestration They are not under the management of the Court,
no more fell under the Sequestration than the feu duties payable by the
Wadsetts –

As this was certainly the Case before the redemption so I cannot
think that the redemption makes any alteration as to that matter – In Effect
no more is done by the redemption than putting the Memorialist in the

place of the Wadsetters and he is Entitled to hold the lands untill the same shall be redeemed from him by the Creditors –

/6/ As I do apprehend that these Subjects do not fall under the Sequestration so the memorialist can very Competently [apply] to the Judge Ordinary to appoint a visitation of the subjects and authouse what repairs shall be found necessary and after these repairs are truely made I should not think it improper to have the accounts of the Tradesmen cognosced –

If the Memorialist is not barred by the Custom of the Country from claiming the repairs from the wadsetters they would no doubt at Common Law be bound to leave houses etc sufficient in which view it would be proper before making any repairs to require the wadsetters under form of Instrument to put the Subjects in repair and a petition may then be given to the Judge Ordinary Praying to appoint a visitation of the Subjects to aut-house such repairs as shall be found necessary and to ordain the wadsetters /7/ to pay the Expence of these repairs to the Memorialist which Petition will fall to be served against the wadsetters and if the Sheriff should refuse to find the Wadsetters liable in these Expenses It will be sufficient Exoneration to the Memorialist and will Entitle him to State the same agst. the other Creditors.

Edinr. 5th. Augt 1762

This and the five preceeding
pages is the opinion of
(signed) Robt McQueen.

REGULATION OF AGRICULTURE IN SEVENTEENTH CENTURY KINTYRE

By A. I. B. STEWART, C.B.E., B.L., F.S.A.SCOT.

Retired Solicitor, Campbeltown

It was with some surprise that I learned of the existence in the Register House among the Breadalbane Muniments, under reference GD 112/17/1, of the afterwritten Acts of Neighbourhood of 10 June 1653 and the subsequent Acts of Bailyerie of 4 November 1672. Both documents clearly relate to Kintyre in which the Breadalbanes and their predecessors, the Campbell baronets of Glenorchy never had any interest. But they were closely related to the Argyll family by a common ancestry and by marriage: the ninth earl was fostered at Taymouth and in his case, as in many, the bond of fosterage was stronger than that of blood. It is not unreasonable to presume that the papers had been provided by him as styles for his kinsmen to follow, though the laird of Glenorchy had published as early as 1621 very comprehensive acts of court. These are to be found in the Black Book of Taymouth.[1]

Archibald, seventh earl of Argyll, had seen the culmination of years of scheming in the grant by royal charter dated 30 May 1607 of the lands of Kintyre. In vain might Sir James MacDonald complain that, 'my race has been for ten hundred years kindly Scotsmen under the kings of Scotland' and plead that His Majesty should give no employment to the Campbells, 'who craves ever to fish in drummly waters'. It was not only a fulfilment of Campbell ambition but of royal policy which placed these lands, along with Islay, granted to Cawdor, in hands which King James might reasonably feel would effectively separate Clan Donald from their Irish kin and act as a deterrent to Irish invasion.

But matters did not go as intended. Sir James MacDonald, last of the successors of the Lords of the Isles, escaped from prison and raised the clan. His defeat by Argyll in Kintyre resulted in his flight to Spain in 1615, where to his surprise he was joined in exile by his persecutor the Earl, who in 1619 was denounced traitor and rebel for the offences of marrying a Catholic lady and entering the service of the king of Spain. He had meantime taken the first step to remove the Clan Donald tribesmen from the Kintyre estates by obtaining decrees of removal in the Court of Session in 1609 and 1619.[2] Very little if anything seems to have been done to enforce these decrees when he resigned his lands of Kintyre to his son by the second marriage, James, Lord Kintyre, who received a charter from King

---

1   *The Black Book of Taymouth*, privately printed by the Marquis of Breadalbane (Edinburgh, 1855) pp. 352 ff.
2   S.R.O., Acts and Decreets, vol. 245, fo. 216 and vol. 340, fo. 79.

Charles I on 12 February 1626. Lord Lorne, later to become the eighth earl and only marquis of Argyll, eventually succeeded in thwarting the plans of his Catholic younger half-brother to convey Kintyre to Ranald McDonnell of Dunluce, recently created first earl of Antrim. The Privy Council intervened and Lord Kintyre in 1636 reconveyed to the Crown who made the lands over to the marquis.

A rental of 1636 is the first evidence we have of the existence of written leases of the Kintyre farms, when existing tenants delivered up their tacks. But for some years to come the marquis had probably too much on his mind to attend personally to the management of his estates. In 1638 at the famous Glasgow Assembly he came out unequivocally on the Covenanting side and from then on he became the leader of that party and possibly the most influential Scotsman of his day. He reached the zenith of his career on 1 January 1651 when he placed the crown of Scotland on the ungrateful head of Charles II. But shortly thereafter he had fallen out of royal favour and of popular esteem and he asked and obtained permission to retire to his estates. From Inveraray he made his peace with the conqueror Cromwell and handed over several of his castles, including Tarbert and Loch Kilkerran (Campbeltown) in Kintyre. His estates there had been devastated by the Civil War when they were for some years occupied by the army of Alastair MacColla MacDonald (Young Colkitto). In June 1647 the remnants of these forces were massacred at Dunaverty and Argyll was then free to arrange his affairs. The granting of leases to new tenants was facilitated by the deaths and destruction caused by the wars and subsequent spread of the plague which followed the Covenanting army.

In 1650 he arranged for a number of Lowland lairds under the leadership of William Ralston of that Ilk, a leading Covenanter friend, to take up tacks in Kintyre. He hoped that the Presbyterian religion and presumably more advanced agricultural skills of the incomers would both provide a stern defence against the Irish who had so recently destroyed his lands and simultaneously improve the value of his Kintyre estate. Ralston himself was given twenty-three and a half merklands at Saddell with the castle as a residence. But Argyll's troubles were not over. His son, Lord Lorne, later the ninth earl, and Alexander Macnachtan of Dunderawe, his chamberlain in Kintyre, took up arms under Lord Glencairn for the King. The marquis dismissed Macnachtan whom he evidently suspected of embezzling rents.

There survives at Inveraray a minute of a meeting of the tenants of the burgh of Campbeltown held on 13 June 1653 at which they each gave evidence as the state of their accounts. The marquis, accompanied by his younger son, Lord Neil Campbell, who had replaced Macnachtan as chamberlain of the Kintyre estates, three days earlier had promulgated the accompanying Acts of Neighbourhood. It is a matter of interest that both documents were dated at Lochheid, the old name. The marquis did not use the new name of Campbeltown created in his honour. These were doubtless the first set of written rules for the governance of rural communities in the West Highlands. It is unlikely that written rules were ever considered necessary by the MacDonald lords of Kintyre and their indigenous tenantry. It may be that the incomers from Renfrewshire and North Ayrshire had found the natural indifference of their Highland neighbours to regulation somewhat burdensome and that their pleas had resulted in the Acts. It is to be noted that both 'Lowland and Hieland' gentlemen had been consulted.

The original does not have numbered paragraphs.

The Court Book of the Barony and Regality of Falkirk and Callendar recently published by the Stair Society shows that several of the matters dealt with in these Acts and in the Acts of Bailyierie concerned that court, whose interests however embraced a predominantly urban population.

The 1653 Acts indicate the existence of a rather offhand attitude to the duties of neighbours towards each other. All the Acts seem to be reasonable though the penalties in paragraphs six and eight may be considered severe by modern readers. The provisions of paragraph nine have a singularly modern look.

The use of 'both plantatiounes' in paragraph thirteen is interesting. At first sight it might be considered to apply to the recent plantation in Kintyre of Lowlanders and Campbells. As mentioned above the marquis had granted tacks or leases to the Lowland lairds led by William Ralston in 1650. In 1652 the forfeited estate of Largie was leased to Donald Campbell of Inverawe – 'the McConnachie' – and at the same time many other Campbells were given leases of lands in Kintyre. McKerral heads his tenth chapter 'The Plantation of Lowland Lairds and Campbells'.[3] But it is unlikely that the indigenous Highlanders, the native Kintyre tacksmen, were excused the education tax to pay the schoolmaster's salary and here the phrase must surely be shorthand for Lowlanders and Highlanders.

Paragraph fourteen indicates that the Statutes of Iona of 1609 had not apparently eliminated the existence of 'idle maisterless men and soarners', who no doubt had increased as a result of the wars.

The marquis was executed in 1661 for his alleged adherence to Cromwell. However, his son was rewarded by Charles II for his unfilial behaviour in serving his monarch in 1653 against his father's strongly expressed wishes and the estates and the earldom though not the marquisate were restored to him. Times were much more settled and the clash of arms was not heard again in Kintyre until the earl fell out with Charles's brother James II over the Test Act and returned from exile in Holland to raise in Campbeltown his standard of rebellion in 1685. He too perished on the scaffold.

Evidently he felt that by 1672 the Acts promulgated by his father were in need of revisal and the results were the accompanying Acts of Bailyierie.

Articles one and three of the earlier regulations are repeated in a revised form in Articles one and two but Article two, the requirement of each township to supply a common herd, is dropped. But the new Acts pay much more attention in general to agricultural methods and to cropping and rotation. Idle beggars, now known as 'thiggers' or thieves still trouble the country and horses are apparently still borrowed without leave. A new rule

3   A. McKerral, *Kintyre in the Seventeenth Century* (Edinburgh, 1948).

regarding thirlage is introduced. Altogether the 1672 Acts indicate that, while there still exists a certain amount of disorder, the state of knowledge of agricultural methods is progressing.

The names of the birlawmen, or arbiters, are of interest. Andrew McKerral[4] estimates that the 1678 Kintyre rental shows 139 tenants of Lowland stock, 103 Campbells and 179 of the old Gaelic native stock. The appointment of the birlawmen shows what seems to be a regard for a fair distribution among these groups. There are fourteen Lowlanders, seven Campbells plus Archibald McGibbon, an Inveraray man, and fourteen Kintyre Gaels, including eight McNeills.

The goodman of Karriskey is McNeill of Carskey. The family had held these lands as native men since at least 1505 but did not take a feudal title till 1704. The use of 'goodman' for a Highlander seems to me unusual. The laird of Sannay is MacDonald of Sanda. Brimmoor is William Hamilton of Brownmuir and Subbar is James Maxwell of Southbar. Cauldwell is John Caldwell of Caldwell. MacKay of Ugadale was the last of his line, holding under a charter of Robert Bruce. Lachlan McNeill (Buidhe) was the founder of the families of MacNeal of Ugadale and of Losset. He was the ancestor of at least eight of the twelve McNeills, in various spellings in the *Dictionary of National Biography*. Major John Campbell rose with the Earl in 1685. He was among the Campbell gentlemen executed at Inveraray and chosen for special treatment, having had his arms hacked off before hanging. He was the grandfather of Rev. John McVicar, Minister of St. Cuthbert's, Edinburgh, in 1745 who had the temerity or courage to pray for King George during Prince Charles Edward's occupation of the city. Charles McEachan of Tangie was the last of the family to hold these lands, though it is believed that the Jura McKechnies are of the same line.

The mediaeval parishes of Kilcolmkill and Kilblaan now form the parish of Southend. Kilchousland, Kilmichael, Kilkivan and Kilkerran are united in the parish of Campbeltown. Killean and Kilkenzie are now one parish. Saddell is united with Skipness in which Argyll held no lands.

The Argyll family held their Kintyre estates till 1950 when they were sold to meet death duties and although the terms evolved over the years the conditions of their leases undoubtedly had their origins in the marquis's Acts of Neighbourhood.

I am indebted to my son Angus Stewart for drawing my attention to the existence of these papers and for the permission of Mr Patrick Cadell, Keeper of the Records of Scotland, to publish them.

---

4   Op. cit.

ACTS OF NEIGHBOURHOOD[1]

At Lochheid in Kintyire the tenth day of June 1653.

The quhilk day the Right honorable My Lord Marqueis of Argyll, Earle of Kintyire Lord Campbell and Lorne and Lord Neill Campbell chalmerlane of Kintyire his lordships sonne, with ane certain number both of Lowland and hieland gentlemen of the countrey Being mett; for the better settleing the conditioun of the country; and for keiping good nybourhood among the severall inhabitants theirof doeth with mutuall consent aggrie to the particullars efterspecifiet.

1.   Imprimis that all merch dykis formerlie buildit, sall be repaired and made up againe by the parties nybouring Betwixt [now] and Hallowmes nixt to cume (in caise of contraversie or debate) or Beltane thairefter anno 1654 at fardest, and that the samen merch dykis sall be keiped wp and maintained both summer and winter And wher ane hieway to kirk and mercat falls to be in a merch dyk That then the gaitt or yett wpon that merch dyik is to be maintained by the nybours proportionablie, as the merch dyike itself is.

2.   As lyikquyse that ther be a comoun sufficient herd presentlie apoynted in everie toune, for whom the tennant or tennants of that toune respectivelie are to be anserable.

3.   Item that ther be poyndfolds appoynted in everie toune, having sufficient water in thame, as formerlie the saids poyndfolds have bein and that the pairtie poynder sall make intimatioun with all possible diligence to the nybours nixt adjacent to the lands wher the goods ar poynded By one of his servants, or any other, whose aithes being taken sall be sufficient probatioun of the intimatioun made: And when the goods ar owned, if the skaith be done in cornes, then it is to be prysed be two or mae sufficient swornemen to be equallie chosen be the pairtie poynder and pairtie owner of the goods And the skaith prysed is to be payed be the pairtie to whom the goods belange Bot if the owners of the goods doe not give satisfactioun to the poynder whether the skaith be in corne or grass so that he be necessitate to complain to any having chairge within the countrey; In that caice the pairtie whose goods ar poynded sall not onlie pay the skaith, bot lykquyse the equivalent of the skaith to any who sall have chairge of the countrey for the tyme Bot if the goods be poynded for being upoun the grass, then the owners of the goods ar to pay tuelve pennies scotts for ilk heid of horse and ky; and for ilk sex heid of scheip or goat poynded. And if the goods poynded be not owned betwixt and the nixt Lords day after the poynding than the poynder of the goods is to make publict intimatioun at

---

1   For an explanation of Scottish terms in the Acts reference may be made to *The Concise Scots Dictionary*, ed. M. Robinson (Aberdeen, 1985) [*C.S.D.*]. Terms which do not appear there or seemed to require some further annotation are explained in the following footnotes.

the kirk door of the paroch, or the nixt adjacent paroch when divyne service is. And that both in Irish[2] and English with the number of the goods poynded And the most remarkable marks of the samen so neir as he can And in caice they sall not be owned notwithstanding of that intimatioun befoir the nixt Lords day Then the lyke is to be done that day also. And if they be not owned within 48 houres efter the second intimatioun upoun the second Lords day efter the poynding then the poynder is to bring the goods to any having chairge within the countrey for the tyme who is to receave the samen off their lands, and to pay him not onlie for the skaith done wpoun his cornes, and proven as is afoirsaid, and the penaltie for eating of the grass for which they wer poynded Bot also sall give him satisfactioun for keiping and intertainment of the goods, during the tyme they were in his custodie from the tyme of poynding till the tyme of delyverie of the samen, And that according to the modificatioun of him who sall have chairge of the countrey for the tyme.

4.   It is lykquise ordained that when any goods sall come and haunt, with any mans goods whatsumever He is to make intimatioun therof within twentie dayes efter the saids goods coming among his, that such goods ar wpoun his ground And the intimatioun is to be maid publictlie at the kirk door of that paroch or the nixt adjacent paroch wher divyne service is and that both in Irish and Inglish with the number of the goods they have haunting among thers, and the most remarkable marks thereof so neir as he can, And in caice they sall not be owned (not withstanding of that intimatioun) befoir the nixt Lords day, then the lyke is to be done that day. And if they be not owned within fourtie eight houres efter the second intimatioun wpon the second Lords day, then the person in whose custodie the goods ar is to bring the samen goods to any having chairge within the countrey for the tyme or in his owne optioun to advertise the officer of the bounds to receave the goods off his land, and he is to be satisfied according to the modificatioun of him who has chairge of the countrey of the tyme And in caice the persones in whose custodie any such wauch[3] goods sall be found doe not make intimatioun in maner as is particularlie abovespecifeit in that caice the saids persone or persones sall be accounted and esteimed to be the stealers or resitters of the saids goods, and they accordinglie proceided against.

5.   Item it is mutuallie aggreit annent swyne that they be keiped aff cornes and infield lands till Hallowday nixt and if they continow in transgressing in either of the above written it is declairit that the pairtie wrongit by thame may then lawfullie kill them, And from Hallowday nixt such as keip thame, ar to keip thame within ther owne ground, and in caice they doe not, It is aggreit wnto that the partie, in whose ground they sall be found to wander, may lawfullie kill thame without prejudice.

---

2   The Gaelic language; Campbeltown still has two parish churches, the Highland and the Lowland.
3   Stray, the equivalent of 'waif' or 'waff'.

6.   Item that no persone presume to take his nybors horse ather to ryde thereon or labour therwith without leave askit and given by the owner And that under the paine of tenpunds toties quoties to be exacted by him who sall have chairge of the countrey for the tyme And that by and attour the prejudice and skaith that the horse sall sustain And in caice the pairtie transgresser be not solvendo, That he sall be scourged throw the towne of Lochheid.

7.   Item that no man presume to cutt off the hair ather taills or meands of nybors horse or meires, wnder the paine of twentie pund of penaltie, of everie one who sall be found guiltie, and in caice the pairtie transgressor be not solvendo, he is to be scourged throw the Lochheid toune.

8.   As also that none sall suffer any of ther stoned horses or colts, to be among ther nybor meires for prejudging them in any tyme of the yeir And if it be found other wayes The pairtie prejudged sall have libertie presentlie to geld such stoned horses or colts as he finds among his meares, without any inconvenience to follow in relatioun to him for gelding therof.

9.   It is also with mutuall consent aggried that at everie dwellinghouse ther sall be a kaillyaird and that the kaillyaird dyike sall be planted with trees round about at an equall distance, and that the samen sufficientlie hayned with libertie alwayes to the planters of the said kaillyairds and tries to cutt for the wse of building and labouring within the ground such trees as sall be wsefull for that effect: provyding they imediatlie plant thrie trees for ilk tree cutted.

10.   As also that all timber of all sorts whatsumever within the countrey sall be hayned: and that, whosoever, without licence fra the heretor, sall cutt or peill any therof for the first fault they sall pay fyve pund; for the second fault ten pund; and for the thrid fault 20 lib, and for the 4 fault fourtie lib. And that by and attour the payment of the timber cutted or peilled. And ther is heirby libertie granted to the possessor of the ground quhair the timber sall be cutted or peilled to take fra the saids persons ther axes, playds horsses or any other thing broght be them for that effect And to present the samen to him who sall have chairge of the countrey for the tyme, and to dilate thir names with libertie also to search in any place suspected of such cutted or peilled timber And ther is also libertie granted that the possessors of the severall lands quhair the woods ar sall have libertie to cutt any such timber as sall be found necessar for building within that land and labouring of the ground therof, provyding it be ordourlie done, and that the woods be not destroyed.

11.   Item that ther be no peitts casten in any medowes or sward ground (if ther be any moss within these lands); And that ther be ane new way taken for casting be way of binks in the laigh or fall of the moss, and that no further holls be casten wnder the paine of fyve pund of penaltie toties quoties as they sall contravene.

12.   Item, that during the wholl summer and harvest tyme, goods be broght and keiped in sufficient faulds; to the effect the corne may be the

better keiped, and the land taitched[4] wnder the paine of halfe a mark of the heid of ilk beast keiped back and not faulded as said is.

13.   Item it is mutuallie aggriet be the gentlemen of both plantatiounes that ther sall be uplifted yeirlie for the wse of a schoolmaster at Lochheid ane groat out of ilk merk land fra the Lairgie syde to the muill of Kintyire inclusive And that by and attour the soume of ane hundreth merks Voluntairlie promised be my Lord Marqueis And in the mean tyme Mr Thomas Orr present schoolmaster is to be payed presentlie two yeires of bygane rests, and to receave the benefit of his present act during his faithfull service.

14.   Item all maisterles and ydle people ar heirby discharged from remaining any longer within his countrey of Kintyire wnder the paine of being taken and apprehended and censured accordinglie as idle maisterles men and soarners And lykwyse all tennants and inhabitants within the countrey quhatsumever ar heirby dischargit from ressaiting or intertaining any such persone or persones: And whosoever sall doe in the contrarie it is aggriet by mutuall consent that they sall be esteimed as airt and pairt of any rimeid and wrongs to be done by such persones and sall be lyable for produceing of them, and making satisfactioun for any skaith they sall doe within the countrey: And lykewyse the ressaitters and intertainers of any such persones as is afoirsaid sall be lyable to the penaltie of tuentie pund so oft as they sall ressaitte and intertein any such persones, And that by and attour the making satisfactioun for the skaith abovewritten.

Argyll.

---

4   Manured – see 'tathe' in *C.S.D.*

ACTS OF BAILYIERIE – KINTYRE 1672

At Campbeltoun the fourth day of November jm vi thrie score twelve yeirs.

Acts made & sett doun be ane Noble Earle Archibald Earle of Argyll & with advyce and consent of the gentlemen and others in Kintyre to be keiped & observed in tym coming.

1.   In regaird of the many debaitts that does ocurr annent the marches of sevrall roumes in the countrey it is enacted and ordained that the haill lands within the sevrall paroches be perambulat and bounded with all conveniences and that march dykes be digged in all touns quhair it may be done and that march stones sheuchs and ditches be made and sett doun be the tenants of the lands be advyce of the persones, efterspecifeit who are to be appointed birlawmen in eatch parroch at the sight of the noble Earle his bailzie.

2.   For the better keping of cornes and grass it is appointed that there be poindfangs[5] made in everie toune of the countrey and that all beastiall that beis found eatting and destroying cornes or grass be putt in the said poindfangs and keipit and detained ther untill the owners be advertised and pay four shillings Scotts for ilk horse or two and eight pennes for ilk sheip or goatt eatch twentie four hours they sall heppen to be in these poindfangs and that for eating of the grasse as weill in winter as summer besyds satisfactiion for eatting cornes according as the samen shall be comprysed and if the said goodes sall be poinded theyre and not releived then it is appointed that the samen be sent to my lords poindfang at Campbeltoun and that the bailzie pay the skaith and be comptable to my Lord for the said goods and in caice any person sall happen to break a lawfull poindfang, quhair ther is grass and watter it is ordained that any such person or persones sall pay an unlaw of twentie punds toties quoties And if owners of poinded goodes beis not found then the goodes are to be publicklie intimate at the paroch kirk the next ensueing sabbath day and if within fourtie eight houres thereafter they will not be releived that they are to be delyvred to the bailzie who is to satisfie for the eatten grass or cornes ut supra and in the mean time untill the march dyks be digged it is appointed that all persones indevour to keip ther goods from eatting ther neighboures grass And that the said act as to the four shilling and eight penneis to be suspendit till may nixt except in the caice of wilfull eatting and destroying the grass and that eatting of moor grass without the head dyiks shall not come under the said fyne.

3.   It is ordained quhair ther is any cornes eatten or distroyed in the countrey that the samen shall be apryssed be two honnest neighbouris and that the owners of the goodes that eatts the said corne sall pay for the skaith and als mutch to the bailzie.

---

5   The equivalent of 'poyndfolds' – see 'fank' in *C.S.D.* 'Fang' is the Irish word for enclosure.

4.   It is appointed that in eavry roume of land the fourt pairt of the croffting be either sown with peize or left lie under the paine of ten pund uppon ilk merk land yeirlie.

5.   It is appointed that the outfield land of ilk roume shall not be laboured above thrie yeirs togidder and to be left ley other thrie yeirs therafter and the transgressors of this act to pay ane unlaw of fyve pund for ilk aicker of land yeirlie.

6.   As for the lands that shall happen to be lymmed it is appointed that the rulles following sall be observed to witt if the lymm be laid on pleiued land, then the samen is to be labored, as other outfeild land but if it be laid on heather or bent land upon that ther shall be butt fyve croups taken in at first and therafter to be left ley for thrie yeirs and then laboured other thrie yeirs etc. And quhen bogg land is taken in that ther be butt fyve crops taken of it at first and then to ly two yeirs ley and therafter laboured four yeirs and it is recomendit to the bailzie and birlawmen to sie this act deulie observed throw the countrey.

(7.   No article 7 in original)

8.   It is appointed that the mosses be casten regularlie and in order in tyme cuming and that none presume to spoill the mosses by making holls therin but that the said mosses be casten uppon a face or bink and that the transgressors of this act shall pay ane unlaw of fyve punds for ilk darg of peitts casten in holls.

It is appointed that the tennants that casts peitts on other folks ground shall give ane sher[6] or pay six shillings scotts for eatch darg and that for spoylling the grass and that none cast peitts in meidow ground under the paine of fyve pund for ilk darg and that the turffs to be laid even that grass may grow theron under the paine off thrittie shilling eatch darg.

9.   Considering that the countrie is oppressed with common thigers and that any course formerlie taken for restraining thereof hes proven ineffectuall therfore it is ordained that whosoever sall give or bestow any thing uppon the said thiggers in tyme cuming shall pay ane unlaw of twentie pund unforgiven except the said thiggers be such as shall have ane testimoniall of ther povertie and indigent conditione from the bailzie or Kirk Sessions.

10.   If any person wanting land or grass in the countrey have ky or horsse passturing on other folks ground it is appointed that all such goodes be seased on and delyvered to the bailzie as oversoumes[7] and waff beasts and disposed of accordinglie the skaith being alwayes satisfied be him to any persons damnified.

---

6   Provide a shearer for a day.
7   Each 'roume' had its 'soume', the total number of beasts it could properly carry. 'Oversoumes' were beasts in excess of this number – see 'owersoum' in C.S.D.

11.   It is appointed for the better preserving of Inclossed ground that no person or persons presume to break doun the dyks thereof nor yitt to travell therthrow be foott or horsse and the contraveiners of this act to pay ane unlaw of fyve pund for ilk horsse or kow and fourtie shilling ilk footman the one half to the bailzie and the other halfe to the owner of the Inclossed ground It is alwayes provydit quhair ther is common high wayes going through the said Inclossers that ther be hinging gatts keiped wp theron.

12.   Wher ther is parks or Inclossed ground with sufficient dyks incaice the samen shall be broken doun and the grass eatten and destroyed, be bestiall It is enacted that the owners of the said goodes shall pay ane unlaw of fyve pund besyde four shilling for the peice of aither kow or horsse that shall be found within the said parks toties quoties unless it can be proven that the dyks wer broken doun of befoir.

13.   In regaird the sevrall tacksmen of the countrey are bound to preserve the woods therfore it is appointed that the said tacksmen dilate the cutters and destroyers of the said woods or be debitours for the destroyed woods themselves and in the mean tyme recommends to the bailzie and birlawmen to sie the act annent cutting of woods be putt in execution and quhair any person is found cutting woods that the tennants of the land take the horsses and axes and send them to the bailzie.

14.   It is recommendit to the bailzies and officares of the countrey to take nottice who plants young trees conforme to the tacks and that for ilk tree that is not planted, yeirlie they shall pay twelve shilling scotts and it is appointed that my lords gardener furnish ash and plain trees to all the countrey twa penneis scotts the peice and that the bailzie and officars give ane accompt of ther diligence heiranent at my lords cuming to the countrey.

15.   It is appointed that whosoever takes away ryde or work other menes horsses without ther oun leive shall pay ane unlaw of fyve pund the on halfe to the bailzie and the other half to the owners besyd satisfaction to any persones damnified.

16.   It is appointed that the lands of ilk suckin sall goe to ther oun mylns with ther cornes and if they cannot be served within ten days therat that in that caise wppon payment of halfe multer to the mylne of the suckin, they shall have libertie too goe to any of my lords mylns and that none presume to goe to any other mylnes of the countrey than to my lords under the paine of ten pund for the first tym twentie punds for the second and lossing the beneffeit of ther tack for the third tyme and for removing of all debaitts betwixt millers and tennants for afterward it is appointed that the twa pairt of all cornes and bear growand uppon the ground seid and horsse corne alenarlie excepted shall pay the ordinarie multers.

It is appointed that ther shall be four birlawmen in eatch parroch who shall have power to concurr with and assist the bailzie in everie thing relaitting to the good of the countrey and to sie the acts befoir written deulie keiped and observed The names of quhich birlawmen are as follows viz:–

For the parroch of Killicolmkeile.
>   The Laird of Ralstoun   The good man of Karriskey.
>   Dugall Campbell   Lachlan McNeill

For the parroch of Kilblaane
>   The Laird of Sannay   The good man of Subbar.
>   The good man of Brimmoor   John McNeill in Cristollach

For the parroch of Kilchousland
>   The good man of Cauldwell   Mackai of Uggodill
>   John Fultoun   James Campbell in Uggodill

For Kilmichall parroch
>   Captaine David Moor   Hector McNeill in Darlochan
>   John Cunynghame of Caddell   James Fleming

For Kilcheivan
>   Lachlan McNeill of Tirwargus
>   Archibald McNeill in Balligrogan
>   John Cunynghame in Balloch
>   Gilbert McLartie in Kilquibenach

For Kilcherane
>   McEcharne   Alexr Forrester
>   Ard. McGibbon and Majour John Campbell

For Kilchenzie
>   Charles McEichan   bailzie Robert Campbell
>   Liutennant Robert Campbell and Dugald Campbell

For Killean
>   Robert Russell   David Forrester
>   Donald McNeill in Balloch And. McNeill in Drumnamuckloch

For the parroch of Saddell
>   Archibald oig Campbell
>   William Wallace
>   Neill McMarcus in Leppinbeg
>   John Wallace

Sic subscribitur   Argyle

INDEX

Anderson's *Historical Essay* has not been systematically indexed but some references picked up in indexing the Introduction or otherwise are included.

Aberdeen, Old, 18
- King's College, 18
Achnacoan, 202, 203n, 205
Achnacone, 202n
Achtriachtan, 201n, 202n
Action, against Viscount Stair, 175
Acts,
- of bailyierie 1672, 212, 214, 220–23
- of neighbourhood 1653, 212, 213, 216–19
- of parliament: Act 1425 c.48, *A.P.S.* ii,9 (c.3), 23; 1469 c.30 (notaries), *A.P.S.* ii,95 (c.6), 23, 24; 1469 c.36 (apprising), *A.P.S.* ii, 96 (c.12), 195; 1672 c.19, Adjudication Act 1672 (c.45), *A.P.S.*, viii, 93, 195; 1681 c.6, Test Act 1681 (c.6), *A.P.S.*, viii, 243, 175, 183, 184, 214; 1690 c.2, *A.P.S.* ix, 111 (c.2) (restoration of Presbyterian ministers), 3; 1695, *A.P.S.*, ix, 481–85 and App. 118 and 124, 141n; 1698 c.37, *A.P.S.*, x, 176, 131n; 1703, *A.P.S.* xi, 66 and App. p. 21, 7; 1704, *A.P.S.*, xi, 140, 135n ; 1704 c.9, *A.P.S.*, xi, 203, 131n; 1705, *A.P.S.* xi, 221, 11; 1707, *A.P.S.* xi, 427–28, 11; Act of Settlement 1701, 4; Clan Act 1715, 200; *Magna Carta*, 84–85, 97, 111; Ordinance for the Government of Scotland 1305, 5, 6; Poynings' Law 1494, 5; Statutes *De donis* 1285 and *Quia emptores* 1290, 6; Statutes of Iona 1609, 214
- of sederunt: on solicitation of judges, 181n, 183, 197; 29 May 1584, 197; 6 July 1688, 132, 142, 144; 25 June 1692, 132, 142

Adjudication, see Wadset
Advocates
- banishment from Edinburgh, 174, 188
Advocates, Faculty of, 47, 131, 132, 133, 139, 140, 142, 146, 148, 157, 158, 159, 160, 171, 190
- Clerks of, 139, 140, 140n
- Dean of, 131, 132, 138, 139, 140, 171, 190
- entry to, 132–33
- membership of, 135
Advocates Library, 4, 14, 15, 146, 149, 150, 157, 160, 164, 171
- fire in, 171, 172
- Keepers of, 14, 16, 139, 140, 148, 161, 171, 172
Agriculture, regulation of, 214, 215, 216–22
Agustín, Antonio, 167
- *Iuris pontificii veteris epitome*, 166
Alciati (Alciatus), A., 150n, 167
Allan, John, 14, 15
Allestree, Richard, 161
Ambrosian Library, 164
Anderson, Andrew, King's printer, 10
- relict of, 10, 10n
- , Andrew, s. of David Anderson, 16
- , Anne, 15
- , David, minister at Perth, 16
- , David, W.S., s. of Andrew Anderson, 17
- , Elizabeth, 15
- , James, W.S., 2, 8, 149
- career, 3–16
- catalogue of library, 15
- Deputy Postmaster-General for Scotland, 13, 14
- education, 3
- family connections, 3, 14, 15–16

Matthaeus, A., 170
Mauchan, Alexander, of
    Overbarnton, 198
Maxwell, James, of Southbar, 215,
    223
Memorial for counsel, see Opinion,
    counsel's
Methodus compendiaria, 145
Milan, 164
Millar, John, 158
Mills, see Thirlage
Monks, forgeries by, 9, 35, 36, 59
Moor, David, Captain, 223
More, Sir Thomas
    – *Enchiridion ethicum*, 161
Mortonhall, see John Trotter
Moscrop, John, of Casselton, 198
Multures, see Thirlage
Municipal law, see Scots law

Natural law, 150–52, 158, 163, 165,
    169, 170
Netherlands, 134n, 137, 138, 175,
    185, 214
New Edinburgh Gazette, see
    Evening-Post and *Scots Post
    Man*
Newabbey, 141
Newton, Isaac, 151, 152, 161
Nicholson, William, bishop of
    Carlisle, 4, 23
Nisbet, see David McGill
– , Mary, 3
Noodt, G, 137, 145, 146, 149
    – *Probabilia*, 138n, 149
    – *De foenore et usuris*, 150
    – *Collegium Grotianum*, 150
Nottingham, Earl of, 165

Opinion, counsel's
    – by Robert McQueen, 209–11
    – on apprising in 1574, 198–99
Overbarnton, see Alexander
    Mauchan
Orr, Thomas, 219
Oxford, 138, 140n, 142n

Padua University, 165
Palaeography, 3, 9, 12, 20
Panciroli, G., 170
Paris, Matthew, 24
Parishes
    – birlawmen for, (*named*) in
        Kintyre, 222–23
    – Campbeltown, 215
    – Dreghorn, 2
    – Kilbirnie, 2
    – Lismore, 202
    – Southend, 215
    – Walston, near Biggar, 1, 2, 3
Parliament
    – British, 12
    – English, 4
    – Scottish, 3, 4, 5, 6, 11, 13, 23,
        131, 141n, 178, 189
Paterson, Sir Hugh, of Bannockburn,
    W.S., 3
– , Thomas, 16
Peats
    – casting of, 218, 221
    – unlawful casting of, 218, 221
Peerage of Scotland, Crawford's, 15,
    189
Perth, 16
Petitus, S., 170
Philology, 141, 145–46, 151, 158, 167
Philosophy, 135, 139, 151, 158, 160,
    167
Pilrig, 135
Pitcairne, David, of Dreghorn, 3
– , Eleanor, 3
– , Mary, 3
Pittendreich, see Sir James Balfour
Plagiarism, 193–94
Poindfangs (Poindfolds), see Cattle,
    damage by stray
Poland, 165
Presbyterian, 16, 18, 170, 176, 180,
    182, 213
    – Declarations of Indulgence 1669
        and 1672, 1–2
    – indulged ministers, 1–3
    – outed ministers, 1, 136n
    – restoration of ministers, 3

THE STAIR SOCIETY

*Instituted in 1934 to encourage the study and
advance the knowledge of the History of Scots Law*

OFFICE-BEARERS 1992

President: PROFESSOR GORDON DONALDSON, C.B.E., M.A., PH.D., D.LITT., HON.D.LITT., F.B.A., F.R.S.E.

Chairman of Council: SHERIFF PETER G. B. McNEILL, Q.C., M.A., LL.B., PH.D.

Vice-Chairman: W. DAVID H. SELLAR, B.A., LL.B.

Council: THE RT. HON. LORD HOPE, P.C., B.A., LL.B., LL.D.; FRANCES SHAW, M.A., PH.D.; PROFESSOR JOHN W. G. BLACKIE, B.A., LL.B.; SHERIFF IAN D. MACPHAIL, Q.C., M.A., LL.B., LL.D.; ATHOL L. MURRAY, M.A., LL.B., PH.D., F.R.HIST.S.; D. ROSS MACDONALD, B.A., LL.B.; JAMES D. CAMPBELL, LL.B; HECTOR L. MacQUEEN, LL.B., PH.D.; WILLIAM G. SIMMONS, LL.B., W.S.

Literary Director: PROFESSOR WILLIAM M. GORDON, M.A., LL.B., PH.D.

Secretary and Treasurer: IVOR R. GUILD, C.B.E., W.S., 16 Charlotte Square, Edinburgh EH2 4YS

Auditor: J. MARTIN HALDANE, C.A.

Secretary for the U.S.A.: PROFESSOR W. ALAN J. WATSON, M.A., LL.B., D.PHIL., The Law School, University of Georgia

Secretary for Japan: PROFESSOR TAKESHI TSUNODA

241

CONSTITUTION

1.   The Society shall be called 'The Stair Society'.

2.   The object of the Society shall be to encourage the study and advance the knowledge of the history of Scots Law especially by the publication of original documents, and by the reprinting and editing of works of sufficient rarity or importance.

3.   Membership of the Society shall be constituted by payment of the annual subscription, and shall cease if this be in arrear for one year.

4.   The amount of the annual subscriptions shall be fixed by the Council from time to time, and shall be payable in advance on 1st January in each year.

5.   The management of the affairs and funds of the society shall be vested in a Council consisting of the President, Vice-President, a Chairman, a Vice-Chairman and not more than ten ordinary elected members.

6.   The President, Vice-President, Chairman and Vice-Chairman shall be elected annually at the Annual General Meeting, to hold office for the following calendar year, and shall be eligible for re-election. Those elected at the Inaugural Meeting shall hold office until 31st December, 1935.

7.   The ordinary members of Council elected at the Inaugural Meeting shall hold office from that date. At every Annual General Meeting thereafter the Society shall elect members to fill any vacancies on the Council that may have occurred, or that may be due to occur at the end of the year, members so elected to hold office from the ensuring 1st of January. The original members of Council shall hold office until 31st December, 1939, and, at the Annual General Meeting to be held in November, 1939, all of these members, except two (selected by agreement or by lot), shall be eligible for re-election. The two so selected shall retire as at 31st December following, and shall not be eligible for re-election for one year. Thereafter at each Annual General Meeting two of the ordinary members of Council shall retire as at 31st December following, and shall not be eligible for re-election for one year. The two members to retire annually shall be those who have the longest continuous period of service, and, as among those of equal service, shall be selected by agreement or by lot.

8.   In addition to the elected members, the Council shall have power to co-opt as additional members of Council any member of the Society who, in their opinion, may be fitted to render special service in promoting the work of the Society. Such co-opted members shall hold office for such period, not exceeding five years, as the Council may in each case determine. At no time shall the co-opted members of Council exceed three in number.

9.   The Society at the Inaugural Meeting, and thereafter at the Annual General Meeting, shall appoint a Literary Director or Directors, a Secretary and a Treasurer, and such other officers as may from time to time be deemed necessary, who shall be subject to the direction of the Council in the performance of their duties, and who shall receive such remuneration as

the Council may determine. Those so appointed shall not be members of Council, but may be invited to attend any meeting of Council.

10. Any casual vacancies in the offices of President, Vice-President, Chairman, Vice-Chairman or elected members of the Council, or among the officers of the Society, may be filled up by the Council, appointments so made to be for the period till the 31st of December following the next Annual General Meeting.

11. In any year in which a volume is published each member who has paid his subscription for that year shall be entitled to receive one copy.

12. The Annual General Meeting shall be held between 1st November and 31st March at such time and place as may be fixed by the Council. If the Meeting is not held until after 31st December in any year, office-bearers and members of Council then due to retire shall remain in office until the Meeting is held. The Council may also at any time call a Special General Meeting of the Society, and shall do so on a requisition from not less than ten members, which shall specify the object for which the Meeting is to be called. Seven days' notice shall be given of all General meetings.

13. The Constitution of the Society as contained in these Rules may be amended at any General Meeting on twenty-one days' notice of the proposed amendments being given to the Secretary and included in the Agenda circulated for the Meeting.

PUBLICATIONS OF THE STAIR SOCIETY

1. *An Introductory Survey of the Sources and Literature of Scots Law*. By various authors. With an introduction by the Rt. Hon. Lord Macmillan, P.C., LL.D., Lord of Appeal in Ordinary. 1936.

1a *An Index to Volume No. 1,* compiled by James Cowie Brown, M.A., LL.B., Ph.D., was issued in 1939.

2. *Acta Curiae Admirallatus Scotiae, 6th September 1557–11th March 1561–2*. Edited by Thomas Callander Wade, M.A., LL.B., Solicitor, Falkirk. 1937.

3. *Hope's Major Practicks, 1608–1633*. Edited by the Rt. Hon. James Avon Clyde, LL.D., formerly Lord Justice-General of Scotland and Lord President of the Court of Session. Vol. I. With portrait. 1937.

4. *Hope's Major Practicks, 1608–1633*. Edited by the Rt. Hon. James Avon Clyde, LL.D., formerly Lord Justice-General of Scotland and Lord President of the Court of Session. Vol. II. 1938.

5. *Baron David Hume's Lectures, 1786–1822*. Edited and annotated by G. Campbell H. Paton, M.A., LL.B., Solicitor, and Assistant to Professor of Law in the University of Glasgow. Vol. I. With portrait. 1939.

6. *Lord Hermand's Consistorial Decisions, 1684–1777*. Edited by F. P. Walton, K.C. (Quebec), LL.D., Hon. Fellow, Lincoln College, Oxford, formerly Director, Royal School of Law, Cairo. With biographical Sketch of Lord Hermand by James Fergusson. With portrait. 1940.

7. *St. Andrews Formulare, 1514–1546*. Text transcribed and edited by Gordon Donaldson, M.A., Ph.D, and C. Macrae, M.A., D.Phil. Vol. I. 1942.

8. *Acta Dominorum Concilii, 26th March 1501–27th January 1502–3*. Transcribed by J. A. Crawford, M.A., LL.B., Advocate. Edited with an Introduction by the Rt. Hon. James Avon Clyde, LL.D., formerly Lord Justice-General of Scotland and Lord President of the Court of Session. 1943.

9. *St. Andrews Formulare, 1514–1546*. Edited by Gordon Donaldson, M.A., Ph.D., with Prefatory Note by David Baird Smith, C.B.E., LL.D. Vol II. 1944.

10. *The Register of Brieves, 1286–1386,* as contained in the Ayr MS., the Bute MS., and Quoniam Attachiamenta. Edited by the Rt. Hon. Lord Cooper, LL.D., Lord Justice-Clerk. Thomas Thomson's Memorial on Old Extent. Edited by J. D. Mackie, C.B.E., M.C., M.A., Professor of Scottish History and Literature in the University of Glasgow. 1946.

11. *Regiam Majestatem and Quoniam Atttachiamenta,* based on the text of Sir John Skene. Edited and translated with Introduction and Notes by the Rt. Hon. Lord Cooper, LL.D. 1947.

12. *The Justiciary Records of Argyll and the Isles, 1664–1705*. Transcribed and edited, with an Introduction, by John Cameron, M.A., LL.B., Ph.D, Vol.I. 1949.

13. *Baron David Hume's Lectures, 1786–1822*. Edited and annotated by G. Campbell H. Paton, M.A., LL.B., Solicitor. Vol. II. 1949.

14. *Acta Dominorum Concilii et Sessionis, 1532–1533.* Edited by Ian H. Shearer, M.A., LL.B., Advocate. 1951.
15. *Baron David Hume's Lectures, 1786–1822.* Edited and annotated by G. Campbell H. Paton, M.A., LL.B., Advocate and Lecturer in the History of Scots Law in the University of Glasgow. Vol. III. 1952.
16. *Selected Justiciary Cases, 1624–1650.* Edited and annotated by Stair A. Gillon, B.A., LL.B., Advocate. Vol. I. 1953.
17. *Baron David Hume's Lectures, 1786–1822.* Edited and annotated by G. Campbell H. Paton, M.A., LL.B., Advocate and Lecturer in the History of Scots Law in the University of Glasgow. Vol. IV. 1955.
18. *Baron David Hume's Lectures, 1786–1822.* Edited and annotated by G. Campbell H. Paton, M.A., LL.B., Advocate and Lecturer in the History of Scots Law in the University of Glasgow. Vol. V. 1957.
19. *Baron David Hume's Lectures, 1786–1822.* Edited and annotated by G. Campbell H. Paton, M.A., LL.B., Advocate and Lecturer in the History of Scots Law in the University of Glasgow. Vol. VI. 1958.
19a *A Supplement to Baron Hume's Lectures.* Edited and annotated by the Editor of the printed volumes. 1957.
20. *An Introduction to Scottish Legal History.* By various authors. With an Introduction by the Rt. Hon. Lord Normand, P.C., LL.D., Lord of Appeal in Ordinary, 1947–1953. 1958.
21. *The Practicks of Sir James Balfour of Pittendreich.* Edited by Peter G. B. McNeill, M.A., LL.B., Ph.D., Advocate. Vol. I. 1962.
22. *The Practicks of Sir James Balfour of Pittendreich.* Edited by Peter G. B. McNeill, M.A., LL.B., Ph.D., Advocate. Vol. II. 1963.
23. *The Origins and Development of the Jury in Scotland.* By Ian D. Willock, M.A., LL.B., Advocate and Professor of Jurisprudence in the University of St. Andrews. 1966.
24. *William Hay's Lectures on Marriage.* Transcribed, translated and edited by the Right Rev. Monsignor John C. Barry, M.A. (Cantab.), D.C.L. (Rome), Rector of St. Andrew's College, Drygrange, Melrose; Consultor to the Pontifical Commission for the Revision of the Code of Canon Law. 1967.
25. *The Justiciary Records of Argyll and the Isles. 1664–1742.* Edited by John Imrie. Vol. II. 1969.
26. *Miscellany I.* By various authors. With a preface by the Rt. Hon. Lord Clyde, LL.D., Lord Justice-General and Lord President of the Court of Session. 1971.
27. *Selected Justiciary Cases, 1624–1650.* Edited with an Introduction by J. Irvine Smith, M.A., LL.B., Advocate. Sheriff of Lanarkshire at Glasgow. Vol. II. 1972.
28. *Selected Justiciary Cases, 1624–1650.* Edited with an Introduction by J. Irvine SMith, M.A., LL.B., Advocate, Sheriff of Lanarkshire at Glasgow. Vol. III. 1974.
29. *The Minute Book of the Faculty of Advocates, 1661–1712.* Edited by John M. Pinkerton, Clerk of Faculty. Vol.I. 1976.

30. *The Synod Records of Lothian and Tweeddale, 1589–96, 1640–49.*
    Edited with an Introduction by Dr. James Kirk of the Department of
    Scottish History, Glasgow University. 1977.
31. *Perpetuities in Scots Law.* By Robert Burgess, LL.B., Ph.D., Senior Lecturer
    in Law in the University of East Anglia. 1979.
32. *The Minute Book of the Faculty of Advocates, 1713–1750.* Edited by John
    M. Pinkerton, late Clerk of Faculty. Vol. II. 1980.
33. *Stair Tercentenary Studies.* By various authors. Edited by David M.
    Walker, Q.C., M.A., LL.D., F.B.A., Regius Professor of Law at the University of
    Glasgow. 1981.
34. *The Court of the Official in Pre-Reformation Scotland.* By Simon
    Ollivant, M.A., Ph.D. 1982.
35. *Miscellany II.* By various authors. Edited by David Sellar, B.A., LL.B., of the
    Department of Scots Law in the University of Edinburgh. With a preface
    by the Rt. Hon. Lord Avonside. 1984.
36. *Formulary of Old Scots Legal Documents.* Compiled by Peter
    Gouldesbrough, Former Assistant Keeper in the Scottish Record Office
    with a Supplementary Essay on Early Scottish Conveyancing by Gordon
    Donaldson, H.M. Historiographer in Scotland. 1985.
37. *The Scottish Whigs and the Reform of the Court of Session 1785–1830.* By
    Nicholas T. Phillipson, M.A., Ph.D., of the Department of History in the
    University of Edinburgh. 1990.
38. *The Court Book of the Barony and Regality of Falkirk and Callendar.*
    Edited by Doreen M. Hunter, M.A., late of the Scottish Record Office.
    1991.

SUPPLEMENTARY SERIES

1. *The College of Justice.* Essays by R. K. Hannay. Reprinted with an
   Introduction and Bibliography by Hector L. MacQueen, LL.B., Ph.D., of the
   Department of Scots Law in the University of Edinburgh. 1990.

JOINT PUBLICATION WITH THE SALTIRE SOCIETY

The Scottish Legal Tradition. New enlarged edition by M. C. Meston, M.A.,
LL.B., J.D., Professor of Private Law, University of Aberdeen, W. D. H.
Sellar, B.A., LL.B., Senior Lecturer in Scots Law, University of Edinburgh
and the Rt. Hon. Lord Cooper, LL.D., late President of the Court of
Session. Edited by Scott C. Styles, M.A., LL.B. 1991.